Death and Burial in Socialist Yugoslavia

Death and Burial in Socialist Yugoslavia

The Politicization of Cemeteries and Ethnic Conflict in the Balkans

Carol S. Lilly

BLOOMSBURY ACADEMIC
LONDON • NEW YORK • OXFORD • NEW DELHI • SYDNEY

BLOOMSBURY ACADEMIC
Bloomsbury Publishing Plc
50 Bedford Square, London, WC1B 3DP, UK
1385 Broadway, New York, NY 10018, USA
29 Earlsfort Terrace, Dublin 2, Ireland

BLOOMSBURY, BLOOMSBURY ACADEMIC and the Diana logo are trademarks of Bloomsbury Publishing Plc

First published in Great Britain 2024
Paperback edition published 2025

Copyright © Carol S. Lilly, 2024

Carol S. Lilly has asserted her right under the Copyright, Designs and Patents Act, 1988, to be identified as Author of this work.

For legal purposes the Acknowledgments on pp. xii–xiv constitute an extension of this copyright page.

Cover image: Jasikovac Orthodox Cemetery, Gospic, Croatia
Photography by Carol S. Lilly

Bloomsbury Publishing Plc does not have any control over, or responsibility for, any third-party websites referred to or in this book. All internet addresses given in this book were correct at the time of going to press. The author and publisher regret any inconvenience caused if addresses have changed or sites have ceased to exist, but can accept no responsibility for any such changes.

Every effort has been made to trace the copyright holders and obtain permission to reproduce the copyright material. Please do get in touch with any enquiries or any information relating to such material or the rights holder. We would be pleased to rectify any omissions in subsequent editions of this publication should they be drawn to our attention.

A catalogue record for this book is available from the British Library.

A catalog record for this book is available from the Library of Congress.

ISBN: HB: 978-1-3502-8582-8
PB: 978-1-3502-8586-6
ePDF: 978-1-3502-8583-5
eBook: 978-1-3502-8584-2

Typeset by Newgen KnowledgeWorks Pvt. Ltd., Chennai, India

To find out more about our authors and books visit www.bloomsbury.com and sign up for our newsletters.

To My Own Beloved Deceased
To my Father—who taught me to ski, drive, and the importance of having a job I love, and To my Mother—who taught me to ride horses, make dinner in half an hour, and always take care of my animals before myself. Despite their best efforts, neither could teach me to love gardening. And To Rick—the muž geroj, *who made me keep my name and in so many ways made my life more various, rich, and strange. I miss them all every day.*

Contents

List of Figures	viii
Preface	x
Acknowledgments	xii
List of Abbreviations	xv
Cemeteries Visited Map	xvi
Introduction	1
1 Burial Cultures of the Region	21
2 Religion, Nationalism, and the State in Socialist Yugoslavia	49
3 Partisan Communities of the Dead	73
4 The Secularization of Cemeteries	97
5 Burial Rituals	125
6 Grave Markers: Messages in Stone	147
7 Ethnic Conflict and Politicization of the Dead	185
Conclusion: Death after Communism	229
Glossary	243
Notes	245
Bibliography	293
Index	317

Figures

I.1	Mostar Partisan Cemetery	2
I.2	Damage to Mostar Partisan Cemetery, summer 2022	3
1.1	Nineteenth-century marker from interfaith marriage, Roermond, the Netherlands	27
3.1	Monuments to fallen soldiers and victims of fascist terror, 1950s–60s, Prizren, Kosova; Vrbaška, Bosnia & Hercegovina; Vrebac, Croatia	85
3.2	Vraca Memorial Park, Sarajevo, Bosnia & Hercegovina	93
3.3	Abstract Socialist memorials	94
3.4	"Generally Yugoslav" grave markers of Partisans	95
4.1	Ethnoreligiously mixed cemeteries, Nova Bežanija and Lešče, Belgrade, Serbia	112
4.2	Segregated Muslim and Jewish cemeteries, Gunja, Croatia and Zemun, Serbia	113
4.3	Stup Cemetery under the M17-M18 highway interchange	117
4.4	Marked cemetery sections	122
6.1	Traditional Muslim graves with male/female turbans	150
6.2	Family grave markers	156
6.3	Typical rural grave marker from the 1940s to 1950s	159
6.4	Grave markers from the 1970s	160
6.5	Use of script	167
6.6	Mixed marriages among Christians. Note the differing crosses and scripts	170
6.7	Mixed marriages: Muslims and Christians	172
6.8	Traditional Muslim grave marker with photograph	174
6.9	Nontraditional Muslim grave markers with Islamic symbols	175
6.10	Cultural adaptations on Muslim grave markers	176
6.11	Partisan grave markers	182
6.12	Partisan grave markers for children	183
7.1	Grave markers with Albanian national symbols	192
7.2	Kosovar soldier's grave marker	193
7.3	Grave markers with Croatian national symbols	195

7.4	Military markers in Bosnia & Hercegovina	196
7.5	Markers with Serbian national symbols	198
7.6	Epitaphs on Serbian markers	199
7.7	Renovated nationalist graves	202
7.8	Krstovdan incident at Grace, Kosova	216
7.9	Damaged and empty graves after the wars of Yugoslav dissolution	219
7.10	Patriarchate of Peć	225
7.11	Grave desecrations	226
C.1	Increased religious elements on grave markers	234
C.2	Capitalism and grave markers	235
C.3	Capitalism and grave markers	236
C.4	Mehmed	237
C.5	Roma grave markers	240
C.6	Hope for the future	241

Preface

I first became aware that there was something wrong with the American "way of death," as Jessica Mitford put it, in my early twenties when my grandmother died. Although it was not the first funeral I had attended, it was my first gravesite experience. I stood with my mother at the grave, waiting for the moment when the casket would be lowered into the ground and they would begin to shovel dirt onto it, wanting that sense of finality and closure, so I could let the emotions wash over me. Like most people, I had read about and more importantly seen many such scenes like this on television and in movies. In the United States of the 1980s and still today, however, no such scene occurred. The short service ended, and we were all gently ushered away, with the casket and body still hovering over an empty hole. I have no idea when or how the casket was lowered or the grave filled in. It was all extremely unsatisfying—there was no sense of closure, the emotions never washed over, in fact, I found I couldn't cry at all.

Some years later, as a graduate student of Yugoslav history I first visited a Croatian cemetery on November 1 for the annual celebration of Day of the Dead. I was moved and impressed by the care and attention lavished on the graves by every family but was even more struck by the cemetery and graves themselves, which were far more interesting and meaningful than anything I had seen in the United States. Most were family graves that housed multiple generations of the same family, providing a sense of history and community impossible to recreate with single-use permanent graves, especially in our highly mobile society. Moreover, graves in Yugoslavia are frequently characterized by the use of personal imagery—photographs and etchings that impart a far more intimate connection to the deceased.

Every time I went to Yugoslavia after that, I sought out cemeteries, but beginning in the late 1980s and well through the wars of Yugoslav dissolution, colleagues and friends from Serbia began to tell me with horror about the desecrations that they said were being perpetrated on Serbian graves mainly by Albanians in Kosovo. I remember being astonished by the frequency with which the subject arose but even more so by the passion with which my friends and colleagues described the desecrations, almost as worse than any form of physical violence against a living person. That was when I first began to consider the idea of a research project focused on cemeteries as sites of ethnic identity and conflict.

The next time I had an opportunity to visit a Yugoslav cemetery and consider the idea was in the early 2000s in connection with a different research project about a Serbian woman and her family, which also enhanced my understanding of local death rituals. As I visited the graves of that family, I was struck by the rapidly changing style of grave markers after the fall of communism. I recall one in particular of a young Serbian man whose full-color, larger-than-life photograph on shiny black marble showed him bare-chested with sunglasses and a gold chain, arms crossed behind his head, with beach umbrellas in the background. Although it contradicted my cultural expectations for funeral imagery, I was fascinated by the intimate view it offered into the persona of the deceased (see Figure C.2).

Ultimately then, this project grew out of a long series of seemingly unconnected events, all of which led me to believe that burial rituals and cemetery structure matter on an individual, communal, national, and transnational level. They have the power to provide comfort and soothe the pain caused by death, but they may also create new wounds and cause further distress to families, communities, and states. While they are not likely the source of tension between ethnoreligious communities, they reflect its presence and may be used as weapons in ethnic conflict.

I began research for this project in 2011. Since then, three members of my immediate family have died: my husband of over thirty years to pancreatic cancer in 2016; my father in 2018; and my mother in 2019. Once again I found myself dissatisfied with the burial culture of the United States: it is expensive, rigid, and often soulless. Recently, however, thanks to the work of progressive death activists like Caitlin Doughty and her colleagues at the Order of the Good Death, it is improving. My research for this book and the classes I now teach on this subject provided me the knowledge and skills to avoid another funeral like my grandmother's, and while the options permitted me in each case were still far from ideal, at least this time I knew what was coming.

Acknowledgments

This monograph is the product of over a decade of research in multiple locations. The number of institutions and people who have contributed to my work is overwhelming, and I fear that I will inadvertently leave someone out. Assuming the worst, I offer in advance sincere apologies and assurances that I have valued every ounce of assistance provided by every individual.

As a faculty member at a small state university, I am particularly conscious of the investment in time and finances required to carry out a project of this nature. Funds provided by the International Research and Exchanges Board Short Term Travel Grants and the National Council for Eurasian and East European Research Title VIII Short Term Travel Grants were critical to my research and I thank them. I am also and especially grateful, however, for the years of financial support and release time provided by my own institution, the University of Nebraska Kearney, from its Research Services Council, the Vice Chancellor for Academic Affairs, the College of Arts and Sciences, and the Department of History.

I extend my appreciation to multiple institutions in regions of the former Yugoslavia where I conducted research for this monograph. In Bosnia & Hercegovina, I am grateful to the staff of the Arhiv Bosne i Hercegovine and, especially, Sandra Biletić, who always sought to ensure that my limited time there was well spent. Thanks go also to the director of the Jugoslovensko Komunalno Poduzeće Pokupno Društvo Sarajevo and Friar Zdravko Andjić of the Parish Church of St. Ilija, Zenica, for providing access to their archives. In Croatia, my thanks go to the staffs of the Hrvatski Institut za Povijest and Hrvatski Državni Arhiv. In Serbia, I am grateful to staffs of the Arhiv Jugoslavije, the Arhiv Srbije, the Istorijski Arhiv Beograda, and the Narodna Biblioteka Srbije. In Kosova, I am indebted to the staff of Agjencia Shtetërore e Arkivave të Kosovës, who graciously provided me access to archival documents, although I had regrettably arrived during the month of Ramadan. Throughout my decade of research, I benefited enormously from conversations and interviews with scholars, experts, and knowledgeable individuals whom I have listed in the bibliography, but if I excluded any I apologize and thank them here. Special thanks also to Almir Methadžović who went out of his way to take and send to me multiple photographs of grave markers that were critical for my research.

In all of these regions, several special individuals made my research activities not only more productive but also far more enjoyable. In Croatia, my thanks go out to Dr. Vjeran Pavlaković at the Faculty of Philosophy at the University of Rijeka, who has always taken time to meet with me, answer questions, and offer suggestions for sources and the best avenues for further research. It was also Vjeran who connected me to Filip Škiljan, my extraordinary research assistant in Croatia. Filip's skills as a researcher are unparalleled, and I am thoroughly indebted to him! In addition, I send my undying gratitude and best wishes to Lela Baća and her family (Željko, Cica, Kristina, Natalja, Željka) in Zaprešić. Lela was the first friend I made in Croatia, and it was thanks to her that I attended my first Dan Mrtvih (Day of the Dead) Ceremony in 1987.

In Bosnia & Hercegovina, I am grateful to Dr. Amir Duranović, at the Department of History in the Faculty of Philosophy at the University of Sarajevo, who always made time to help me find sources and to share insights and coffee. My greatest ally and friend in Bosnia & Hercegovina, however, is Selma Hadžihalilović. Selma always and unerringly found me the right people to talk to and the best cemeteries to visit to work through every research question. She was also an ideal sounding board, helping me think through each interview and visit, questioning my assumptions, and asking me new questions. This monograph would have far less depth without her contributions, but more important, my life would be far less interesting.

In Kosova, my thanks go out to Mrika Limani Myrtaj who served as translator and guide during my research trip there in 2019. Mrika is a fairly recent acquaintance, but we found that we had a great deal in common and, at least from my perspective, we made excellent travelling companions. As an extremely talented historian, she was not only a superior guide but also wonderful company. I have only the best memories of our time together.

In Serbia, I thank all of my colleagues at the Institut za Savremenu Istoriju who have treated me as a colleague and offered me exceptional research assistance since my first trip to Belgrade in 1987. Most of all, however, I thank the former director of the institute and friend Dr. Momčilo Pavlović who has always gone miles/kilometers out of his way to ensure that my research efforts are as successful as possible. More to the point, he is a dear friend who has offered companionship, advice, humor, a roof over my head, and more than a few glasses of good red wine and rakija. The times I spent with him, his wife, Tanja, and their now adult children (Pavle and Ana) mean more to me than any book ever could.

Bloomsbury Press has been an absolute pleasure to work with—timely and responsive at all junctures. I thank their editorial staff as well as the anonymous reviewers whose judicious intervention made this monograph far better, however imperfect it undoubtedly remains.

Many dear colleagues, friends, and family members in the United States have also paid into this final product. My thanks to all past and present members of the History Department at the University of Nebraska Kearney for their intellectual support and friendship over decades, with special appreciation to Dr. Will Stoutamire for his insightful comments. Many other colleagues, friends, and family members also read multiple chapters and/or provided moral support over the past years. While none of those mentioned earlier or later bear any responsibility for this book's errors, they may claim credit for any praise it may garner. I am therefore particularly grateful to Amy Rundstrom, Jill Irvine, John Buchanan, Carla Jaffe, Melissa Bokovoy, Catherine Higgs, Ann Marie Park, Nick Miller, Sabrina Thomas, Kathryn Dunbar, Donald Lilly, Stephanie Dunbar, Daniela Garvue, Max Garvue, and Barry Garvue. My love to you all.

Abbreviations

AP	Autonomous Province
BC(M)S	Bosnian/Croatian/(Montenegrin)/Serbian
CARC	Council of Affairs of Religious Cults (Soviet Union)
CAROC	Council of Affairs of the Russian Orthodox Church (Soviet Union)
CPY	Communist Party of Yugoslavia (KPJ)
CRQ	Commission for Religious Questions (KVP)
HDZ	Hrvatska Demokratska Zajednica (Croatian Democratic Community)
IVZ	Islamska Verska/Vjerska Zajednica (Islamic Religious Community)
JMO	Jugoslavenska Muslimanska Organizacija (Yugoslav Muslim Organization)
JNA	Jugoslovenska Narodna Armija (Yugoslav People's Army)
KLA	Kosovo Liberation Army (UÇK)
LCY	League of Communists of Yugoslavia (SKJ)
LDK	Lidhja Demokratiike i Kosovës (Democratic League of Kosovo)
NDH	Nezavisna Država Hrvatske (Independent State of Croatia)
OSCE	Organization for Security and Cooperation in Europe
PLA	People's Liberation Army (NOV)
RS	Republika Srpska (Serbian Republic)
SFRY	Socialist Federal Republic of Yugoslavia (FNRJ)
SUBNOR	Savez Udruženja Boraca Narodnooslobodilačkog Rata (Allied Unions of Fighters from the People's Liberation War)
ZAGS	Civil Registration of Births, Weddings, and Deaths (Zapis' Aktov Grazhdanskogo Sostoianiia—Soviet Union)
ŽFT	Žrtva Fašističkog Terora (Victim of Fascist Terror)

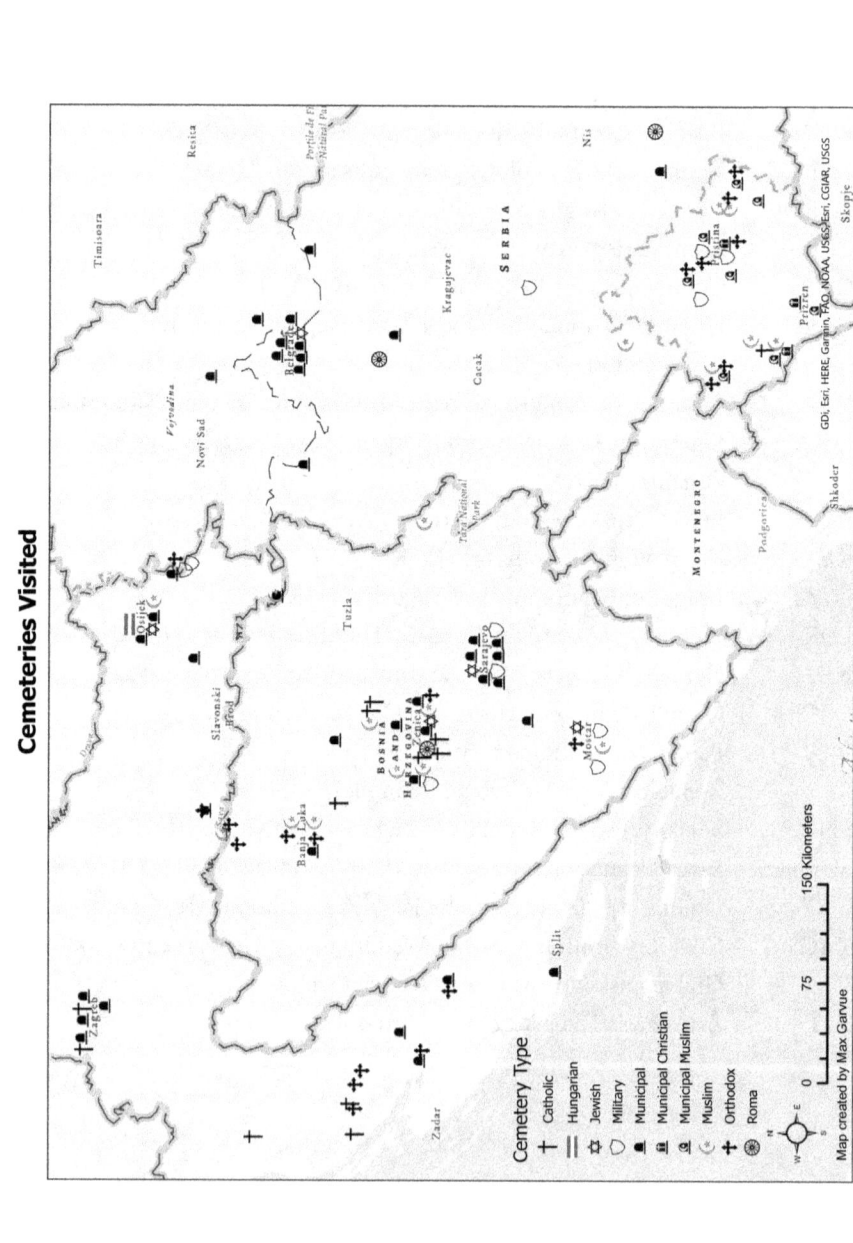

Introduction

In the summer of 2022, I visited the Partisan Cemetery in Mostar, Bosnia & Hercegovina. This was my last research trip to the republics of the former Yugoslavia for this book, and just one week before my departure, on June 14, I was devastated to read of its desecration in what was described as a "neo-fascist rampage."[1] I arrived at the site on July 3 with my 73-year-old guide Mirad Čupina, a machinist, self-proclaimed anti-fascist, and member of the local successor to Yugoslavia's Partisan Veteran's Organization. Having never been to the cemetery before, I was struck by its beauty and the brilliance of its design, even in its damaged and sadly dilapidated state. Conceived by architect and sculptor Bogdan Bogdanović in 1960 and unveiled in 1965, it was one of the first major Partisan cemeteries and among the earliest of Yugoslavia's famous modernist art monuments.[2] Bogdanović's goal was to join old and new—the dead and the living of Mostar. From its post at the top of a hill above the city, water runs from a fountain, joining the two sides of the memorial park and symbolizing the role of the Neretva river in connecting Mostar's two largest nations—Croats on the West bank and Muslims on the East. The entrance of river rocks is guarded by two abstract lions, at which point the park splits around the waterway and visitors ascend a path on either side. The path moves along six successive terraces, along which were placed several hundred flower-shaped stones as cenotaphs inscribed in cursive with the names and dates of birth and death of Partisan soldiers from the region who died in the People's Liberation War. The remains of over 800 local Partisan and civilian victims are interred in an ossuary to the right of the terraces. Massive symbols of the sun, stars, and planets are placed at the top where the fountain begins, drawing on designs and architecture from ancient civilizations (Figure I.1).

The entire structure was bombed during the wars of Yugoslav dissolution and suffered continuing desecration and neglect in the decades to follow. According to Čupina, the local veteran's organization had been trying for years to pressure the

Figure I.1 Mostar Partisan Cemetery. For more photographs on this theme see: https://yugcemeteries.omeka.net/exhibits/show/monuments

Bosnian government take over repairs and maintenance, and it was proclaimed a national monument in 2006, but all renovations have been carried out by volunteers with EU funding. Even so, no water has flown from the fountain since the early 1990s and the lack of maintenance is evident. Most disturbing, however, was the extraordinary desecration of June 14 whose perpetrators remain at large. The destruction wrought on that date was clearly deliberate and extensive as nearly every single tombstone was smashed (Figure I.2). As Čupina put it, "This was not just vandalism, but terrorism," or, as I will suggest later, a hate crime. As we were leaving the area, another older man walking his dog stopped and asked for information about the cemetery. It started out friendly but within a few moments he and Čupina began to argue. First, the man suggested that the site could not really be considered a cemetery as, he claimed (incorrectly),

Figure I.2 Damage to Mostar Partisan Cemetery, summer 2022

it housed no remains, and from there the conversation quickly deteriorated.[3] When Čupina began one of his responses with "I am an anti-fascist," the other replied, "*And I am a fascist.*" I have replayed that moment of conversation over and over in my mind since, trying to imagine if I misunderstood or misheard it. Although Nazi and Ustashe symbols have regularly been painted on walls of the Memorial Park, I had never heard anyone admit to such position and even now it seems inconceivable. Yet beyond what it suggests about the disturbing polarization of society, it also revealed how easily the cemeteries that we think of as sites of mourning and piety can become spaces and even sources of division and hatred.

Cemeteries have often been described as communities of the dead—sites of unity and comfort where families, friends, and communities of the living gather to mourn and commemorate their deceased loved ones. As such, and as places where people from all walks of life gather for private and public rituals of mourning and remembrance, they have the capacity to help create a collective identity. The very architecture, landscaping, and symbols displayed in a cemetery, as well as the rituals performed, are all intended to reflect the culture of those interred below and surviving above. Like communities of the living, however, cemeteries are not only inclusive but also exclusive. Every community is based on the concept of belonging, and those who do not belong may be deliberately and brutally expelled. In the United States, African Americans, Latinos, and Asians were long barred from "white" cemeteries as part of racial segregation and the Jim Crow Acts.[4] Even today non-white and Jewish graves in the United States remain frequent targets of grave desecration.

Burial sites, memorials, and dead bodies themselves are regularly weaponized in both internal and international conflicts across the globe. Charles Van Onselen provided a vivid and astonishing portrayal of what he called the "desecration industry" in South Africa resulting from poverty, inequality, and bureaucracy.[5] Mehrdad Amanat noted that there is a long history of exhumations and the burning of corpses in Iran, going back at least to the nineteenth century and possibly further; a particularly strong wave of desecrations followed the 1979 Revolution as Islamic radicals demanded the removal of leftist victims from Tehran's Muslim cemetery.[6] From 2011 to 2013, a wave of bombing attacks devastated Sufi shrines throughout Northern Africa.[7] In all these cases and many more, the living have found the destruction and mutilation of the dead and their burial sites to be a powerful instrument of social, political, and ethnic conflict. While considerable international attention and some scholarly works have recently focused on attacks against a nation's broader cultural heritage in wartime, there has been very little analysis about the significance of violence perpetrated on the dead and how it may affect those still living.

As a country made up of six republics, multiple nations, and five major religions (Catholics, Orthodox, Muslims, Jews, and Protestants) with their diverse burial cultures, Socialist Yugoslavia is an excellent case for investigating how cemeteries and burial rituals may both unite and divide individual citizens and entire communities. This monograph focuses on the Yugoslav republics of Bosnia & Hercegovina, Croatia, and Serbia (including its autonomous provinces of Kosovo and Vojvodina) during the period of Communist rule beginning in 1945 and up through the wars of dissolution that lasted from 1991 to 1999.[8]

The Communist Party of Yugoslavia (CPY) that took power in the aftermath of the Second World War clearly understood the importance of creating a new and stronger collective identity in postwar Yugoslavia. Foreign occupation, civil war, and genocide, resulting in over one million wartime deaths, had not only shattered the interwar state but also deeply traumatized and divided its citizens. Among the tools that the CPY utilized to create that new collective identity was the institutionalized memory of the Second World War, including the monuments, ossuaries, and cemeteries dedicated to its victims. Those wartime cemeteries and monuments were generally successful in helping Yugoslav citizens mourn their loved ones killed by foreign occupiers and other enemies of the new regime. Most were also reasonably effective as war cemeteries or monuments that offered certain common values to citizens, including a unified Yugoslav state, the "brotherhood and unity" of Yugoslavia's nations and nationalities, and Socialist construction in its various and changing dimensions. Those Partisan cemeteries that were characterized by abstract modernist architecture and symbolism seemed particularly well suited to the goals of identity creation.

In contrast, however, the party paid very little attention to the role of civilian burial culture or civilian cemeteries as potential communities of the dead. Central party and state leaders gave no statements or speeches and passed almost no federal laws affecting the burial culture of ordinary citizens, and its broader policies toward civilian burial culture failed to reinforce secularism, pluralism, or brotherhood and unity. Although the Communist regime often sought to secularize cemeteries and modernize funerals for hygienic purposes, it did so inconsistently, while at the same time, it largely left the previous system of ethnoreligious segregation in place. Throughout Socialist Yugoslavia, Muslims and Jews were buried in separate cemeteries or at least in separate sections of cemeteries, but in many cases, so too were Catholics and Orthodox, and in some, even Protestants and Atheists.

Moreover, the Socialist regime made funerals and civilian cemeteries into legitimate spaces for political discourse by politicizing the funerals of its supporters and encouraging the placement of its own emblem, the five-pointed red star, on the graves of its supporters, while prohibiting any other political or national symbols. By the late 1980s and early 1990s as nationalist sentiments escalated and Yugoslavia disintegrated, even civilian grave markers and cemeteries had become an instrument in the arsenals of escalating ethnic conflict, making these sacred spaces increasingly vulnerable to desecration. Violence perpetrated against the dead served only to amplify and intensify violence among the living. Inasmuch as the Communist regime created its own communities of the dead, it did so only within Partisan war cemeteries, failing to expand that community to graveyards intended for civilians. Its policies thus only further divided Yugoslavia's communities of the dead, both on ethnoreligious and political bases, contributing to the cultural violence associated with Yugoslavia's wars of dissolution.

When the CPY took power following the Second World War, it had a vision for a new society based on Marxist-Leninist ideology but modified to accommodate Yugoslavia's diversity and history of ethnoreligious conflict. While burial policies were not themselves a high priority, they fell directly into the nexus of two extremely sensitive issues—religion and nationalism. Although the Communist party was sometimes ruthless in its treatment of religious leaders, it could not always risk the consequences of hostile relations when mediating conflicts between Yugoslavia's diverse ethnoreligious communities. Precisely because national and religious identities were so closely connected in Yugoslavia, party leaders often feared that attacks on any given religion could lead to confrontations with the associated national community. Therefore, they generally confined their criticisms to clergy and religious institutions. While the Communist regime did gradually secularize many (though not all) cemeteries, it accepted their continued ethnoreligious segregation. The regime further permitted individuals and ethnoreligious communities considerable freedom in the practice of religious burial rites and commemoration of the dead. Yet that did not mean that it entirely ignored all funeral rites and burials. The regime was concerned with burial culture, however, less for its value as a social or human practice than its ability to influence its hold on power.

Immediately following the Second World War, the Communist party focused considerable attention on the sacrifices made by Partisans fighting for the People's Liberation Army (PLA) waged alongside European campaigns of the Second World War. The regime thus mobilized regional veteran's organizations to gather the remains of soldiers and civilians killed by occupying forces during the war into special cemeteries or ossuaries, create specific rituals for reburial ceremonies, and decorate their graves with five-pointed stars. These efforts represented both a legitimate desire to respond to the real needs of families and survivors to mourn their losses and a more utilitarian effort to appropriate those emotions for the goals of the state. In contrast, those who had died in the war's ethnic conflicts largely went unremarked and any occupation soldiers or Yugoslav citizens who died on the opposing side of the war were not only officially unmourned but also often left in deliberately unmarked or even eradicated graves contrary to the Geneva Convention.

Further, while most citizens were left to carry out burials as they wished without interference, the Communist regime expected all party, or even trade union, members to be buried in a strictly secular manner and sometimes harassed those relatives who sought to incorporate religious rites. Similar complications sometimes arose for relatives of deceased veterans from the PLA, regardless of their party membership. Although permitted religious rites, families had to organize the ceremony in cooperation with the Veterans Association (VA), sometimes resulting in complex negotiations and disputes between the VA and religious figures.

The most obvious arena for such political discourse were the cemeteries. Partisan cemeteries and sections were exclusive to those members of the PLA who had died during the war or immediately thereafter. Although many larger cemeteries, like the one in Mostar, were entirely abstract in concept and included little or no political symbolism, soldiers' graves within most locally designed and constructed Partisan cemeteries were obligatorily marked with the five-pointed star and occasionally also the hammer and sickle. Similarly, any members of the PLA who survived the war and died later, along with any members or even just supporters of the Communist party, were buried in civilian cemeteries in graves conspicuously marked with the five-pointed star. Some also included images of the deceased in Partisan garb or, again, the Soviet hammer and sickle. As the communists had a monopoly on both political power and imagery, neither burial rituals nor grave markers could indicate support for any political organization other than that of the Communist party. Thus, while the regime was willing to tolerate religious rites, religious symbols on grave markers, and ethnoreligiously segregated cemeteries, it insisted on complete political conformity even after death.

To be sure, relatively few citizens had funerals that included any political elements and only a minority of graves in civilian cemeteries bore the Partisan five-pointed star; yet any citizen who attended the funeral of a veteran or visited any Yugoslav cemetery recognized the extent to which politics had penetrated burial culture. By the mid- to late 1980s, some citizens had begun to see cemeteries as not only an ethnoreligious but also a political space. As early as 1985, some Kosovar Albanians had begun to place the double-headed eagle (the Albanian national symbol) on graves as a sign of both national and political resistance to the regime. By the late 1980s, the Serbian media had begun to carry regular (sometimes exaggerated) stories about the Albanian desecration of Serbian graves in Kosovo. By the time ethnic violence broke out in the 1990s, cemeteries and grave markers had become well known throughout the region as sites and symbols of not only one's own revered ancestors but also one's national and political enemies—their graves clearly marked and set aside for anyone to find and defile. Among those graves and cemeteries most commonly desecrated in the wars of Yugoslav dissolution were not only those of the ethnoreligious enemy (Serbian Orthodox, Catholic Croats, Muslims) but also Partisans.

Historiography

A considerable English-language literature on cemeteries and burial culture has developed since the 1977 publication of Phillip Aries's seminal work, *The Hour of Our Death*.[9] Thomas Laqueur's 2015 *The Work of the Dead* seems almost a bookend to Aries's in its scope and eloquence.[10] I am indebted to both, but especially Laqueur, for the concept embedded in his title, which speaks to us about why the dead matter on an individual and communal level, as well as for his chapters on cemetery secularization in Western Europe. While not entirely applicable to the Yugoslav case, his lucid descriptions of the distinction between churchyard and cemetery present a model for how those who sought to modernize the cemetery imagined their future.

Many scholars—historians, ethnographers, sociologists, and others—built on Aries's initial insights but focused their work on specific topics such as professionalization of the funeral industry, grave marker and cemetery design, public commemorations for war dead, public health and science in the funeral and cemetery industry, theological conflicts between Protestants and Catholics concerning burial rites, epitaphs and obituaries, and the use of cremation as a means of disposal.[11] Further, they often approached their topic from a regional or even strictly local perspective and over limited time periods of one or two centuries.[12] There is a great deal to be said for the local approach. Despite the truism that only death and taxes are universal, it seems equally true that when it comes to burial rituals, "everything is local." The importance of the local context is particularly apt in postwar Yugoslavia where both burial rituals and cemetery organization differed not only from republic to republic but also region to region and sometimes village to village.

Even more significant are the distinctions found between urban, provincial, and rural contexts where the most obvious differences concerned not only the educational level and religious sentiments of the local inhabitants but also the degree of control exercised by central governing institutions. Several recent historians, including Julie Rugg, Monica Black, and Felix Schulz, have emphasized the temporal continuity of communal and religious values as well as important variations in cultures that have persisted both geographically and between rural and urban sites.¹³ Their contributions are critical to my analysis, but the case in Communist Yugoslavia was even more complex, where the interactions between multiple religiously based cultures and an ideologically driven secular regime resulted at best in misunderstandings and in some cases direct conflicts.

At the same time, I welcome Schulz's call for more comparative studies in the field, at the micro and macro levels, both to see how a broad variety of societies across time and space have responded to death and to trace the roles played in them by religion, politics, ideology, and economics.¹⁴ Schulz himself does quite a bit of that comparative work in *Death in East Germany, 1945–1990*, consistently cross-referencing the conclusions of his findings in Eastern Germany to those of scholars who have worked in Britain, France, and the United States. Among his conclusions is that by the twentieth century, "there was still a large gulf between the city and the countryside and certainly differences between individual countries, but ultimately Western countries shared a sepulchral culture dominated by individualization, professionalization, secularization, sanitation, regulation, and rationalization."¹⁵ While Schulz's argument is apt, it only reinforces the need for more comparative work as it leaves out the more economically or religiously diverse Western countries to say nothing of those with non-Western burial cultures.

In fact, much of the existing scholarship on the topic has focused on Britain and France, although Black and Schulz wrote on death and cemetery culture in Germany, and there are important works on Mediterranean Europe as well.¹⁶ In contrast, there are many fewer scholarly pieces available in English on the burial culture of Judaism or of Orthodox and Islamic countries, though Leor Halevi's work is a striking exception.¹⁷ Several excellent books address, at least in part, the burial culture and policies of the Soviet Union and other state Socialist regimes. While essential for their content and as comparative works, they do not focus on the multiethnic or multireligious character of those countries or seriously address any problems they may have posed.¹⁸ The few works (mainly articles) that have looked seriously at ethnoreligious conflicts in cemetery policies focused on Catholic-Protestant conflicts from the sixteenth to seventeenth centuries in France and Northern Ireland, and Islamic sects in modern Turkey, where the state's interest was certainly very different from that of the Yugoslav Socialist regime.¹⁹ Another exception is an excellent edited volume that investigates cemetery segregation in America's ethnic cemeteries.²⁰

While there has been substantial scholarly attention to ethnoreligious conflict per se and more recently to the concomitant destruction of cultural buildings such as libraries, universities, and religious objects, including cemeteries, very little of it specifically analyzes the desecration of graves and cemeteries as a weapon of war or a "hate crime."[21] Andrew Herscher accurately argued that for the Serbian Orthodox Church "patrimonial monuments were not simply *symbols* of identity but irreplaceable *components* of it."[22] How much more so must be the graves of their sacred ancestors, and for individual Serbs, Croats, or Muslims, those of their own mothers and fathers? As Laqueur pointed out, "The willfully brutal disposal of the dead … is an act of extreme violence, an attack on the order and meaning we look to the dead to maintain for us."[23]

Literature produced on cemeteries and burial culture in the local languages is almost entirely national or regional in focus but includes several excellent religious histories and studies of local cemeteries.[24] Ethnographic and religious works in each region describe and analyze local burial rituals, placing them in the framework of both religious and often pre-Christian traditions.[25] These works have been invaluable for their deep and detailed information regarding religious and burial traditions, cemetery formation, and relations between and among all groups during the period under examination.

Finally, an entirely separate but related field of literature focuses not on cemeteries, per se, but on history and memory more broadly, often including the roles of cemeteries and memorials. Pierre Nora is particularly revered for his seven-volume edited library on French "lieux de memoire" (sites of memory). Nora's concept has been widely applied in the scholarship of other historians writing on memory and memorials including most prominently Jay Winter, who expanded our understanding of them to include also "sites of mourning."[26] More recently, their approaches have also been applied to regions of the former Yugoslavia by multiple scholars including Jelena Djureinović, Heike Karge, Andrew Lawler, Donald Niebyl, and Jelena Subotić.[27]

While building on this existing literature, my work illuminates the cultural and historical background as well as the practical policy decisions that contributed to an egregious set of grave and cemetery desecrations at a time of severe ethnic conflicts. It is a particularly interesting case, as the Socialist Federal Republic of Yugoslavia was both extremely diverse and under the governance of a regime that had every reason to promote a burial culture that was both pluralistic and integrated but did not. In order to support its stated goals of secularism, pluralism, and brotherhood and unity, the Communist regime should have worked toward multiethnic and multireligious communities of the dead that would foster and endorse comparable neighborhoods, villages, and republics. Instead, the party focused exclusively on retaining its monopoly on political power and imagery. Thus, the Communist party not only failed in these broader goals but also strengthened the very unity between national and religious identity that it had hoped to dissolve.

Theoretical Framework and Definitions

In this work, I use the terms "burial culture," "burial rituals," and "burial policies" in the broadest possible manner to include all beliefs, practices, and activities associated with death, mourning, body disposition, and commemoration, including the sites and architecture surrounding death as well as visual representations on grave markers. Burial cultures, like all others, are not static but evolve over time and are subject to political, ideological, economic, and class influences. Nonetheless, they are distinct from those influences and reflect longer-term cultural values and beliefs and intimate social relations. Burial rituals are traditional and symbolic practices often having religious or pagan origins that provide both comfort and unity to family, friends, and the wider community. Burial policies are specific and deliberate decrees, rules, and laws concerning commemoration and disposal of the dead intended to achieve a public goal.

This investigation of the Communist regime's policies toward burial culture is comparative in multiple dimensions as it (1) examines differences between policies in three republics, (2) compares the regime's policies directed toward its multiple religious communities in each republic, and (3) considers differences in those policies as implemented between rural and urban constituencies. Moreover, while most studies of commemoration focus on either private (burial rituals and grave markers) or public (memorials and military cemeteries) forms, this study crosses the boundaries between public and private space as well as public and private mourning.[28] Scholars have applied the terms "private" and "public" as well as the distinction between their presumed separate spheres in multiple ways over a long expanse of history from Ancient Greece to the present, engendering an enormous scholarly literature. Without dissecting that literature in detail, I would like to clarify my definitions and address how those spheres functioned within Socialist Yugoslavia.

Most understandings of the public/private dichotomy in modern society place it in the context of a Western liberal democracy. Two influential theorists of the public/private dichotomy, Hannah Arendt and Jürgen Habermas, provide much of the background and vocabulary relevant to this study. Habermas described the public sphere as a place where private individuals could come together for purposes of rational political debate, while the private sphere represented the space for commodity exchange, social labor, and the conjugal family, or "intimate sphere."[29] Hannah Arendt made a similar distinction but described that intimate sphere in more detail, as comprising all those things considered properly hidden, including the "bodily part of human existence" and all aspects of the life process, especially the realm of birth and death, "because it harbors the things hidden from human eyes and impenetrable to human knowledge."[30] Over time, the liberal conception of the public/private dichotomy established firm boundaries between the two spheres in order to protect private life from intrusions by the state. Thus, the liberal conception claims that the public sphere provides and protects equal rights for individual citizens while treating private economic activity, family life, and religion as entirely separate and secure from public interference.[31]

In that context, the term "private" very often focuses mainly on issues related to commerce, trade, and labor, which are understood to be privately owned in liberal democracies. Obviously, postwar Yugoslavia was not a liberal democracy. One of the first critiques of the private–public dichotomy came precisely from Marxists who noted that individual political rights applied only to citizens of wealth and property and that only the elimination of private ownership of property could result in true equality.[32] Those Marxists and their subsequent state-socialist regimes thus abolished private commerce, trade, and labor and sought to entirely eliminate the private realm by extending state/communal control into all areas previously considered private.[33] Even so, most communist-dominated countries left some activities to function within the private sphere, whether it be those related to economic survival on small private plots or the hidden life processes, like burial practices. In this work, "private" and the private sphere mainly refer to those intimate personal decisions and life processes that take place within the family and household.

The term "public" in the Western liberal democratic context can also have multiple meanings associated either with the marketplace of ideas (as in public debate and opinion) or state/municipal administration, thus involving politics more directly.[34] In a state-socialist regime, even one as relatively open as Yugoslavia's, we cannot really use the terms "public debate" or "public opinion" without considerable caveats. Therefore, in this work, "public" should be understood to be synonymous with state or municipal—a large category given that the state-socialist regime had taken over much of what had previously been private.

One important question for purposes of this work is where religious communities and institutions fit within this dichotomy. In fact, the public/private dichotomy has been challenged on religious grounds by many scholars who note that while religion was relegated to the private sphere as early as 1648, it "was never in every sense private—any more than it was always conservative."[35] Yet while very few states instituted a strict separation of church and state, Marxist regimes were certainly among those that tried. Nonetheless, Socialist Yugoslavia's religious policies were deeply inconsistent as they were sometimes far more hostile and aggressive toward religious communities than permitted by law, while in other cases, just the opposite. In particular, the regime preferred to leave matters relating to death and burial within the private sphere as much as possible. More importantly, in the Yugoslav context, religious communities and organizations were widely recognized as representatives for the nation, particularly in regions of the former Ottoman Empire where the millet system had formalized rights based on religion, which then became equated to the nation.[36] Rights and privileges granted to religion in the private sphere thus accrued to the associated nation and vice versa. Another exception to the Socialist encroachment on private property in Yugoslavia critical to this work involved the continued ownership of cemetery property by religious communities for several years following the Communist takeover of power. Yet, while much religious life properly belongs in the private sphere, it is difficult, for the reasons discussed earlier, to describe confessional (i.e., religious) cemeteries as entirely private.

Indeed, another critical flaw in the private/public dichotomy is its failure to clearly define the important sphere of activity and interaction that takes place in-between the public (the state) and private (the intimate sphere). Habermas acknowledged this somewhat indirectly and obscurely.[37] Again though for Habermas, all that intermediary activity and interaction still took place within urban democratic societies, while Yugoslavia of the post-war period was not only state-socialist but in many areas also deeply rural. Yugoslavia's urban citizens may indeed have struggled to find a sphere outside the home that had not been taken over by the state, but its rural inhabitants participated in a wide variety of social networks at multiple levels within village neighborhoods and those still-functioning religious communities. Tone Bringa has described how rural neighborhoods (often multiethnic), along with kinship and religious networks, functioned to create "relationships of mutual obligations, exchange, and support," manifested in home visits. Those visits, engaged in mainly (but not exclusively) by women, took place among close neighbors on a daily basis and with others on special occasions for rituals associated with life-cycle events like births, weddings, sons departing for the military, and funerals.[38] These social networks both informed and likely restricted private rituals, including burial and memorial practices. Thus, while this work speaks in terms of public and private forms of burial culture and memorialization, it also recognizes the critical role played by those groups situated in-between—whether construed on local, national, or religious foundations—or some combination of the three.

Finally, as Susan Gal has noted, much of the literature on the private/public dichotomy has correctly elaborated the many ways in which the concept is deeply flawed, with references to "blurred," "unstable," "shifting," "renegotiated," and "intersecting" boundaries. While these terms are useful, Gal's own portrayal of the private/public relationship as a fractal distinction—a term drawn from geometry, which illustrates "how a single pattern recurs inside itself … often with multiple nestings"—is compelling. These nestings, she explains, can then be "reproduced repeatedly by projecting it onto narrower contexts or broader ones."[39] Gal's examples of a home, which is private space but which holds within it the living room as a public space, wherein private conversations may also take place, or a street as public space, while the store front or alley/driveway are private, are instantly transferrable to both cemeteries and funerals. The cemetery itself is clearly a public space; nested within however, each individual gravesite and marker is considered private. Nonetheless, those markers are subject to public regulations and may be seen by members of the community or public passing by, commenting on them in their private conversations. Similarly, a funeral is generally organized by the family for a largely private audience but often takes place in a public setting, with the participation of community or public figures depending on the deceased's role in society and/or nature of the burial rituals.

My research investigates the fractal patterns of these spheres by looking at how private forms of commemoration—specifically grave markers and burial rituals—are mediated by local and ethnoreligious communities, in the context of the new public legal burial culture instituted in Yugoslavia following the Second World War. When this work investigates the legal structure and organization of cemeteries in Socialist Yugoslavia, it focuses on public/state goals and expectations for burial culture. In contrast, those chapters that examine burial rituals and grave markers tell us something about how individual citizens of the former Yugoslavia privately mourned and memorialized their deceased relatives, mainly within public spaces. In all cases, the local and ethnoreligious communities influenced both public policy and private commemorations. In short, there can be no clean boundary between the public and private burial cultures as all spheres influenced one another through a series of complex and sometimes contested negotiations over form, ritual, structure, and content.

Origins, Methodology, and Organization

My original questions when I began this research were simple—how did the Socialist system influence and/or change cemeteries and burial culture in the former Yugoslavia? What did cemeteries look like in a socialist but also multireligious and multiethnic society like Yugoslavia? How were they different than they had been previously? Were they organized differently? Did the grave markers look different? How did the regime effect such changes? Were these changes the same in all regions? And then, what happened to those cemeteries when the Communist regime and Yugoslavia itself fell apart?

My methodology for approaching the topic consisted of three parts. My first research goal was to investigate regime policies and discussions on cemeteries and burial culture. This meant finding any laws and policy decisions relevant to the topic in federal, republic, and municipal organs of power. In addition, I examined Federal and Republic Archives of the Commission for Religious Questions for the entire period of its existence from the end of the Second World War to the mid-1980s, inasmuch as they were available, as well as most of those from the Association for Fighters from the People's Liberation War. Second, I sought interviews with select individuals in all three republics, including cemetery and funeral directors, religious figures, and appropriate academics. Finally, my third goal was to visit and photograph cemeteries and grave markers in cemeteries throughout the region to see if and how they had changed over time. In the process of my research, I visited nearly 120 cemeteries and memorials: 34 in Croatia, 41 in Bosnia & Hercegovina, 18 in Serbia, and 26 in Kosova. I specifically sought out a mixture of larger municipal and smaller rural cemeteries, religious, secular, and military, some homogenous, but especially those with ethnoreligious diversity. In a period of approximately ten years, I took well over 2,000 photographs, which serve as a primary source and form of evidence, clearly demonstrating the continuing segregated nature of most cemeteries, the existence of and limited burial options available to those in mixed marriages, and the face of politicized grave markers. My approach was unlike that of scholars who focus on one or a very few small cemeteries, methodically mapping out every grave within it. I did not create a statistical database and was not seeking numeric data but rather broad comparative patterns evident among a large number of cemeteries in different areas. Those patterns should not be understood as absolute or applicable in all cases but indicative of larger trends. Hence this research crosses the boundaries between traditional and public/digital history. My photographs are accessible to the public on my Omeka website: Death and Burial in Socialist Yugoslavia (omeka.net). I also provide a link to a Google Earth map of the cemeteries I visited.[40]

This work is inherently interdisciplinary as it covers topics and interrogates problems that might best be approached by scholars trained in the disciplines of not only history but also religious studies, ethnography, anthropology, sociology, linguistics, and architecture. It is, therefore, likely to raise as many questions as it answers. Far from the "final word," on *Death and Burial in Socialist Yugoslavia*, it is an investigation into how policies of the Socialist regime in Yugoslavia affected the multiple burial cultures in the three BCS-speaking republics of Croatia, Serbia, and Bosnia & Hercegovina. I hope that the monograph may open a forum for discussion, encouraging others to engage in further research and oral histories on how the state, ethnoreligious communities, and private individuals negotiated and experienced burial culture and cemetery structure not only in the former Yugoslavia but also in other multiethnic and multireligious countries.

I have organized this monograph into seven chapters along with an introduction and conclusion. Seeking to make this monograph accessible to a broad spectrum of readers, Chapters 1 and 2 provide background information necessary for the remaining chapters. Chapter 1 describes the burial cultures of each of the major religious groups in the former Yugoslavia (Catholicism/Protestantism, Orthodoxy, Judaism, Islam). It further discusses the development of a Socialist burial culture in the Soviet Union, which provided a model for the early attempts of the CPY in the postwar era. Chapter 2 provides a historical background of Yugoslavia up through the wars of Yugoslav dissolution and specifically addresses the relationship between religion, nation, and the state in the three Yugoslav republics examined in this monograph (Croatia, Serbia, including Kosovo/Kosova, and Bosnia & Hercegovina).[41] A second section describes the Communist regime's legal and political structures and those agents that organized its postwar policies toward religious communities and burial culture.

Chapter 3 describes the postwar creation of cemeteries and memorials for soldiers and civilians killed during the Second World War by enemies of the Communist regime. Though they were often poorly funded, I argue that these cemeteries largely succeeded in helping both to overcome private grief and create a collective identity based on common values including the continued existence of the Yugoslav state, the brotherhood and unity of Yugoslavia's nations, and Socialist construction. As the Partisan cemeteries were ethnoreligiously integrated and largely egalitarian, they came close to creating a new community of the dead based on the Communist party's stated goals. Those designed in the abstract modernist style for which Yugoslavia later became famous may have been particularly successful by promoting universalist goals without the use of Communist symbols. Even so, because they excluded the remains of domestic soldiers who had fought against the Communist regime, they were nonetheless explicitly political.

Chapter 4 then moves to an investigation of Communist party policies toward civilian burial culture in postwar Yugoslavia.[42] It begins by focusing on efforts to remove the administration of cemeteries from the hands of religious communities and the creation of new municipal cemeteries, particularly in urban centers. While the Communist regime secularized cemeteries in Croatia and Serbia by the mid-1960s, it was never fully able to do so in Bosnia & Hercegovina. Moreover, in contrast to the Partisan cemeteries, where Serbs, Croats, Muslims, and Jews were buried side by side without distinction, almost no effort was made to integrate Yugoslavia's civilian cemeteries or create from them new "communities of the dead." As a result, both the old and the newly created cemeteries in all three republics remained nearly as segregated by religion and nationality in 1991 as they had been in 1945.

Chapter 5 addresses private forms of commemoration with a focus on burial rituals. It briefly examines different approaches to burial ritual in the differing cultures, religions, and republics and the extent to which those forms interacted with state regulations. The communists usually avoided interfering with private burial rituals unless either the deceased or presiding religious figures were politically active. Yet, while the Communist regime gradually came to recognize the importance of rituals, it did very little to introduce new burial rituals that might spread its own values among the civilian population. Two exceptions include cremation, which it promoted mainly for pragmatic reasons, and, more significantly, the funerals of veterans from the PLA, whom it considered a main source of political legitimacy.

Chapter 6 investigates the conflict between private and public forms of mourning by examining grave markers within Socialist Yugoslavia as reflections of religious, national, political, and personal identity. It traces how those symbols of identification on grave markers evolved over time in response to changing economic, social, and political conditions. The chapter also considers several specific ways that identity may be reflected on grave markers. One concerns the use of Latin versus Cyrillic script, another addresses the design and placement of grave markers for those in mixed marriages, while a third interrogates the meaning behind changing forms of Muslim grave markers.[43] Finally, it explores how grave markers for soldiers and other supporters of the regime politicized civilian cemeteries up through the mid-1980s.

Chapter 7 focuses on burial policies and burial culture during the period from the rise of nationalism in the 1980s through the wars of dissolution from 1991 to 1999. Specifically, it considers the "graves and bones" politics of mass graves, the use of national symbols on grave markers, and how the desecration of cemeteries and individual grave markers became a weapon in the developing ethnic conflict and war. It describes when, where, by whom, and for what purposes the desecrations took place and how they were understood by people on all sides of the conflict. I argue that the Communist regime's failure to integrate cemeteries while simultaneously making them into legitimate spaces of political discourse had, under these new conditions, also made them into spaces of ethnic and political conflict. The resulting violence against the dead even further divided the living.

Finally, the conclusion outlines the current status of cemeteries in the former republics that are now independent states. It further elaborates on the changing nature of postcommunist cemeteries and grave markers not only under conditions of nationalist politics but also under capitalism and a consumer society. It also includes a brief section on Roma burial culture.

Burial culture and commemoration is a deeply sensitive topic. As Thomas Laqueur noted, caring for the dead is fundamental to human civilization.[44] Yet, while all those living will experience death and most of us will attend a funeral and visit a cemetery, we do so with expectations and values conditioned by our individual cultural traditions, beliefs, and lifetime experiences. According to Caitlin Doughty, mortician and founder of the Death Positive movement in her *Order of the Good Death*, funeral homes are famous for prominently displaying the purported words of William Gladstone: "Show me the manner in which a nation cares for its dead and I will measure with mathematical exactness the tender mercies of its people, their respect for the laws of the land and their loyalty to high ideals." In fact, she argues, not only are these words likely not those of Gladstone at all, moreover, the presumed "merits of a death custom are not based on mathematics (e.g., 36.7 percent a 'barbarous act') but on emotions, a belief in the unique nobility of one's own culture. That is to say, we consider death rituals savage only when they don't match our own."[45] Heeding Doughty's warning, I consciously seek to treat all burial traditions, religious or secular/atheist, traditional or modern, urban or rural, with full respect and as equal in merit. Even more sensitive are those aspects of this work dealing with death caused by ethnic conflict and war, mass burials, and desecrations. No one who has worked in this field for over thirty years is without friends on differing sides of the conflict, painful memories, and opinions. As a historian it is my goal and responsibility to maintain a balanced perspective, avoid generalizations, and present information that is accurate and verifiable. As a human being, I have a responsibility to defend those who have suffered and died and call to account those whose actions caused such harm. I take both responsibilities equally seriously.

1

Burial Cultures of the Region

Veneration of the dead is part of what makes up civilized society. Scholars still debate when exactly the oldest deliberate human burial took place, but most seem to agree that it was sometime in the Middle Paleolithic Era, that is, about 100,000 years ago. One may argue about specific details, but human burials have been a part of human culture for a very long time.[1] Though humanity's relationship toward death is complex and subject to change, the dead matter to us deeply, as individuals and as societies.[2] For many, the essence of that relationship is fear, whether of death, the deceased, or just the unknown. Others have succeeded in replacing fear with hope based on belief in the afterlife and even glorification of the deceased. While differences in the rites and practices relating to funerals and burials often emanate from their disparate religious foundations, those religions exist within a particular cultural and historical context and are in a constant state of evolution and adaptation. This chapter summarizes the differing burial cultures associated with the religious communities of Yugoslavia following the Second World War, including those from Catholic and Protestant Europe, the Orthodox world of the Balkans and Russia, European Judaism, and Islam in the Balkans.

Catholicism and Protestantism in Western and Central Europe

Initially, fear of the dead caused societies in Western and Central Europe to build cemeteries far from urban dwellings. As they developed a more supplicating attitude toward the deceased, first saints and eventually all deceased ancestors were increasingly seen as beneficent mediators between those remaining on earth and the all-powerful God who would determine their fate after death. Cemeteries were built closer to towns where descendants of the deceased could pray to them and present them with regular offerings in hopes of getting a better deal after death.[3] Most cemeteries were connected to a religious building, as the ground surrounding that building was understood to be hallowed. Pope Gregory I (590–604) officially endorsed burial near churches so that worshippers might be reminded to pray for the souls of the deceased. Although officially against church law, beginning in the early Middle Ages, the clergy and especially sacred or important lay persons were permitted burial within the building itself. Over time, clerical authorities relaxed restrictions on who could be buried inside the church in order to raise funds.[4] Even so, most people were buried outside church walls.

Cemeteries in the Christian world thus reflected existing social divisions, and people remained as unequal after death as they had been in life. Those of greatest value to society were allotted highly desirable burial plots within the church, as close to the altar as possible, where the prayers of the faithful could ensure their rapid rise to heaven and they could be enlisted to help wealthy and important descendants in their earthly endeavors and in the afterlife. A hierarchy of status also determined the placement of those buried outside the church. Only the very richest could afford individual gravesites with permanent monuments. Most cemeteries were divided into "cemeteries of the rich" and "cemeteries of the poor" both of which included some individual sites but also mass graves, which became the final resting place for many.

As space was increasingly in short supply, particularly in years of plague, the mass graves were periodically excavated and the clean bones placed in an ossuary or charnel house—either a vault under the church or a separate building. Various religious institutions and activities developed to ensure that the bones would remain safe and prepared for Resurrection.[5] In other cases, cemeteries operated on a rotating basis and individuals were buried first only in one section of the cemetery and then in another and another so that the bodies of those buried in the first had plenty of time to decompose before the rotation came around to it again.[6]

The traditional orientation of Christian burials was East to West with feet to the East so that at Resurrection when they sat up they would be facing their Lord in the East.[7] Most were buried on the South side of the church, then some on the East and West, but the North side was considered the "Devil's side" and was avoided or reserved for the burial of suicides or other outcasts.[8] Conventional belief that the land surrounding the church was sacred meant that certain categories of people were excluded from burial on church grounds including not only suicides but also serious criminals, unbaptized infants, and those belonging to different religious groups.[9]

Burial rituals among Catholics remained largely consistent from the Middle Ages to the French Revolution and to a considerable degree beyond. One of their most important burial rituals—critical to securing a satisfactory afterlife—was receiving last rites and sacraments just before death. Deathbeds in the premodern world were far more public places where family and friends gathered to make their final farewells and where the dying might engage in acts of repentance and forgiveness. The most important act of preparation for death among many believers was the final confession and reception of the Eucharist as a kind of provision for the journey to the other world, ideally as close to the moment of death as possible. The earliest written reference to last rites was in Paulinus's *Life of St. Ambrose* from 422, but they had apparently long been in practice. Under the secularizing tendencies that developed in eighteenth- to nineteenth-century France, deathbeds could become sites of tension between Catholics and anti-clericals. In more traditional regions, however, public deathbeds and confessions were still standard practice well into the twentieth century.[10]

After death, the decedent was placed in a coffin with arms crossed on the chest. Then the body was sprinkled and anointed with holy water and scent. The body was then usually placed in a chapel or mortuary, though in rural regions it could also stay at home until the funeral, which could not take place for at least twenty-four hours to prevent premature burial. A mass was read over the body on the day of death, with a second mass to follow three days following the death, then another after seven days, thirty days, one year later, and on All Saints Day. On the day of the funeral, the deceased was taken from the chapel or home and the priest read a mass for the dead over the body. A cleric carrying the cross and children carrying candles led the procession from the chapel or home to the church and cemetery; additional clerics followed, carrying the censer with incense and a vessel of holy water. The priest wearing his ceremonial robes followed them, then the coffin carried by pall bearers, and finally close family and all others. At the church, the priest read the Requiem Mass over the coffin. Then the procession continued to the gravesite, where a final brief service took place, and the burial was complete.[11]

By the late sixteenth century and into the seventeenth century, two important developments led to changes in West European burial culture. The first related to the Protestant Reformation and gradual secularization of cemeteries, while the second was the rapidly increasing population and urbanization, which resulted in massive overcrowding of urban cemeteries, combined with changes in attitude associated with the Scientific Revolution and Enlightenment.

Protestant Reformation and Secularization of Cemeteries

The Protestant Reformation introduced theological innovations that significantly altered burial culture. Most important was rejection of the concept of purgatory, which eliminated any need for intercessory prayers for the soul of the deceased. Although some disagreement remained about exactly where the soul went after death, all Protestants agreed that the soul's fate was sealed and prayers were of no further value. Accordingly, the funeral had no spiritual function and served only to dispose of the body and offer comfort to the living.[12] Protestants also adopted a more reserved and simple approach to funeral services, stripping them of the pomp provided by priests, candles, incense, torches, and the ringing of bells. At the extreme, Protestants did not even require that the deceased be buried in consecrated ground; nor did they see any need to preserve bones in their sacred state, contributing to the gradual disappearance of charnel houses and ossuaries in much of Western Europe.[13]

These theological distinctions led to conflicts between Catholics and Protestants throughout Europe that seemed on the surface to be about burial rituals and cemetery access but really reflected deeper anxieties relating to cultural change and the maintenance of familial connections. Particularly intense conflicts occurred between the Huguenots and Catholics in sixteenth-century France and Protestants and Catholics in sixteenth- and seventeenth-century Ireland. In both cases, the Protestants offended their Catholic neighbors by publicly rejecting elaborate funerals in favor of simple ascetic ones and insisting on the absence of intercessory prayers. In response, Catholics refused burial to the Protestant "heretics" in their graveyards considering them a pollutant. In many ways, the Catholic reaction was historically and theologically consistent since outcasts, suicides, and nonbelievers had always been buried outside church territory in nonconsecrated ground. The French Catholics directly asked the Huguenots why they would even wish to be buried in Catholic graveyards since they did not believe in the need for burial in consecrated ground. The Huguenots, however, naturally wished to be buried with family members and did not mind being buried next to Catholics as long as they could use their own rituals and clergy, which was precisely what the Catholics refused to permit. Irish Catholics and Protestants faced the same issues but, according to historian Clodagh Tait, sought to avoid open conflict whenever possible. Frequently, both sides looked the other way and pretended not to notice the existence of the other in their common graveyards, seeking to preserve community-based and family gravesites.[14]

Even so, conflicts arose in both locations, though more often in France than Ireland, leading to situations where usually Protestant corpses were left unburied or only partially buried, with limbs exposed, or were left to rot in latrines, buried and then exhumed, and tossed in ditches or fields, reflecting what historian Penny Roberts refers to as "extreme hatred and contempt for the deceased."[15] Although the Huguenots started out by resisting Catholic efforts to exclude them from their graveyards, by the late sixteenth century they began constructing their own, albeit under a variety of legal conditions and restrictions. Most compelling in these stories of religious groups facing a hostile majority is the determination of individuals to bury near loved ones. Peter Jupp has argued that even more in premodern than modern societies, family graves and community rites serve as a bond against death. Julie Rugg also concluded that it was more the desire of family members to be buried close to one another than any ideological or religious conflict that served as the primary motivating factor behind most changes to burial practices in the rural Yorkshire communities she studied.[16]

Despite the violence associated with some of these cases, it was not until the eighteenth century that France first moved toward a system of municipal and secular cemeteries where eventually all could be buried in the same space. Not surprisingly, the first steps took place in the context of the French Revolution. Among the many visionary projects created in those years were some that imagined cemeteries as entirely secular and egalitarian in nature, lacking not only mausoleums but even any religious symbols.[17] French cemeteries were gradually secularized, though not as quickly as the revolutionaries anticipated. In the first years of the French Revolution, the cemeteries were secularized but retained religious sections separated by walls. The Napoleonic Decree of 1804 abolished all confessional cemeteries. By 1881, separate religious sections within cemeteries were also banned, and a law in 1905 banned the use of religious symbols on the public parts of cemeteries, although they could be used on individual grave markers.[18]

Few other European countries adopted as strict a form of the separation of church and state in cemeteries as did France, however. While most accepted the need to create municipal public cemeteries by the early nineteenth century, they also accepted the legal continuation of confessional cemeteries and many also permitted religious sections to be created within public cemeteries. In the Netherlands, an 1827 law required each municipality to either create its own or share a cemetery with a neighboring municipality, while the first funeral law of 1869 allowed Catholics, Protestants, and Jews to either purchase their own cemeteries or, if that was too expensive, create separate sections within the public cemeteries. In Great Britain, Germany, and Sweden, public secular and confessional cemeteries coexisted in a variety of configurations.[19]

These very different models of secularization have had an important impact on local burial practices. The rigid French laws have complicated the ability of its Jews and Muslims to comply with their own burial rituals as we will see in more detail later. At the same time, those countries applying a broader approach and offering more options to the various religious communities have had unintended effects on the ability to bury family members together, specifically those in interfaith marriages. For example, the law in the Netherlands that allowed each religious community to purchase a confessional cemetery or section of one also gave it full control over those cemeteries and sections, including the right to exclude burial privileges to nonmembers. Such a right included the refusal to permit burials of spouses from differing religious denominations, resulting in the photograph of two linked graves of a nineteenth-century Catholic woman and her Protestant husband. Unable to be buried together in the Chapel graveyard near Roermond, they arranged to be placed as close together as possible, directly opposite one another, in their separate sections (Figure 1.1).

Demographic Change and Public Hygiene

The second major issue that influenced the organization and development of graveyards and cemeteries was the combination of the constantly increasing population and a new concern for public hygiene under the influence of the Scientific Revolution and Enlightenment in the sixteenth to seventeenth centuries. Urban graveyards had always experienced pressures for space to which they had responded with rotations and periodic emptying of mass graves into ossuaries. The enormous growth of West European cities during the early modern and modern eras greatly increased the pressure on graveyards. When possible, churches extended their graveyard space, but the more common response was simply to pack more bodies into existing mass graves with predictably horrifying results. By the eighteenth century many graveyards had become so overused that heaving corpses raised the level of urban cemeteries above the surrounding land and streets. Moreover, because the soil had been exhausted, bodies were no longer decaying properly but only festered and stank. At the same time, the eighteenth century saw new values that promoted public hygiene as a source of good health along with a determination to eliminate contact with any form of bodily fluid, including those emitted from corpses.[20]

Burial Cultures of the Region 27

Figure 1.1 Nineteenth-century marker from interfaith marriage, Roermond, the Netherlands

In France, enlightened officials began to agitate in the mid-eighteenth century for an end to burial in churches and the transfer of all cemeteries outside city limits. Using the language of science and medical terminology, they described the deleterious and contagious effects of noxious fumes emanating from mass graves and overfilled pits on all urban citizens but especially those living in proximity to churches and cemeteries. A particularly egregious event occurred in late 1779 when the fumes from an overflowing mass pit at the Cemetery of Les Innocents in Paris spread into the cellars of an entire neighborhood and caused an overwhelming stench and illnesses among inhabitants for several months. In response, the administration of Paris finally took drastic steps, closing all urban cemeteries and requiring that the deceased of Paris henceforth be interred in cemeteries outside city limits. The example set in France was followed in several other European countries as burial in churches was forbidden in Sweden in 1783, and cemeteries within city limits were banned throughout the Austrian Empire between 1784 and 1788 and in Bavaria in 1803.[21] By the early nineteenth century, a series of regulations instituted throughout German cities placed cemeteries outside city limits and with strict hygienic rules.

In the years after the closing of Les Innocents and through the years of the French Revolution, intense discussions took place among officials and cultural elites about the new character of French cemeteries. Although a wide variety of projects—some quite extraordinary—were proposed, there was general agreement that future cemeteries would be "fields of rest" characterized by space and nature and filled with trees, shrubbery, and flowers. There were to be no mass graves, although the individual ones would be rotated on a six- to ten-year schedule.[22] In the meantime, however, and especially in the early years of the French Revolutions up through the Terror in 1794, the cemeteries were nothing more than empty receptacles for mass graves into which bodies were unceremoniously dumped. Funeral services, if they existed at all, took place within the city, after which the body was transported out of town for burial by municipal employees. Stories soon emerged that during the lengthy trip from Paris to the cemetery, the porters stopped so frequently for liquid refreshment that by the time they reached the cemetery they were barely able to complete their duties.[23]

In the era of the Directory and Thermidor following the Terror (1794–9), French authorities made a concerted effort to reform funeral and cemetery practices. Blaming all previous atrocities on the egalitarian impulses of the revolutionaries, social and religious distinctions in burial culture as in all else returned with a vengeance. The churches regained control over funeral rites, and the government called on citizens to act according to their wishes and economic abilities, "You modest people, be content with a simple urn; you wealthy ones, raise tombs that nourish the architect, the painter and scores of workmen whom you employ."[24] The final reforms of the Napoleonic Era were not as radical as earlier reformers had hoped but did include a ban on the reuse of coffins and assured that even the poorest citizens would have a shroud and coffin financed by the burials of the wealthy. They also secured a stable government-organized form of transportation from the city to the cemeteries, ensuring conformance to standards of public hygiene and decency, and procured funds for the purchase of land to create the famous Père Lachaise cemetery, which opened in 1804.[25]

That same year, Napoleon issued the Imperial Decree on Burials, which again forbade burials in closed places of worship and within the city and further stated that there were to be no more common graves; thereafter in France each person had the right to an individual grave over which they could erect a grave marker. Even so, it was expected that those graves would be reused after five years. Later, under continuing pressures for space, common graves were reintroduced but now with the stipulation that bodies could never be "stacked" but only buried side by side in trenches and must be in coffins. A further section of the law allowed individuals who provided endowments to the cemetery to reserve space for their family members, thus creating the concept of hereditary family gravesites that remained theirs in perpetuity. The founders of the law had imagined that only a very few individuals would take this opportunity, but in a relatively short time it became extremely popular and indeed the standard, further exacerbating the problems of space.[26]

In much of the rest of Europe, including Great Britain, cemetery reform developed in a more gradual and haphazard manner and was connected with the growth of Protestantism. Dissenters of various kinds, having no need for burial in consecrated ground, began as early as the sixteenth century, to establish a few small cemeteries separate from churches and often outside of town in Geneva and several German states, as well as Great Britain.[27] As early as 1581, the first Reformed mayor of London called for the removal of cemeteries outside the cities, probably mainly for hygienic reasons. Nonetheless, in Britain, these small separate cemeteries remained atypical; most dissenters were still buried in church graveyards, and for over 200 years the main response to demographic growth was to pack more bodies into the same space.[28] One hygienic improvement was that the use of coffins increased steadily such that by the early eighteenth century even paupers were buried in coffins in many parishes.[29]

In the first half of the nineteenth century, one short-lived "solution" to the problem of space was the development of private and joint stock cemetery corporations for the lower and middle classes. Although these corporations were able to provide some non-Anglican burial grounds, they did not solve the larger issue of overcrowding, particularly as some of them decided to maximize profits through a policy of "high-density burial."[30] By the middle of the century, British urban cemeteries had become, in the words of historian James Curl, "exceedingly nasty places" attracting the attention of a wide variety of scientists, public health officials, and reformers. A series of reports published between 1839 and 1850 detailed the unsanitary conditions associated with not only the cemeteries themselves but also local funeral practices. As in eighteenth-century France, the reports spoke of exposed, dismembered, and partially decayed bodies, which posed a significant threat to the public as they spread such contagious diseases as cholera, typhus, typhoid, diphtheria, and dysentery. The reports further exposed corruption and fraud within private cemetery and funeral enterprises, recommending the creation of national secular institutions.[31]

Despite public horror and outcry, it seemed the reports would have accomplished little had it not been for the cholera outbreak of 1848, which resulted in the Public Health Act of 1850 and creation of National and Municipal Boards of Health authorized to close down and/or forbid further burials within churches and church cemeteries. In contrast to France, however, as Rugg's study has shown, the Municipal Boards of Health worked with local communities to ensure that decedents were buried with family members whenever possible. In many cases, municipal leaders mediated between religious groups, in others they allowed parishes to buy additional land to expand their church cemeteries or create new ones, while in others they simply bent the rules or looked the other way.[32]

By the nineteenth century, cemeteries in most of Western Europe had begun to look more or less as we imagine them today. Depending on the country, some remained small, intimate church graveyards, but most cities also had large publicly administered and carefully planned park-like spaces, meticulously designed and landscaped, with chapels and public memorials, and filled with grave markers of widely varying sizes and styles indicating the religious and social identity of the deceased individual or family.[33] European graves may be individual, joint, or family with corresponding markers, which may thus have only one date inscribed or as many as eight to ten. In some, the gravesites belonged to the individual or family in perpetuity, but that rule also varied from country to country. In others, they were leased for a specific period, ranging from five to sixty years, after which time if the lease was not renewed, both the bones and grave marker would be removed and the site opened for lease to a new customer.[34]

One important development associated with these changes was the dramatic increase in the use of cremation as a means of body disposal. Although cremation existed in pagan and other cultures, it was forbidden by Christians on the assumption that the physical body must be intact at the moment of Resurrection. The concept revived in the late eighteenth and nineteenth centuries given the hygienic catastrophes that had resulted from overcrowding. It was mentioned in early projects for new French cemeteries during the Revolutionary era but to no great response and then again among mid-nineteenth-century anti-clerical Italians. An early apparatus was displayed at the International Exposition in Vienna in 1873, and the following year a Cremation Society formed in London. The first working crematorium was built in Gotha, Germany, in 1879, and crematoria were constructed in Great Britain during the 1880s–90s. Père Lachaise cemetery gained its crematorium in 1887 though not its first customers until two years later.[35]

Nineteenth-century opponents to cremation continued to argue that those cremated would not be accepted at the time of Resurrection and that cremation destroyed evidence of criminal misconduct. Proponents, who came to include many European governments, insisted that God could receive bones made into ashes as easily as those reduced to dust and that issues of public health and the environment outweighed all other concerns that could be addressed with reasonable legislation. Over the next century, cremation became increasingly popular in most West European countries, particularly after a Vatican Council decision in 1965 finally reversed the ban on cremation for Catholics. Two additional reasons for the growth in popularity for cremation were cost and continuing problems with space. By the middle of the twentieth century, improvements in technology and the construction of additional crematoria had reduced its price below that of a traditional burial. Moreover, once permanent or long-term gravesites became more common, cemeteries again quickly filled up and in many urban cemeteries almost the only way to ensure burial near one's family members was through cremation. Cemeteries closed to traditional burial would still accept urns or ashes. By the 1980s, between 40 and 60 percent of citizens in a variety of West European countries were choosing to be cremated. In Britain, whereas in 1919 only 1 percent of all citizens had chosen cremation, by 1998 72 percent were cremated after death.[36]

In many countries, family members are not permitted access to the cremated remains, which must be buried, stored in a columbarium, or disposed of by cemetery authorities. In the earliest years of cremation, most cemeteries created special sections for the storage of urns in columbaria or the burial or scattering of ashes in "memorial gardens." These special sections provide permanent sites where families may, as with traditional in-ground burials, visit their deceased loved ones on a regular basis; they have sustained the institution of cemeteries as public and communal sites of memory. In other countries, families are free to take possession of the ashes and bury or scatter them in approved locations, though enforcement is nearly impossible.[37]

Orthodox Christianity

In many ways, the burial culture of Orthodox Christianity is similar to that of Catholics. They certainly shared the same early ideas about burying their dead near religious buildings and the relics of saints. Most early graveyards were associated with and connected to a church or chapel, and as among Catholics, especially sacred or important lay people were permitted burial within church buildings. Those of highest rank were placed in the nave, others in the narthex, or inside porches, side chapels, under the floor, or in crypts; all others were buried outside. According to canon law, the deceased were to be buried individually and in coffins but that did not always take place, particularly in times of plague or famine. In cases of disease, the bodies were covered with lime before being covered with dirt. The Orthodox also did not provide funeral services for the burial of non-Christians, schismatics, unbaptized children, and suicides (except for the mentally ill) and sometimes excluded them from sacred ground. Thus, for example, Moscow before 1917 had seven cemeteries for Christians, two for dissenters, such as the Old Believers, and separate cemeteries for Armenians, Karaims, Muslims, Germans, and other foreigners.[38]

Yet several important features distinguish Orthodox from Catholic and Protestant burial cultures. Perhaps most important is that Orthodoxy has a more fully developed cult of the dead and of ancestors. The cult may derive from a particular Byzantine value placed on the social bonds of family and friendship. According to Nicholas Constas, this value reflected theological anxiety about "kindred recognition"—a fear that the deceased might not recognize one another after Resurrection due to bodily disfigurement. As Constas puts it then, "Concern for the dead was an extension of concern for society as a whole and honoring the memory of the departed was a way to cherish and celebrate life itself."[39]

Furthermore, according to Orthodox theology, while death does mark an important transition to a better life, that transition is characterized by a strong sense of mystery and awe. Other scholars suggest that the roots of the cult of death and ancestors lie in pre-Christian pagan traditions.[40] More than in Western Europe, though not necessarily Central Europe, Orthodox burial culture developed in combination with extant rituals derived from pre-Christian pagan religions. This merging of religions has been described in Russia as *"dvoeverie"* or "dual belief," but the same process took place throughout the Balkan Peninsula and in much of Central Europe as well.[41] It is characterized in burial culture by the introduction of a series of elaborate rituals before, during, and after the funeral intended to ensure safe passage of the soul of the deceased from this world to the next and prevent harm to those left behind. Despite variations between the precise rituals practiced by different national groups and even in different villages, striking similarities are also evident.

The line between official Orthodox theology and pre-Christian pagan traditions is often unclear. According to Monk Mitrofan, the author of a nineteenth-century primer of death in Russia, the immediate aftermath of death can be terrifying for the deceased; the soul remains on earth for three days in the company of its guardian angel, revisiting important sites and analyzing their meaning for the future of the soul. Afterward, the soul visits God who offers a preliminary assessment, but the final judgment comes only after forty days. In the meantime, the prayers of the living are critical, particularly on the ninth and fortieth day.[42] Certainly, many Orthodox rituals derive from this belief that it takes some time for the soul to leave the body and reach its final resting place. In the meantime, traditional rituals often treat the body as if it were in a state of limbo, simultaneously both alive and dead, and needing extra care and protection from vampires who would deny eternal peace and salvation to the deceased, damning them to the endless life of the undead.

Before the funeral, the deceased most often remains at home surrounded by lit candles for a period of one to three days where family and friends bringing food and gifts visit the body, often greeting it with a kiss. Measures to ease the soul's transition and prevent vampirization may include covering all mirrors and other reflective surfaces, such as TV screens, leaving doors and windows open, placing a basin of water under the deceased, and ensuring that cats and other animals stay out of sight.[43] Mourners attending the funeral and those who come to visit later bring food and drink for the deceased and leave it in the vicinity of the grave. Some also bring clothing and other gifts, which they sometimes place inside the coffin or grave. Another common feature of Orthodox funerals is the loud lamentations of women both during the procession and at the gravesite. The laments are original creations, not only describing important details from the life of the deceased but also connecting them to national and local values and traditions. Following the funeral, a meal is held at the home of the family with a special place setting reserved for the deceased. Visitations to the gravesite with gifts and food for the deceased follow seven days after the funeral, then again after forty days, at six months, one year, and then yearly. The Orthodox calendar includes several special days for visiting the deceased, known in Serbia as "Zadušnice" (Days of the Dead) when some believe the soul returns to earth in material form to visit its grave. That is why, according to the Orthodox, it is so important that the body be buried whole and not cremated.[44]

While facing several important dissident movements, the Orthodox Church avoided a disruption comparable to the Protestant Reformation that divided Western Christianity from the sixteenth century onward. By avoiding major internal religious challenges, Orthodox burial culture was able to retain a greater degree of stability. On the other hand, many countries with an Orthodox majority included populations observing other religious faiths, including Catholicism, Protestantism, Judaism, and Islam. Its challenges, then, came not from within but outside their religion, perhaps encouraging an even more determined adherence to its own traditions.

Due to the lower level of urbanization and modernization in Eastern Europe and Russia, Orthodox burial culture also suffered less from the challenges of overcrowding and its hygienic consequences. Fewer (though still some) reports described Orthodox cemeteries overflowing with bodies inadequately buried and failing to decompose properly due to overburdened soil. Even so, large cities in Orthodox countries responded to overcrowding and sanitary problems in ways not unlike those in the West. By 1657, burial inside the Kremlin walls was forbidden and after the plague of the 1770s, Russia's enlightened monarch Catherine II oversaw the construction of eight new cemeteries outside Moscow's city limits.[45] Most municipal cemeteries in the Balkans were not built until the latter half of the nineteenth century, but they too followed West European models.

Orthodox cemeteries may also have experienced fewer hygienic problems because the practice of providing long-term leases for burial sites was slower to develop within them and they were more systematic in their approach to body and bone removal. The Byzantine Greeks had already developed the practice of exhuming bodies after a certain number of years, cleansing the bones and placing them in ossuaries. In the Mediterranean Orthodox countries, exhumation of the deceased had become an important part of the funeral ceremony by the nineteenth century. Five years after the initial burial, the family reconvened at the cemetery and meticulously exhumed the body seeking to ensure that the bones were fully white, as an incompletely decomposed body signified that the deceased had not yet been cleansed of their sins. In that case, the family carried out prescribed rituals to ensure that the soul found peace and did not become vampirized.[46]

Judaism in Europe

Judaism is the oldest of the Abrahamic religions, dating back nearly 4,000 years; it is thus unsurprising that Jewish burial culture has changed a great deal in that time. Some of these changes stem from the reality of Jewish diaspora as Jews have been forced to accommodate themselves to different regions, host countries, and an enduring history of discrimination and persecution. Others have resulted from theological disputes among Jews about death and the afterlife, particularly the concept of Resurrection.

Early Jewish burials were in caves. Archaeologists have discovered many highly decorated Jewish catacombs for the period in the centuries before and leading up to the Christian era. At approximately the first century, Jews began to bury their dead in the ground in communal cemeteries, perhaps in deference to the biblical idea that bodies should return to dust. The earliest known Jewish public cemetery is the Mount of Olives in Jerusalem, which dates back to 2400 BCE. It was not originally used by Jews but came to be used by them as well as by Christians and Muslims.[47]

Unlike Christians, Jews do not build their graveyards near religious buildings. Perhaps in connection with pagan fears associated with death, they were most often built on the edges of town; Talmudic Rabbis ordered cemeteries to be placed at least 22 meters from any residence. The separation between cemeteries and synagogues is related to the Jewish law that prevents high priests (*koheni*) from having any contact with the deceased, including entering cemeteries.[48]

That did not mean that cemeteries were not considered holy ground. On the contrary, according to the Rabbi Elyokim Schlesinger, head of the Rabbinical Board of the Committee for the Preservation of Jewish Cemeteries in Europe, a cemetery is more sacred than a synagogue. Schlesinger describes the integral connection in the Jewish faith between the soul and the body, which does not end after death. Rather, he claims, the soul returns to the body for occasional visits, particularly on the anniversary of the individual's birth and death, on the eve of a new moon, and when people come to pray. Jewish cemeteries represented ideal sites from which to seek divine intervention as those visiting souls represent direct messengers to God.[49]

For Jews the cemetery is considered sacred ground in perpetuity and must be preserved. Therefore, Jews have extremely strict injunctions against the disturbance or disinterment of remains. Noted authority Rabbi Yechiel Ya'akov Weinberg explained the restrictions as stemming from the deep respect Jews give to the deceased and their belief that any disturbance of the grave would be perceived by the corpse as pain and humiliation. The proper treatment of the corpse, he explained, further affirms faith in Resurrection.[50] Jews who accept Resurrection believe that since the soul returns to the body on regular occasions, its remains must not be disturbed for any reason and monuments cannot replace the sacred ground on which they stand. According to Rabbi Schlesinger, removing even one single bone will cause great pain to the soul and the greatest kindness one can provide for the body is to leave it in peace.[51]

Unfortunately, that has not always been possible given the traumatic history of the Jewish nation. The Jewish diaspora that developed slowly over centuries resulted by the early Middle Ages in the dispersal and settlement of Jews throughout Europe, Africa, and the Middle East. Those Jews eventually divided into two regional groups: the Ashkenazi of North, Central, and Eastern Europe and the Sephardic Jews primarily located in Iberia, North Africa, and the Middle East. In nearly all European countries Jews faced considerable, if not always consistent, persecution, which also influenced the development of their burial culture. Many countries, like England, required Jewish cemeteries to be located on or just outside the edge of town while others allowed them inside the city.[52] Cities with large Jewish populations often responded by ghettoization, forcing city administrators to address the issue of burial space head on, providing them space for cemeteries. It is believed that the oldest Jewish cemetery in Europe is in Worms, Germany, where the oldest still visible grave marker dates from 1058/9.

Urban Jewish cemeteries soon faced the same problems with lack of space as did all others but with several complicating factors. First, as a persecuted minority, Jewish religious communities were rarely provided sufficient burial space to begin with. Further, as noted earlier, Jewish law prohibits the disruption or transfer of graves—a closed grave cannot be reopened. Therefore, the concepts of removing bones to ossuaries and reusing or rotating gravesites are both anathema, even if the cemetery is no longer in use and the tombstones have been removed.[53] Finally, Jewish law prohibits the construction of mass graves—each body must have its own individual site with each body separated by at least six "hands breadths" (50–60 centimeters, according to Rabbi Schlesinger) of solid material. After the fourteenth-century plague in Prague left thousands of bodies to be buried within a very short time, the Jewish community devised a solution. It is estimated that between the fifteenth and eighteenth centuries 100,000 Jews were buried in a long trench, twelve layers deep, each layer separated by six hands breadths of dirt.[54] Anyone visiting an old urban Jewish cemetery is immediately struck by the evident lack of space as grave markers are pressed in among one another with almost no intervening space.

Even when European Jews were not facing direct persecution, the differences between their burial restrictions and those of the host country could cause problems. Theoretically, Jewish cemeteries have always been strictly segregated from all other faiths. Officially, at least, even today non-Jews cannot be buried in Jewish cemeteries and vice versa. In practice, there are ways around the restrictions. Jews can be buried in Gentile cemeteries as long as they are in sections separated either by a wall or at least six feet.[55] Even so, the restrictions resulted in some conflict by the late nineteenth century as cemeteries in Western Europe became increasingly secularized and homogenized. In France, separate cemeteries were banned as early as 1804 and separate sections in cemeteries in 1888. Mayors were not legally allowed to make any special provisions on the basis of religion though they did have some flexibility if specific requests were made in writing by the deceased or bereaved family members. Still, not all chose to apply that option and have not always allowed Jewish sections within municipal French cemeteries or permitted Jewish communities to purchase land for the creation of religious cemeteries.[56]

The French law of 1881 also provided for gravesite leases of fifteen, thirty, and fifty years after which time any untended graves could be repossessed by the state for reuse and the bones removed to an ossuary. Again, it was up to the discretion of the mayor of each city to decide whether or not to create a separate Jewish section that would be exempt from these laws—some did, others declined. In Belgium, plots are leased only for fifty years, although the leases are renewable and there are no known cases of conflict. Even so, some Belgian Jews have preferred to be buried in the Netherlands, which offers burial sites in perpetuity.[57]

Theoretically, cremation is out of the question for Jews, particularly among those who believe that Resurrection is impossible for bodies that have been artificially disintegrated. Nonetheless, already by 1898 some Reform Rabbis had begun to sanction it and in the interwar period, reform Jews in Germany created a section in Berlin's famous Weissensee Cemetery for the burial of cremated ashes. They also, however, created a section where no ashes would be permitted to assuage the concerns of those members of the faith insistent on a more rigid adherence to rules. Not surprisingly, the events of the Holocaust added a new context to the Orthodox Jewish ban on cremation.[58]

In the past century, increasing interfaith marriages among Jews led to some moderation of their practice of strict segregation. Some Jewish cemeteries agreed to bury Gentile spouses rather than force couples to be buried in separate cemeteries. Theoretically, however, they were to follow the same restrictions as for Jewish burial in Gentile cemeteries and must not permit the use of any non-Jewish religious symbols on the grave markers.[59] Thus, in interwar Germany, Weissensee Cemetery permitted the burial of the Christian wives of Jewish men, though again the cemetery also then created a special section open only to Jews to satisfy concerns of the Orthodox.[60] Yugoslavia's Jewish cemeteries also permitted the burial of non-Jewish spouses after the Second World War with the argument that the community had become so depleted that they could not justify such exclusionist behavior.[61]

Obviously the most serious problem facing Jews in European diaspora was periodic expulsion. One famous case took place in Spain where Jews and Catholics had managed an uncomfortable coexistence until the mass conversions of the fourteenth century. In the following century, many Christianized Jews, called "Conversos," lived a double life, publicly conforming to the precepts of Catholicism while attempting to maintain their Jewish faith and traditions in secret. Official intolerance of such dualism led to the Spanish Inquisition of 1480, when a decade of persecution, torture, burnings, and ultimately mass expulsions led many to flee to more tolerant regions of Europe, such as the Netherlands, Italy, and the Balkans.[62] Although this is a famous case, it was far from unique. Jews were frequently forced to leave their homes throughout Europe, often on a moment's notice, leaving behind not only many of their belongings but perhaps also, most painfully, deceased relatives in graveyards. These cemeteries were then subject at the very least to neglect by local inhabitants, if not outright desecration.

By far the most famous case of Jewish persecution in Europe took place before and during the Second World War at the hands of the Nazi regime in Hitler's Germany. Already by 1934 the effects on burial culture could be seen in the refusal of members of the NSDAP to be buried at Heerstrasse Municipal Cemetery in Berlin, considering it a Jewish cemetery. By the late 1930s, the Nazi regime decided that while it could not forbid burial to Jews in municipal cemeteries, it did insist that just one crematorium be designated for use by Jews. As the position of the Jews in Germany further deteriorated, some cemeteries, where nonreligious but "racial" Jews had previously been buried, were "Aryanized," banning all further burial of Jews. The few like Weissensee that still permitted Jewish burial increasingly became places of refuge where Jewish children played and sacred scrolls and runaways could be hidden.[63] In the immediate postwar period, Jewish cemeteries were often subject to further desecrations but some, like Weissensee, were also restored. Unfortunately, the separation of Germany and Berlin meant that Jews in the West could no longer visit relatives buried there.[64]

Jewish burial culture is highly ritualized but intended to ensure equality after death. The Jewish burial society, known as the Hevra Kadisha, is responsible for preparing the body before the funeral. The body is washed, eyes and mouth closed, limbs straightened, wrapped in a shroud, and candles lit at the head and feet. From that point onward the body must never be left alone and there must be no food or drink in the death chamber. Theoretically, the body should be buried before nightfall on the day of death but at least as soon as possible. The funeral is also simple and egalitarian, with the body placed in only a wooden coffin. Embalming, cremation, and mausoleums are all banned.[65]

Judaism also prescribes a set of rules for mourning, specifying who must mourn, for how long, and in what ways. One tradition is "rending of garments" or vertical cutting along the lapel of the shirt of a family member, which symbolizes the tearing apart of the deceased from family. The torn shirt must then be worn for a period of up to thirty days. The Jewish period of mourning is also strictly proscribed. The first seven days is called the week of Shiva. During that week family members must perform no labor or other productive activities. The first three days after the funeral are often private days of weeping, but after that relatives and friends visit, bring food, and share memories and stories. The kaddish or mourning prayer is traditionally recited twice every day that week, then again at thirty days, on the first anniversary, and every year on four specific days, Yom Kippur, Passover, Shavuot, and Sukkot. The next twenty days are less intense, but even so laughter and rejoicing are avoided. After thirty days, the family takes a walk to symbolize the return to normal life. At the end of the year, the tombstone is unveiled.[66]

Islam in Europe

Islamic religious doctrine regarding burial culture draws partly on the *Qur'an*, understood to be the word of God as transmitted to Muhammad in the seventh century, but also on a set of texts, known as the *Hadith*, which are said to make up the body of Muhammad's other teachings, deeds, and sayings. Not only may these differ from the *Qur'an* but different branches of Islam, such as the Sunnis and Shi'a, draw from different collections. As the monotheistic religion with the world's second largest following (just behind Christianity), Islam exists within a wide variety of nations and countries whose burial cultures reflect not only their religious values but also the historical contexts within which they function. However much Islamic clergy and jurists wish to enforce religious doctrine, they also recognize and are themselves subject to these cultural forces and some adaptation is inevitable.[67]

I will be describing only the burial culture of Islam as it has existed in the Balkan Peninsula under the influence of the Ottoman Empire where it developed under very different conditions than in the Middle East, Africa, or Southeast Asia. It has, perhaps, more in common with conditions in the Caucasus and Central Asia, but those Muslims are more often Shi'a while Muslims in the Balkans are nearly all Sunni or Sufi. Islam came to Europe with the Ottoman conquest of the Byzantine Empire from the thirteenth to fifteenth century. As a religion, Islam did not and does not require or even encourage religious conversion. Nonetheless, in areas where religious diversity already existed, such as Bosnia & Hercegovina and Albania, significant numbers of the extant populations did convert, gaining freedom from taxation and association with the ruling class. In these regions, the Muslim population also increased due to colonization by conquering Turks. The burial practices of Islam in Bosnia & Hercegovina and Kosovo/Kosova were thus influenced not only by the Ottoman Empire but also by those of the extant population, which included Catholics and Orthodox, and in Bosnia & Hercegovina an independent Bosnian Christian sect whose massive grave stones, or *stećci*, are still scattered throughout the countryside.[68]

Whether as Slavic converts or Turkish conquerors, the Muslims have been generally perceived as highly unpopular among their Christian neighbors. Much literature of the eighteenth and nineteenth centuries refers to them as apostates and oppressors who must be obliterated from the landscape before the nation can regain its glory.[69] Under the influence of nineteenth-century nationalism, religious and nationalist wars pitted Christians against Muslims in a series of violent struggles as Bulgarians, Serbs, Greeks, and other Balkan nationalities sought Great Power assistance in achieving independence from the Ottoman Empire. Nonetheless, it is easy to overstate the religious element of that violence and worth remembering that in the Second Balkan War of 1913, Orthodox Serbs and Bulgarians applied precisely the same, if not higher, levels of violence and brutality against one another in seeking to establish the boundaries between their two Christian states.⁷⁰ Further, lengthy periods of peace and calm also prevailed, when good neighborliness and civilized behavior characterized relations between the various religious groups.

The transition from Christianity to Islam among some inhabitants of Bosnia & Hercegovina and in Kosovo/Kosova, which began after Ottoman conquest in the fifteenth and sixteenth centuries, did not take place overnight. Noel Malcolm describes a degree of syncretism among the three religions in Kosovo/Kosova and significant cases throughout the seventeenth century where Christians officially converted to Islam for the tax benefits but secretly maintained adherence to Christian ritual. Similarly, according to Amila Buturović, the first generation of Bosnian Muslims was often buried together with Christians. As with the Catholics and Protestants in Western Europe, family ties were more important than religious dogma. Only in the eighteenth century did the religious separation become consistent both geographically and stylistically.⁷¹

Nonetheless, even in periods of peace, Muslim burial cultural in the Balkans often met with considerable disapproval from their Christian neighbors. Every Balkan citizen of every denomination knows the aphorism to pass a place "as if by a Turkish graveyard" with an implication that the space has been ignored and neglected. Muslims themselves often acknowledge the accuracy of the proverb while denying any suggestion that they lack respect for the deceased or history. According to Bosnian Muslim cleric and scholar Mustafa Sušić, while Christians have a religious obligation to care for graves, the Muslim approach simply reflects a different view of death that sees it as just another phase of life.⁷²

It is a testament to the proscriptive power of the *Qur'an* that there is no "cult of death" among Muslims as exists among the other Abrahamic religions and especially the Orthodox. This distinction lies partly in Islam's complex attitude toward the relationship between the soul and the body after death. As Halevi explains it, "In the Qur'anic understanding, then, a person (*nafs*) becomes fragmented unto death when the soul (*nafs*) leaves the body."⁷³ The soul and body are thus in different worlds, and the *Qur'an* says nothing about the treatment of dead bodies or burials. The implication, however, is that prayers are of no value to the corpse, and Islamic Law was unalterably opposed to the concept of prayers to the deceased on the behalf of those still living. Theologically speaking, then, there is no good reason to visit the grave.⁷⁴

The *Hadith*, however, is more ambivalent about prayers for the dead, indicating that they may be of service to Islam and like Christians, many Muslims clearly believe in a median existence for the soul between death and the afterlife and a space where the soul can provide assistance to those still living. In fact, while the *Qur'an* itself does not address the fate of the body between death and Resurrection, some Muslim scholars developed a belief in a kind of Muslim purgatory known as the "tortures of the grave." In this view, the soul returns to the grave after death and is reunited with the body where, up until the moment of Resurrection, it suffers nightly tortures in expiation for sins committed during life on earth. Relatives of the deceased may be able to alleviate these tortures by means of prayer, epitaphs on the tombstone, and candles.[75] Many Muslim cemeteries are indeed located close to mosques or a holy shrine regularly visited by the faithful who come to pray for aid despite the objections of clergy. In postwar Bosnia & Hercegovina, some pilgrimages have even received clerical sanction as they help build Muslim religious identity through prayer and commemoration.[76]

By the eighth century, Islamic burial rituals had developed that are similar in many ways to those of the other Abrahamic religions. The corpse is washed, usually by a member of the same sex, oiled with scent, and wrapped in a white shroud. They are then placed on a flat wooden board, called a *tabut*, and covered with cloth, usually green, the color of Islam. Like Jews, Muslims require that burial take place as soon as possible after death, preferably before sundown on the day of death or at least the next day. A critical part of the funeral is the procession from the home of the deceased, hospital, or mortuary to the mosque where prayers are read and then to the cemetery for the final prayer and burial. Traditionally, the closest male family members take turns serving as the pall bearers and the procession is followed by all male members of the family and community. It can be considered an act of religious virtue to join a funeral procession, even of an unknown person.[77]

While Muslims believe in the afterlife as do Christians and Jews, they conceive of paradise in more tangible terms as a real place where the saved will enjoy a pleasurable bodily existence. In theory, therefore, one should not dread death but look forward to it. Thus, while weeping is acceptable, excessive displays of mourning such as wailing and rending of clothing are inappropriate, a view that likely contributed to women's exclusion from these burial rites.[78] Muslim women in Socialist Bosnia & Hercegovina, however, held regular *tehvids*—communal religious meetings—usually at the home of a relative of the deceased. During these meetings, held on the day of the funeral, then after seven and forty days, six months, and one year, the women read prayers for the deceased, as well as engaged in social networking activities.[79]

Muslims generally insist on individual graves, though one may see husbands and wives sharing a grave marker. Once in the ground, the deceased is placed on their right side, facing Mecca, and certain specific prayers must be read including the shahada—a statement of witness that God is one and Muhammad is His last prophet.[80]

Burial Culture in Socialist Regimes

Much of Central and Southeastern Europe fell under the control of state-socialist regimes following the Second World War. Some were originally Orthodox, like Russia, others were Catholic and Protestant, and several, like Yugoslavia, were multireligious and multiethnic. The influence of state socialism over burial culture has likely varied considerably, although this is difficult to document since so little research has been carried out in this area.[81] Regardless, to the extent that the Communist Party of Yugoslavia relied on any Communist country for advice or precedent, it looked only to the Soviet Union.

Existing literature indicates that the impact of the Communist revolution on burial culture in major cities of the Soviet Union was extensive and entirely negative. Although the Bolsheviks theoretically believed in complete equality after death as in life, here too they failed to live up to their own standards. By 1905 they had developed highly elaborate Red Funerals to commemorate the deaths of those martyred in the fight for revolution. Whereas traditional Orthodox funerals were draped in white to indicate "the other light," these were characterized by red banners, flags, ribbons, and wreaths, symbolizing the blood of martyrs. While Red Funerals were not revived in the Soviet era, elaborate funerals and burial privileges for party elites remained.[82]

In the immediate aftermath of the revolution in accordance with the policies of War Communism, the Bolsheviks nationalized the entire funeral industry. The new production quotas assigned to grave diggers as government employees required them to dig graves for only two adults or four children per day. The problem was that these new regulations went into effect at the end of the First World War and in the middle of a Civil War when thousands of people were dying daily and the bodies just kept accumulating. By 1918, mountains of corpses were stacked at the gates of every city cemetery in the country. Inevitably, ordinary families were forced to adopt alternate solutions, whether that meant bribing cemetery employees or burying the bodies themselves wherever they could find a spot.[83]

In contrast, high-level party members and other political elites received privileged treatment. From 1917 on, their funerals were well-publicized honorary events and their remains were placed in special locations designated for Soviet dignitaries. Red Square was by far the most prestigious as it housed the graves of the first 238 revolutionaries killed in 1917 and in 1924, Lenin's Mausoleum. Ultimately eighty-seven members of the Communist Party of the Soviet Union would be placed in the Kremlin wall, the last being Party Secretary Konstantin Chernenko in 1985.[84]

During the era of the New Economic Policy from 1921 to 1924, the funeral industry was reprivatized—just long enough for conditions to return to normal—and then it was again nationalized in 1929 and merged with the bureaucracy charged with the registration of births and weddings known as ZAGS. Apparently recognizing the serious organizational and philosophical issues involved, the Soviet regime focused more in its first decades on suppressing old religious rituals than on creating new ones. As Victoria Smolkin has put it, the role of ZAGS was "to enforce Soviet legal norms; it was not to solemnify rites of passage or endow life with meaning."[85] As a result, Western observers visiting Russia in the 1930s remained horrified by the lack of dignity and ceremony they witnessed in funerals other than those for elites.[86]

During the Second World War, likely in connection with the regime's improved relations with the Orthodox Church, the Soviet regime created two organizations, the Council of Affairs of the Russian Orthodox Church (CAROC) and the Council for Affairs of Religious Cults (CARC), to mediate between the government and the leaders of religious communities on questions of faith that required resolution. The organizations were expected to provide preliminary review regarding such questions, gather data, create reports, elaborate drafts for laws, submit them to the government, and supervise their implementation.[87]

By the 1960s, the Khrushchev regime finally sought to inject some ceremony into the system, noting that the lack of Socialist rituals had clearly contributed to the continued popularity of religious rites. The February 18, 1964, Council of Minister's Decree "On the Inculcation of New Civic Rituals into Soviet Daily Life [Byt]" established a central council to oversee the creation of new rituals. While much of the decree focused on rites relating to marriage and birth ceremonies, it also instructed municipal authorities to clean up cemeteries and improve the organization of civil funerals, producing models for "mourning pavilions" and preparing objects for funeral rituals.[88]

Whatever the council's and municipal authorities' intentions, their results were decidedly mixed. The municipal authorities often complained of inadequate resources, while the creative intelligentsia assigned to assist them had ambiguous intentions. A typical ZAGS funeral service in the late Soviet era took place in the "Hall of Ritual" and lasted only fifteen to twenty minutes. Some were more luxurious than others, depending on cost (music and flowers were extra), but the employees were predictably bored and sure to loudly inform family members exactly when their allotted time was up. The standard ritual, according to Catriona Kelly, "always boiled down to two elements: wreaths and speeches. The latter were invariably in a strict pecking order: first the director, 'and then say the trade union boss. ... Friends? Right at the end.'"[89] The entire process was also fraught with corruption, entailing bribes at every step to secure the gravesite, necessary paperwork, grave diggers, transportation, and grave marker so that while burial costs were ostensibly quite low, requiring as little as 200 rubles, in practice they could cost up to 15,000–20,000 rubles. Predictably, however, and reflecting the system's hierarchical structure, the one ritual that the regime did create and encourage was a visit by newlyweds to Lenin's Mausoleum.[90]

Communists in the Soviet Union, as well as in all of Central and Southeastern Europe, also encouraged cremation as an egalitarian, hygienic, and inexpensive alternative to in-ground burial. The Soviets turned to cremation as early as 1919 as a desperate response to the piles of unburied bodies that followed their nationalization policies. However, the challenges they faced were enormous, not only because the Orthodox Church remained adamantly opposed to the concept but also because they lacked the technological skills for the task. The first crematorium opened in 1920 had very low capacity and burned to the ground within a year. Later crematoria were more technically successful and were popular with some of the Communist party's leading members; even so, many of their main customers were also drawn from the country's expanding prison population. Only in the 1960s under Khrushchev did the regime try seriously to promote cremation among the wider public. Here again, they were not very successful and in as much as they did gain proponents, it was either among confirmed atheists or those anxious to gain entry for deceased relatives near family in an otherwise "full" cemetery.[91] According to Kelly, the regime in Leningrad aggressively promoted cremation in part by making access to traditional burial sites extremely difficult and unappealing. It closed old cemeteries and declined to provide adequate transportation or landscaping for new ones. In contrast, the crematorium site with its massive columbarium outside Leningrad/St. Petersburg is beautifully landscaped and has a well-appointed bus that runs frequently but is nearly always empty.[92]

Despite Soviet efforts to promote atheism, the regime did not ban religious worship and families were permitted to include whatever religious symbols they preferred (or none) on grave markers. Cemeteries throughout Russia thus remain filled with Orthodox crosses. Although the Communist regime sought to restrict access to religious rites by limiting registration of clergy, a kind of underground church made up of itinerant unregistered priests emerged. Somewhat more astonishing was the phenomenon of religious funerals conducted in absentia by correspondence, according to which family members in locations lacking a priest would send a small amount of dirt from the grave by mail to a priest who would conduct a service over it and return it to be placed on the gravesite. According to official figures (which included at least some of the "correspondence funerals"), some 40 to 70 percent of all funerals in the Soviet Union from the 1920s to 1980s were religious. Not surprisingly, the highest percentage of religious funerals was in the 1920s and 1980s, while the lowest was in the late 1960s during the height of Khrushchev's anti-religious campaign.[93] Obviously these figures varied enormously in different areas of the country. As Catherine Merridale pointed out, the lasting attachment to Orthodoxy was clearly seen in the continued visitations to and use of village cemeteries. People outside the cities continued to visit their family graves on Saturdays, Sundays, or any day that they could, leaving behind, as in the past, flowers, food, bread, and drink.[94] Meanwhile, at least some regions with multiple religious populations provided separate cemeteries for them. For example, Tashkent, the capital city of Uzbekistan, had cemeteries for its Orthodox, Armenian, Jewish, Muslim, and even atheist citizens.[95]

Since the fall of communism in the Soviet Union and Central and Southeastern Europe in the early 1990s, open adherence to religious faith has returned with considerable speed and energy. In many cases, it is difficult to clearly differentiate sincere spiritual faith from a more cultural and political connection between religion and national identity. Either way, religious symbolism has been more clearly reflected in the burial culture of succeeding decades.

Conclusion

These then are the burial cultures that made up the main religious communities of and influences on Socialist Yugoslavia, though they functioned and coexisted quite differently in its diverse republics, cities, towns, and villages. In some cases, people of differing religious backgrounds worked, lived, and died together with relative ease. They knew each other intimately, shared their secrets, love, and tragedies, and joined together to celebrate all rites of passage. In other cases, they lived almost entirely separate existences with little or no knowledge of the "other" and what they did know might be a mixture of superstition and misinformation as they imagined that other living in a world of barbarism. Most often, however, reality lay somewhere in between, as they shared some parts of their lives, saw each other in public fora, on the streets, in the markets, and at work, exchanged polite conversation but their relationships lacked intimacy and depth and they remained largely indifferent to each other's loves and tragedies. Their daily interactions were also guided and shaped by political developments and social relationships of the communities and state in which they lived.

2

Religion, Nationalism, and the State in Socialist Yugoslavia

As a country Yugoslavia is more often remembered for its failures than its successes. A substantial proportion of the books written on its history include in their title terms such as "Breakup," "Conflict," "Collision," "Death," "Demise," "Destruction," "Fall," "Failure," "Fragmentation," "Ruin," and "Unraveling." These choices are hardly surprising considering that while the two Yugoslavias (Interwar Yugoslavia 1918–41 and Socialist Yugoslavia 1945–91) experimented with several forms of government, including democracy, dictatorship, and socialism, both ended in civil wars that pitted nations and neighbors against one another. This book seeks to neither condemn nor rehabilitate what has been called "the Yugoslav experiment."[1] Rather, it studies the intersection between Socialist Yugoslavia's burial culture and the ethnoreligious conflicts that confounded political life during the Second Yugoslavia. It suggests that although Communist policies relating to burial culture could have served to mitigate ethnic conflicts, they instead likely exacerbated them.

This chapter establishes the historical context for Socialist Yugoslavia and then more specifically the republics of Croatia, Serbia (including the Autonomous Province of Kosovo), and Bosnia & Hercegovina with an emphasis on the relationship between religion, nation, and the state. Moreover, it describes the legal, political, and social framework within which all burial policies in those republics took place, along with those assigned to implement them, from the end of the Second World War in 1945 until the wars of Yugoslav dissolution that ended in 1995 in Croatia and Bosnia & Hercegovina and 1999 in Kosovo. It thus provides the foundation for discussions in later chapters regarding the organization and structure of military and civilian cemeteries, rules and regulations regarding burial rites and grave markers, as well as conflicts in and between the Socialist state and various ethnoreligious communities and nationalist ideologies on these topics.

The regions that would unite in the First Yugoslavia in 1918 were divided between the Ottoman and Austro-Hungarian Empires from the fifteenth through much of the nineteenth century. With the rise of nationalism in the late eighteenth and early nineteenth centuries, several of the Balkan nations began to seek and achieve greater autonomy and/or independence, often creating rivalries with one another over the creation of their borders. Yet by the end of the First World War, three major South Slavic nations in the region (Serbia, Croatia, and Slovenia) had agreed to unite in one country, hoping to protect those borders and increase security against the Great Powers of Germany and Russia. Originally called the Kingdom of Serbs, Croats, and Slovenes (later Yugoslavia), the new country also encompassed (willingly and not) a large number of other Slavic and non-Slavic nations and nationalities.[2]

Although the idea of a unified South Slavic state made some sense both demographically and geographically, Croat and Serb governing bodies held radically differing concepts of state organization with the result that many citizens never accepted the new state's authority. As relations between and within national units became increasingly violent, the Serbian monarchy installed a dictatorship on January 6, 1929, further eroding any hope for legitimacy. By the late 1930s, the threat from Nazi Germany finally inspired the Yugoslav government to build unity through compromise, but the opportunity for negotiations had long since passed. The Axis occupation of Yugoslavia in 1941 was thus accompanied by a brutal civil war as nationalist tensions exploded into violence.

The Communist Party of Yugoslavia (CPY) was first formed in 1919 and after being outlawed in 1921 remained relatively insignificant throughout the interwar period. Nonetheless, under the leadership of Josip Broz Tito in the mid-1930s it became more disciplined, "bolshevized," and most importantly adopted the "popular front" line, allowing it to cooperate with other anti-fascist parties. Further, it was the only political party in Yugoslavia then or later that was not affiliated with any one nation or nationality. Once the Communist party entered the Second World War as the People's Liberation Army (PLA) or Partisans in July 1941, that fact and its slogan of "brotherhood and unity" allowed the party to stand outside and above the fratricidal struggles ravaging the country as it fought against foreign occupiers. Given the nature of the war, the PLA did not fight only the foreign occupiers but also a wide variety of domestic forces collaborating with them, including the Croatian fascist Ustashe and Serbian nationalist Chetniks. As the Partisans' military successes grew, so did their popular front policy, and increasing numbers of ordinary citizens with no interest in communism or the party joined the Partisans and their mass organizations: the People's Front, the People's Youth, and the Anti-Fascist Front of Women.

As the war ended, the Yugoslav Communist party, with both Soviet and British assistance, gradually established first military and then political control over the country. Seeking to prevent the nationalist conflicts of Interwar Yugoslavia, it created the second Socialist Yugoslavia as a federation of six equal republics (Serbia, Croatia, Slovenia, Bosnia & Hercegovina, Macedonia, and Montenegro). Serbia also included the two Autonomous Provinces of Vojvodina and Kosovo. The CPY was expected to provide the unifying moral authority that would hold the republics and nations together, and certainly in practice all real power lay with the party rather than the state. As a result, specific policies in relation to the national question were often ambivalent and somewhat contradictory. On the one hand, the party was careful to avoid any suggestion that it was promoting cultural assimilation or the creation of an overarching Yugoslav identity. In fact, it explicitly encouraged the cultural autonomy of certain national minorities and, as Paul Shoup noted, was "not averse to providing a safe outlet for national feelings." At the same time, recognizing the inherent risk of a return to the violence seen during the Second World War, the regime immediately included within its criminal code articles that banned the incitement of national, racial, or religious hatred.[3]

In the first years after the Second World War, from 1945 to 1952, the CPY clearly modeled itself and many of its policies on the Soviet Union under Stalin. In the spring and summer of 1948, however, Soviet–Yugoslav relations suffered an irredeemable rift leading to Yugoslavia's expulsion from the Soviet bloc. Once party leaders recovered from their initial shock, they began to reread the classics of Marxism-Leninism and by the early 1950s had determined to de-Stalinize and purify the party, returning it to the original Marxian goals of "worker's self-management." Reflecting that shift, the party changed its name in 1952 to the League of Communists of Yugoslavia (LCY).

By the 1960s, leaders of the LCY worked ever more to decentralize both the party and state. Yet while the initial objectives of decentralization were in line with plans for worker's self-management, they were increasingly associated with the specific economic goals of each republic and then more directly yet with nationalism. For example, the "Croatian Spring" of 1971 combined demands for economic reforms and greater democratization, with calls to reinvigorate the Catholic Church, strengthen use of the Croatian language, and reintroduce Croatian national symbols. While Tito ultimately repressed the Croatian Spring, he simultaneously offered the republics significant concessions in the direction of greater decentralization, leading to the 1974 Constitution, which significantly increased the rights of republics and especially the Autonomous Provinces of Vojvodina and Kosovo.

Tito's death in 1980, combined with a burgeoning economic crisis, set the stage for Yugoslavia's economic and political decline throughout the decade. Nonetheless, the sparks that set the fires for the Yugoslav conflagration were unquestionably lit by the rise of nationalism not only among Croats, as in 1971, but almost every nation and nationality in Yugoslavia including Kosovar Albanians, Slovenes, Macedonians, Montenegrins, and Bosnian Muslims. That spark of nationalism burned most openly and fervently, however, among Serbs, where it kindled national flames among nearly every other ethnic group in the former Yugoslavia.

In the mid- to late 1980s, Serbian nationalist politics were also associated with the rise of Slobodan Milošević, leader of the Serbian League of Communists, and increasing involvement in politics by the Serbian Orthodox Church. The most famous expression of Serbian nationalist politics came with the September 1986 publication of the *Memorandum of the Serbian Academy of Arts and Sciences*, outlining what it claimed to be systemic economic and political discrimination against Serbs of catastrophic proportions. It focused first on the purported existential threat facing the Serbian population in Kosovo and then on Serbs in Croatia and Bosnia & Hercegovina.

Although the *Memorandum* blamed the threat to the Serbian nation mainly on the Communist regime (which, it claimed, kowtowed to the national interests of Slovenia and Croatia), Milošević, then a mid-level Communist official, was quick to grasp the potential of nationalism and soon used it to oust his rivals and take control of the Serbian Communist party. Milošević's 1987 visit to the site of the famous Battle of Kosovo Polje was a turning point in both his career and Yugoslavia's fate as he called on the emotive power of Serbian history and traditions to restore Serbian control over the Autonomous Provinces of Kosovo and Vojvodina.

In the following two years, as Communist regimes throughout Europe were collapsing one by one, Communist leaders in the Socialist Federal Republic of Yugoslavia made multiple attempts to preserve the state, but its time had also come. In the spring of 1990, the republics of Slovenia and Croatia held multiparty elections resulting in victories for noncommunist governments; both then declared independence from the federation on June 25, 1991. The remaining republics and provinces (except Serbia and Vojvodina that remain together to this day) eventually also declared independence between September

1991 (Macedonia) and May 2008 (Kosova). The declarations of independence did not lead to war in all cases. Macedonia and Montenegro withdrew without conflict. Even Slovenia, the first to go, was able to depart after "only" a Ten-Day War in which approximately 70 people were killed and 328 wounded.

Yugoslavia's wars of dissolution took place in Croatia and Bosnia & Hercegovina from 1991 to 1995 and then in Kosovo in 1998–9. Statistics on casualties in the wars have been extremely difficult to calculate but suggest that approximately 135,000–140,000 people were killed: as many as 100,000–104,000 in Bosnia & Hercegovina, approximately 20,000 in Croatia, and 11,000–13,500 in Kosovo.[4] Long-standing and severe violence took place not just in multiethnic regions but mainly in those with significant Serbian Orthodox populations, targeted by Serbian nationalist politics.

The following sections provide more detail on the historical background of Croatia, Serbia, Bosnia & Hercegovina, and Kosovo/Kosova, focusing on relations between the religious communities, developing nationalist organizations, and the state.

Croatia

Croatia is a boomerang-shaped country, bordering the Adriatic Sea, Italy, Slovenia, Austria, Hungary, Serbia, Montenegro, and Bosnia & Hercegovina. It existed as an independent kingdom briefly in the tenth to eleventh century, but in 1102 a succession crisis led it to accept a dynastic union with the Hungarian kingdom. After the Hungarians lost the Battle of Mohacs to the Turks in 1526, Hungary became part of the Habsburg Austrian Empire where it, and Croatia with it, remained until the end of the First World War. Croatia was Christianized by Catholic missionaries in the ninth century, and a large majority of Croats are Catholic. However, in 1578 hoping to fend off Ottoman invasions, the Habsburg dynasty invited Orthodox Serbs to colonize its borderlands, mostly along the inside edge of the boomerang. The Serbs were offered free land and religious rights in return for their agreement to fight the invading Turks. The area where the Serbs settled became known as the Military Frontier—Vojska Krajina or often just the Krajina. At the end of the seventeenth century, anticipating the imminent demise of the Ottoman Empire, more Serbs moved out of Kosovo/Kosova and into the regions of Eastern Slavonia and Vojvodina, across the Danube River from Serbia, believing that they would be able to return home in the near future. In fact, however, the Ottoman Empire persisted for another

200 years, and they became permanent residents of the region. As a result of these migrations and others, Croatia came to include a substantial Serbian Orthodox minority (approximately 14.5 percent of the population in 1948) along with smaller numbers of Protestants, Muslims, and Jews.[5]

At the end of the First World War, Croatia agreed to form the Kingdom of Serbs, Croats, and Slovenes, later renamed the Kingdom of Yugoslavia. Although the Croats joined the union voluntarily, it was never a happy marriage. Croatia had envisioned the union as a loose confederation of fully equal partners, whereas the Serbs always imagined themselves as first among equals in a highly centralized union. These differences led to increasing polarization, particularly between the Serbs and Croats and, despite some belated efforts at compromise, brutal conflicts during the Second World War.

Croatia was occupied by Germany during the war, but the Germans also worked with the Croatian fascist Ustasha regime, which sought to exterminate not only the region's Jewish but also its Serbian population. The role of the Croatian Catholic Church in those policies has been the subject of considerable debate. While most members of the Catholic hierarchy cannot be held responsible for Ustasha atrocities against Serbs and Jews, nor did all members of the Catholic clergy do all they might have to prevent them. Some clergy members participated in mass conversions of Orthodox Serbs to Catholicism, but others refused, while still others claimed they did so only to save Serbian lives. What is beyond doubt is that the Church was unalterably hostile to the Communist party itself.[6]

Nonetheless, the Partisan movement in Croatia, as elsewhere, downplayed its Communist agenda and willingly accepted the cooperation of all those willing to join the fight against fascism, incorporating clerics from all of Yugoslavia's religious communities, including a few Catholic priests. At the end of the war, the Partisans made further efforts to achieve some kind of modus vivendi with the Catholic Church. On June 2, 1945, in an interview with Catholic Bishop Salis-Seewis, Tito, "speaking as a Croat," criticized the behavior of one part of the Catholic clergy and urged them to form a more "national" (nacionalni) church, suggesting they should break from Rome and form a schismatic Catholic Church. He emphasized his own desire to create great community of South Slavs, both Orthodox and Catholic.[7]

That goal was very likely what had inspired the cooperation of Monsignor Svetozar Ritig who had served as secretary to the well-known supporter of South Slavic unity, Bishop Strossmayer, before the First World War. At the age of sixty, Ritig joined the Partisans and, at the war's end, returned to Zagreb where he became minister without portfolio in the federal government and head of

Croatia's Commission for Religious Questions. Ritig's support for the regime had never been ideological and his loyalty to the church was unquestioned, but he believed that only the Communist party could hold the different federal units together based on the slogan of "brotherhood and unity."[8]

Ritig further argued that technically the regime did not persecute the Church, because it never interfered with its internal structure but limited itself to the prosecution of individuals. Nonetheless, it carried out some of those prosecutions with great vigor. Most prominently, the party carried out a public war crimes trial against Archbishop of Zagreb Alojsius Stepinac whom it considered a direct enemy of the state, ultimately convicting him of treason and collaboration with the Ustashe regime and sentencing him to sixteen years' hard labor.[9] Multiple other priests at all levels were also arrested, beaten, imprisoned, and even killed sometimes in the absence of any legal proceedings.[10] Ultimately, the Communist party always considered Catholic loyalty to the Pope a threat to national patriotism. As a result, Communist party activists generally took a harder line against Catholic priests and the Catholic Church than against any other religious community in Yugoslavia. Relations were so strained in the early years after the war that the Yugoslav government formally broke off relations with the Vatican in December 1952.

Beginning in the mid-1950s and continuing throughout the 1960s, however, regime relations with the Catholic Church gradually improved due to renewed efforts from both sides. As early as 1953, Tito condemned violence against the clergy, and in 1959 Politbureau member Aleksandar Ranković sent an internal memo to all republic organizations advising against the use of "administrative measures" in work with religious communities. Just as important were the decisions of the Second Vatican Council from 1962 to 1965 that fundamentally reexamined interactions between the Catholic Church and non-Catholics. Under these improved conditions, formal diplomatic relations were gradually reestablished leading to a 1965 agreement that guaranteed the Catholic Church freedom of action in religious affairs and rituals in return for Vatican promises that the priests would not abuse church activities for political purposes.[11]

After a brief period of relative calm, the Catholic Church reappeared on the scene during the 1971 Croatian Spring when, according to Vjekoslav Perica, lay Catholics experienced a "golden age." Churches were overflowing and religious symbols ubiquitous. The Church promoted the cult of the Virgin Mary as the national symbol of Croatian Catholics and organized a series of jubilees and celebrations at the shrine of Marija Bistrica. Perica describes the function of the Marian Cult as being as much national as religious, citing Cardinal Kuharić who claimed that it "reasserted Croatian Catholic identity and unity." At Marijan celebrations in 1971, pilgrims dressed in national folk costumes and sang national songs along with religious hymns, and one bore the slogan "Let Our People Not Lose Their Identity" while the Archbishop offered a "Prayer for the Croatian People."[12] The connection between nationalism and religion was precisely what made the Croatian national movement so disturbing and dangerous to the unified state and its ideology as it worked directly counter to the regime's original goals to disassociate national and religious identity. Although Tito and the central regime crushed the Croatian Spring, carrying out a mass purge of the Croatian Communist party and arresting many of its main leaders, it was unable to suppress the revival of Catholicism, which continued throughout the 1970s–80s.[13]

By the spring of 1990, the revival of Croatian nationalism was increasingly evident in the republic's first multiparty elections, which saw the emergence of Franjo Tudjman and the Croatian Democratic Community (HDZ). Building on connections that had developed between the Croatian national movement and Catholicism during the 1970s, Tudjman sought an alliance between the HDZ and the Catholic Church during his election campaign and following his 1992 victory made a highly visible pilgrimage to the Marian Shrine at Marija Bistrica outside Zagreb. Later he also supported the Catholic Church in promoting the beatification of Archbishop Alojzie Stepinac as a martyr to the Communist system.[14]

Within a very short time the Catholic Church had reasserted its dominant role in society and political life. The national ideology of Croatia as it developed by the early 1990s under Franjo Tudjman combined an emphasis on the historic continuity of the Croatian state and the primacy of the Croatian nation over national minorities, particularly the Serbs. Tudjman's speeches consistently referred back to Croatia's historic traditions and glory, and he made a point of resurrecting symbols from the past, including those appropriated by the fascist Ustashe.[15] The most important of these was Croatia's checkerboard flag (šahovnica), which is also prominently featured on its state herald.[16] In addition, the new Constitution of Croatia, passed under Tudjman in December 1990, dropped Serbs as a constituent nation and relegated them to the status of a minority. The Constitution also eliminated Cyrillic, the script most commonly used by Serbs, as one of the official scripts in use by the state.[17]

The revival of Croatian nationalism engendered considerable anxiety among the resident Serb population, particularly given the Ustasha atrocities against Serbs during the Second World War. Serbian nationalists in Serbia proper deliberately intensified their fears, leading many Serbs in the Krajina to begin forming armed militias as early as August 1990 and by March 1991 to declare the secession of the self-proclaimed Autonomous Region of Krajina and its union with Serbia.[18] Once Croatia declared its independence from Yugoslavia in late June 1991, the war was on. Much of the war also took place in eastern Slavonia, near Osijek and Vukovar, with aid to the Serb minority coming from Yugoslav People's Army (JNA), which had become almost entirely Serbianized by September 1991.[19] Another critical part involved the JNA's bombardment and siege of Dubrovnik. The European Community's recognition of Croatia and the UN-imposed Peace Agreement in December 1991 largely ended the official participation of Yugoslavia and the JNA in Croatia, although the civil war continued for the next four years. In 1995, the Croatian military engaged in two serious planned attacks on the Serbian resistance code-named Operations Flash and Storm. Operation Flash began on May 1 in Western Slavonia while Operation Storm focused on the Krajina in early August. Both were fully successful in defeating the insurgency but resulted in almost the entire exodus of the Serbian population from Croatia. Serbian civilians, young and old, men, women, and children, fled their homes, carrying with them everything they could, including sometimes their deceased relatives.[20] In 1991, Serbs had made up 12.2 percent of the population of Croatia; according to the next official census in 2001, they were only 4.5 percent.[21]

Serbia

Serbia lies in the central Balkan Peninsula and is currently bordered by Hungary, Romania, Bulgaria, Macedonia, Kosova, Montenegro, Bosnia & Hercegovina, and Croatia. It too had an independent empire from the tenth to fourteenth century, until the Ottoman conquest culminating with the famous Battle of Kosovo Polje in 1389. Serbia gradually regained its independence throughout the nineteenth century, always aspiring to increase its territorial holdings both to the west into what is now Bosnia & Hercegovina and to the south into what is now Macedonia. It considers the area that is now the Republic of Kosova to be the heartland of Serbian civilization, and some Serbs also have territorial aspirations into Croatia on the basis of its Serbian population there.

Serbia was Christianized by Orthodox missionaries, and a large majority of Serbs are Orthodox, having had their own Patriarchate since the thirteenth century. Nonetheless, several areas connected to Serbia contained ethnic and religious minorities. The regions of Kosovo/Kosova and the Sandžak of Novi

Pazar have had substantial Muslim populations since the fourteenth century, while multiple ethnicities belonging to Protestant, Catholic, and Jewish religious communities reside in Northern and Eastern Serbia but particularly, the region known as Vojvodina, north of the Danube. Because Vojvodina was part of the Austro-Hungarian Empire for several centuries, its burial culture reflects West European influences far more than is true of Serbia proper.

Although the government of the Kingdom of Serbia was mainly interested in territorial acquisition, it agreed to the creation of Yugoslavia at the end of the First World War as a way of uniting all Serbs within one state. During the war, many Serbs had come to see themselves as heroic warriors who had sacrificed for all south Slavs and had thus earned a leading role in Yugoslavia. They were disappointed and hurt, therefore, when most of their Slavic brethren reacted to them with resentment and distrust rather than gratitude. Nonetheless, by the end of the First Yugoslavia, many Serbs were equally dissatisfied with its results and especially the 1929 dictatorship of King Alexander. While some hoped for a better future under the new Communist regime, many felt unfairly painted with the brush of "Serbian hegemony."

Relations between the German occupying forces and the Orthodox Church during the Second World War were far less cooperative than those between the Catholic Church and Ustasha regime. The Orthodox hierarchy made a concerted effort to appear politically neutral, but its sympathies were clearly on the side of Draža Mihailović's nationalist Chetniks who, though officially a resistance group, sometimes collaborated with the Germans. Even so, some Orthodox priests also participated in the Partisan struggle, and relations between the Communist party and the Serbian Orthodox Church were less hostile than those with the Catholic Church. Though far from friendly toward the communists, the Orthodox Church had a long tradition of accommodation with the state and was better able to continue in that mode, particularly as the Patriarch of the Russian Orthodox Church had also reached an accommodation with Stalin during the Second World War. Because the Orthodox churches had no equivalent to the Pope, their conflicts with a given state had no international implications. On the contrary, each Orthodox Church was a national church, and the Communist regime's main concern about the Serbian Orthodox Church was its potential for promoting Serbian nationalism.[22]

Relations between the state and Orthodox Church began to deteriorate in the 1960s due to increased nationalist tensions in Kosovo. Tito had responded by first crushing the rebellion of Albanian nationalists in Kosovo, but also a group of Serb nationalists centered around Aleksandar Ranković and Tito also provided greater cultural rights and opportunities to ethnic Albanians. While Serbia's political nationalists had been eliminated, opposition to Tito's actions festered within the Orthodox Church, which increasingly saw itself as the source and center of Serbian identity and national salvation. By the late 1960s, it organized a series of religious rituals intended to mobilize popular sentiment around national themes.[23]

By the early 1980s the Orthodox Church had emerged from enforced passivity toward expanding activism on behalf first of the Serbian minority in Kosovo and eventually the entire Serbian nation. Serbian political nationalism was also increasing as seen in the 1986 *Memorandum of the Serbian Academy of Arts and Sciences* and the rise of Slobodan Milošević. Although Milošević manipulated Serbian nationalism to enhance his own power base, as a communist, his ability to collaborate with the Serbian Orthodox Church was somewhat limited. Even so, they shared a common agenda with regard to the grievances of Serbs in Kosovo and Croatia. Nonetheless, Milošević was far from the most extreme among Serbian nationalists, including those in Croatia and Bosnia & Hercegovina.[24] Since most of them were not communists, they had greater support from the Serbian Orthodox Church. Moreover, most of the noncommunist nationalists, like Vuk Drašković and Vojislav Šešelj, were far more willing to draw on the history and traditions of the anti-communist Chetnik movement from the Second World War.

The election of noncommunist governments in Slovenia and Croatia in 1990 distracted Serbia's main attention from Kosovo but not from the larger issue of what it perceived as a threat to the Serbian nation outside Serbia proper. The more immediate threat now appeared to be toward the Serbian population of Croatia, particularly in the borderland regions—such as the Krajina and Eastern Slavonia. Growing Croat nationalism under Franjo Tudjman had inspired a return of nationalist symbols many of which were associated with the fascist Ustashe regime. As soon as Croatia declared independence in June 1991, and with the explicit support of the Milošević regime, the Serbian populations of the Krajina and Eastern Slavonia initiated a series of uprisings that soon led to open war between Croatia and the JNA.

Although the December 1991 UN-brokered Peace Agreement ended official JNA involvement in Croatia, many Serbs remained deeply concerned about the fate of their conationals. Some now chose to defend their nation by joining a variety of unofficial nationalist paramilitary organizations active in both Croatia and Bosnia & Hercegovina like Arkan's Tigers, Šešelj's White Eagles, and many others. According to Maria Vivod, the Milošević regime trained volunteers in as many as fifty-five paramilitary organizations, financing them with stolen and looted goods from the former Yugoslav republics. The men (and a few women) in these paramilitary organizations would be responsible for many of the most horrific war crimes and atrocities carried out in Croatia, Bosnia & Hercegovina, and later Kosovo.[25]

Although Serbia was never officially involved in the war in Bosnia & Hercegovina, it was nonetheless considered its main architect, and Milošević engaged in endless and entirely fruitless peace negotiations with the United Nations, European Union, Russia, and the United States until finally NATO air strikes forced him and the Bosnian Serbs to sign the Dayton Peace Accords in November 1995. In the aftermath of Dayton, Milošević began gradually to lose popularity at home while he also faced growing active resistance from Albanians in Kosovo. By 1998, the increasingly violent conflict in Kosovo forced him into another series of international peace negotiations, this time at Rambouillet. But where he had proved willing to sacrifice the interests of the Bosnian Serbs for peace, Milošević was far more stubborn when it came to Kosovo. At the same time, however, US negotiators drew on the lessons learned from both Serbian atrocities in Bosnia & Hercegovina and the success of NATO air strikes. Accordingly, when Milošević dug his heels in, NATO again began air strikes, this time not only on Kosovo but on Serbia itself, leading to the end of the war in Kosovo. By 2000, Milošević had been ousted from power and by 2008, Serbia's borders had been reduced to only those of Serbia proper and Vojvodina, just a bit larger than what they had been before the First World War. The Serbian minority populations in Croatia and Kosova had largely been expelled from the newly independent countries and those remaining lived under conditions much worse than what they had been previously.

Kosovo/Kosova

The region known as Kosovo/Kosova is currently bordered by Serbia to the north and east, Macedonia to the south, Albania to the southwest, and Montenegro to the northwest. It has been inhabited over the centuries by both Serbs and Albanians. Albanians were likely among the first inhabitants of the Balkan Peninsula and specifically the region of Kosovo/Kosova, although Slavs also migrated into the area as early as the sixth century. Both groups were originally Christianized in the ninth century, but while the Serbs have always been uniquely associated with the Orthodox faith, Albanians accepted both

Catholicism and Orthodoxy. Perhaps because of their greater religious diversity, a substantial proportion of Albanians throughout the Balkans converted to Islam in the centuries that followed under Ottoman rule, though many also remained as Catholic and Orthodox Christians. As a result, Albanian national identity has never been based on religion but mainly on language, history, and culture.[26] The Serbian connection to the Orthodox Church only grew stronger under Ottoman rule, particularly as the Ottoman millet system allowed non-Muslim religious communities considerable economic and local administrative autonomy. Demographic statistics in the region vary considerably but most seem to suggest that by the late nineteenth and early twentieth centuries Albanian Muslims made up approximately 60 percent of the population in Kosovo/Kosova. After the collapse of the Ottoman and Austro-Hungarian Empires following the First World War, an Albanian independent state was created, but in 1918, Kosovo/Kosova was absorbed into the Kingdom of Yugoslavia as part of Serbia.

Although Kosovar Albanians were described as citizens of Yugoslavia, they were systematically denied rights guaranteed by the Treaty for the Protection of Minorities established by the Paris Peace Conference, particularly regarding the right to use of their own language. Thus, unlike Czechs, Germans, Hungarians, and Turks in Yugoslavia they had no access to education or publications in their native language. Many Albanians responded by joining active resistance movements, which were also consistently suppressed. The Serbian regime hoped to reduce the Albanian demographic majority by providing substantial free land grants to Serb colonists from Vojvodina and even the United States while at the same time encouraging Albanian emigration to Turkey.[27]

During the Second World War, Kosovo/Kosova was divided and occupied by various fascist regimes as part of their occupation of Yugoslavia. Most of the region was occupied by Italians, one section was under Bulgarian rule, and a final small region, including the strategically important copper mines, fell under German occupation but was left mainly under the administration of Serbian collaborationist forces. Kosovar Albanians showed no particular attraction to the ideology of fascism and were reluctant to participate in the war outside Kosovo/Kosova, but some did collaborate with the occupying forces as they were considered preferable to Serbian rule and a possible route to eventual independence. Some Kosovar Albanians also used the opportunities provided by wartime to take revenge on ethnic enemies for outstanding insults, injuries, or crimes. During this period over 30,000 Serbian and Montenegrin colonists were driven out and their villages burned. Some of them were allowed to return in the postwar period, but not all, and many also chose not to.[28] By the end of the war all efforts to change the demographic composition had achieved very little and according to the 1948 census, Albanians still made up 68.4 percent of the population and Serbs and Montenegrins 27.5 percent.[29]

Although the Socialist regime worked throughout Yugoslavia to mitigate ethnic tensions, promoting its ideology of national equality and brotherhood and unity, those efforts in Kosovo encountered significant challenges. In the first decades after the war, the party's centralized approach to governance worked to the advantage of the Serbs who, though a minority of the population, held a majority in the local branch of the Communist party and thus also the local government. Only the 1966 dismissal of Aleksandar Ranković, marking federal support for decentralized economic policies, increased the voice for Albanians in Kosovo. During the 1950s and 1960s, Serbs and Montenegrins held 50 percent of party and 68 percent of administrative and leading positions in government, although they made up only 27 percent of the population. In contrast, by the late 1970s, Albanians made up over 60 percent of the members of the League of Communists of Kosovo and by 1981 held 75 percent of positions in the police and security forces.[30] As educational, employment, and governing opportunities increased for Kosovar Albanians, those opportunities correspondingly declined for the minority Serb population along with their demographic proportions. Whereas Albanians still made up approximately 68 percent of the population in the 1961 census, they began increasing steadily through the following decades until by 1991 Albanians made up 82 percent and Serbs/Montenegrins only 11 percent.[31]

These real demographic and political changes, while due to a variety of causes, were reflected in increasing nationalist rhetoric from the Serbian Orthodox Church, Serbian nationalist intellectuals, and the Milošević regime. In their writings, the Serbian Orthodox clergy explicitly blamed Islamic fundamentalism for a whole series of problems in Kosovo, from its changing demographics to attacks on Serbia's cultural and religious heritage and purported rapes of Serbian women. In fact, not only is Albanian national identity distinct from religious identity but Albanian nationalism as an ideology remained almost entirely secular. Albanian nationalist policies from the 1960s on, far from being religiously oriented, were led mainly by Marxist students and intellectuals.[32] The first Albanian demonstrations followed the ouster of Aleksandar Ranković in the late 1960s and were directed toward gaining an Albanian university, though the demonstrators also shouted "Kosovo Republic" and "Long Live Enver Hoxha." The next demonstrations in 1981, initially about living conditions at the university, were even more clearly secular. According to Aydin Babuna, not a single Imam or religious figure participated in the demonstrations. Instead, the protest was mainly composed of nationalist students, along with some leftist underground groups.[33] Islam did not become involved in the question of Kosovar independence until the late 1980s, and by then the Catholic religious community was equally engaged.[34]

In October 1988, Milošević abolished the autonomy originally granted to the Provinces of Kosovo and Vojvodina by the 1974 Constitution, removing or arresting Albanian leaders and ultimately amending the province's own Constitution to ensure complete subordination to Serbia. Over the following years, Kosovar Albanian employees in nearly all areas of civil service were forced from their jobs while a Serbian curriculum was reimposed in the school system. In response, the Albanian majority simply took their educational system underground. In December 1989, the Democratic League of Kosovo (LDK) was formed as a secular, liberal democratic political party in opposition under the leadership of Albanian literature professor, Ibrahim Rugova. While the LDK's main goal from 1989 to 1998 was national independence, its methodology was entirely premised on peaceful resistance.[35]

Up until the 1995 Dayton Accords, a kind of stalemate persisted based upon the Kosovar Albanians' belief that leaders of the international community would address their situation along with all other Balkan concerns at the peace negotiations. When the Dayton Accords did no such thing, many Kosovar Albanians began to lose faith in peaceful resistance. Already in 1993, a small guerilla organization, eventually known as the Kosovo Liberation Army (KLA), had formed and begun preparing for active and armed resistance against Serbia. The increase in armed attacks against Serb policemen beginning in 1998 by locally famous Albanians like Adem Jashari sparked correspondingly high levels of Serbian repression against Kosovar Albanians, including the massacre of the entire Jashari clan on March 3, 1998, which left fifty-eight people dead, including eighteen women and ten children.[36] Such atrocities captured the attention of the international community, which acted more quickly and decisively this time, and by March 1999, NATO had begun air strikes against Serbia, eventually ending the war and resulting in Kosova's official declaration of independence in 2008. That independence, however, remains a matter of international controversy. As of 2022, 119 of 193 member states of the United Nations had recognized Kosova's independence, but approximately 20 had later withdrawn recognition, leaving the true number closer to 99.

Bosnia & Hercegovina

Bosnia & Hercegovina is located in the middle of the Balkan Peninsula, sandwiched between Croatia on the north and west, Serbia on the east and southeast, and Montenegro to the south; it also has a tiny outlet to the Adriatic Sea at Neum. The independent Kingdom of Bosnia thrived during the thirteenth to fourteenth century, particularly under King Tvrtko I (1353–91). The lands of Bosnia & Hercegovina were conquered by the Ottoman Turks in the mid-fifteenth century. Toward the end of the nineteenth century in 1879, the decline of the Ottoman Empire and Great Power competition in the region resulted in the Treaty of Berlin, which allowed the Austro-Hungarian Empire first to administer and then by 1907 annex Bosnia & Hercegovina. At the end of the First World War, which saw its origins in Sarajevo, Bosnia & Hercegovina became part of the newly created Kingdom of Yugoslavia.

Slavs in Bosnia & Hercegovina converted to both Western and Eastern branches of Christianity during the ninth century, based more or less on location. By the mid-thirteenth century, however, the region also had its own autonomous cult, the Church of Bosnia.[37] Perhaps as a result of this religious diversity, more inhabitants of Bosnia & Hercegovina converted to Islam after the Ottoman conquest than in most other parts of the Balkan Peninsula. By the end of the seventeenth century, 75 percent of Bosnia's population was Muslim, but that percentage declined with the fall of the Ottoman Empire to only about 30 percent by the end of the Second World War.[38] Meanwhile, as nationalism developed elsewhere in the Balkan Peninsula, those portions of the population that remained Catholic increasingly identified themselves as Croatian, while simultaneously those who were Orthodox came to think of themselves as Serbian. Their proportions of the population also waxed and waned over time, but according to the 1948 census, Serbs made up approximately 44 percent and Croats 24 percent of Bosnia & Hercegovina.[39] The region also included minority populations of Jews and various protestant sects.

Already during the period of Austro-Hungarian administration, Bosnian Muslim nobles, in defense against the nationalism of their Christian neighbors, had begun to develop a sense of identity termed *bošnjaštvo*.[40] During the first interwar Yugoslav state, the Yugoslav Muslim Organization (JMO) was formed to defend the interests of Muslims in Yugoslavia, although its candidates ran for office only in Bosnia & Hercegovina. At this point, the JMO did not claim that Bosnian Muslims made up a "nation," but it was a step in that direction. During the Second World War, most of Bosnia & Hercegovina fell within the fascist quisling Independent State of Croatia (NDH). Since Catholics Croats made up only about 50 percent of the NDH, the Ustasha regime consciously sought an alliance with Bosnian Muslims. In 1943, the Nazi regime created a specifically Bosnian Muslim SS Division—the Waffen Handžar Division—to reinvigorate the fight against the Partisans. Bosnian Muslims meanwhile had hoped to gain more power relative to the Ustashe and, ultimately, autonomous status. In fact, neither aim was achieved.[41] While the Division certainly damaged Muslims' reputation, they remained caught between the aggressive nationalism of others, a fact that helps explain why Bosnia & Hercegovina has so often been described as the birthplace of the Partisan movement with its slogan of "brotherhood and unity."

In the immediate postwar period, the CPY established working relations with the Muslim religious community in Bosnia & Hercegovina, allowing it to retain Islamic institutions such as the Reis-ul-ulema, the Vakuf Commission, and Vakuf Assembly.[42] Bosnian Muslims, perhaps more than any other group, had reason to support the postwar Yugoslav regime. Indeed, it was the Communist party, though theoretically dedicated to the end of nationalism, that finally recognized Bosnian Muslims as a nation. Discussions in support of recognizing the Bosnian Muslims as a constituent nation began in the mid-1960s, and by 1968 the League of Communists of Bosnia & Hercegovina passed a resolution declaring them as Yugoslavia's sixth nation.[43] The federal leadership supported the decision, and the term appeared in the 1971 census and the Yugoslav Constitution of 1974. In the following years, Bosnian Muslims became increasingly attached to the concept of Yugoslav federalism both as a form of protection against Serbian and Croatian nationalism and as a framework for the development of Muslim identity. As Xavier Bougarel has argued, though Bosnian Muslims only minimally contributed to the formation of a Yugoslav identity, they were probably the last to sincerely believe in it.[44] By the mid-1980s citizens in the republic's urban regions had developed a strong sense of identity based on ethnic pluralism, seen in relatively high levels of interethnic marriages.[45]

The development of nationalism in neighboring republics influenced not only the Serbs and Croats of Bosnia & Hercegovina but also Bosnian Muslims. In 1983, thirteen Bosnian Muslims, under the leadership of Alija Izetbegović, began to develop a kind of religiously based Islamic nationalism that would win prison sentences for eleven of them. By the late 1980s, however, they had been released and as the federal government's credibility declined, Izetbegović's popularity increased. Nonetheless, Islamic nationalism remained a minority ideology within Bosnia & Hercegovina, even among the clergy, most of whom promoted collaboration with the Yugoslav state, and unity among all Muslims, both religious and secular.[46]

Only as Yugoslavia began to disintegrate and ethnically based political parties formed and won elections in Bosnia & Hercegovina, did most Muslims join the Party of Democratic Action (SDA) led by Izetbegović, who had by then adopted a more moderate tone. The war began in Bosnia & Hercegovina in April 1992 after competing referendums showed strong determination by Muslims and Croats to achieve independence but overwhelming support among Bosnian Serbs to remain in Yugoslavia. In fact, many Bosnian Croats imagined independence from Yugoslavia as the first step toward Hercegovina's separation from Bosnia and unification with Croatia. Accordingly, while Bosnian Muslims and Croats were united against the Serbs in the first months of 1992, by late October violent conflicts broke out between Muslim and Croat forces that lasted until early 1994.

On April 7, 1992, the nationalist Serbian Democratic Party (SDS) led by Radovan Karadžić formally declared the independence of the Serbian Republic (RS) and began military operations with support from Belgrade. By the time hostilities broke out, the Bosnian Serb army already had troops stationed on high ground surrounding the capital city of Sarajevo, which remained under siege for 1,425 days, the longest in modern military history. At the same time, the Bosnian Serb army carried out a deliberate policy of ethnic cleansing and engaged in widespread human rights violations, including mass rapes and massacres. Although Croats and Muslims also carried out atrocities, Bosnian Serbs have been held responsible for many more cases, not only because they were in the stronger position but also because the Serbian leadership deliberately employed ethnic cleansing and rape as strategies of war. The massacre at Srebrenica in July 1995 resulting in the slaughter of over 8,000 Muslims, along with Bosnian Serb attacks on other "Safe Areas," eventually convinced NATO leaders to order air strikes against Bosnian Serb forces beginning August 30, 1995. Within two weeks, Bosnian Serbs had begun to comply with NATO demands and were prepared to engage in peace negotiations. The war in Bosnia & Hercegovina came to an end with the signing of the Dayton Peace Accords in November 1995.

Scholars still disagree about the extent to which Izetbegović and the SDA genuinely supported a multiethnic and multireligious or a strictly Islamic state.[47] In his public statements up through the end of the war, Izetbegović consistently referred to himself as a European-style Muslim fighting for an integral Bosnia & Hercegovina that included Serbs and Croats but in which the genocide of Muslims could never again take place.[48] Serbs and Croats were explicitly welcomed within the Bosnian state, and some served in the Bosnian army and government. Even so, there were indications during the war that Islamization had begun to degrade the state's multiethnic and multireligious character to the extent that that non-Muslims began to feel unwelcome or like second-class citizens. Within the ostensibly multiethnic Bosnian military were several exclusively Muslim units including both local and foreign recruits who spoke openly about Jihad. By October 1993, Foreign Minister Haris Silajdžić admitted that the war cabinet was entirely composed of Muslims from the SDA, which, he argued, made sense as they made up the vast majority of soldiers. Indeed, the percentage of Serbs serving in the military had declined significantly, from 13 percent in the early stages of the war to an estimated three to six percent by the summer of 1994. It was also clear by this time that although Serbs and Croats were still part of the government, their voices had been effectively marginalized.[49]

Bosnian Muslims developed two competing national ideologies in the decade following the war. Those who called themselves "Bosnians" based their identity on citizenship in the state, while those who referred to themselves as "Bosniaks" based their identity on Islam. The SDA revealed its continuing ambivalence in the 1996 electoral campaign with two contradictory slogans: "For a sovereign, united and democratic Bosnia" and "For our own land and in our own faith."[50] It still remains unclear whether the goals of the state are established in accordance with its previous identity as a multiethnic and multireligious secular entity or are ever more coherent with those of the Bosniak Islamic national ideology.

The postwar constitutional order of Bosnia & Hercegovina established by the Dayton Accords has further contributed to this uncertainty. The Constitution itself is extremely controversial and has become subject of multiple lawsuits and international discussions.[51] According to the Dayton Agreement, postwar Bosnia & Hercegovina is comprised of three sections: the Federation of Bosnia & Hercegovina, the Bosnian Serb Republic, and the Brčko District comprised from sections of each but belonging to neither. As of 2013, Bosniaks made up approximately 70.4 percent of the federation, Croats 22.4 percent, and Serbs now only 2.5 percent. Serbs made up 82.9 percent of the population in the Bosnian Serb Republic of Bosnia & Hercegovina, Muslims made up 12.7 percent, and Croats 2.2 percent.[52] Theoretically, the state is a parliamentary representative democracy, with a central presidency that rotates among three chairs: a Croat, a Serb, and a Bosniak. The ethnic component of the Constitution has become the subject of most criticism and debate, for while it was presumably intended to enforce ethnic equity, it not only requires individuals to choose an ethnic identity to practice their rights as sovereign citizens but also systematically discriminates against any who do not belong to the three main ethnic groups.

The system is in any case chronically dysfunctional as both the Federation of Bosnia & Hercegovina and the Bosnian Serb Republic act as separate entities to prevent the proper operation of the whole.

Agents, Policies, and Laws

The CPY thus took power in 1945 in a country of multiple nations, nationalities, and religious communities, many of whom had been living together for centuries but others for less than thirty years. They did not all share a common set of values, nor were their relations either with the new state or one another entirely promising. In many cases, those wartime relations had been extraordinarily violent. The party's goal was to repair those damaged relationships, along with the country's shattered economy, through policies of modernization, secularization, and the equality of all nations in a federal Yugoslavia.

Given the enormity of the practical and political tasks facing the Communist party, policies toward death and burial were not high on its list of priorities. But neither could they be avoided as countless Yugoslav citizens were still deeply enmeshed in the process of finding, burying, and mourning those missing and killed in the war. Moreover, the Communist party sought to create an institutionalized memory of the PLA through the burial and commemoration of Partisans killed in battles as integral to its legitimacy. To do so, the CPY relied on the services of the Veteran's Association, Savez Udruženje Boraca Narodnooslobodilačkog Rata or SUBNOR.[53] Created in 1947, SUBNOR's purpose was to mobilize former active members of the PLA for the purpose of building socialism. While the tasks of the organization included ensuring the material well-being of veterans, they also involved building brotherhood and unity, securing peace, developing patriotism among youth, and, critical for this work, cultivating the traditions of the PLA by commemorating historical events and monuments from the war, and establishing, organizing, and maintaining the graves of soldiers to "permanently preserve the memory of our fallen comrades."[54] The term always used for the establishment of soldiers' cemeteries and graves was "uredjenje." While no one English word adequately substitutes for the meanings encompassed by this term, I have variously translated it in this work as "created," "established," "organized," or "arranged" depending on context. Ultimately, it implies the need to create order out of disorder. In short, the task required SUBNOR organizations not just to build cemeteries but also bring together the scattered individual and mass graves hastily dug during the war and arrange them within a thoughtful, politically, ideologically, and artistically coherent space that would inspire piety, gratitude for their sacrifice, and renewed devotion to the cause for which they had died. Thus, the arrangement of the cemetery must "express the meaning that our socialist Fatherland attributes to defending and guarding the memory of our holy and glorious days of struggle."[55]

Veterans joined a SUBNOR Association at the Communal (Opština/Općina) level and its delegates were then united into progressively higher Associations at the District (Srez) or Autonomous Region (Pokrajina), Republic, and finally Federal level located in Belgrade. Each Association included multiple Commissions assigned to specific tasks such as concern for war invalids, prisoners of war and internees, national defense, and, most relevant here, the "Commission for the Cultivation of Revolutionary Traditions." Just as leadership of the PLA had always stayed in the hands of trusted members of the Communist party, so too were the leaders of SUBNOR not only seasoned veterans but longtime members of the Communist party. SUBNOR chose Tito himself as its first president, and though he soon became only an honorary lifetime president, all other presidents, not only of the federal associations but also the republic associations, were trusted communists.[56] Leaders of the Commission for the Cultivation of Revolutionary Traditions were also party members but included representatives from other social-political organizations and experts from disciplines relevant to the task, including history, literature, art, architecture, civil engineering, landscape design, and so on.[57]

Civilian burial culture was even lower on the priority list than that intended for soldiers. Nonetheless, people continued to die and had to be buried, and the intimate connections between burial culture and religion meant that the process of burial had the potential to create conflicts between differing religious communities as well as with the state. In response, the regime designated primary responsibility for the work of burial to extant and experienced personnel, placing them under the supervision of politically reliable organizations and individuals in each republic. The state organization responsible for mediating all debates and conflicts between religious communities and the Communist regime was the Commission for Religious Questions (CRQ).

Likely based on comparable Soviet organizations created during the Second World War (CAROC and CARC), the CRQ was an advisory body created at all levels of the state (federal, republic, district, municipal, and communal) whose purpose was to thoroughly investigate all issues regarding church–state relations and advise the state on the best course to take. The make-up of the commissions was essential to their functioning, and most republics, at least in the early decades, made a concerted effort to include not only representatives from the Communist party but also individuals with religious background and credibility who were also loyal to the new state.[58] For example, the head of Croatia's CRQ in the first years after the war was Monsignor Svetozar Ritig, described earlier in this chapter, whose religious credentials and loyalty to the Partisans were both unparalleled. He saw his role as mediating between the church and authorities, and his influence with the government was in his powers of explanation and persuasion.[59] Ritig was not an isolated case as the CRQ in Bosnia & Hercegovina included a famous pro-Partisan Muslim, Hasan Ljubunčić, who later wrote a travelogue about his hajj. Given the participation of individuals like Ritig and Ljubunčić, the CRQ was often more sensitive to the concerns of the religious communities than either the Communist party or legislative and executive organs of the state, and it sought to facilitate compromises between them.[60] But while the CRQ had a great deal of responsibility and some good will, it had no actual power; it accepted complaints, gathered information, and gave advice but could not make the final decision. Nonetheless, there is some reason to believe that its conclusions were valued and given due consideration.

Those organizations and individuals assigned to work in burial culture did so within a legal and institutional framework that theoretically at least established a clear separation between church and state and stringent limits on private ownership of property. The First Yugoslavia, during the interwar period, had taken a median line in its religious policies between establishing a state church and declaring the separation of church and state. Certain recognized religious communities, which included the Serbian Orthodox, Catholic and Greek Catholic, Evangelical, Islamic, and Jewish communities, were provided a special position with special privileges. The recognized religious communities were all declared equal and religious education within them was theoretically optional (at the determination of parents) but in practice required. Marriage was possible only by religious rites, and marital disputes were resolved by the religious communities, which also maintained the birth, marriage, and death registries, known as *matične knjige*. Larger religious communities could also establish and maintain their own schools, orphanages, hospitals, and, of course, cemeteries.[61]

The Yugoslav Communist regime, like all states based on Marxist-Leninist principles, was theoretically based on the primacy of the working class and considered religion antithetical to the long-term interests of humanity.[62] In theory then, it sought to both industrialize and secularize society but, more than most, had also to weave its way cautiously among the multiple ethnoreligious communities. In devising its policies the Yugoslav communists looked first to the Soviet Union. However, Yugoslav reliance on Soviet experience was never blind and party leaders were just as likely to learn from Soviet mistakes as to follow its precedents. Accordingly, Yugoslav policies toward religion were both more nuanced than those of the Soviet Union and, in any case, Soviet policy toward religion changed significantly from the radicalism of the early revolutionary era toward one of greater moderation and cooperation during the Second World War. More significant was the party leaders' conviction that the legacy of ethnic and religious conflict in Yugoslavia required a multilayered approach. Seeing religious and ethnic hatred as fatally entangled, the party insisted on the separation of church and state, not only due to reliance on Marxist-Leninist ideology but also in hopes of eventually disconnecting religious and national identity.[63]

Already in 1934, the Yugoslav Communist party had adopted the Comintern's anti-fascist National Front Policy, which recommended cooperation with all those opposed to fascism, including religious organizations. Throughout the Second World War, Partisan units carefully included members and religious leaders from all of Yugoslavia's constituent religious communities. Priests wore Partisan caps with crosses sewn inside the Partisan star and participated in the celebration of religious holidays, weddings, baptisms, and funerals.[64]

In the immediate postwar period up until late 1947, although the party officially continued its policies of tolerance, still focusing on common goals of unity, they were increasingly also interspersed with incidents of revolutionary radicalism. For example, despite wartime cooperation and postwar guarantees of freedom, many priests and other religious personnel suffered extensive official and unofficial persecution from the Communist party and state both during but especially in the early years after the Second World War.[65] According to Serbian historian Radmila Radić, from the end of the war to April 1953, 1,403 religious leaders from all of Yugoslavia's religious communities were convicted of serious political crimes.[66] Priests were also harassed, beaten, and killed often entirely without cause. Although such behavior was considered counterproductive by party leaders, these cases were never pursued by the regime and at most resulted only in a "verbal reprimand."[67]

Officially, however, and in keeping with its broadly cautious approach, the first postwar Constitution published in January 1946 guaranteed freedom of religious worship and granted equal status to all religious communities in the state. Religious worship was legally described as a private matter, and all citizens had an equal right to belong to a religious community and participate in religious rites but also not to. The state could, but was not obliged to, provide material support to the religious communities. Religious education was permitted but only within religious buildings and outside of regular school hours, and, by 1946, official recognition of religious holidays had been eliminated. Separation of church and state also meant that the state had the sole right to maintain birth, marriage, or death records in the *matične knjige*, though it was not to interfere with or prevent the free expression of religious belief or religious rites. Political organizations could not be formed on religious bases, nor could any individual use or abuse churches and religion for political purposes.[68]

The Law on Agrarian Reform and Colonization passed in August 1945 also had an important effect on religious communities. By expropriating a significant amount of land held by religious communities for redistribution among peasants and for colonization, the law erased much of their economic power practically overnight.[69] Because all nonarable land was explicitly excluded from the law, cemeteries theoretically remained with the religious communities. In practice, however, many of them were also expropriated on other grounds. Specifically, the Law on Expropriation published on April 4, 1947, established that the state (at any level from local to federal) had the right to appropriate private property when necessary for the "social-economic and cultural elevation and development of the people," including for the construction of public utilities, industry, agriculture, and military, educational, health, cultural, and sports facilities. The original owners were to be compensated in cash or in property of comparable value.[70]

The Law on the Legal Status of Religious Communities, published on May 23, 1953, officially established the religious communities as legal entities. While many of its twenty-four articles reconfirmed the rights and freedoms guaranteed by the Constitution, it also established limits on them. Specifically, Article Five forbade the misuse of religious activities, classes, media, rituals, and/or religious sentiments for political purposes.[71] That article could be broadly interpreted, allowing the state to intervene more or less at will. Eventually each republic would publish its own version of the law, though not immediately. Serbia's law, for example, was not published until 1962.[72]

The complex ethnoreligious composition of the former Yugoslavia and its history of religious, national, and ideological conflict in the twentieth century make it a particularly productive case for studies of burial culture. The diversity of the region is mirrored in its cemeteries. SUBNOR and the CRQ sought to harmonize those diverse cemeteries with the ideological goals of the Communist regime. They did so, however, in very different ways and with differing results, though in both cases, the political needs of the state reigned supreme.

3

Partisan Communities of the Dead

Cemeteries and memorials dedicated to soldiers who died in battle are simultaneously private and public forms of commemoration. The title of Jay Winter's classic work *Sites of Memory, Sites of Mourning* eloquently clarifies their dual purpose for the formation of collective identity and mediation of individual grief. Writing about the period following the First World War, Winter argues that cemeteries and war memorials "used collective expression, in stone and in ceremony, to help individual people—mothers, fathers, wives, sons, daughters, and comrades-in-arms—to accept the brutal facts of death in war."[1] This need for both such acceptance and a new collective identity was equally dire in Socialist Yugoslavia where years of occupation, civil war, and genocide took the lives of some 6.5 percent of the population, leaving an entire generation deeply traumatized and in need of solace. Yet for the Communist Party of Yugoslavia, the role of military cemeteries and war memorials in promoting stability and state legitimacy was equally important if not more so.

This chapter evaluates the extent to which cemeteries, ossuaries, and monuments created in remembrance of those killed by enemies of the new regime during the war were effective in helping to overcome private grief and create a sense of collective identity in the postwar period. Given the enormous number and diversity of such spaces and monuments created, it is impossible to address this topic comprehensively. As of late November 2022, Andrew Lawler's website and Facebook page, which seek to document the condition of all monuments and memorials created in Socialist Yugoslavia, included 3,679 just in Bosnia & Hercegovina.[2] Certainly some of the memorials were more effective in their goals than others. As whole, however, I argue that they were quite successful in the private sphere as a means to alleviate grief and reasonably so in the public as sources of a common identity. Although the country for which they were created has since dissolved and many of the monuments vandalized or destroyed in the process, the very fact that such desecration occurred and is still occurring suggests that the cemeteries achieved their goals and represented a threat to the nationalist successor states that followed. After all, why would anyone bother to destroy monuments and cemeteries that held no meaning or value? Yet they might have been even more effective and less vulnerable to desecration had they also been more inclusive and less politically charged.

War Cemeteries

The first use of military cemeteries in Europe occurred in the aftermath of the First World War and was likely modeled on the example provided by the United States following the Civil War. Previously, most ordinary soldiers had been buried where they fell, in mass graves that, if marked at all, were indicated with only one large memorial, occasionally with names but usually without. A few others had been fortunate enough to be returned to their families for burial at home.[3] The length and brutality of the Civil War, resulting in the death of at least 618,000 Americans, inspired the American public and its government to engage in the first conscious attempt to account for and publicly acknowledge the sacrifice of all soldiers killed in battle. By 1864, the American government had created seventy-three national cemeteries and many more were to follow.[4]

By the Law of December 29, 1915, France was the first European country to establish a military cemetery, but others quickly followed its lead and members of the British Red Cross were diligent in noting the precise position of fallen soldiers so that their bodies could be gathered together in large military cemeteries, each in an individually marked grave. The change likely developed from the immobility of trench warfare and, as in the United States, the sheer volume of dead bodies, perhaps as high as ten million, which both necessitated an organized disposal process and stimulated a new belief that every individual should be accorded value and the enormity of their sacrifice recognized.[5]

Those countries most active in creating and designing military cemeteries abroad during and in the immediate aftermath of the First World War were, of course, not only victor nations like France, Britain, and the United States but also smaller countries like Yugoslavia. They were mainly concerned with the need to appropriately honor their own war dead whose bodies would be difficult if not impossible to repatriate. In those countries, the military cemeteries might more accurately be described as "war cemeteries" in that they usually house the remains of only those soldiers who died in a particular war or even just one battle. Those cemeteries are often nationally segregated, with each section being maintained by the nation whose soldiers are interred within. For example, Zeitenlik World War I Allied Military Cemetery in Thessaloniki, Greece, has sections for the remains of soldiers from Great Britain, France, Italy, Russia, and Serbia who perished on the Macedonian Front from 1915 to 1918.[6]

These military cemeteries located outside each nation's home territory are easily recognizable as national cemeteries, but scholars have argued that military cemeteries more broadly represented the first national cemeteries and often made a significant contribution to the development of national consciousness. Benedict Anderson focused on cenotaphs and tombs of unknown soldiers as uniquely national, claiming that there is never "any need to specify the nationality of their absent occupants. What else could they be *but* Germans, Americans, Argentians ...?"[7] More directly, Susan-Mary Grant argued that America's National Military Cemeteries were created precisely because the Civil War was fought by volunteer troops and that final victory required an investment in the nation's collective will and morale. Ultimately then, those National Cemeteries represented not only a validation of patriotic sentiment "but of America as a nation. The revolutionary generation had staked a claim to the land, but it was the Civil War dead who, finally, established it as American."[8]

The deceased soldiers from defeated armies have also normally been provided with sections in war cemeteries. During and immediately following the Civil War in the United States, the bodies of Confederate soldiers were often buried in the same cemeteries as those of Union soldiers for reasons of practicality, though they were excluded from honors and their families often removed them later. Although the topic was and remains highly contentious, the United States ultimately agreed to allow Confederate soldiers burial in military cemeteries, understanding the political consequences of denying them that right. Currently some 12,000 Confederate veterans are buried or memorialized within VA cemeteries, though sometimes in separate sections and with slightly modified headstones.[9] In Europe, the Treaties of Versailles, Trianon, Lausanne, Sèvres, and Neuilly following the First World War required that each nation care for the war dead of enemy soldiers on its own territory.[10] That duty, predicated on assumptions about the honorable disposal of the bodies of deceased soldiers in wartime, would later be included in the Geneva Conventions of 1929, 1949, and 1977, which guarantee the personal dignity of the dead and the relatives' and states' right to know the fate of and have access to the burial site of the deceased soldiers.[11] Yet despite the best efforts of the Geneva agreements, not all soldiers who died in subsequent wars were either repatriated or buried in marked graves where they died and then made accessible to their families.

During the Second World War, dead bodies were frequently used as a means of establishing territorial gain in a way that inevitably politicized their graves. According to Monica Black, burying German soldiers where they died in battle abroad "was indelibly linked to the project of conquest, to making foreign soil German. In effect, the fantasies of Nazi poets about generations of the dead nourishing the soil of a new Germany now became state policy."[12] The Cold War politics that split Europe following the Second World War further complicated the division between "winners" and "losers." Thus, although both Germany and Italy were defeated powers, West Germany and Italy eventually allied with "winners" like the United States, Britain, and France, while the Soviet Union and Yugoslavia, at least initially, joined up with defeated powers like East Germany, Romania, and Bulgaria. Under these highly politicized conditions, neither the creation of cemeteries for enemy dead nor their repatriation was guaranteed. Only after the collapse of the Soviet Union could the private German foundation known as *Volksbund Deutsche Kriegsgräberfürsorge* begin the process of collecting and burying all German soldiers who died in former Soviet territory.[13] Similarly, Greece was able to begin the process of repatriating the remains of 6,800–8,000 soldiers who perished during the Second World War in Albania only in 2018.[14]

Yugoslavia ended the Second World War with remains of soldiers from both allied and enemy armies on its territory, though the perception of who counted as an ally and an enemy changed with time. Immediately following the war, Red Army soldiers were treated as heroes, and monuments commemorating their sacrifice appeared in cities and towns throughout the country, including the capital of Belgrade. After the split with the Soviet Union, however, most of those memorials were removed. Nonetheless, in 1954, 711 Red Army soldiers' remains were gathered and reburied, along with the remains of 1,386 Partisans, in a mass grave in the newly opened "Cemetery to the Liberators of Belgrade" in Novo Groblje cemetery beneath a statue by the famous sculptor August Augustinčić.[15] When relations with the Soviet Union improved during the Khrushchev era, the state carried out a massive federally funded campaign to create cemeteries for those Soviet and Bulgarian soldiers who died on its territory during the last months of the war in the regions of Vojvodina and Croatia.[16]

Yugoslavia's treatment of occupying soldiers killed on its territory was both simpler and less admirable. The purpose of international laws regulating honorable treatment of all wartime dead was to ensure human dignity and provide comfort and humanity to their families, regardless of political conflict. The Communist regime that took power in Yugoslavia following the Second World War, however, had no wish to provide dignity to the dead soldiers of those armies that had invaded and occupied Yugoslavia or to their domestic collaborators; nor would it offer comfort to their families. On the contrary, it was determined to eradicate any trace of their presence, as if they had never existed. According to Vladimir Geiger, the Ministry of Internal Affairs for the Democratic Federation of Yugoslavia passed Decree 1253 on May 18, 1945, for the removal and destruction of the graves and cemeteries of "occupiers" and "enemies of the people." The planned removal included the graves and monuments of German, Hungarian, and Italian soldiers as well as those of domestic collaborators including Ustashas, Chetniks, and Slovene Homeguards. Republic and local organizations were instructed to remove all foreign, religious, and other markers, as well as all walls and fences, and entirely level the ground in order to erase every trace of the fascist regime. While the bodies were not to be disturbed or the areas used for new burials, all distinguishing marks and inscriptions on any material removed from the graves were to be thoroughly eradicated before it could be reused. The availability of supporting documentation varies, yet Geiger's evidence strongly suggests that the decree was carefully executed in all of Yugoslavia's republics.[17]

Belgrade's Novo Groblje Cemetery thus includes military sections for Russian, French, Italian, Bulgarian, and Austro-Hungarian soldiers from the First World War, as well as a section for soldiers of the English Commonwealth who died in Yugoslavia during the Second World War, but no German section, although Belgrade was occupied by the Germans from 1941 to 1945.[18] In 2007, an Austrian woman travelled to Serbia seeking the grave of her father, a soldier in the German defense forces. Her mother had been told that he died in 1944 and was buried in Čačak's military cemetery in grave number 33. The daughter found no military cemetery in that city but was eventually directed to a park where she was told the bodies of German soldiers had been secretly taken and reburied one night in 1947.[19]

The cemeteries created by the regime for soldiers and other victims of war in the immediate postwar period were, therefore, first and foremost exclusive. They were cemeteries for the winners, not for either occupiers or those domestic soldiers who had fought against the Communist regime and lost. *Their* bodies were explicitly barred from the official war cemeteries and if their graves were not also razed, they were to be buried quietly, without ceremony or any indication of their military activities.[20] Max Bergholz documented the fate of an Orthodox priest in the Serbian village of Brezna, who in 1956 sought to publicly commemorate the deaths of all Serb combatants—Partisan and Chetnik—who had died in war, inscribing their names on a plaque in the Church. For his efforts, he was convicted of abusing his position in the Church for political purposes and sentenced to twenty months in prison.[21] These exclusions were not only political, however, but almost visceral. Several SUBNOR documents worried that the wrong remains might inadvertently be included within memorial cemeteries or ossuaries. While some expressed concern about the possible political consequences of such an error, others had a more emotional reaction. One report described with horror a case when a group of survivors from the 1943 battle of Ljubin grob at Sutjeska went to visit the site where so many of their comrades had fallen, only to see columns of youth who had also come to pay their respects inadvertently turn the wrong direction and stand in reverent silence over the ground where German soldiers had died and been buried. The survivors were torn between wanting to instantly publicize the mistake and not wanting anyone, especially German tourists, to know about it.[22]

Nonetheless, cemeteries for the war dead could also serve as a powerful inclusionary tool for the state. In the years following the Second World War, the Communist Party of Yugoslavia (CPY) sought to institutionalize the memory of the war as one way of "concretizing" a new collective identity that would secure peace, social stability, and its own position in power.[23] The most important values associated with this identity were acceptance of Yugoslav state identity, the brotherhood and unity of Yugoslavia's nations and nationalities, and support for socialism. Yugoslav state identity meant belief in the continued existence of a unified state of Yugoslavia but not a Yugoslavian national identity, which had been thoroughly discredited by policies of the interwar regime. Rather, the new state was constructed as a federation that explicitly promoted existing national identities on a basis of complete equality, within the concept of brotherhood and unity. That brotherhood and unity was understood to have been forged during the course of the Partisan struggle when members of all of Yugoslavia's nations and nationalities participated in the liberation of the country under the leadership of the CPY. Communist party leadership continued in the postwar Yugoslav Federation, which by late 1947 openly proclaimed its goal of building socialism. At that point, the party promoted such goals as industrialization, the elimination of private property, and socialization of the countryside. Although the specific tasks associated with building socialism evolved with the split from the Soviet Union, the development of "worker's self-management" and political decentralization, the collective identity associated with a unified Yugoslav state, brotherhood and unity, and socialism remained consistent.

One of many tools that the Communist party employed to help create that collective identity was the institutionalized memory of the Second World War, which it assigned to the Veteran's Association, SUBNOR. Among the tasks SUBNOR engaged in to create that memory was the design and construction of graves, cemeteries, ossuaries, and monuments for fallen soldiers of the People's Liberation Army (PLA). The creation of these cemeteries was a long slow process that passed through several chronological phases associated with political and social developments from the late 1940s up through the 1980s. Yet in all of them we see the differing but overlapping roles for soldiers' cemeteries in alleviating private grief and the promotion of a collective identity. Heike Karge's monograph *Sećanje u kamenu-okamenjeno sećanje?* brilliantly addresses that tension between private mourning and institutionalized remembrance in postwar Yugoslavia from 1947 to 1970. Discarding what she sees as a crude dichotomy between official and subversive forms of commemoration, Karge directs her attention to the ambivalence and diversity that characterized practices of memory cultures among local, republic, and central actors and the negotiations and compromises regularly reached among them.[24] Karge and others agree that while private and public goals with regard to cemeteries for fallen soldiers could work in harmony, they did not always.[25] After all, private mourning focuses on the deceased individual, while the state selects, prioritizes, and highlights specific forms of remembrance to promote collective identity, while ignoring others. However sincere the state's desire to create an institutionalized memory, one critical issue that complicated the creation of cemeteries and monuments throughout the entire period of Socialist Yugoslavia was a lack of funding.

Funding the Memory of Death

Creating a collective identity isn't cheap. The process of doing so in the aftermath of a war that left over a million victims often hastily buried in widely dispersed rural and inaccessible locations was particularly challenging. According to Karge, in the mid-1950s the average cost to transfer the remains of 200 deceased soldiers and put up a plaque in their honor was two million dinars.[26] Although this was a task that the Communist regime took seriously and on which it would ultimately expend massive amounts of money, it did not do so immediately or consistently. To be fair, the regime faced enormous financial and existential challenges in the first fifteen years of its rule. The competitors for funding were real. Yet the delays and obstacles in financing commemoration impeded the very goals they sought to attain.

Despite early expectations, almost no cemeteries or memorials to soldiers or civilians killed in the war were funded at the federal level. In 1952, the Commission for the Arrangement and Commemoration of Historical Places, referred to by Karge as a central "think tank" of remembrance, was founded in Belgrade. Directly financed by the Federal Executive Council, its purpose was to determine, design, finance, and oversee the construction of a limited number of specific sites of remembrance considered to be of general Yugoslav (opštejugoslovenksi) significance. Yet the criteria for that term were never clearly established before the Commission was dissolved in 1963, presumably in connection with the more general decentralization of those years. Over the course of its existence, several mass burial sites from the PLA made their way on to and off of the list for possible federal financing, but ultimately only one—Tjentište, the site of the Battle of Sutjeska—was actually completed. All other monument parks financed by the Commission were chosen for their political significance relating to the wartime achievements and location of the Supreme Staff of the PLA and the Central Committee of the CPY.[27]

Funding for all other cemeteries and memorials to fallen soldiers and civilian victims of fascism, large or small, came from the republics or the local communes where they were located, SUBNOR associations, and voluntary contributions in cash, kind, and labor. In the earliest years after the war, nearly all cemeteries and memorials were strictly locally funded. Beginning in the mid-1950s, all three republics regularly sent surveys and instructions to Communal associations of SUBNOR about the need to create and maintain cemeteries and memorials. In almost all cases, they received back dutiful reports, describing modest achievements and great ambitions but also usually ending with pleas for financial assistance, few of which were met, perhaps because SUBNOR was also strapped for cash. While the organization seemed to have sporadic access to state subsidies, its only official sources of funding were membership dues and publication sales.[28] SUBNOR also lacked sufficient personnel at the local level to carry out all of the tasks assigned to it. In one meeting of the Central Council, a Serbian delegate insisted that SUBNOR could not be made responsible for maintaining cemetery records

> because in most cases we don't have there even one paid individual to do such things. Our organizations in many districts do not function normally, they don't meet regularly but only on occasion. ... Often they don't have their own space ... Under these conditions, we cannot not tell them to keep good solid records unless we secure someone to do that work, unless we resolve the cadres question.[29]

In theory, a 1954 federal law placed the graves and cemeteries of fallen soldiers and the victims of fascist terror under public protection, stating that Local People's Councils must be responsible for their establishment and care. In practice, however, this law had little effect. Nor did the revised version from 1961, which focused mainly on federal responsibility for the graves of allied and foreign soldiers on Yugoslav territory. With regard to graves for soldiers and victims of fascism within Yugoslavia, it stated only that their arrangement and maintenance would be regulated by the republics through their own legal decrees.[30] In short, republics were expected to create their own laws and by the mid-1960s, most did, but at different rates and in differing ways. Bosnia & Hercegovina was the first to do so in 1962, Serbia in 1964, and Croatia in 1965.

A decentralized approach to commemoration was consistent with the country's federalized structure and allowed for local initiative but also had some problematic side effects as those areas facing the greatest need for postwar cemeteries were also among the poorest. Specifically, a majority of battles, mass death sites, and wartime losses were located in Bosnia & Hercegovina. Yet Bosnia & Hercegovina was also one of the poorest of the Yugoslav republics, and the regions where those battles and mass death sites took place were among the most underdeveloped. For these reasons, SUBNOR associations of Bosnia & Hercegovina were among those most committed to the tasks of grave and cemetery arrangement in the 1960s. Bosnia & Hercegovina was the first to pass a Law on Graves for Soldiers, including a deadline for completion by 1967 and a rule book for its application. Indeed, early efforts by Bosnia's SUBNOR Council were so impressive that by 1964, SUBNOR's Central Council in Belgrade sent documents and laws from Bosnia & Hercegovina to other republics to use as models.[31] Another obvious success from Bosnia & Hercegovina was the early creation of the Partisan Cemetery in Mostar financed entirely by the city and citizens of Mostar with the aid of Volunteer Youth Labor Brigades.[32]

Despite what seemed like a stellar beginning, local SUBNOR associations in Bosnia & Hercegovina often struggled to fulfil their self-imposed goals. A 1967 report claimed that as of 1964, of the 132,129 known remains in that republic only 41,648 (31.5 percent) had been properly buried.[33] By mid-1967 an additional twenty-seven cemeteries holding 4,189 soldiers had been completed at a cost of 244,646,200 dinars. While approximately half of that money had come from the District Assemblies as required by law, in 1964 the republic had also begun to include resources for this work within its budget. The amounts, ranging from 30 to 50 million dinars per year, were then divided among the districts based on their submitted requests. As a result, the republic had accomplished more in the last two years than the entire previous decade. Nonetheless, the 1967 deadline could not be met. At the end of 1969, nearly 40 percent of the cemeteries in Bosnia & Hercegovina were still in partial or complete disarray and the deadline was extended again until December 31, 1971.[34] Finally, by 1975, a SUBNOR report claimed that it had in recent years achieved "significant results" and fulfilled the tasks established by the law with regard to the creation of cemeteries for fallen soldiers in almost all communes, though it still had much to do for those of victims of fascist terror.[35]

Although the other republics had not included deadlines in their laws, Serbia reported in 1974 that it had recently spent approximately 5 million dinars on the construction of Partisan cemeteries and that of the 11,834 deceased soldiers and victims of fascism in Serbia, 7,751 were in individual graves and 4,083 in mass graves and ossuaries. Of those in individual graves, 2,793 (36 percent) were under the direct care of their relatives, mainly in village cemeteries, presumably placing the other 4,958 in Partisan cemeteries.[36]

Croatia did not pass a separate Law on Cemeteries for Soldiers at all but rather included it as a separate Chapter within its more general Law on Cemeteries in July 1965. According to a 1979 report, that Chapter's lack of precision was the source of multiple problems. First, it remained vague in terms of securing financial resources for soldiers' cemeteries with the result that out of ninety-two districts surveyed, only eleven explicitly included funding for soldiers' cemeteries in their budgets. Several other aspects of the report indicated that most soldiers' remains from the PLA in Croatia had not been formally gathered into Partisan cemeteries or even sections of cemeteries. The report explicitly noted that because the law provided no deadline for gathering soldiers' remains into established cemeteries, a great many still remained as individual graves buried on private property, alongside roads, and in places increasingly affected by urbanization. Although the report did not say so, it seems that many others were distributed within local municipal cemeteries. What it did say was that, in practice, care for nearly all soldiers' graves both in and outside of cemeteries remained the responsibility of the families and SUBNOR associations, which could be unreliable and sporadic. The most serious flaw, according to the report, was that Article 9 of the Law on Cemeteries established the legal usage of a cemetery lot at approximately fifteen years after which, if not maintained, it could be sold to another customer. As a result, any graves of soldiers that were not cared for often simply disappeared and with them all evidence of the sacrifices made for the liberation and "our obligatory respect toward those sacrifices."[37]

By the mid-1960s, SUBNOR organizations had begun to devise alternate solutions for the care and maintenance of soldiers' graves and cemeteries including patronage arrangements with schools, youth, working, and other mass organizations. Theoretically, such arrangements would serve a dual purpose, both ensuring the care for the graves and promoting proper Socialist and patriotic education among youth and the broader citizenry.[38] A 1975 symposium on monuments of the PLA in Bosnia & Hercegovina called for more direct self-managed social influence, which eventually evolved into Self-Managed Social Agreements by economic enterprises (radna organizacija), social-political organizations (like the Youth Organization or SUBNOR Councils), or local governing bodies (such as the District Assemblies or Local Communities). Organizations signed a four-year contract setting aside 3 percent of their yearly income for the maintenance of a particular cemetery, grave, or monument. For example, the District of Slavonska Požega prepared a list of 175 Monuments of the Revolution, including plaques, busts, graves, cemeteries, monuments, commemorative buildings, and fountains along with specific organizations to be contracted for their maintenance.[39] By the time of Yugoslavia's disintegration, many individual soldier's graves were undoubtedly still being cared for by relatives; many others, however, and especially those in Partisan cemeteries, had become the responsibility of various mass, labor, and educational organizations many of which would soon dissolve within the new states. The break up of Yugoslavia thus left no organization behind to protect them or ensure their continued maintenance.

Overcoming Grief

The most immediate goal of a military cemetery is to provide proper burial for battlefield dead, honoring their sacrifice and providing comfort and a space for mourning to families, friends, and comrades. For some families, the ultimate goal is to return the body home where it may be interred in the local, often confessional, cemetery. In the heat of battle, however, and often for years after, such a task may be overwhelmingly difficult. As one relative, himself a soldier, later explained, "In the course of the war, I couldn't do anything to carry out the exhumation and transfer the remains of my sister home to the [local] cemetery. The battles were cruel and difficult and there were other concerns besides grieving and thoughts of the dead."[40] In any case, others prefer that the soldier's remains stay with their comrades, in a setting where their sacrifice is visible to all and regularly honored with public rituals.[41]

Despite theoretical support from the Communist regime, the arrangement of most military graves and cemeteries from the end of the war until the early 1960s was largely spontaneous. Karge has accurately described this period of commemoration as "bottom-up" rather than "top-down."[42] Yet we must be careful not to draw a sharp line between the private and public tasks assigned to soldiers' cemeteries. For while the goals of private mourning clearly predominated during these early years, there is no clear end to the process of mourning. Even after all those who knew the deceased must themselves have died, military cemeteries may still be understood as "sites of mourning." Nor were regime efforts to use memory of the dead to build a collective identity temporally constrained, though they clearly strengthened over time. As early as 1949, Central and Republic SUBNOR Councils instructed local associations that they must "urgently" create teams and go out to all places where "in the course of the People's Liberation War our comrades were killed, tortured and shot, cremated and buried" and take all necessary measures to arrange and mark their graves, preparing potential cemetery sites with fencing, landscaping, and flowers.[43] By 1953, these instructions had become far more elaborate, specifying that the graves of soldiers be marked with a five-pointed star or, if they were members of a proletarian brigade, the hammer and sickle.[44] Nonetheless, the initiative and actual work in each of these cases was directed mainly by family, friends, and local SUBNOR organizations; was characterized by a high level of emotional intensity; and focused on the goals of private mourning.

Because so many regions had to deal with large numbers of soldiers' and civilians' remains from battle and killing sites, SUBNOR associations often opted to build ossuaries or common mausoleums as a simple and relatively inexpensive means of commemoration. Even so, the task of finding, exhuming, and gathering the remains of multiple identified and unknown soldiers from particular battle sites, along with those of individual soldiers buried outside cemeteries, and then placing them into commemorative ossuaries, vaults, or obelisks was complex, time-consuming, and expensive. The ossuaries and obelisks might be placed at the site of the battle itself, in a town square or park, or within a local cemetery. They usually included a metal plaque providing available information about the deceased, and how and when they had died, though the amount and accuracy of that information varied considerably (Figure 3.1).

These were the memorial acts most akin to those described by Jay Winter in that the graves, cemeteries, and monuments were initiated, designed, funded, constructed, tended, visited, and valued by people for whom the act was deeply personal.[45] Yet, as we have seen, these locals usually worked with very limited

Figure 3.1 Monuments to fallen soldiers and victims of fascist terror, 1950s–60s, Prizren, Kosova; Vrbaška, Bosnia & Hercegovina; Vrebac, Croatia. For more photographs on this theme see: https://yugcemeteries.omeka.net/exhibits/show/monuments

resources, meaning that the graves, memorials, and cemeteries they created were usually built and inscribed with only the materials and information at hand. Nonetheless, according to Karge, the 1950s in Yugoslavia saw the construction of more monuments to the Second World War, including especially fallen soldiers, than any other decade. For example, of 2,700 memorials raised in Croatia by 1960, over two-thirds were dedicated to soldiers and civilian victims of fascism. Of the memorials Lawler has thus far documented in Bosnia & Hercegovina, approximately 20 percent of those created in the 1950s and 1960s consisted of graves, cemeteries, and ossuaries.[46] Those sites were ripe with symbolism and full of emotional intensity for the relatives and friends of those interred, many of whom had donated cash, kind, and labor for their creation. A significant portion of the population, particularly family members and veterans, attended cemetery openings and then visited them on a regular basis, especially state holidays, considering them "holy places."[47] Yet as we will see in later chapters, Partisan cemeteries and memorials included only those who fought with the Partisans and were not equally valued by all local residents, particularly those whose relatives had fought on the other side of the war or rejected the Communist agenda.

Besides those cemeteries and memorials founded for soldiers who lost their lives in the People's Liberation Struggle, mass graves and ossuaries were also created for civilian victims killed by enemies of the regime during the war.[48] In the official language of the Communist party, those individuals were referred to as "Victims of Fascist Terror"—*Žrtva fašističkog terora*—often abbreviated to ŽFTs. Nearly every document from the 1940s through the 1980s relating to the creation of cemeteries and other forms of commemoration for the deceased officially described them as being prepared for "soldiers of the People's Liberation Army and Victims of Fascist Terror." Scholarly literature on this topic has established a clear hierarchy in commemorative activity that prioritized soldiers over civilian victims of war not only in Yugoslavia but in all postwar Europe. The Holocaust and its victims did not begin to gain serious public attention until the 1960s even in the West and were left entirely out of official mourning in the Soviet Union and most Socialist states throughout their existence.[49] Given that reality, Socialist Yugoslavia was generally more conscious of and interested in commemorating the deaths of its civilian, including Jewish, victims of fascism than were most other countries. Certainly, monuments and cemeteries dedicated to soldiers from the PLA received a higher priority, but a significant number of memorials and cemeteries were created for civilian victims both early on and continuing throughout the existence of Socialist Yugoslavia.[50]

Nonetheless, the regime had good reasons to prioritize commemoration of deceased Partisan soldiers whose heroism and sacrifice for the future of a united Yugoslav state represented precisely those values it hoped to promote among new citizens. The stories associated with victims of fascism were less heroic and often contradicted the official narrative of brotherhood and unity. Yet, their commemoration was consistently fueled from below by grieving survivors, fellow camp inmates, and relatives who gathered in remembrance, creating ad hoc memorials and pressing for more official ones in letters and editorials. Central and republic SUBNOR archives include numerous private letters, sent even to Tito himself, expressing their interest in commemorating sites where civilian victims were killed. Karge has argued that despite official reluctance at the highest levels of the Yugoslav Communist Party, Jasenovac was nonetheless created thanks in part to pressure from below by former camp inmates and other victim survivors in the late 1950s and early 1960s.[51] At the local level at least, such initiatives were generally welcomed as SUBNOR, government, and party activists often had relatives and close friends among the victims. For example, Dušan Misirača, the head of SUBNOR in Bosnia & Hercegovina, was among those most committed to the construction of soldiers' cemeteries in general but was also among the main forces behind Bosnia & Hercegovina's involvement in Jasenovac. Misirača eventually published two articles on Jasenovac and one on cemeteries and, although the information is inconclusive, it is possible that one or more of his relatives were killed at Jasenovac.[52]

Nonetheless, SUBNOR activists officially placed victims of fascist terror in a different category arguing that their remains should ideally be kept separate from those of soldiers of the PLA and for whom the rules of commemoration were on a different level. For example, while the graves of soldiers were ideally (though not consistently) to be individual, providing all possible personal and military information, it was entirely acceptable for the remains of victims of fascist terror to be combined within ossuaries or a mausoleum listing only their names on a plaque.[53] Indeed, according to Lawler's statistics, of the 207 cemeteries he has thus far documented in Bosnia & Hercegovina, 184 were for Partisans only, 5 were for victims of fascism only, 5 were mixed, and 2 are unknown. Nonetheless, he estimated that approximately 90 percent of the 146 mass graves commemorated only victims of fascism, while the 168 ossuaries were largely mixed.[54] A 1969 report sought to justify such segregation from a historical and functional, rather than hierarchical, perspective, arguing that it was not because the victims of fascist terror were "less notable for their active participation in the battle and their contribution to the front line, but because the contents differed by historical standards and in every respect."[55]

Different rules applied, however, when it came to the commemoration of those killed between and among Yugoslavia's multiple ethnoreligious groups. While the mass murder of Serbs, Jews, and Roma by the Ustashe at Jasenovac in Croatia was problematic for the Communist regime, it simply could not be ignored due to its size and infamy. However, in the bloody civil war that accompanied foreign occupation during the Second World War, citizens from Yugoslavia's multiple ethnoreligious communities sometimes carried out brutal atrocities against neighbors and even former friends, either in connection with the occupying powers or on their own initiative. Such cases of intercommunal violence in the rural towns and villages of Bosnia & Hercegovina, as well as in some parts of Croatia, Serbia, and Kosovo/Kosova, were much more difficult to negotiate historically, politically, and with regard to commemoration. This is an extremely sensitive topic and one that has received a great deal of political, but fortunately also scholarly, attention.[56] Following the war, the Communist regime placed the blame for all such atrocities on foreign occupiers and their domestic collaborators, while many domestic citizens with blood on their hands escaped all responsibility, particularly if they had later joined the Partisans. Although monuments to the "victims of fascism" were erected throughout Yugoslavia, those victims were described in abstract terms without reference to their ethnoreligious identity or any intercommunal violence. Perhaps the regime felt that it had little alternative—the complexities of ethnoreligious and political conflict were so overwhelming and the traumas so deep that the party saw no way of resolving them. Instead, it simply papered over many atrocities in the interests of promoting brotherhood and unity, laying all blame on outsiders and those whose hostility to the new regime was implacable.

Max Bergholz describes just such a case in Kulen Vakuf, a village in Northwestern Bosnia nearly on the border of Croatia, with a mixed population of mainly Bosnian Muslims but also Catholic Croats and Orthodox Serbs. During the early part of the Second World War in 1941, Kulen Vakuf experienced a number of massacres, first by Ustashe units that included both Croats and Muslims against Serbs and then, in retaliation, Serbs against Muslims. Ultimately, thousands of Serbs and Muslims were drowned in the river or more commonly shot and thrown into limestone pits. Only in 1981 did the town erect a monument to commemorate the "victims of fascism." But the commemoration ceremony mentioned neither the violence nor the actual victims. Indeed, one of the speakers at the opening celebration was a Serbian Communist who, before joining the party, had attacked his Muslim neighbors and may have participated in their massacre. The monument itself symbolized the unity of Yugoslavia as a central flower surrounded by eight smaller flowers, representing each of the six republics and two autonomous provinces. The only names engraved on the four plaques were those of 147 local Partisans who had died in the war.[57] The monument style typified by the abstract flower in Kulen Vakuf, however unsatisfying it surely was to the families of those killed by their neighbors, nonetheless, may have represented Socialist Yugoslavia's most successful attempt at the creation of a collective identity through public forms of commemoration.

Creating a Collective Identity

While the cemeteries, ossuaries, and mass graves constructed in Yugoslavia following the war were initially created by and for families, friends, and comrades of the deceased, they also had an important role in the creation of a new Yugoslav identity. Already in the mid-1950s, but ever more aggressively in the 1960s and beyond, the regime and SUBNOR began to think about war memorials and cemeteries less as spaces for grieving and more as sources for the education of youth and even tourism. Accordingly, they focused their attention more on location and quality of presentation. Karge refers to this period as marking the end of a phase primarily oriented on overcoming grief to one focused more on the future; it thus represented a transition period in which the regime's concerns shifted from the wartime survivors to later generations. The new challenge was how to pass on the memory of the war.[58] In terms of cemeteries, the regime sought to move away from the locally directed, emotional forms of commemoration, typical of the first fifteen years following the war, toward those that would help create a collective identity.

Increasingly through the 1960s, SUBNOR activists emphasized the role of cemeteries in developing brotherhood and unity and patriotism, while educating youth in the revolutionary traditions of the People's Liberation Struggle. Given the political and national debates wracking the country from the late 1960s and into the 1970s, that task was considered increasingly vital, and officials developed more innovative ways of promoting their ideals. Hence, they sought to make Partisan cemeteries and wartime memorials as much into spaces for tourism and recreation as sites of mourning. Future Partisan cemeteries were to be located near major highways, or alternatively in massive nature parks, and equipped with hotels, restaurants, information booths, and multiple activities. Most important, they were to inspire hope and enthusiasm for the future, rather than thoughts of death and mourning.

Dr. Smail Tihić, the author of several tourist guides for Bosnia & Hercegovina, enthusiastically promoted a different way of thinking about and designing Partisan cemeteries.[59] In April 1969, Tihić pointed to the enormous public interest in the cemeteries of fallen soldiers,

> Citizens young and old come to [these cemeteries] most often and spend the most time in them. They come individually and in groups, on holidays, but also on ordinary days. Most often they come to pay their respects to the fallen heroes, but historians and other scholars, foreign guests, and domestic passers-by also

come. They read the inscriptions, they search in the memory of the near and the familiar, they search for friends and acquaintances.[60]

Yet according to Tihić, many cemeteries in Bosnia & Hercegovina were failing in their public and educational function. To satisfy their educational goals, they must be easily accessible, clean, and attractive, providing clear, unambiguous information about the soldiers, allowing visitors maximum opportunity to identify each individual buried there. Thus, he recommended that the currently existing multiple small, inaccessible, badly built, and neglected cemeteries be centralized into one representative object for each commune that could not only count on a "permanent life and function, but would be one of the beauties of the city, a place of 'pilgrimage' for residents of the region and for all citizens, foreign and domestic, who come to the city, students and school excursions."[61] Placement in such cemeteries, he argued, would also provide a better option for those Partisans still buried in confessional cemeteries, mixed in among ordinary citizens.

Throughout the late 1960s and 1970s reports complained about the inadequacy of existing Partisan cemeteries, referring to serious problems with the quality of commemorative markers and monuments, including grammatical errors, incorrect use and choice of language, inaccurate historical context, and low artistic value.[62] Yet disagreements also developed between and among SUBNOR activists and others over the appropriate solution and, specifically, whether additional legislation, centralization, and supervision would improve quality and prevent anarchy or simply destroy authenticity, while hindering creativity and initiative.

That tension between the need for improved quality and the desire for authenticity was most clearly manifested in a debate in the Republic of Bosnia & Hercegovina over which laws should be applied to the creation and design of cemeteries for soldiers and victims of fascist terror. During the 1960s additional laws were passed throughout Yugoslavia to promote the "Commemoration of Historical Events and People" and for the "Defense of Monuments of Culture."[63] The Republic Commission for Commemoration in Bosnia & Hercegovina played an important role in applying these laws, including also to the organization of cemeteries. In October 1968, Bosnia's SUBNOR requested that only the Law on Cemeteries and Graves of Yugoslav Soldiers be applied to cemetery creation, but the Commission for Commemoration declined, stating that (1) the cemeteries and graves of soldiers and victims of fascism were also historical monuments and thus protected by that law; (2) newly constructed cemeteries and ossuaries must also be treated as cultural/historical monuments and historical documents; and (3) there was no conflict between the laws.

SUBNOR disagreed, citing considerable confusion since the Rulebook for the Law on Cemeteries described them as based on plans created by authorized organizations while the Law on Commemoration required a public competition between artists/sculptors and so on. Moreover, serious conflicts had arisen due to noncompliance with Article 2 in the Law on Cemeteries, which referred only to the exhumation of soldiers' remains from individual disorganized graves and not the removal of entire local cemeteries where tens or even hundreds of soldiers or victims of fascism were buried as had frequently occurred. The report cited examples, such as Vlasenica, Sanjski Most (both sites of mass killings), and Jasikovac, the location of the Central Hospital of the Partisan Supreme Staff, where hundreds or even thousands of bodies were exhumed and transferred, eradicating authentic sites of historical significance, presumably for the sake of convenience.[64] Although this and many similar conflicts remained unresolved throughout the existence of Socialist Yugoslavia, the gradual development of the Partisan Cemetery in Sarajevo provides an excellent case study in how many of these debates evolved over a period of twenty years. It exemplifies not only the transition from private mourning to public identity formation but also concerns over where and how to best commemorate both military and civilian wartime deaths and the consequences of inadequate funding.

Immediately following the war, the City of Sarajevo commemorated its war dead with two memorials: an Ossuary to the People's Heroes in Veliki Park and a temporary monument to the Liberators of Sarajevo in front of the old National Bank. Although about fifty soldiers were buried in an unarranged cemetery at Koševo (near the current Olympic Stadium) as well as a comparable number in Vraca, atop a hill on the South side of the city, plans for the construction of a central and major Partisan cemetery had come to naught by the mid-1960s.[65] The failure stemmed both from a lack of funding and disagreements over its appropriate location and character. While all agreed that the cemetery must be a visible marker of the sacrifices made by those who fell in the struggle for the liberation of Sarajevo, many also felt it should have a less sacred character and be more like a park, one that the citizens of Sarajevo, and especially its youth and children, could enjoy while visiting those who had sacrificed for their freedom. "It should inspire confidence in the power of our peoples, not the sadness which is often demoralizing."[66]

The design of the Memorial Park during the mid-1960s provided an opportunity for multiple lengthy debates on this and other topics, as members of the committee considered whether it should have mausolea/vaults/ossuaries or individual graves, if remains should be moved to the site at all, and how to distinguish People's Heroes, Liberators of the City, Partisans, and Victims of Fascist Terror from one another.[67] By 1964, the decision was made to build the cemetery at Vraca thanks to its magnificent view of the city and surrounding landscape as well as for the Austro-Hungarian Fortress located on the site, which seemed ideal for a monument park.[68] The most serious alternative had been the creation of a Partisan section within the newly created Municipal cemetery at Bare, but many feared that not only would it lose significance within that enormous complex but its educational value would be made more difficult by the proximity to religious rituals and ceremonies held there. Following a 1965 competition, Vlada Dobrović and two collaborators were selected to design the Memorial Park and Partisan Cemetery, though debates long continued over whether to keep or demolish the fortress and whether to include a museum, lodgings, and restaurant.[69]

As it turned out, complications due to funding and design delayed construction of the cemetery for fifteen years, and when the grand opening took place on November 25, 1981, the final product included no individual soldiers' graves but rather multiple monuments, including an eternal fountain and flame and seven terraced memorial walls bearing the names of 9,091 Sarajevans who had died during the war—both soldiers and victims of fascist terror—listed together in alphabetical order. The only actual remains on-site are those of Sarajevo's twenty-six People's Heroes interred in a cube-shaped granite ossuary at the top of the walls (Figure 3.2).[70]

Apart from one monument to Tito, which includes his likeness and a Partisan Star, the rest of the architectural design at Vraca is entirely abstract, lacking any specific references to communism.[71] Indeed, Socialist Yugoslavia has become particularly well known for its early commitment to massive avant-garde monumentation and architecture. Already by the mid-1950s, in response to its conflict with Stalin, the Yugoslav Communist party abandoned Soviet Socialist realism and opened the doors to artistic and architectural experimentation. That experimentation was seen remarkably early in monumental works commemorating victims of fascism with Bogdan Bogdanović's 1952 Memorial to Jewish Victims of Fascism in Belgrade and Edward Ravnikar's Memorial Complex for the Kampor Concentration Camp on the Croatian island of Rab. Beginning thus in the 1950s, but particularly in the 1960s and 1970s, monuments and memorial parks throughout Yugoslavia were characterized by extraordinary abstract designs that drew on multiple coexisting artistic trends, while creating new forms of their own (Figure 3.3).[72]

Figure 3.2 Vraca Memorial Park, Sarajevo, Bosnia & Hercegovina

The abstract forms and inspiration inherent in so many of these new works, while likely inspired mainly by the artists' own vision, also ably served the Communist regime's ideological goals in multiple ways. First, they allowed the CPY to clearly separate itself from Stalinist approaches to Socialist construction, presenting itself not only as allowing more artistic freedom but also as manifestly "cutting edge." Abstract forms also better suited commemorative needs in those cases where memorials that might identify the national or religious culture of victim or perpetrator would damage the cause of "brotherhood and unity." Similarly, in those cases where military and civilian victims were impossible to separate, an abstract memorial made their collective remembrance relevant to all. Finally, as the decentralization of Yugoslavia increased during the 1960s and 1970s, abstract memorials allowed for the inclusion of local cultural markers, without risking an all-out descent into nationalism.

Figure 3.3 Abstract Socialist memorials
• Mostar Partisan Cemetery, Bosnia & Hercegovina
• Monument to the Jewish Victims of Fascism, Belgrade, Serbia
• Monument to Fallen Partisans, Jasikovac Orthodox Cemetery, Gospić, Croatia

Indeed, Partisan cemeteries had a significant advantage in that they were never ethnoreligiously segregated. In this sense, the Partisan cemeteries were drawing on the European example set during the First World War when, for the first time, soldiers of all ranks, socioeconomic backgrounds, ethnicities, and religions were buried side by side without distinction. Moreover, while several European countries at that time chose a cross as the grave marker for each soldier, the Imperial War Graves Commission and the British Parliament decided in 1920 to adopt the principles of secularism and egalitarianism in creating a standard rectangular and secular memorial for each British Imperial victim of the First World War seeking to eliminate any distinctions of class, caste, race, and

Figure 3.4 "Generally Yugoslav" grave markers of Partisans
Banja Luka and Mostar, Bosnia & Hercegovina and Zagreb, Croatia

religion and ensure that each victim's sacrifice was equally valued.[73] Similarly, the graves of deceased Partisans were always placed side by side regardless of national, ethnic, or religious background, nor did the inscriptions indicate any ethnoreligious identity. For example, the names of soldiers buried in Mostar's Partisan Cemetery and in the Partisan sections of Mirogoj in Zagreb and of the Municipal Cemetery in Banja Luka are inscribed on stones placed or scattered along the ground. In that sense, these cemeteries were truly "generally Yugoslav" (opštejugoslovenski) in a way that, as we will see, Yugoslavia's civilian cemeteries were not (Figure 3.4).

Partisan cemeteries were also far more likely to be egalitarian than were civilian cemeteries. To be sure, as we have seen in Vraca, Kulen Vakuf, and elsewhere, the Yugoslav Communists did not reject all hierarchical distinctions. As in Revolutionary Russia and the Soviet Union, the military cemeteries and graves of postwar Yugoslavia honored first and foremost its leaders and those designated as "People's Heroes" during the Partisan Struggle. For example, the Tomb of the People's Heroes constructed in 1948 houses the remains of four prominent Yugoslav Communists under a large marble slab supporting their busts in Kalemegdan Park overlooking the Danube River in Belgrade. According to Goran Miloradović, Milovan Djilas devised the concept in the midst of the Soviet-Yugoslav split as a means of increasing unity and providing a symbolic parallel to the Kremlin Wall.[74] Nonetheless, those Partisan cemeteries whose symbolic imagery was entirely abstract and bereft of political symbolism came closest to creating true "communities of the dead" for its inhabitants and for all Yugoslavia's citizens. Like the Civil War soldiers buried in National Cemeteries in the United States, the dead interred in those universalist cemeteries came closer to making the land that had been claimed for Yugoslavia in 1918 actually "Yugoslav."

Whether as ossuaries, monuments, cemeteries, or more elaborate monument parks, they provided a simple space of mourning and remembrance *but only* for those killed by enemies of the current regime. Where they fell short was in their exclusion of those domestic soldiers—citizens of their own country—but who had fought against the regime. Thus, even these much more effective cemeteries were deeply politicized, a characteristic that would have lasting consequences. Nonetheless, the integrated and egalitarian Partisan cemeteries might have served as a model for civilian cemeteries and, had that model been adopted, might have created there too a kind of Yugoslav "community of the dead" based on new values and ideals. Instead, most civilian cemeteries remained ethnoreligiously segregated throughout the Socialist era. Moreover, in contrast to the deliberately abstract and universalizing approach adopted for many Partisan cemeteries, the graves of Partisans and communists buried in civilian cemeteries were far more openly and deliberately politicized.

4

The Secularization of Cemeteries

The title of Thomas Laqueur's masterful *The Work of the Dead* refers to his argument about how the dead "dwell in us—individually and communally ... how they give meaning to our lives, how they structure public spaces, politics, and time ... and how we invest the dead ... with meaning."[1] Laqueur's comment draws attention to the intersection between private and public forms of commemoration. While the organization of funerals and selection of grave markers take place within the private sphere of the family, secularization and cemetery structure are very much a matter of public concern.

This chapter first describes the Communist regime's efforts to secularize the administration of civilian cemeteries by removing extant burial spaces from the control of religious communities. A second section investigates the structure and design of new municipal cemeteries created in the three republics. The importance of creating secular and integrated cemeteries might be considered self-evident for a regime that sought to reduce the role of religion in society and restructure communities on multicultural rather than ethnoreligious foundations. Cemeteries were certainly not the starting point for that agenda, but what would be the point in creating a pluralistic society based on secular forms of identity that encourages interfaith and interethnic marriages if all citizens are still buried separately in cemeteries that reaffirm ethnoreligious ties and separate them from the "other"? To realize their ideological agenda the communists might logically have planned new cemeteries entirely dissociated from ethnoreligious sources of identity, and in rare cases they did. Overall, however, it seemed that Yugoslav communists failed to appreciate "the work of the dead" and what the dead might do for them.

Laqueur traced the transition from confessional churchyards to secular cemeteries in Western Europe, arguing that we may see it as a shift from *gemeinschaft* (community) to *gesellschaft* (society). While the churchyard provided for the dead of a religious and ethnic community, those buried in a cemetery were likely unrelated and unknown to one another, possibly of differing religions, nationalities, and political beliefs. The churchyard, as he saw it, was "ancient, crowded, hierarchical, exclusively for the use of a small community, grounded in faith, and seething with new burials that all faced east to await the resurrection and displaced older ones in constantly reused land in the heart of the living community." The secular cemetery, in contrast, was "spacious, open to anyone who could pay, landscaped, garden like, with huge and diverse communities of the dead serenely planted in specific graves, many owned in perpetuity, gathered at the periphery of the settlements of the living and oriented toward a calm, melancholy, but sweet eternal repose."[2] According to Laqueur and others, this transition from churchyard to cemetery came about in Western Europe during the eighteenth and nineteenth centuries, due to a broad combination of factors associated with modernization, including the Protestant Reformation, Scientific Revolution, urbanization, secularism, and the rise of individualism.

The transition from churchyard to cemetery in Western Europe was not always easy and certainly involved the conflicts associated with modernization and the limited religious pluralism that existed between Catholics, Protestants, and Jews.[3] Moreover, though eventually successful, the transition was not absolute, even in Western Europe where confessional and communal cemeteries persist into the present, particularly in rural regions.[4] In Central and Southeastern Europe, the transition from *gemeinschaft* to *gesellschaft* occurred far more slowly if at all, since many of the preconditions for it were either absent or delayed and political conditions differed rather dramatically. A few municipal cemeteries had been created in the major cities of Zagreb and Belgrade by the late nineteenth century, but they were exceptional. In many regions of Yugoslavia, religiously controlled and ethnically dominated churchyards remained the rule until the Communist takeover of power in 1945. When that transition finally began to take place, it was in a largely rural, multireligious, and multinational environment fraught with tension following the Second World War and under the auspices of an ideological regime that sought to change not just institutions but culture and human beings themselves by nondemocratic means. These factors influenced both policy decisions and their outcomes, though not always in ways that might be expected.

Key to understanding Yugoslav laws on civilian death and burial is that they were slow to materialize and entirely decentralized. Party and state representatives held no substantive discussions about the role of cemeteries in new Yugoslavia and passed almost no federal laws guiding their activities. While the new state quickly restricted the authority of the church over the registration of births, marriages, and deaths, it moved far more slowly regarding control over cemeteries.[5] Lacking direction from above and with respect for existing burial traditions, cemetery administrators left the old structures and divisions in place. The diversity of burial cultures and traditions and the weight of its other responsibilities also likely inspired the federal government to delegate responsibility for burial policies to the republics and municipalities.

The very first law that the federal government passed concerning cemeteries was the 1946 Law on People's Councils (Narodni Odbori), which stated only that among the many tasks of the section for social welfare and national health in local People's Councils was also "management of cemeteries."[6] The law provided no explanation as to who exactly should administer the cemeteries or when and how their transfer to the local councils should take place—a significant lapse considering that many cemeteries remained in the hands of religious communities.

Having placed management of cemeteries in the hands of municipalities, the federal government took an almost entirely hands-off approach to the issue, leaving it up to republics and municipalities to pass and enforce laws and regulations relating to burials and cemetery management. Most cities, including Belgrade and Zagreb, passed municipal laws dealing with disposition of the dead and cemeteries in the 1950s, while the first republic laws were not passed until 1960. The early municipal laws shared many similarities as they all reflected an effort to promote modernization and public hygiene.[7] The municipal People's Councils faced a far greater challenge in asserting management rights over cemeteries. Although certain similarities arose in the process, particularly regarding the nature of relations with specific religious communities, there were also critical differences. After all, both secularization and the creation of new municipal cemeteries were public activities that developed in accordance with each republic's legal and historic context. The details of both processes also relied not only on each republic's ethnoreligious diversity but also on the relationship between its Communist party and religious communities. Nonetheless, despite important differences in their processes, both Serbia and Croatia were able to successfully secularize cemeteries by the mid-1960s, while nearly one-third of cemeteries in Bosnia & Hercegovina still remained in the hands of the religious communities by the mid-1980s. Yet in all three republics, ethnoreligiously segregated burials remained the rule, whether in separate cemeteries or separate sections of cemeteries, municipal or confessional.

Cemetery Secularization in Serbia and Croatia

Serbia's burial culture is based on the Eastern Orthodox version of Christianity but is complicated by the fact that some Serbs lived within the Ottoman Empire while others resided in the Austro-Hungarian Empire. Thus, sections of what would become Serbia inherited their public and legal burial culture from entirely different systems, while migration and colonization by different ethnic groups create additional diversity. Even by the Second World War, Serbia's rare modern municipal cemeteries existed only in a few large cities and in some mixed communities of the former Austro-Hungarian Empire. Novo Groblje Cemetery in Belgrade, for example, was founded in 1886 as an Orthodox cemetery and only during the interwar period did it agree to set aside seventeen sections for the burial of Catholics and Protestants and two for Muslims. Two Jewish cemeteries were also originally connected to Novo Groblje. The Ashkenazi one located inside Novo Groblje is no longer in use, while the Sephardic Jewish Cemetery across the street is still active.[8] While Serbia's cemeteries were generally segregated by religion, the majority of Orthodox cemeteries in Serbia belonged to and were traditionally managed by local municipalities or villages rather than the church. Since those cemeteries were already considered communal property, their takeover by the People's Councils was rarely an issue of contention. There were some important exceptions to this rule: Vojvodina included Catholic and Protestant cemeteries that owned the deeds to their cemeteries, and Muslim cemeteries in the Sandžak of Novi Pazar and Kosovo were usually the property of the Islamic vakuf (waqf—charitable foundation), which also held the deed to the property.

As constituent parts of the Austro-Hungarian Empire, Croatia and Vojvodina had been subject to laws on cemetery reform enacted by Joseph II in the eighteenth century and by the mid- to late nineteenth century, cemeteries in those regions had begun to approximate those in the rest of Western Europe but with a more sharply defined urban–rural divide. In the outskirts of cities, provincial towns, and villages, most cemeteries remained as the property of the Catholic or, in Vojvodina, the Protestant Church, a fact that clearly complicated the party's secularizing agenda. At the same time, larger cities had already begun to build municipal cemeteries in the European garden style, replete with chapels, monuments, and grave markers of varying sizes and styles reflecting the wealth, status, and faith of the decedent. To the extent that these cemeteries were often more modernized than those in either Serbia proper or Bosnia & Hercegovina, Croatian and Vojvodinian burial culture was better situated to facilitate certain regime goals in the area of cemetery management, such as the mandatory use of mortuaries to improve hygiene.[9]

Many of these cemeteries were already accounting for the religious diversity of the region as well. When Croatia's capital city of Zagreb built its first large municipal cemetery, Mirogoj, in 1876, it included four sections—one each for the city's Catholics, Orthodox, Protestants, and Jews. Theoretically, the interconfessional law of 1879 eliminated these divisions, but in practice they are still evident for Jews and Muslims, though less so for the Orthodox population.[10] Within a decade, Mirogoj had also constructed a public mortuary and had begun to provide transportation for the deceased, though its use was not obligatory.[11]

Several regional laws passed just after the turn of the century sought to ensure that all religious communities had equal access to burial space. In 1906, a law in the region of Croatia-Slavonia specified that each religious community had the right to create its own cemetery but must dedicate space in it for the burial of members from other religious communities and those of uncertain status. Alternatively, locales with multiple religious communities might decide to build a common cemetery with separate sections for each.[12] A 1907 law on religious relations stated that churches and religious communities may not refuse burial in their cemeteries to members of another faith if another nonbeliever was already buried in that cemetery or if no cemetery for members of that religious community existed in the area.[13] Finally, statutes on village cemeteries from interwar Yugoslavia stated that they may be either communal or confessional. A communal cemetery should bury members of all faiths equally and be administered by a district official and doctor along with four elected council members chosen from among the believers of the religions buried there. A confessional cemetery was to be administered by a cemetery council made up of the church pastor, the district official, the doctor, and four representatives chosen from the appropriate religious group.[14]

While all these laws lost legal power following the Second World War, they might have provided some degree of precedent in case of conflict. Even so, in most cases individual Catholic churches within Croatia owned their cemetery land and thus retained the right to determine where, and, even if, to bury individuals within them. Traditionally, most Catholic communities have been exclusivist, refusing burial within the cemetery to a variety of outcasts including nonbelievers, criminals, suicides, and unbaptized babies. The exclusion of "nonbelievers" affected the burial of members of religious minorities, Communist party members (by definition atheists), and non-Catholic spouses of members of the congregation all of whom were, at best, offered space on the very edge of the cemetery or, more likely, outside cemetery walls contradicting the Communist regime's pluralistic goals and slogan of "brotherhood and unity." This policy provided the Communist regime both an ideological and a practical reason to pursue cemetery secularization. Nonetheless, the 1946 Law on People's Councils stating that they had the responsibility for "management of cemeteries" did not specifically mention confessional cemeteries, though it also did not exclude them, a lacuna that different constituents interpreted in very different ways. Some understood it to mean that the confessional cemeteries were to be exempted from the law, while others clearly believed that the confessional cemeteries must be taken over by the People's Councils.

Already in February of 1947, the District People's Council in Zagreb decided to take over the cemetery of the Church of St. Ivan Zelina in the outskirts of Zagreb. The Catholic priest protested that doing so was a violation of the Constitution and of Roman Catholic decrees, so the People's Council turned to the Zagreb Commission for Religious Questions (CRQ) for help. Having examined both previous and existing laws for guidance and considering the topic's sensitivity, the CRQ punted; that is, it advised the Croatian Republic's legislative committee (the Department for the Construction of People's Power and Legislation) that the regime would not be able to change administration and ownership simply by decree. Therefore, "administration of the confessional cemeteries ought to be left in the hands of the previous organs, under the eventual supervision of the district People's Councils, until there is a new legal order for the entire cemetery matter."[15]

A similar problem arose in the summer of 1948 in Zagreb's suburb of Šestine. In this case the complaint regarding a cemetery takeover came directly from the Archbishop of Zagreb who reminded the CRQ that cemeteries had been explicitly excluded from expropriation in the Agrarian Reform of 1945. Having received no response from the government on the previous matter, the CRQ sent another request for guidance.[16]

An unsigned document in the CRQ Archive from February 1949 stated even more directly that the state must absolutely publish a decree on cemeteries in the near future. Yet even that, it warned, would be insufficient since the cemeteries in Roman Catholic parishes were all written into the legal cadastres, or property books, and excluded from the agrarian reform. Nonetheless, it urged that the problem be resolved as it was obviously wrong to leave public property in private hands.[17]

By late 1949 the Republic of Croatia at the suggestion of its Ministries of Communal Affairs and National Health finally submitted a "Decree on

Cemeteries" reiterating that they were all to be administered by local and municipal People's Councils, which were also responsible for their maintenance and expansion. The decree further clarified that cemeteries must provide for the burial of the deceased of their region regardless of confession but could have special sections for members of certain religious communities if they wished and if conditions permitted. Cemetery administrators were not to prevent or hinder religious burial rituals or the placement of religious symbols on grave markers under threat of punishment. All religious organizations were to remit their cemeteries along with all other related property, funds, cash, and other valuables to the local People's Councils by November 1, 1949. The decree was to go into effect on the date of its publication in the press. In fact, there is no evidence that this decree was ever published or put into effect.[18]

Nonetheless, on November 3 the Osijek People's Council decided to take over all of the city's confessional cemeteries, informing all religious communities, church institutions, and special councils that they had fifteen days to comply.[19] In response, the Bishopric of Djakovo filed an official complaint to the CRQ on behalf of the three Osijek Parishes and personally contacted Monsignor Ritig for advice.[20] Ritig wrote to the Federal CRQ and the Federal Committee for Legislation and the Construction of People's Power in Belgrade, pointing to the lack of unity in this matter between Croatia and Serbia. For while Osijek had decided to appropriate all confessional cemeteries, the Serbian government had just passed a law stating that it would do so only if confessional cemeteries were abandoned or in serious disrepair. Worried that such divergent decisions could cause serious problems between republics and religious communities, Ritig urged the federal authorities to reach a unified decision as soon as possible.[21]

Ritig reiterated these concerns a month later but was even more pointed in his criticism of the Osijek decision, urging that it be delayed for the time being. The final decision about whether or not to take over confessional cemeteries, he argued, must be taken by federal authorities fully conscious of the complex issue of sacred objects found in and around cemeteries, that cemeteries had been exempted from the agrarian reform, and that the relationship of religious communities toward their cemeteries must be treated equally throughout Yugoslavia.[22] Nonetheless, by April 1950, officials in Osijek had received the blessing of the Zagreb CRQ and Ministry of Communal Affairs to move ahead with appropriation.[23]

Early actions in Osijek seemed to imply Zagreb's support for the takeover of confessional cemeteries. Yet events in the months and years to come suggest a more complex interpretation, as most parts of the republic witnessed a move back toward the maintenance of religious administration of confessional cemeteries. Perhaps Ritig's memos had been effective, for even in Osijek secularization was delayed until 1957.[24] Throughout the early 1950s, members of the CRQ debated questions such as: What was the difference between ownership and management of a confessional cemetery? Did it matter whether a confessional cemetery had been written into the legal books or not? Who had legal rights to cut/sell the grass/hay in confessional cemeteries? Who was legally responsible for their upkeep and maintenance? Not uncommonly, the commission recommended legal solutions that favored the religious communities, although the documents do not usually say if their suggestions were adopted.

For example, in May 1952 the CRQ argued that the District of Zagreb had been mistaken in taking over several confessional cemeteries, apparently in opposition to a priest who had sought to bury an unbaptized child in a section of the cemetery reserved for that purpose. According to CRQ member Roko Rogošić, that practice was entirely in conformance with canon law and as the priest had not forbidden the burial, this was only a dispute over where in the cemetery the deceased should be buried.[25] Moreover, since there had been protests, the priests allowed them to bury the child wherever they wanted. Therefore, as the Constitution guaranteed private property and the separation of church and state, the Legislative Councils for Croatia and Serbia for the Republic of Croatia determined that the actions of the People's Council for the District of Zagreb were incorrect and that the cemeteries in Grešina, Čučerje, and Brdovac should be returned to the administration of the church.[26]

Debates and conflicts occasionally surfaced also in Serbia's Autonomous Region of Vojvodina and in Muslim majority regions from 1949 up through the late 1960s, especially when cemetery grounds included potential profit-making opportunities from harvesting hay or fruit trees.[27] The latter seemed particularly common in the Autonomous Region of Kosovo to the consternation of the region's Islamic Religious Community (IVZ). More disturbing was the fact that many People's Councils clearly intended to take over Muslim cemeteries, not to administer but to destroy them, seeking to use the land for other municipal purposes.[28]

The response of the Serbian Commission for Religious Questions in dealing with such disputes was similar to that of the Croatian CRQ. First it sought additional guidance from the state with equally disappointing results and was then also inclined to recommend that cemeteries remain in the hands of religious communities, particularly in cases where legal ownership was clear. Thus, it described certain takeovers of both Christian and Muslim cemeteries as an "incorrect interpretation" of Article 31 of the Law on People's Councils since "taking over the administration of cemeteries certainly does not also mean taking over ownership of confessional cemeteries."²⁹ In a rare case in Serbia proper, the CRQ chided the local People's Council for confiscating old headstones to use for construction purposes. "It is true that according to Law, the People's Councils are allowed to administer the cemeteries, but they should not conclude from that that they can also take over the headstones, which are private property."³⁰ Archival documents from the CRQ in the Autonomous Region of Kosovo were unavailable, but reports from the Islamic Religious Community, though far from expressing satisfaction, seemed to indicate that legally at least, the situation had been resolved in their favor. For example, one complained that even though the dispute with the People's Councils had theoretically been settled, some Vakuf councils did not defend themselves with sufficient energy, allowing the People's Councils to continue to cut hay illegally.³¹ While CRQ policies throughout the 1950s often supported the religious communities, the commission's continuing appeals to the state for guidance left no doubt that it believed a proper decision would eventually resolve the debate in favor of the state, placing cemeteries firmly in the hands of municipal bodies.³²

A discussion in Croatia from December 1952 may help illuminate the regime's reluctance to follow through on the secularization policies first initiated in 1949. The discussion in this case focused on the differences in the legal status of churches in Yugoslavia and in the Soviet Union. Addressing a conflict over who had the right to cut hay in a cemetery in the Imotski district, the CRQ noted that this was really an issue of cemetery ownership. In the USSR, it explained, all churches, cemeteries, and all properties of churches and monasteries had become people's property in 1918. In Yugoslavia, by contrast, the religious communities remained free, and the agrarian reform law had left a certain amount of the land to the church. Moreover, it explained, in Croatia there were two kinds of cemeteries: those owned by former municipalities belonging to the people but others that had been written into the books as church property and which remained as such unless expropriated or nationalized. On this basis, the Legislative Council of Croatia determined that the right to cut hay in church cemeteries belonged to church organs.³³

In an era when the Yugoslav Communist party was elaborating on the theoretical distinctions between its version of Marxism-Leninism and that promoted and enforced by Stalin's Soviet Union, party leaders likely found it convenient to highlight the differences in their policies toward religious communities. Indeed, it is possible that the regime's decision to retreat from immediate appropriation of cemeteries in the late 1940s and early 1950s related to security concerns based on the potential threat of Soviet invasion and the corresponding need to ensure domestic unity. This was not the time to start a fight with the religious communities over cemeteries.

Yugoslav authorities did not seek to resolve Ritig's concerns about the enormous divergence between cemetery laws and practices within Yugoslavia until the early 1960s when comparable (though not identical) laws on cemeteries were passed in all federal republics.[34] Otherwise, when changes took place in burial practices over the following decades they were made at the municipal level, where specific laws continued to be passed throughout the decade. Oddly, most of these laws still failed to fully settle the confusion between administration and ownership.

Croatia's law stated only that cemeteries are communal objects under the supervision of districts that make decisions about their use and administration. "They are administered by the local communities which may decide to form special bodies for that purpose, or they may entrust it to worker's organizations." Nonetheless, the law specified that district People's Councils were to take over the administration of all cemeteries within two years.[35] The state's intentions attained legal backing from a 1962 Croatian Supreme Court case, which concluded that cemeteries "cannot be the subject of legal trade among citizens, that is, among civil legal persons, and therefore cannot be the object of their ownership." Since religious communities were legal persons according to Law on the Legal Status of Religious Communities, they could not own cemeteries.[36] Similarly Serbia's Law on Burial and Cemeteries passed in April 1961 did not discuss cemetery ownership, but a related decree passed one month later clarified that "cemeteries are public objects administered by organs determined by the municipal councils of the Commune (opština) regardless of who owns the land on which they are located." If the land belonged to an individual or legal institution, it explained, they must enter into a contract with the municipality regarding its use or the land will be expropriated.[37] Similar laws were passed in municipalities throughout the republic. For example, a Cemetery Law passed in the Municipality of Ferizaj, Kosovo, in December 1961 stated more explicitly, "The land on which cemeteries will be built should be public property, and if there is no corresponding land, then the land will be provided via expropriation on the basis of a contract between the municipality and the owner of the land."[38]

Regardless of the legal explanations, the point had been made: all cemeteries in Croatia and Serbia were to come under secular and state control. That fact, along with the establishment of a legal deadline, was precisely what district and municipal People's Councils had required and/or been waiting for. The process of taking over cemetery management in Croatia required a bit more than two years but had largely been completed by mid-decade. Similarly, by the mid-1960s, debates and discussions regarding cemetery secularization had almost entirely disappeared from the minutes of the CRQ in Serbia.

In May 1966, responding to requests from the representatives of religious communities who cited multiple examples of severe neglect and the abandonment of cemeteries under the new administration of municipal authorities, Croatia's CRQ commissioned a report on cemeteries from every municipal district in the republic. From a list of 111 municipal districts, the CRQ received 64 reports from all areas of the country, though not in equal measure.[39] While the largest municipal districts with forty or more cemeteries were well represented, many reports also came from very small districts with fewer than ten cemeteries. Since the request for information was quite vaguely stated, the reports also varied wildly, ranging from one or two paragraphs to multiple pages. Still, most did include certain common elements, including who was administering and maintaining cemeteries, the status of fences, walls, and other structures and whether or not there had been complaints in their district from members of the religious communities.

Nearly all the reports confirmed that by 1966, cemeteries throughout Croatia had passed into the administration of secular authorities. In short, the Laws on Cemeteries from 1960 and 1965 had been successful.[40] After 1966, very few exceptions appeared regarding the secularization of cemeteries in Croatia. One concerned the Jewish Religious Community in Dubrovnik, which sued for and received an exemption from secularization by claiming its cemetery as a cultural-historical monument and promising to maintain it at its own expense while also cooperating fully with the Dubrovnik Funeral Enterprise. The Dubrovnik Municipal authorities and CRQ agreed to accept the situation as it served the interests of all involved.[41]

As a conflict that evolved most frequently (though not exclusively) between the Catholic religious community and the Communist regime, the establishment of secular control over cemeteries in Croatia and Serbia might be understood as a private/public clash specifically between church and state. The Church and its confessional cemeteries represented remnants of the private sphere that still owned private property used for public ends, which the state sought to abolish by making public municipal governments responsible for cemetery financing, maintenance, and administration. Yet confessional cemeteries were never "private" in the sense of ensuring the rights of individuals and families to make personal intimate decisions about life processes. Church officials and hierarchies made those decisions, as seen in their refusal to bury not only members of other religious communities and atheists but also unbaptized children, suicides, and spouses from a congregant's interfaith marriage. While many, perhaps even most, Catholics within Yugoslavia likely accepted these rules as legitimate, they were not included in the decision-making process. Once the Communist regime appropriated the cemeteries, it took over the right to make decisions about burial rights and space, again without seeking input from private citizens. Secularization, then, was less a conflict between public/private spheres than between differing institutions about control over a space utilized by private individuals.

A case that exemplified that shift in decision-making power took place in the Zagreb suburb of Granešina. On June 23, 1956, Katica Šehman, a Croatian member of the minority Seventh Day Adventist Church, died at the home of Dora Ilić in Granešina. Since Šehman had no relatives, Ilić, as a representative of the Adventist Church, arranged and paid for her burial. She called a number of neighbors and asked them to dig a grave for Šehman next to that of her own parents in the nearby Catholic cemetery. One of those she initially contacted, Ivan Šamec, told her she must first ask permission of the priest, Martin Bešanić. When she failed to do so, he contacted Bešanić himself, but by the time Bešanić and Šamec arrived at the cemetery, the grave was well underway. Beside himself with fury, Father Bešanić hurled insults at the gravediggers, who, he said, should be ashamed of themselves for digging such a grave for money. He saved his worst attacks, however, for Ilić and the deceased Šehman. Referring to himself as the "boss" of the cemetery, he insisted that as Šehman had renounced Catholicism and Christianity, she had no place in a Catholic cemetery and would *never* be buried in Granešina's. Miroševac municipal cemetery, he reminded them, had only recently been built just a mile or two away, shouting, "There is the military cemetery! So go there, as there is no place for her remains in Catholic Granešina!" Finally, though, he ordered the gravediggers to bury her body in the corner of the cemetery where a spot was reserved for nonbelievers, unbaptized or illegitimate babies, and suicides. Within six weeks, however, Ilić had successfully appealed his action to the Communist regime and Šehman's body was moved back to the regular part of the cemetery, next to Ilić's parents. By June of the following year, the regime had charged Bešanić with violating Dora Ilić's human rights and eventually sentenced him to eighteen months in prison.[42]

As Šehman's burial took place in a cemetery still owned and administered by the Catholic Church, Father Bešanić had the legal right to determine who was buried there.⁴³ Moreover, Šehman could indeed have been taken to the municipal cemetery nearby. In fact, however, several comments from participants suggest that the case against Bešanić had very little to do with Šehman and her burial rights but with Bešanić himself, whom they described as having regularly crossed the boundary of his spiritual occupation and engaged in political activities hostile to the regime. He had allegedly spread negative rumors about the government and used his sermons for political purposes. The municipal council accused him of bullying those who declined to tithe the parish and of pressuring parents to christen their children and send them to religious studies class.⁴⁴ Yet even if anti-Communist politics lay at the root of Bešanić's arrest, his uncivil treatment of another religious denomination allowed the party to take the high ground in the conflict between the state, the church, and private mourning and claim that it was supporting the rights of a private individual and religious minority to practice their faith against the repressive behavior of the Catholic Church.

New Cemeteries in Croatia and Serbia

A second critical step in the secularization process was creating new cemeteries administered by municipal authorities. Beginning in the 1950s, Croatia's urban cemeteries became seriously overcrowded due to a rise in population associated with postwar industrialization policies. Zagreb experienced a particularly rapid increase in population from 1948 to 1971 as did other urban centers in Croatia, though to a slightly lesser degree.⁴⁵ Discussions about overcrowding in Zagreb's municipal cemetery, Mirogoj, began even during the interwar period and in the course of the Second World War, though they then focused mainly on the need for more efficient use of space as Mirogoj had already expanded as much as possible.⁴⁶ The next obvious step was the creation of Zagreb's second municipal cemetery, Miroševac, which opened in 1952, and then its third, Markovo Polje, in 1969.⁴⁷ Other Croatian cities also began to open new municipal cemeteries in the postwar decades, though their ability to do so was curtailed by funding shortages. For example, shortly after taking over existing cemeteries, Osijek's Communal Enterprise, "Vrt" (Garden), recommended the creation of a new "Central" cemetery. In 1962, the General Urban Plan determined its location and by 1964 approved land for its construction. According to the cemetery report from 1966, all sixteen of the municipality's cemeteries were overcrowded and the plans for the new cemetery were ready to go, awaiting only state funding. The report also noted, however, that the Osijek Parliament for that year had not dedicated a single dinar for investment in the region's cemeteries, to say nothing of funds for the construction of a new cemetery. As it turned out, the new cemetery's construction would not begin until 1978 and was not ready for use until 1984.[48]

Cemeteries were even more congested in Belgrade, which served both as Serbia's and Yugoslavia's capital but did not receive serious attention until the early 1970s. The problem was particularly acute in Belgrade's Novo Groblje and across the Danube River in Zemun, as the amount of space in each had remained the same, while the size of the population increased fivefold. A report prepared by Belgrade's Council of Communal Affairs in 1971–2 planned in the short term to rely largely on family plots and reburials but agreed that new construction and cremation would be necessary in the future.[49]

By June 1973, a second report described the situation regarding burials in Serbia as "critical" since existing capacity had been exhausted. Belgrade had four to six times less space than required to meet the needs of its one million citizens. The high demand had led to intensive reburials that sometimes resulted in personal conflicts. It was estimated that graves in some Belgrade cemeteries contained an average of five to six bodies. The number in Novo Groblje was said to be six and yet pressure among citizens to be buried there remained very high thanks mainly to its superior infrastructure and maintenance.[50]

At that time, however, only one new cemetery was under construction—Nova Bežanija—though it was quite large and on the verge of accepting its first burials. The initial plan for Nova Bežanija, located in New Belgrade across the Danube near the site of an existing village cemetery, had been worked out as early as 1963 and a more detailed one in 1968. Due to disagreements over water sources, however, no funds were made available until 1971. By December of that year, the Communal Enterprise had purchased 19 hectares of land and hoped to acquire twenty-five more. While funding issues remained, the Communal Enterprise planned to open the cemetery by the end of 1973 with 15,000 spaces which it expected to last five years based on an estimated 3,000 burials per year.[51] Nova Bežanija opened in August 1974 and is remarkable as one of only two civilian cemeteries I have seen in any of the three republics where all citizens are buried side by side regardless of religion or ethnicity. There are no sections of any kind based on visible criteria. It is a truly an "All-Yugoslav" cemetery that represents the *gesellshafft* described by Laqueur comprising "diverse communities of the dead."[52] The only other comparable example is Lešče Cemetery, also on the outskirts of Belgrade, which opened in 1980.

Integrated cemeteries like Nova Bežanija and Lešče may have had the potential to promote the kind of multiethnic and pluralistic society the Yugoslav Communist regime hoped to achieve. Creating a public space where all citizens regardless of religious and ethnic identity could be buried side by side, they offered multiple religious communities an opportunity to interact during important life events and become familiar with each other's burial customs. At the very least, cemetery visitors would see the grave markers of other ethnoreligious groups intermingled with their own and might come to recognize the relatives who came to care for them. In that way, parcels of an integrated cemetery might have become something like integrated neighborhoods or villages where individuals of differing nations, nationalities, and religious communities nonetheless find they have something in common despite their differences (Figure 4.1).

And yet there is no particular indication that the Communist regime had such lofty ambitions for them; at least the documents on Nova Bežanija's design and construction did not mention them. Moreover, beyond those two exceptions, both the old confessional cemeteries now under municipal administration and the newly created municipal cemeteries in Serbia and Croatia continued to include ethnoreligious sections.[53] In the older, previously confessional cemeteries, the continuing segregation was perhaps inevitable since gravesites in the region most often belong to families rather than individuals. Multiple members of each family are buried in the same location, and hence both graves and sections show continuity over time even as ownership of the cemetery has changed. These sections are not marked, nor are they consistent, and certainly in larger municipal cemeteries, Orthodox graves are scattered among the Catholic ones or vice versa and are often indistinguishable from them. Others, however, particularly in Croatia's region of the former Military Frontier and Eastern Slavonia, still have separate sections for Orthodox and Catholics.[54] Those parts of Serbia within Vojvodina, as well as some regions in Eastern Serbia, which saw substantial in-migration during the nineteenth century, are particularly ethnically and religiously diverse; even the small provincial towns of Titelj (5,247) and Kostolac (13,637) have Orthodox, Catholic, Protestant, and Muslim grave markers with names indicating Serbian, Montenegrin, Macedonian, Croatian, Slovenian, Russian, Hungarian, Romanian, Vlah, Slovak, and Roma national origin. Some, like Titelj, still have vaguely separate sections for Orthodox and Catholic/Protestant graves, while in many others, the Christian markers can be difficult to distinguish; in all cases, however, any Muslim graves were placed in a separate section. Indeed, nearly all of the cemeteries in both Croatia, Vojvodina, and Eastern Serbia have distinct sections, if not entirely separate cemeteries,

Figure 4.1 Ethnoreligiously mixed cemeteries, Nova Bežanija and Lešče, Belgrade, Serbia

for Muslims and Jews. Osijek, for example, has several municipal cemeteries containing Catholic, Orthodox, and Protestant graves but then also a separate Jewish and Muslim cemetery as well as a Hungarian one. The town of Gunja (population 4,267) on the border of Bosnia & Hercegovina has one cemetery

Secularization of Cemeteries 113

Figure 4.2 Segregated Muslim and Jewish cemeteries, Gunja, Croatia and Zemun, Serbia

clearly separated into Catholic and Orthodox sections and then another entirely separate Muslim cemetery, despite the existence of a 1962 memo from the Zagreb CRQ explicitly recommending against it as the Law on Cemeteries did not allow for the creation of cemeteries on a religious basis (Figure 4.2).[55]

In Central and Southern Serbia, cemeteries are much more likely to be homogenous and/or entirely segregated. This is true even (or perhaps especially) in ethnically mixed communities, which most often included Muslims and Roma. According to Professor Šefedin Šehović, of the Teachers School at the University of Novi Pazar, cemeteries in that region were strictly segregated and Muslim cemeteries were entirely managed by the religious communities throughout the Socialist period.[56] Cemeteries in Kosovo/Kosova are also strictly segregated but look very different from those elsewhere in Serbia or Yugoslavia. First, many people in that region are buried outside of formally established cemeteries, whether religious or municipal, presumably on family-owned ground. Many of these burial sites are easily visible from the road and may include as few as a handful or as many as two dozen gravesites. Other cemeteries remain connected to religious sites such as churches or mosques and some at least were administered by the religious communities throughout the Communist period as in Novi Pazar. Nonetheless, most cemeteries in Kosovo/Kosova are municipal but are then segregated into separate Muslim and Christian cemeteries or sections. The Christian cemeteries are further segregated into Orthodox and Catholic sections, sometimes also including a Jewish section. Moreover, as we will discuss further in Chapter 6 on grave markers, the municipal Muslim cemeteries in Kosovo/Kosova are among the most secular in the region. The community they represent is thus national rather than religious.

In short, with the remarkable exceptions of Nova Bežanija and Lešče cemeteries in the suburbs of Belgrade, both old and new cemeteries in Serbia and Croatia largely remained ethnoreligiously segregated, though the extent and visibility of segregation is certainly much lower among the Christian denominations. The establishment of separate cemeteries and separate sections in these municipal cemeteries undoubtedly reflected the wishes of private individuals and religious communities that see cemeteries as an extension of their community and congregation. Like Catholics, the Muslim and Jewish communities have strict rules forbidding religious integration in cemeteries. Again, however, these decisions were made by religious hierarchies and institutions likely with the consent but not the direct participation of private individuals. The Communist regime, while willing to transfer cemeteries from religious to public administration in Serbia and Croatia, declined to interfere with these rules. In this way, it revealed the extent to which it remained unable or unwilling to disrupt the extant ethnoreligious communities for purposes of social integration and enforce any transition from *gemeinshafft* to *gesellshafft*.

Cemetery Secularization in Bosnia & Hercegovina

The secularization of old and the creation of new cemeteries in Bosnia & Hercegovina differed considerably from what had occurred in either Serbia or Croatia due to the region's ethnoreligious diversity, rural nature, and the more harmonious relations between the local regime and religious communities. While each religious community in Bosnia & Hercegovina has its own burial culture, each has also been influenced by the other ethnoreligious communities, by the Ottoman conquest, and by the legal culture of the Austro-Hungarian Empire that ruled it for forty years. In Catholic Croat regions or among their populations, most cemeteries in 1945 were confessional and under the legal ownership of the Catholic Church as in Croatia. Similarly, in Serbian regions and among Serb populations, cemeteries would be strictly Orthodox but likely owned by local communities. The burial culture of the Bosnian Muslims is based on Ottoman Islam, and cemeteries were the legal property of the Islamic religious community. Because Islam lacks a "cult of death" and does not encourage prayers to deceased relatives or saints, many of the older cemeteries had been more or less abandoned by 1945.

The Communist regime's policies in establishing secular control over cemeteries in postwar Bosnia & Hercegovina were very different from those in Croatia and Serbia. The question of who should administer the cemeteries was barely mentioned in any documents of the Bosnian Commission for Religious Questions until 1963, three years after the first Law on Cemeteries was passed. No further discussion on the matter took place for another twelve years, though afterward, the discussions continued nearly up to the end of Yugoslavia's existence. The differing approach in this case may derive from the more amicable relationship between the Communist regime and the Islamic religious community.[57] The issue seemed to have been settled at a meeting between the Federal CRQ and Reis-ul-Ulema and the Secretary of Islamic Elders in April 1953 at which Džemal Bijedić, then a member of the CRQ and later president of the Republic of Bosnia & Hercegovina and prime minister of the Socialist Federal Republic of Yugoslavia, agreed that Muslim graves should remain the property of those "to whom they are currently recorded in the legal cadastres."[58]

While initially content to leave functioning cemeteries in the hands of religious communities, the Communist regime put considerable effort into taking over older "abandoned" cemeteries for urban development. Most documents dealing with cemeteries, therefore, focused on the legal expropriation of cemeteries and their reuse for more modern purposes such as sports stadiums, Houses of Culture, student dormitories, parking lots, and so on. Most of the expropriation cases mentioned in CRQ documents during the early 1950s referred to Muslim cemeteries, and most stated that the Vakufska Direkcija (Director of the Foundation which held the deed of ownership) had agreed to the expropriation and reuse.[59] Even so, open conflicts arose in cases where, for example, construction had begun without any attempt at exhuming the existing remains; the local government had failed to secure the agreement of the Vakuf; or it had neglected to provide the Islamic community with compensation in the form of an alternative burial site. In most such cases, the CRQ apparently worked to mediate the conflict and seek a resolution, but ultimately the land remained with the state.[60]

Documents from the Roman Catholic Church in Zenica, however, tell a less harmonious story. Its own documentation, along with a Register of Deeds provided to the Church from the Zenica District in 1991, records the expropriation and nationalization of multiple religious properties, including many cemeteries, from all three religious communities for a ten-year period from 1949 to 1959. Based on those documents, one Orthodox cemetery of 2,206 square meters, three Catholic cemeteries totaling 5,448 square meters, seven Muslim cemeteries totaling 8,936 square meters, and four additional cemeteries of indeterminate denomination totaling 175 square meters were expropriated. Of the 16,590 square meters of cemetery land expropriated, 53.8 percent was from the Muslim religious community, 32.8 percent from the Catholic Church, and 13.2 percent from the Orthodox Church. Given Zenica's postwar demographics of approximately 58 percent Muslim and 21 percent each of Serb and Croat citizens, it appears that the Catholic Church was singled out for harassment, while the Orthodox Church was treated with unusual leniency, but that may only reflect the unusually large size of one expropriated Catholic cemetery (5,350 hectares) from the Franciscan monastery. Although the registry briefly describes the property, its previous and future owners, and date of transfer, it does not tell us whether the transfer included any exchange of property and/or how it was accepted by the religious community involved.[61] Previous documents from Croatia, Serbia, and AP Kosovo, however, suggest that all three religious communities deeply resented the appropriation of cemeteries. Additional evidence that the state often violated its own laws regarding the expropriation of cemeteries comes from Aleksandar Ranković who strongly advised against such practices in his 1959 memo designed to improve state relations with the religious communities.[62] One case where an older cemetery with separate Catholic and

Figure 4.3 Stup Cemetery under the M17-M18 highway interchange Sarajevo, Bosnia & Hercegovina

Orthodox sections was not expropriated for "public use" but severely encroached upon is Stup Cemetery currently hidden beneath the cloverleaf exchange of the M17 and M18 freeways just south of downtown Sarajevo. The intersection above it was built in 1978 and is, according to Wikipedia, "one of the most frequent interchanges in the Balkans with over 60,000 vehicles each day" (Figure 4.3).[63]

The first Law on Cemeteries was passed in Bosnia & Hercegovina in March 1960. Although Article 2 of the law described cemeteries as communal objects that were administered by the municipal People's Councils, Article 20 recognized the region's largely rural character, explaining that while cemeteries in urban regions would be managed by municipal People's Councils, those in nonurban regions would be managed by the local councils or, if there were none, "by the institutions of the previous system" (*"organ iz prethodnog stava"*).[64] Given this caveat, it is no wonder that little action took place in the first years after the law's passage. One substantive CRQ discussion about cemetery administration occurred in January 1965 when a member from northeastern Bosnia, near the town of Bijelina, pointed to a number of problems regarding cemeteries. Not only were many old Muslim cemeteries in the region entirely neglected, serving as playgrounds for children, but there had been several recent cases of discrimination: Catholic priests refused to bury Old Catholics (a denomination formed in interwar Yugoslavia), Muslims refused to bury members of the Roma community, and various churches harassed families who wished to bury their Communist relatives in religious cemeteries. The discussion concluded that the regime must work with religious communities to resolve these difficulties but over the longer term must build new common cemeteries with sections and parcels for each religion.[65]

The issue did not reappear, however, until a decade later in spring 1975 when two substantial reports addressed secularization as a serious and outstanding issue. Both noted that the Law of 1960 had not been applied in much of the republic, especially in suburbs and rural regions. Whereas cemeteries had long since been taken over in other republics, many in Bosnia & Hercegovina remained in the hands of religious communities or, worse yet, were taken over by municipalities and then later given back. Now those religious communities were even seeking permission from the Ministry of Internal Affairs to build new cemeteries. Further, cemeteries' unresolved status had resulted in conflicts and problems for Bosnia's citizens who are "treated differently in situations, just when their lives are most difficult anyway." The reports referred to problems dealing with mixed marriages and the burial of atheists/communists, financial pressures from religious communities, and conflicts relating to burial placement—that is burying "undesirables" at the edges of the cemetery along with suicides, criminals, and unbaptized babies. They also noted increased nationalist and political agitation within cemeteries, claiming that some clergy had begun holding nationalist and/or anti-Communist lectures within cemeteries.[66] These latter comments likely reflected the impact of the Croatian Spring on Catholic areas of Bosnia & Hercegovina.

Six months later, Muhamed Bešić, a member of the Bosnian CRQ and later secretary of the Socialist Alliance of Bosnia & Hercegovina, suggested that although the delay in taking over cemeteries in Bosnia & Hercegovina often appeared to be a legal property issue relating to expenses of maintenance, it must occur regardless of cost. "It must be made possible for relatives of different religions and beliefs to be buried in the same cemetery. This is a political question which limits freedom: people will begin to be afraid of mixed marriages." Drago Barić agreed but suggested that they first survey all district CRQs to find out which cemeteries had been taken over and if not, why not, how many and which confessions had cemeteries, and who cared for them, and in the meantime that they extend the time for taking them over by one year.[67]

The extension clearly continued longer than one year. The survey was finally sent out only in 1984, in an environment of growing ethnic tension, which saw the arrests for nationalism of Alija Izetbegović and Vojislav Šešelj. When completed, the survey included broad questions on relations with the religious communities but confirmed ongoing problems with cemeteries and a general indifference to their resolution. Several questions queried the kinds of issues that arose between the state and religious communities and while those relating to cemeteries never topped the list, they were always present somewhere in the middle.[68] Nonetheless, fewer than 15 percent of the CRQs surveyed had included any analysis of the problem of funerals and cemeteries in their yearly program.

By 1985, the Social Political Council and Presidency of the Parliament of Bosnia & Hercegovina insisted that problems related to cemeteries were widespread and excuses could no longer be tolerated. Claiming that some 6,000 cemeteries throughout the republic still remained in the hands of religious communities, the presidency demanded urgent implementation of the Law on Funeral Activity and the Maintenance and Administration of Cemeteries; further delays were simply another example of the general irresponsibility and inconsistencies affecting the broader society. The report especially criticized those communities that had decided to leave cemeteries in the hands of the religious communities to avoid the costs of maintenance. As a result of similar neglect, other cemeteries had come to "offer a truly sad picture of a 'no man's land,'" inspiring demands for their return by religious communities. Some municipalities had even given in, allowing the religious communities to build chapels and mortuaries in the cemeteries, contrary to the law.[69]

This report from on high finally apparently had the desired effect, and beginning in the mid-1980s municipal councils even in rural regions of Bosnia finally sought to take control over cemeteries, though by now it was mostly too late. Although an October 1989 report still decried the appallingly slow rate at which cemeteries were being taken over and administered by municipal secular authorities, progress had been made. While the 1985 report had stated that 6,000 cemeteries remained in the hands of religious communities, by 1989, the CRQ claimed that of 7,217 cemeteries in the republic, religious communities still owned 3,210, though they administered only 2,635 of them. In other words, forty-five years after taking power, and only two years before it would lose it again, municipal councils of the Communist regime had established administration over only 63.5 percent of cemeteries. While that marked clear improvement since 1975, the council was far from satisfied and expressed a reasonable concern that in many cases, the progress made was likely more formal than real.[70]

Friar Zdravka Andjić from the Parish Church of St. Ilija in Zenica confirmed much of this documentary evidence from the last decades of Yugoslavia as well as the party's explanation for its reasons. According to his description, before the 1980s, ownership and management of cemeteries in the region varied—while in the cities it was the municipal council, in the villages they were controlled by the religious communities (in his case the Catholic parish, monastery, or bishopric). But during the reform of the 1980s, the cemeteries in some villages were turned over to the municipal council and it was written up in the registry of deeds of the church. Perhaps what happened, he said, was that the church had begun repairing and expanding the chapels in the cemeteries and using them more as churches and for other purposes such as for religious education. They had done this early on too and sometimes got arrested or fined for it. They now also tried to build chapels in cemeteries that didn't have them. He also agreed that Catholic cemeteries had not wished to bury non-Catholics, saying they could be buried only outside the fence. To gain permission for burial in a Catholic cemetery, families had to provide proof that the deceased had been christened as a Catholic. As a result, any atheists or mixed marriages would have a hard time of it, but from his perspective there were few such people and, perhaps unsurprisingly, he was not very sympathetic to them. Speaking to me in 2013, Friar Andjić retained a view of cemeteries as an integral part of the ethnoreligious community. Each should have and maintain its own cemetery, separate and distinct from one another. In post-Communist Bosnia & Hercegovina, that reality had never disappeared and any boundaries that had blurred in the previous decades were quickly being reestablished.[71]

The documentary record of painfully slow progress toward removing religious control over cemeteries in Bosnia & Hercegovina is confirmed by the structure of new cemeteries created in the region. While it was unquestionably difficult to confront the republic's multiple religious communities on their own turf, the Communist regime was no more successful in dealing with them when creating its own cemeteries.

New Cemeteries in Bosnia & Hercegovina

In 1945, the Sarajevo region included 114 cemeteries—103 Muslim, 4 Orthodox, 4 Catholic, 1 Jewish, and 2 military, but by the early 1960s most had reached capacity. The Communist regime initially considered the construction of a common municipal cemetery not only a practical necessity but also an important step toward secularization and the blurring of ethnoreligious boundaries. In early discussions, one urban planner suggested that plots within the new cemetery be allocated irrespective of religious denomination, stating, "Since we live together in one city, surely we can be buried together." That plan, however, encountered such fierce resistance from some religious communities that it was quickly scrapped, and the City Council agreed that the new cemetery would have separate sections for each confession.[72]

Indeed, the CRQ was careful to consult all of Sarajevo's major religious communities regarding their opinions about and special requirements for what was then called Central Cemetery and is now known as Bare Cemetery, before passing any laws regarding cemeteries and burials.[73] By June 1964, when the cemetery was nearing completion, CRQ reports revealed that they had received plenty of feedback, though not all positive. According to Drago Rubić, the Jewish community was showing particular resistance as some older members had informed him that "if they could not be buried in the old Jewish cemetery, they would emigrate from Sarajevo because that was all that was connecting them to the city."[74] According to Dr. Eli Tauber, the problem was resolved by means of a compromise according to which Sarajevo's Jews agreed to be buried in new cemeteries and in return the state agreed to maintain the old Jewish cemeteries.[75] When the new Central Cemetery opened in January 1966 it indeed provided specially marked sections for Orthodox (P), Catholics (K), Muslims (M), Jews (J), Evangelists (E), Adventists (D), Old Catholics (S), and Atheists (A). Other municipal cemeteries in Bosnia & Hercegovina adopted a similar system. Although most others did not use lettered markers, they provided clearly designated sections for each of the main ethnoreligious groups, including atheists. Those from mixed marriages were usually buried in the Atheist section (Figure 4.4).

By 1983, the city of Sarajevo had begun plans for construction of Vlakovo municipal cemetery on the western edge of the city. Based on the urban development plan from 1986 to 2015, it was to be a "park cemetery" with an area of 77 hectares and a crematorium. Based on existing and future demographic projections, 40 percent of the included gravesites would be Muslim, 20 percent Orthodox, 18 percent Catholic, and 22 percent Atheist and other. Burials began at Vlakovo in September 1985 and from 1985 to 1989 a total of 3,139 individuals were buried there, accounting for 29 percent of those who died in the city during those four years. Vlakovo continued the tradition of burials according to religious confession, here too in explicitly marked sections.[76]

In Bosnia & Hercegovina, the Communist regime made the least effort of all to realize the transition from confessional churchyard to municipal cemetery.

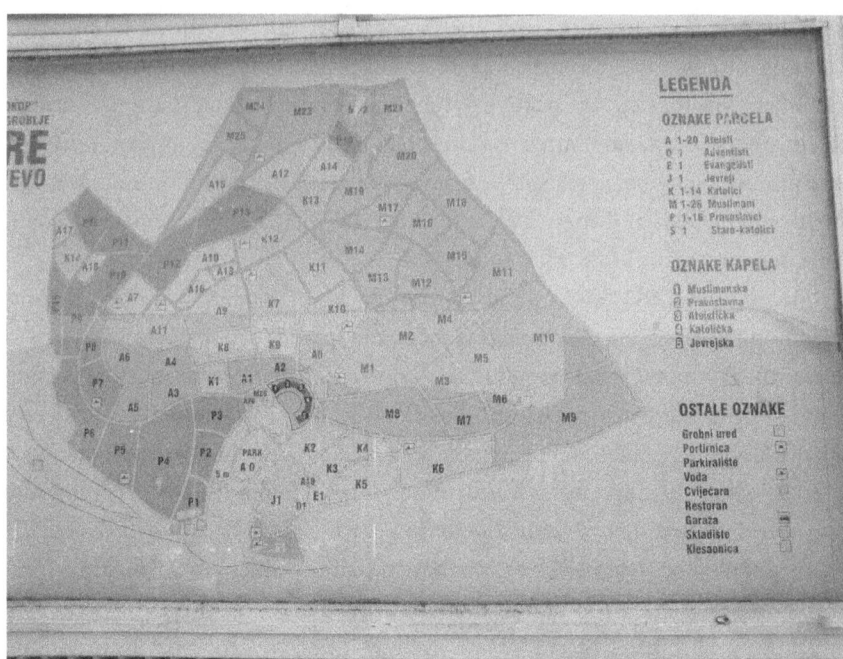

Figure 4.4 Marked cemetery sections
Bare Cemetery, Sarajevo, Bosnia & Hercegovina

There, in the most religiously diverse and rural of the three republics, the regime took the most cautious approach toward change but by the mid-1970s and 1980s found that there was a price to be paid for inaction and that inattention did not translate to tolerance. Careful not to disable the old communities, the regime also failed to produce its own, and that failure compromised the viability of the secular and pluralist society it had hoped to create.

Conclusion

By the late 1980s, as the Communist system was declining throughout Europe and as Yugoslavia itself was beginning to disintegrate, most cemeteries in Croatia and Serbia and perhaps even a slight majority in Bosnia were under the administration of secular authorities. Nonetheless, they remained largely segregated by religion and ethnicity. In many cases, ethnoreligious communities were buried in entirely separate cemeteries, but where they shared the same cemetery, they were often segregated into separate sections. Significantly, separate and segregated cemeteries were predominant in the most ethnoreligiously mixed and volatile regions such as the old Military Frontier and Eastern Slavonia in Croatia, Novi Pazar and Kosovo in Serbia, and throughout Bosnia & Hercegovina.

Differences in the way the Communist regime approached the process of secularization in the three republics reflected the highly localized nature of laws and policies relating to death and burial practices as well as differing sociopolitical conditions and burial cultures in each. The process was most fraught with conflict in Croatia due in part to the contentious relationship between the Catholic Church and the state but mainly because of Croatia's more complex legal infrastructure guaranteeing church property rights. The matter was fully resolved in that republic, although not until the mid-1960s, a full two decades after the takeover of power. The process was least complex and most easily resolved in Serbia proper since its cemeteries were most commonly already in municipal hands, while in Bosnia & Hercegovina, the regime initially ignored the question, due to friendly relations between the state and the Islamic Religious Community along with the region's extreme urban–rural divide and religious diversity, which complicated the legal status of cemeteries and threatened to incite ethnoreligious tensions.

Similarly, each republic approached the creation of new cemeteries from a slightly different perspective. But for each, the primary goal was to resolve problems of overcrowding rather than create a secular and pluralistic community of the dead, appropriate to a proclaimed new era with new values. Certainly, there were no published speeches or theoretical discussions relating to its higher function. In Bosnia & Hercegovina, initial idealistic hopes by an anonymous urban planner for a more egalitarian cemetery were dashed early on and highly visible ethnoreligious markers were provided instead. Even in Belgrade, where such cemeteries were created at Nova Bežanija and Lešče, the outcome seemed more the result of accident than deliberate planning.

One likely disincentive to changing the ethnoreligious structure of cemeteries were the decentralizing reforms of the 1960s and 1970s, which strengthened the position of each republic/nation at the expense of Yugoslavia as a whole. Although integral Yugoslavism had been entirely discredited during the interwar period, the Communist party had cautiously revived a federalized version of Yugoslavism under the slogan "brotherhood and unity" during the Second World War. Once the decentralizing reforms of the 1960s–70s took off, even that level of attachment to the concept of an overarching Yugoslav identity came under suspicion, particularly in Slovenia and Croatia. In the years after Tito's death in 1980, increasing forms of ethnoreligious nationalism spread throughout the country. Only then, did the Communist regime in Bosnia & Hercegovina seem to recognize that the refusal of confessional cemeteries to bury atheists, families with mixed marriages, and members of religious minorities exposed a serious threat to the pluralist identity, not only of Yugoslavia but also their own republic.

The regime's failure to integrate Yugoslavia's civilian cemeteries was due to a lack of trying. It represented a failure of vision and an inability to grasp the role of cemeteries as cultural communities. Even where the state successfully secularized cemeteries, it did so to undermine religion, not to promote its own agenda in the cemeteries. There were no substantive discussions about how cemeteries could cease to represent only ethnoreligious communities and become common spaces where members of a pluralistic multiethnic and multireligious society might gather to commemorate the dead. In the absence of such theoretical discussions and plans and facing strong ethnoreligious burial traditions, cemetery administrators left the old structures and divisions in place, which remained visible to all. Visitors to a cemetery could always tell which graves belonged to whom and what that meant about their history, values, beliefs, friends, and enemies. The cultural significance of cemeteries could not be denied but the connections they created only sparked painful memories of the country's turbulent past.

5

Burial Rituals

Rituals associated with death and burial are an intrinsic part of human existence stretching back even into the time of the Neanderthals, but their purpose and meaning has changed over time. Originally intended to prevent the dead from returning to harm the living, they then became associated with religious beliefs and helping secure safe passage for the deceased individual's soul to the afterlife.[1] In the modern era, funerals and memorial practices have more often been described as rituals that help families commence the process of working through grief and confronting loss.[2] They allow the bereaved to make connections to the deceased and initiate a process of healing. More broadly, burial rites (like other life-cycle rituals) connect friends and family of the deceased to one another and the wider community, whether religious or secular. They foster a sense of belonging and create identity among what Katherine Verdery refers to as an "audience of mourners," further clarifying "who is in and who is out."[3] Burial rituals originate in the private sphere of the family but expand outward to those groups that lie in between the private and public spheres: friends, neighbors, religious organizations, and perhaps also ethnic groups. They often take place, however, in public settings and may intersect with the public sphere on other occasions, depending on the identity of the deceased.

This chapter investigates the response of the Communist regime to the multiple burial rituals and memorial practices among the religious communities in Croatia, Serbia, and Bosnia & Hercegovina. While regime responses to them were framed by federal laws and ideological premises, once again the specific policies differed based on each region's burial cultures and relations with the religious communities. As ceremonies and practices that had the potential to foster a new sense of belonging and identity, burial rituals in the new Socialist state should have been intensely important to its goal of creating a new secular and pluralist community. As we will see, however, the Communist regime in Yugoslavia did relatively little either to counter existing or create new burial rituals. During the first fifteen years after the war, the state sometimes interfered in private burial rituals, especially those associated with the Catholic Church and usually when the deceased had a political connection to the regime. Over the next thirty years, however, the state made only two serious attempts to create new rituals: one—the promotion of cremation—was motivated almost entirely by practical considerations, while the other was strictly for veterans. Neither was sufficient to help create a new community of the dead for all citizens of the state.

Benign Neglect

In an effort to promote unity during and just after the Second World War, the Communist party had sanctioned official Partisan participation in religious holidays and celebrations, allowing them to provide Yule logs for Christmas, stand guard before "Jesus' tomb" on Good Friday, and approving the celebration of St. Sava Day in Serbian schools in 1945. Perhaps the most extreme example of Communist participation in a religious ritual related specifically to burial culture came in November 1944, when the Orthodox Church held a requiem liturgy for all Russian and domestic heroes who had fallen in the liberation of Belgrade. At the end of the mass, various high representatives of the regime, including longtime communists and atheists Moša Pijade, Arso Jovanović, and Peko Dapčević, shared in the final sacrament, kissing the cross and accepting the wafer from the priest.[4]

Nonetheless, despite the freedom of worship guaranteed by the 1946 Constitution, the new regime simultaneously banned state commemoration of all religious holidays and established the exclusive right to provide and maintain birth, marriage, or death records in the official registries.[5] Already in January 1945, the Municipal Funeral Office (Gradski pogrebni zavod) had been formed in the capital city of Belgrade under supervision of the People's Council of Belgrade. Its purpose was to carry out burials of deceased citizens in Belgrade at a moderate price, to provide and sell to citizens all supplies and equipment necessary for funerals, to provide transportation from the hospital to the mortuary and from there to the place of burial, and to carry out all other services in connection with the burial. Similar enterprises would eventually be formed in municipalities throughout Yugoslavia, though with some delay. For example, a comparable institution—"Municipal Cemeteries" (Gradska Groblja)—was formed in Zagreb only in 1953.[6]

At the same time, most funeral societies commonly, though not exclusively, formed on ethnoreligious bases during the interwar period to help individuals save and prepare for funerals were disbanded. For example, a secular funeral society formed in Zagreb as early as 1835 to serve members of the city's guilds and crafts was liquidated in 1948, all its equipment and assets then becoming "the general people's property."[7] There were two major exceptions to this rule. The first were the funeral societies of the Jewish community, or Hevra Kadisha, which were permitted to exist in all three republics throughout the Socialist era. Initially banned in Croatia in 1946 as a "funeral enterprise," the organization appealed to the CRQ, which agreed that it was a religious institution and therefore must be allowed to exist. Moreover, the properties it administered included cemeteries, which were exempt from the Law on Agrarian Reform.[8]

The second exception involved funeral societies in Bosnia & Hercegovina, which were widespread among nearly all religious communities. In 1923, seven Sarajevan Muslims formed the Funeral Society "Jediler" to prevent brokers from becoming involved in and profiting from the misfortune of others.[9] Catholic and Orthodox funeral societies with similar missions also developed not only in Sarajevo but throughout the region, including Zenica, Mostar, Tuzla, Banja Luka, Travnik, and Doboj. They collected yearly membership fees in return for which they secured free funeral services for their members and transportation for clergy and immediate family members from the home to the cemetery.[10]

Whether due to Bosnia & Hercegovina's diverse religious character involving multiple funeral rituals or out of financial need, the Communist regime tolerated the continued existence of these ethnoreligious funeral societies, though under new and highly restricted conditions. They were registered as religiously based nonprofit "citizens' associations," nearly all of their previously owned property was nationalized and in some cases their names were also changed. For example, the Catholic Funeral Association in Sarajevo founded in 1921 as "The Brotherhood of St. Ante Padovan" was renamed immediately followed the war as "The Croatian Funeral Society."[11] By the mid-1970s, likely in response to the events of the Croatian Spring, when the Bosnian regime first began to take seriously the secularization of cemetery culture, it also addressed the question of these ethnoreligiously based funeral societies. At the 1975 meeting held to discuss revisions to the Law on Cemeteries, Muhamed Bešić suggested that in the future, funeral societies must be state rather than church institutions and must not be allowed to serve as extensions of the hand of the church. Thus, it was important to avoid giving them names like "The Serbian Orthodox Funeral Society."[12] Consequently in 1978, "The Croatian Funeral Society" was forced to change its name again, this time to the neutral "Palma." In 1991, it returned to its second name, "The Croatian Funeral Society." The Muslim Funeral Association,

"Jediler," which means "seven" in honor of its seven religiously motivated founders, was renamed "Bakije," a name it has retained to this day. Both Catholic and Islamic Funeral Associations also continued to exist in the provincial town of Zenica throughout the postwar period. Although these organizations described constant struggles with the state to secure adequate space and the necessary equipment to continue their activities after the state had nationalized nearly all of their previous equipment and property, it is remarkable that they were able to exist at all.[13]

Even as municipal bodies established control over most institutions involved in the burial process, private citizens practiced their traditional burial rituals largely without interference from and sometimes even with the assistance of state organizations. These "private" rituals were not limited to the immediate family but engaged and often required the active participation of local communities, including extended family, neighbors, and ethnoreligious groups. The public sphere was involved usually only to the extent that the actual burial relied on municipal funeral services and took place in a municipal cemetery.

Although clearly in conformance with Christian religious rites, many Catholic and Orthodox inhabitants of the Balkans also have a rich and highly developed set of local burial rituals, hearkening back to a pre-Christian heritage, that share many characteristics but also vary from region to region.[14] These rituals retained their intensity for those who have lived in their native villages for centuries or longer but even for those who recently migrated. For example, Edit Petrović claims that even the atheist Partisan Montenegrins who colonized Vojvodinian villages after the Second World War brought their burial traditions with them as a way of maintaining their ethnic identity and continued them in some cases up to 1980s and perhaps beyond. While dispensing with such religious components as priests and candles, their funerals included many of the traditional elements such as keeping the deceased at home for three days before the funeral for visitation by family, friends, and neighbors, ritualized kissing of the deceased by visitors, covering all mirrors and TV screens in the house, opening all windows and doors, placing a basin of cold water under the deceased, and ensuring that cats stay out of the house. After three days, the burial ceremony took place at the cemetery, followed by a meal either on-site or at the family home. In this way, the atheist colonists distinguished themselves from believers but retained their ethnic identity.[15]

Some Serbs and other Balkan Orthodox also engage in a practice known as secondary burial or a "meeting with the dead," which involves the exhumation and reburial of the deceased anywhere from forty days to seven years after the initial interment. Apparently, this tradition stretches back into antiquity but has been outlawed by secular governments since the nineteenth century and usually also by religious authorities. Because it has long been considered illegal, the practice generally takes place in secret and at night. Scholars assume, therefore, that while rare, it likely occurs more often than is reported.[16] According to Milka Jovanović, the two most common reasons for secondary burials in Serbia were an attempt to free the soul of the deceased from "vampirization" and a desperate wish on the part of the family to see their loved one again. However, some Serbs (though this was more common in Macedonia and Greece) also practiced secondary burial after approximately five years as an integral part of the burial rites. In this case, the priests participated, though various pre-Christian beliefs and rituals were also present. Family, friends, and neighbors attended the exhumation to witness the state of decomposition, which was thought to reflect on the virtue of the deceased. Full decomposition within the proscribed time indicated an absence of sin, whereas remaining areas of rotting flesh suggested that the earth had refused to accept the body as unworthy.[17]

In Muslim funerals of Bosnia & Hercegovina, though women were banned from attending funerals, they often participated in *tehvids* where prayers were read for the deceased. The *tehvids* were usually held in the home of the deceased, the first one on the day of the funeral, then on the seventh, fortieth days (when the soul is said to leave the body), at six months, and one year. The first *tehvid* was for family only, but after that Muslim women from throughout the community were also invited to attend, coffee and food was served, and the event provided an opportunity for socializing. According to Tone Bringa, "The *tehvid* is the most frequently held ritual in the region and … the most frequent legitimate occasion for women (or wives) to socialize outside the immediate neighborhood and village."[18]

As a rule, the Communist state sought to avoid interfering with these traditional burial rituals, seeing them as highly personal and relating to ethnoreligious identity. According to Aleksandra Pavićević, while the Communist regime worried about the ideological effect of organized religion, it did not consider pagan practices harmful and was even concerned to document and preserve them as "folklore."[19] Thus, while some traditional rites were legally banned as inconsistent with modern hygienic practices, efforts at enforcement were unreliable at best. For example, every law on cemeteries in Serbia included an injunction against leaving food items at the gravesite and every cemetery I visited posted rules that included one banning this practice. Yet that rule was and is almost never enforced. Indeed, in 1960, the Serbian CRQ recommended removing the article banning meals at cemeteries from the Law on the Status of Religious Communities, arguing that such meals were too deeply rooted in tradition to eradicate and it would be better to let the local governments deal with such issues than regulate them at a federal or republic level.[20] Similarly, although placing items inside the grave with the deceased is banned by law, that also clearly occurred. A Serbian ethnologist related one story of a village funeral where the crowing of a rooster could be heard to come from under the grave for three days.[21]

Muslim burial traditions also faced occasional legal barriers with varying expectations of enforcement. All laws passed after the Second World War specified that deceased persons must be buried in a sealed coffin. According to Muslim tradition, however, the deceased are wrapped only in cloth and placed on a board (*tabut*), not in a coffin. While this law was apparently enforced with regard to Muslims in Belgrade and likely in other large northern and central cities, it was not enforced in the majority Muslim region of the Sandžak of Novi Pazar or at all in Bosnia & Hercegovina.[22]

Moreover, there is evidence of some cooperation between the state and the Muslim community in Serbia. During a time of shortages just after the war, the Serbian CRQ was careful to ensure that the Belgrade Muslim community had access to the appropriate oils needed to perform its normal burial rituals.[23] Then in the early 1960s, Islamic Imams collaborated in a campaign to eliminate blood feuds by refusing to provide burial services for those killed in such feuds leading to a decline from thirty-seven killed three years previously to only five or six in the last months of 1963.[24]

The regime also worked closely with religious communities in Sarajevo before opening Bare Cemetery in 1966. Within the parameters of what they considered to be a modern hygienic system, members of the Sarajevan CRQ were anxious to offer respect and consideration for the burial rituals of each religious community and actively sought their cooperation in reaching appropriate compromises.[25] Most of those I interviewed in Bosnia & Hercegovina, regardless of their political views, confirmed that the regime never interfered with specific burial rituals. Even so, several documents note official efforts to encourage the use of mortuaries in place of in-home funerals and especially to eliminate the Muslim practice of funeral processions. Carrying the deceased to the cemetery and the slow funeral procession on foot had traditionally been an important part of the Muslim funeral service, yet the Communist regime considered it backward and increasingly problematic in a major city with increasing traffic.[26] Nonetheless, Sarajevo's municipal authorities gained at least the tacit cooperation of the

Sarajevo Funeral Society, Bakije, in this and other efforts to modernize Muslim burial practices. In a 1961 memo, Bakije noted that in accordance with its important and difficult task of burying Muslims in a cultured and contemporary manner, it had already constructed a modern and hygienic bathing room for the deceased so that the washing and preparation of the body would no longer take place in private homes or unclean circumstances. Further, and "in order to eliminate from the city the ugly sight of carrying the dead on people's shoulders through narrow and busy streets," the society had purchased an automobile for the transport of the deceased and had made much progress in introducing this custom. Its initial purchases, however, had been used and in need of considerable repairs. At this point, the society continued, if we want to completely eliminate previous practices and particularly in preparation for the opening of the new common cemetery, the society clearly needs a more appropriate and specially prepared vehicle. In the following years, it requested and received the necessary funding and aid from the city.[27] Despite this broad sense of harmony or perhaps simply benign neglect surrounding burial rituals, some conflicts did develop, particularly in the early years following the Second World War from approximately 1945 to 1960.

Conflicts

The first type of dispute over burial rituals developed mainly, if not exclusively, in dealings with the Catholic Church in Croatia with which the Communist regime had a deeply hostile relationship. On a day-to-day basis many Catholic priests in Croatia found themselves under constant suspicion and were inhibited even in their efforts to carry out such crucial services as providing last rites for the dying and funeral masses.

In the years from 1946 to 1960 both the CRQ and the Ministry of Health in Croatia fielded multiple complaints from the Catholic Archbishopric that dying patients in hospitals seeking final sacraments throughout Croatia had either been denied access to a priest by nurses or simply had no way of asking for one when close to death. In some cases, a vigilant relative had come to the rescue and managed to secure a priest at the last moment, but other patients had died unshriven. Such behavior undeniably represented a violation of the state's guaranteed freedom of worship and in every case, the Ministry of Health and CRQ assured the Archbishop that the law must provide reasonable access to a priest and any failure to do represented errors by individuals. In most cases, they then urged the priests and hospital administrators to work together to find a solution.[28]

Perhaps the strongest case for patient's rights was made in early 1952, when the Bishop of Split requested greater access for priests to hospitals, arguing that the mere right to call a priest for last rites was entirely inadequate. By that time, he argued, it was often too late: the ill person might not always have someone nearby to call the priest for them, and clearly hospital personnel were not always willing to help. Moreover, a priest should be available to offer comfort to any ill patient, not just the dying. Nonetheless, the Director of Health Services declined to provide the requested regular access on the argument that establishing specific hours during which priests of all religions would be able to make the rounds of patients would disturb the order and the peace of patients. The Croatian CRQ, however, supported the Bishop, pointing out that the constitutional right of every citizen to the free practice of religion belonged also to those in the hospital who were most in need and whose rights must not depend on whether a relative was nearby to provide assistance.[29]

The Law on the Status of Religious Communities passed approximately one year after this case provided a rather poor compromise. Article 16 stated that persons in hospitals and nursing homes may be visited by priests and fulfill their religious rituals within the limits of the rules of the hospital/home.[30] It did not, therefore, limit the priests' visits only to those in need of final sacraments, but it also gave the hospital or nursing home administrator the last word on how and when they might visit. Perhaps unsurprisingly, therefore, complaints continued into the late 1950s and even 1960s suggesting an atmosphere of continued hostility toward religion, at least in Croatia.[31] The absence of complaints about such issues in Serbia and Bosnia & Hercegovina does not indicate that similar cases did not occur there, only that they may have been less common.

The abuse of private death rituals by the state in this case was so egregious and unnecessary that it nearly defies explanation, but it may also lie in the public/private dichotomy. Once all medical and health care facilities had been nationalized in 1948, hospital and nursing home administrators may have perceived themselves as guardians of a strictly secular and hygienic public space—a role they believed empowered them to protect patients from the well-meaning ignorance of family and friends. Whatever the cause, these kinds of complaints almost entirely ceased in the 1960s when relations between the state and the religious communities (including Catholics) in Yugoslavia eased considerably.

In contrast to those described earlier, nearly all other conflicts over burial rituals in Yugoslavia, from 1945 up through the wars of Yugoslav dissolution, revolved entirely around issues of politics. By 1946 it had become perfectly obvious that in postwar Yugoslavia only the Communist party would be permitted to exist as a political organization, and any individual, group, or organization that sought alternative political options or criticized the Communist party's behavior would face immediate consequences. Further, everyone knew that religion and politics did not mix. The new laws clearly stated that religion must not be misused for political ends, and obviously high-ranking Communist politicians would not have religious funerals. A document signed by Josip Broz Tito in 1967 on the burial honors provided to military veterans stated, "Individuals buried with religious rites, cannot as a rule also be buried with military honors, unless otherwise ordered."[32] But the boundaries between what counted as private and public mourning were not always clear; they varied from place to place, person to person, and using Gal's concept of "nesting," funerals could be simultaneously political and private. Conflicts thus sometimes arose even over the funerals of those who were only moderately political—such as members of Trade Unions or Veterans of the People's Liberation Struggle—if their families sought to commemorate their deaths with religious funerals.

These were precisely the types of conflict I had imagined when investigating burial rites and communism. I expected to find many cases where the Communist party refused priests the right to provide religious services to those who were themselves inclined toward atheism but whose families were not. In fact, I found evidence of only a limited number of cases, again all in Croatia and mostly during the first decade of Communist rule. It is likely that more cases existed than were documented, yet the evidence suggests that religious participation in funerals most often encountered difficulty when private and public forms of commemoration collided, resulting in a mixed audience of mourners.

Between 1946 and 1956 representatives of the Catholic Church sent three complaints regarding blocked religious funeral services to the Croatian CRQ. All three involved deceased factory workers and Trade Union members. In the first case in 1947, the deceased worker's wife in Split requested three priests, but the next day a young man representing the family came to cancel the request, saying the family had received an "order" from the Trade Union that there must be no priest at the funeral. The wife, he said, was at home in tears. The funeral was held without a priest, but they held a mass at home the following day.[33] In the second case in October 1956, a brick factory worker's family in Lepoglava asked a priest to please come to his funeral in street clothing because they wanted a priest present but had been told by the Trade Union that they could not have one. The priest had essentially told them they had to choose between God and the

Union, which led to heated and unpleasant discussions between all three sides with the Union warning of "serious consequences." Not surprisingly, the funeral was held without a priest.[34] The third case in July 1956 involved the funeral of a railroad worker and veteran in Koprivnica. No priest was present, but a fellow railroad official, Mijo Sremec, who knew his colleague to be a believer, spoke in a religious manner at the funeral. Following the funeral, Sremec was called to account by the Department of Internal Affairs, which claimed he had "slandered the socialist social order and praised religion, using enemy words with which he did moral harm to the other employees of the Yugoslav Railway." As a result, he lost his job of twenty-one years at the railway. The General Vicar defended Sremec, insisting that he certainly had not slandered the Socialist social order and reminding the CRQ that Politbureau member Aleksandar Ranković had recently spoken in the Croatian Parliament recommending greater contact between the church and local governments with the goal of seeking positive solutions to concrete problems. The outcome of this conflict is unknown.[35] One similar case occurred over a decade later in 1968 when a priest from Pula complained in a letter to Marshal Tito that the mother of the Croatian "People's Hero" Antun Ciliga had been denied a religious funeral, though she had been a devout Catholic and requested it. Her daughter-in-law had planned to carry out her wishes but had been pressured by district and police officials who said that the state would only pay for the funeral if no religious figures were present.[36]

What is notable in all these cases is that while the decedents were not described as party members, they were all sufficiently connected to the regime that their funerals were considered a matter of public, not private, concern. Yet families and close friends obviously remained engaged in the process, making their wishes known. Ultimately the public nature of the funeral speeches empowered the state to override or dismiss the interests of the family, insisting on the prioritization of public values. At these funerals, as with its creation of Partisan cemeteries, the Communist party was making some effort to create a new collective identity and a society in which there would be no room for open believers. In the first case, the family easily bowed to pressure and cancelled their initial plans to have a priest at the funeral but then had a private mass at home the following day. In the second case, the family tried to get around the public/private conflict by asking the priest to wear lay attire, but when he refused, they had to submit. In the third case, it was a lay person and friend of the family who introduced religion into the public funeral speech and ended up paying a heavy price for it. We have much less information about the reaction of Ciliga's family, but it is likely that they also bowed to the state's social and economic pressure.

The party's response to burial rituals in these cases was crude and surely ineffective in terms of building a community. And while they likely only affected "borderline" individuals with both connections to the regime and traditional ties to Catholicism, their negative impact on the friends and neighbors of those individuals was surely more significant. Given the highly decentralized nature of Yugoslav society, however, it is probable that personal relations between the religious community and the state in each district were a greater predictor of conflict than anything else.

Several factors in the late 1950s and early 1960s worked to reduce conflicts of this nature, including the official missive from Politbureau member Aleksandar Ranković in July 1959 regarding policies toward the religious communities. While the memo never mentioned cemeteries, it emphasized the continuing sensitive nature of relations between religious communities and the state. Ranković noted that while relations with most of the country's religious communities (Orthodox, Old Catholic, Islamic, Jewish, and most Protestants) had already been normalized, those with the Catholic Church, though improving, remained difficult as certain reactionary individuals within the Church continually worked to sharpen those relations. In response, he argued, party members should not overreact but emphasize the positive and work with those who want to work with them. "We must always think about the political aspect of these questions and avoid resolving them by administrative means wherever possible … because such measures do not achieve the most effective results in developing positive tendencies among those churches that wish to adapt their work to new social-political conditions and develop normal relations with the state."[37]

Even so, by the early 1970s the religious revival associated with the Croatian Spring may have emboldened some Catholic priests to renew their political activism but now with a more nationalist agenda. In 1971, a priest in Karlovac refused to allow Serbs into the church at a funeral, allegedly stating, "Only Catholic believers have the right to enter the church, not Serbian cattle; remove the cattle! I want here only pure-blooded Catholics, not Serbian oxen." While denying those exact words, the priest admitted that, provoked by drunks, he had said that the religious ritual could be attended only by Catholics who knew how to behave and not by drunken cattle unable to control themselves. Moreover, he insisted that as the representative of the religious community, he had the right to decide who could and could not attend its religious rituals, just as the Communist party had the right to decide who could and could not attend its meetings. While the document did not say so directly, it seemed likely that the party was less concerned by the priest's assertion of his religious rights than the incident's potential to incite ethnic conflict and he was sentenced to six months' imprisonment on criminal charges for offending national feelings.[38]

Confirmation for that interpretation may be found in the party's more lenient response to a 1974 incident where a Catholic priest in Sinj offended communists attending the religious funeral of a fellow factory worker. Possibly noticing them in the audience, the priest had praised the deceased for his loyalty to the Church in contrast to others who sold out "for a handful of beans." He further honored the deceased for being "true to the Croatian nation and Croatian heart," concluding his eulogy with a traditional Croatian epitaph with nationalist overtones, "Neka Ti je Laka Hrvatksa Zemlja" [May You Rest in Peace in Croatian Soil]. The case was further politicized by the fact that the deceased had been not only religious but also had joined *Matica Hrvatska*, the Croatian cultural organization and founding organization of the Croatian national movement in 1971. Although the priest's words earned him a criminal investigation, he was not actually punished, perhaps because they were unlikely to incite ethnic conflict.[39] By the mid-1970s, however, members of the Communist regime had finally begun to consider a different approach to conflicts between private and public forms of commemoration.

Creating New Rituals

In accordance with its vision for a new society, one might have expected the Communist regime to create and implement a broad series of new rituals and commemorative practices from the moment it took power. After eliminating any official celebration of religious holidays and traditions, the regime would then need to create new secular traditions and rituals in harmony with its new values and goals. Yet its approach to this task was at best slow and half-hearted in all realms of the life cycle, and nowhere was it more ineffective than with regard to death and burial. Apparently, the state gave the issue no thought at all at least up until the 1960s, and even then it largely backed away from the challenge.

Croatia's CRQ first addressed the need for new burial rituals in a 1961 report, which pointed out that the republic's religious communities all had well-constructed and thoughtful ceremonies that had been tested throughout centuries for christenings, weddings, and funerals—indeed for every significant event in life. In this way, the church had successfully integrated itself into the entire life of each person so that every family holiday had a religious imprint.

In contrast, "our social and political organs do not pay sufficient attention to important events in people's lives such as the birth of a child, and official registration of its birth, marriage, death, day of the dead. These questions have not been fully regulated in our legal acts." While some urban areas had begun to address the problem, most small regions remained hindered by a lack of resources.[40] But while recognizing that lack, the party had done little or nothing to correct the problem in the preceding decade.

Accordingly, the CRQ raised the possibility of legalizing the Catholic holiday of Day of the Dead, or All Saints' Day, celebrated on November 1 as a day of memory and caring for the dead when all family members bring flowers and wreathes to cemeteries. After all, it noted, the lack of official Communist holidays was only further enhancing the influence of the Catholic Church, which had a preponderance of holidays including New Years, Christmas, Easter, Nikolina, and Day of the Dead. Moreover, while Communist organizations had taken no position with regard to Day of the Dead, religious communities were using it to great purpose and carrying out all kinds of propaganda about it in religious classes and the press. Nonetheless, no action was taken either in 1961 or in 1964 when it was again revisited: All Saints' Day was not legalized, nor were secular alternatives provided.[41]

The likely problem was that legalizing even one religious holiday raised the question of official tolerance and/or acceptance for all religious holidays. This issue was indeed one of considerable complexity since Yugoslavia was a secular state, made up of multiple officially equal ethnoreligious communities. Not only had the state banned official observance of all religious holidays after the war, it had instituted a six-day work week that remained in effect until 1963.[42] Even so, the regime knew that it could not expect immediate or complete adherence to its system and had been forced to practice a considerable degree of tolerance toward those who continued to celebrate religious holidays, particularly given the constitutional guarantee of freedom of worship and the right provided by the Law on the Legal Status of Religious Communities to freely practice religious rituals. The problem, one member of the CRQ explained, was that "we have to adopt a uniform position with regard to holidays." A colleague agreed: "If we allow the celebration of religious holidays for Catholics, we must automatically also allow it for others too." Ultimately, therefore, they agreed to "stay within the borders of toleration and reject any official recognition [of any religious holidays] in any kind of document. As soon as we make it official, we would immediately get demands from other religious communities."[43] That rejection thus also included Day of the Dead.

While CRQ members in Croatia briefly considered officially recognizing some religious holidays but fell back on tolerance, those in Serbia had come to fear that even tolerance could have negative side effects for socialism. By the early 1960s, Serbian CRQ reports worried that even many Communist party members were again participating in religious rituals: some Communist Muslims were celebrating Ramadan, while Orthodox party members were christening their children and sending them to religious studies classes. Their first response was to call for an increase in "ideological work," insisting that they must fight against "backwardness and mysticism" but above all must not imagine that "the problem will solve itself."[44] By 1970, however, some within the CRQ of Vojvodina began to suggest that the problem might lie in the almost complete lack of Communist ritual available to serve as an alternative. One CRQ leader expressed dismay at having found that while a clear set of burial rituals existed for churchgoers, there was nothing similar for those who were not believers. "It is almost as though a non-believer can't be buried because there are not even pall bearers, the church won't bury a non-believer and no other method has been established."[45] In 1976, the Serbian CRQ described a comparable issue concerning funerals in the central Serbian city of Niš where, it said, religious activity had revived lately and the participation of two or three priests in nearly every funeral had become rather fashionable. It explained the increase in religiosity due to the lack of protocol or music provided by the local Funeral Enterprise for those who wished to be buried without religious rites.[46]

Comparable concerns had also emerged among leaders of the funeral industry. In the fall of 1973, a conference of thirteen experts from all six republics created and adopted for general Yugoslav use a "Guide to Funeral Services" (*Kodeks Pogrebne Usluge*), which was then sent free of charge to Funeral Enterprises in all Yugoslav municipalities. The eighty-nine-page guidebook addressed a broad series of topics relating to death, funeral, and burial services, including the history of burial culture among Yugoslavia's religious communities, their burial rites, laws relating to cemeteries and burial, cremation, exhumation, and the international transportation of corpses.[47]

Among the more important topics were precisely those relating to ethics and ritual. The Guide's authors agreed that there were not as yet in Yugoslavia any agreed-upon rituals for the funeral of an ordinary atheist party member— no wreath, no speech, no ceremony. Indeed, they pointed out, this was true for not only burial rituals but all important life events—marriage, graduation, retirement, and so on. In contrast to Soviet authors writing at approximately the same time, however, these authors cautioned patience, arguing that it takes time to create traditions appropriate to modern civilization.[48] The creation of a new ritual is "a very sensitive question which touches upon the historical and cultural essence of the given nation. It must take into consideration its traditions, and ethical and spiritual values."[49] Further, they noted, "it is difficult to reconcile rationalism and ritual and thus to create a rational ritual." They declined even to suggest what elements might be included in a new funeral ritual since, as they said, "in our country, where so many different cultural and religious influences intertwine, any imposition of a ritual might only provoke spite and resistance." The best they could recommend was that Yugoslavia might follow the example of Hungary where those who did not want a religious ceremony were simply provided free music.[50]

The cultural sensitivity exhibited by the authors of the *Kodeks* is commendable and their concerns accurate. Rituals cannot be created overnight, nor can they be forced upon an unwilling populace. Nonetheless, even new rituals must begin somewhere and there is a difference between sensitivity and outright abdication. Despite the infamous failure of most rituals promoted by Soviet authorities, some, like those associated with Soviet weddings, were eventually quite successful. As Smolkin puts it, "By the end of the Soviet period, many socialist rituals had become important parts of Soviet life—so much so, in fact, that it is now difficult to imagine Soviet life without them."[51] Although the new Soviet rituals did not so much replace older rituals as supplement them, they contributed to a sense of common identity among those citizens who participated in them. The refusal of the *Guidebook*'s authors to provide any suggestions for secular rituals, even while recognizing their importance, likely reflected the growing decentralization of the era and their inability to reach consensus on the issue. While they might reasonably have recommended sample rituals from which the municipal enterprises or individuals could choose, perhaps even that was too contentious. Ultimately, the Yugoslav Communist regime added only two new sets of rituals to those already in existence—rituals for cremation and rituals for veterans.

Cremation

As a means of body disposal cremation was not entirely new to the Balkan Peninsula. The idea of cremation came to the Balkans, as it had elsewhere, in the mid-nineteenth century where it found support among physicians, scientists, and other members of the intellectual elite. In Serbia, it was first promoted by the poet and doctor Jovan Jovanović Zmaj. In 1904, Vojislav Kujundžić, MD, established *Oganj* (Flame), the Association of Cremation Supporters in Belgrade. The Serbian Orthodox Church, however, was and remains adamantly opposed to cremation, insisting that the body must remain whole to ensure successful Resurrection. Yet in many cases its reasons seemed less theological than cultural, connecting the practice to paganism and irreligion and seeing it as a threat to the Orthodox cult of the dead and especially relics.[52] The Catholic Church opposed cremation until 1963 and Islam and Judaism remain so to this day.[53] Unsurprisingly, then, the interwar Yugoslav regime did not pursue the practice.

The Soviet Union began to promote cremation as early as 1919 as an inexpensive, labor-saving, and hygienic alternative. Postwar Yugoslavia soon took up the idea also, and Article 5 of the first Republic Law on Burials and Cemeteries in Serbia in 1961 specified, "The remains of the deceased may be incinerated before burial. The incineration of remains will be carried out in a communal object designated for that purpose (that is, a crematorium)."[54] The first actual crematorium was constructed three years later in Novo Groblje Cemetery. Serbia's revised "Law on Cemeteries" from 1965 provided additional guidelines, specifying that cremation was possible only in cases of death by natural causes, only if the family requested it, and the deceased had not explicitly opposed it. The resulting ashes must be buried in a grave, mausoleum, columbarium, or scattered in a special place (Rosarium) within the cemetery but could not be turned over to members of the family or anyone else.[55] Some two decades after his death, Vojislav Kujundžić, the founder of *Oganj*, finally got his wish to be cremated. In June 1968, his remains were exhumed, cremated, and his urn placed in Rosary No. 1. Preceding him in Novo Groblje were urns of prominent Belgrade citizens who had been cremated abroad and had their remains returned home and placed in family vaults.[56] The Serbian Orthodox Church never officially accepted cremation, insisting that any member of the Church who knowingly consented to the practice would have to be buried without a church service. Yet it did apparently agree to provide funeral services for those members of the Orthodox Church whose family members had decided to have them cremated without their previous consent. In effect, this compromise allowed both sides to "wink" at the practice when necessary.[57]

Although Yugoslavia's first crematorium opened in 1964, regime efforts to promote cremation as an alternative to traditional burials really began only in the early 1970s mainly in connection with a more general crisis of cemetery space in Belgrade. By the early 1970s, leaders of the Belgrade Municipal Council for Communal Services had concluded that the future of burial was in cremation and that it was critical to resolving Belgrade's burial problems. Thus, it sought to raise the percentage of citizens who selected cremation to 30 through more active propagation, promoting its social and economic value, pointing to its significant price advantage, and activating the cremation society.

In 1971 and 1973 two Belgrade reports, one by the Communal Enterprise for Funeral Services and the second by the Institute for Communal and Urban Activities, discussed cremation as an important part of the larger solution to overcrowding. Thus far, they argued, Belgrade had managed with its existing cemeteries thanks to a low mortality rate of 6.7 percent based on demographics. By 2000, however, that mortality rate would double to 12 percent, while the city itself would continue to expand, increasing the need for burial space.[58] Since the construction of the crematorium, Novo Groblje had added a Cremation Funeral Hall, a Columbarium, and a Memory Garden, or Rosarium, for scattering ashes. Most important, from the perspective of burial rituals, however, was Belgrade's plan to improve the aesthetic ambience of the Crematory Hall and Columbarium and develop attractive and contemporary cremation ceremonies.[59] Although lacking religious symbols or paraphernalia, the enormous Cremation Funeral Hall at Novo Groblje, built in the old Synagogue, with an altar-like pedestal in the back to hold the coffin, was designed to resemble a Byzantine Orthodox church. By the end of the Communist era, the rituals established for cremations were similar to those of traditional Orthodox funerals, though offering somewhat greater flexibility. The coffin normally remained closed and the family could choose its own music, but flowers and candles were common, and the ceremony was often followed by a gathering with food and drink but a less elaborate formal meal than after traditional funerals. According to more recent surveys, the likelihood of relatives to visit the remains of cremated deceased on the seventh and fortieth day, six months, and one year after death seemed just as likely as for those buried.[60] In that sense, the rituals provided for cremation were only nominally secular and, as they were so clearly directed toward members of the Orthodox faith, did little to promote ethnoreligious diversity.

The Communist regime never achieved its goals with regard to cremation. The second crematorium in Nova Bežanija was never built, although currently cremation services are available also at Zemun and two other Belgrade cemeteries besides Novo Groblje. A crematorium was constructed at Zagreb's Mirogoj cemetery in 1985, and the 1989 plan for Vlakovo cemetery in Sarajevo also included one, though it has yet to be constructed.[61] It is also unlikely that the goal of 30 percent cremations was achieved during the Communist era. According to Pavičević, the proportion in Serbia in 2014 was 21.4. Even so, there is no doubt that a larger percentage of Serbs have opted for cremation than in any other part of the Orthodox Christian world.[62] Many of those cremated during the Communist era in Serbia were likely supporters of the Communist regime and/or atheists who may have cared little for a religious service. Some were also true believers in cremation who supported it for standard modernist reasons relating to hygiene and the environment and who sought to promote the idea that "religious superstitions about life after death were a matter of the past."[63] Others, however, may have opted for cremation as the only way to ensure entry for their loved ones into the highly desirable but overcrowded Novo Groblje cemetery. As the authors of the 1973 report explained, the fact that most families opted for burial of ashes in the ground suggested that the relatively high percentage of cremations was "not the result of high consciousness and breaking with tradition but rather that they want to have the funeral rituals at Novo Groblje."[64] The enhanced rituals may have improved the experience for those who chose cremation but did not likely change many minds and did not seek to create a secular pluralistic burial culture.

Rituals for Veterans

In the end, and perhaps entirely predictably, the only organization that committed to creating a secular all-Yugoslav funeral ritual was the Yugoslav veteran's organization, SUBNOR. Once again, politics triumphed. Victory in the People's Liberation Struggle remained the Communist party's main source of legitimacy and those who had served were its greatest heroes, deserving of all possible honors in life and death. According to Goran Miloradović, death rituals for Partisans provided assurance that membership in the elite group survived even death and that its values were eternal.[65] During the 1970s, as veterans who had survived the war died in increasing numbers, SUBNOR took action to more properly commemorate the funerals of "ordinary" veterans. In May 1976, SUBNOR published a rulebook outlining the specific obligations and provisions for military funerals to ensure the equality of honors offered to deceased veterans throughout Yugoslavia.

According to that rulebook, all deceased veterans were to be provided a wreath, homogenous in form and size, ideally made of forest branches with a circumference of 50 centimeters and a red five-pointed star in the middle made of fresh or artificial flowers. It must also include a ribbon from the colors of the Yugoslav flag inscribed on the left side with the name of the deceased and

SUBNOR on the right. The wreath was to be placed alongside the stage and carried in the procession by a member of a unit of the territorial defense, civil defense, or People's Liberation War. The honor guard was to stand alongside the stage, right before the procession departs. Its composition was to be determined by the social-political organization of the local community or district. In the procession, a pillow bearing any medals, plaques, or awards was to be carried just ahead of the coffin. Either a member of SUBNOR or someone from another social-political organization was obligatorily to give a farewell speech.[66] These honors could be denied to a veteran who had explicitly in writing or orally rejected them while alive, had been convicted of crimes against the state or other serious crimes, or had been expelled from SUBNOR. While providing specific guidelines, SUBNOR also instructed district councils to allow for the inclusion of local traditions. Moreover, a letter from the Croatian SUBNOR on June 24, 1976, reminded all local committees that while the rules did not say so explicitly (and contrary to Tito's statement a decade earlier), it should be understood that military honors must still be given to those buried with religious rites. In doing so, however, organizations must work first to consistently apply the rules about military honors, harmonizing the religious rituals with the ceremony in such a way that satisfies expectations without giving religion primary significance.[67]

Indeed, already in April 1976, the Union of Orthodox Priests forwarded a complaint to the Croatian CRQ concerning the funeral of one of its flock, a participant in both World Wars and member of SUBNOR. When the family had requested a religious funeral and invited priests to preside, members of SUBNOR protested and threatened to withdraw use of funeral equipment. Even after the SUBNOR rules had been clarified, documents throughout the late 1970s and into the early 1980s reflected continuing ambivalence and conflicts. As with earlier conflicts from the 1940s to 1950s, it is likely that personal relations in local regions were a leading factor.[68]

A common issue of contention, however, concerned the order of objects in the funeral procession. The main honorary object presented by SUBNOR to the deceased at the funeral was the wreath described earlier, decorated with the tricolor sash of the Yugoslav flag and Communist party's red five-pointed star. In accordance with the directive that religious rites not be allowed to take center stage, SUBNOR representatives regularly insisted that the wreath be placed at the head of the funeral procession. Catholic doctrine, however, is equally insistent that the cross must lead the funeral procession and behind the Catholic determination lies a belief in eternal salvation or damnation. As one priest from Bjelovar explained in 1983, he served God alone and would be punished if he allowed the wreath and star to precede him. Accordingly, he left the funeral and said he would go to the cemetery by car and rejoin them there. Negotiations continued almost until dark, disrupting the entire funeral until SUBNOR members finally relented and agreed to place the wreath atop the coffin and behind the cross and the priest.[69]

As conflicts of this nature reveal, the private wishes of the family with regard to mourning were frequently subordinate to those of the state or, as in this case, were entirely lost in the greater conflict between the church and state. At the same time, these conflicts and the ensuing negotiations help to clarify exactly when and under what circumstances the state chose to become involved in private burial rituals and just how far it would go. As we saw in the 1950s, the regime only became involved in funerals when politics were at stake and it only made the effort to create new secular burial rituals when the deceased were its own veterans. Even then, if a serious conflict between private and public forms of mourning developed, most state representatives still saw burial rituals as a highly sensitive issue that could easily backfire. Accordingly, they pushed their agenda far enough to significantly delay, but not so far as to entirely derail, the burial of a veteran. Private forms of mourning could not trump public ones, but they were allowed to coexist.

Conclusion

Except in the first years after the war and mainly in Croatia, the Communist regime in Yugoslavia did little to prevent religious communities from providing traditional burial rituals designed both to secure safe passage for the soul to the afterlife and comfort those remaining in this one. Perhaps fearing to cross the line between religious and national repression, it often declined even to enforce bans on those rituals it had deemed unhygienic (rightly or wrongly) and hopelessly backward. Except in those first years, both Catholics and Orthodox continued to provide last rites to the dying; village funerals remained lengthy affairs focused in the home and offering regular meals, including some at the grave; some Orthodox continued to bury items with the corpse and engage in secondary burials; Islamic burials rarely used coffins and when possible processed the body through town.

Only when the regime (at any level) determined that an individual's burial merited public attention did it seek to ensure that the accompanying rituals reinforced state values. Even so, the state did remarkably little to create new secular rituals that could provide comfort to its own audience of mourners, the sole exception being those provided after the mid-1970s for Veterans of the People's Liberation War. As a result, while non-Communist citizens of Socialist Yugoslavia might complain that burials had been "politicized," those who accepted its values, or even just renounced the ethnoreligious divisions of the past, found they had few alternatives when it came to burial rituals.

6

Grave Markers: Messages in Stone

As the name implies, grave markers were originally intended simply to mark the site of burial and provided only the most basic information. By the nineteenth to twentieth centuries, however, they had come to play a critical role in the grieving process and became increasingly personalized, as families sought to emphasize and elevate the character, status, interests, and achievements of the dead through variations in the markers' size and shape, as well as imagery, symbols, and epitaphs inscribed upon them. Grave markers are thus an important form of communication—between the living and the dead and among those left behind. As primary sources of material culture, grave markers come closest to giving voice to the dead themselves, particularly in an era when many individuals design and place their own grave markers prior to death.

Yet the markers also represent a critical medium of private–public communication. As a private form of commemoration, they provide a means of expressing love, tangible evidence of remembrance, and a placeholder for those memories. As a means of communicating with friends and the public, grave markers allow the family (or the deceased) to display the decedent's most important characteristics and status within the community. Beyond that they inform us about the family's ethnoreligious and historical background. But the public is neither silent nor passive in the process as long-standing social conventions guide and constrain commemorative options, and cemetery administrators (religious and secular) have traditionally played an important role in regulating the placement, size, and style of markers within their larger public function in building and preserving communities of the dead. Socialist regimes may also restrict the ways that families choose to memorialize their deceased loved ones, while commemorating their own honored dead in ways that politicize gravesites and death itself. As a result, grave markers—their size, style, and placement—expose frictions between private and public concepts of mourning, making their social and political interpretation challenging and inexact. Even so, grave markers undoubtedly reflect extant patterns and can hint at social relationships that might otherwise go unnoticed. While chronological changes in the design of grave markers in Socialist Yugoslavia mirrored the evolving social and political context, a more focused investigation of themes like the use of script, the problem of mixed marriages, variations among Islamic grave markers, and treatment of war dead offers insights into the forces of cultural adaptation and political polarization.

Shape, Symbols, Images, and Epitaphs

The grave markers of Catholic, Orthodox, and, to a lesser degree, Jewish families in the Balkans are in many ways comparable to those found in Western Europe. Most were set on either joint or family gravesites leased for periods of ten to fifty years, depending on the locality. The size and shape of the markers, however, varied depending on class, wealth, ethnoreligious background, and time of placement. According to cemetery expert Harold Mytum, the original purpose of the gravestone was not so much to memorialize the deceased as to mark the site of the burial and protect it from disturbance.[1] After the Catholic Church began to encourage burials on sacred ground within a fenced area on church property, most people were simply buried in mass graves without any marker, their bones later being moved to charnel houses and ossuaries. Only elites were permitted burial within the church, and therefore most of the early extant graves are inside church buildings. The first ones from the twelfth century were carved slabs sealing coffins with more elaborate stones set above. As space inside the church filled, tombs were set in the floor, in the walls, and in catacombs underground. Later, walled galleries were constructed outside larger churches whose walls were also eventually filled with tombs. Until the seventeenth century, grave markers outside the church were rare, particularly in stone. Wooden crosses may have been more common but have not survived.[2]

After the mid-seventeenth century, most cemetery monumentation in Europe moved outside, leading to greater diversity in style and size. Following the French Revolution, Napoleonic laws guaranteed every citizen the right to an individual grave but could not ensure that every citizen had the means to pay for a stone marker. Thus, many still had to make do with a painted slab of wood or a wooden cross that would disintegrate over time leaving an unmarked grave whose lease would soon be up. Meanwhile, the old elites, previously buried in churches, and, perhaps even more important, the new elites had the income to express their individual and social status as clearly after death as in life. Some built elaborate chapels and mausoleums within which their entire family would be interred, and others commissioned exquisite sculptures to stand guard above the remains of a deceased loved one. Those in between purchased simple rectangular stones or cross-shaped monuments, now inscribed with the name and date of birth and death of the deceased.

Islamic graves are expected to emphasize the egalitarian quality of death. Oral traditions claimed that the prophet had prohibited plastering and building over a grave, some also adding a prohibition against inscriptions on grave markers. In many Arabic Muslim countries, graves are essentially mounds marked only by bricks or rocks.[3] But despite proscriptions and the insistence of official clergy, tombstones with inscriptions, as well as large, elaborate, and colorful mosques atop graves, developed within only a few centuries after the death of Muhammad. Moreover, the Ottomans are world famous for the epigraphic artistry displayed on tombstones and other forms of sepulchral architecture.

By the fifteenth century Islamic tombstones throughout the Balkans were deliberately imitative of the Ottoman style. They began to adopt the white flat or post pillar headstone, sometimes accompanied by a footstone, which is now ubiquitous throughout the region, adopted Arabic script, and turban tops on headstones for deceased males and caps for females. Women's tombstones were also usually smaller and more frequently decorated. By the eighteenth to nineteenth centuries, all the tombstones became more elaborate, as the shape, style, and size of the turban provided specific information about the class, educational level, and occupation of the deceased. After the military reforms of 1832, the ranked turbans on tombstones for deceased agas were replaced with the newly created fez required for all Turkish officers living or dead (Figure 6.1).[4]

One of the most obvious forms of communication on any grave marker concerns religious affiliation. We have come to expect gravestones to reflect an individual's faith and are accustomed to seeing religious symbols on gravestones or in its fundamental shape as a sign of piety and a mark of belonging to a particular religious community. Yet that was not always the case and is not so today. Christian crosses, for example, were not regularly used as markers on gravesites until about the tenth century and were not especially common even for those few elites who merited individual graves within churches themselves or church graveyards.[5] Even as the use of funeral monuments began to increase, it remains unclear how commonly crosses were placed on them since the various Christian denominations seem to differ on its symbolic meaning. Crosses appear almost omnipresent either as symbols on gravestones or as the grave

Figure 6.1 Traditional Muslim graves with male/female turbans
Sarajevo, Bosnia & Hercegovina

markers themselves within Catholic cemeteries. According to Thomas Kselman, the cross was widely used in nineteenth-century Catholic death rituals as the preeminent symbol of both grief and hope; it was ever present at the bedside of the terminally ill and held by them as they received last sacraments; an altar boy carried a cross at the head of the funeral procession to the church and then to the cemetery; and it decorated the shroud and most grave markers.[6] Over time, Catholics often added other religious design elements on grave markers, including crucifixes, angels, doves, and the Virgin Mary. The graves of deceased children also frequently bear cupids and lambs.

As a symbol, the cross is far less common among the grave markers of many European and American Protestants who considered them "popish" and preferred simple rectangles bearing no religious designation at all. Other English Protestants, however, vastly preferred the cross to crucifixes or worse yet such classical decorations as urns, torches, and pillars, insisting the cross was entirely appropriate as long as it remained simple in form. German Protestants also came to adopt a simple cross for most funeral monuments. Even today, however, use of the cross among Protestants on gravestones is by no means universal and many Protestant grave markers have no symbol at all.[7]

Other stylistic (nonreligious) symbols and images began to appear on Christian gravestones as early as the seventeenth century. Among the first and most common were those associated with the concept of death such as the skull and crossbones and the hourglass, both of which were intended to remind visitors to the grave of the passage of time and that they too would die. By the eighteenth century with the onset of the Enlightenment, such memento mori were increasingly replaced with classical decorations, such as pillars, torches, and urns, and then a wide variety of flora and fauna, including willow trees, lilies, fish, and deer.[8]

Orthodox graves nearly always include a cross, but the shape of the Orthodox Cross is often quite distinctive. The Russian Orthodox cross has an additional bar on top and a slanted bar near the bottom while the Serbian Orthodox cross has a knob on all four ends. In fact, however, the Orthodox are not alone in their use of the knobbed cross, and it may be found on Catholic churches in Italy and Croatia as well as on some Croatian grave markers. It is therefore unreliable to distinguish Croatian and Serbian graves (especially older ones) based only on their type of cross. The Orthodox are not inclined toward excessive decorations of any kind on grave markers. In rural communities, wooden crosses are most common, sometimes enhanced only by an icon.

The most common religious symbol on Jewish graves is the five-pointed Star of David. Although it was an ancient symbol for good fortune, which was not necessarily Jewish, it also has archaic connections in Judaic history based in the legend that King David's shield was in the shape of a hexagram. Thus, the Star is often referred to as Magen David—the Shield of David. It was believed to have been first used as an official Jewish symbol by the Prague Jewish community in 1527 and became popular on synagogue doors in the 1600s. In its relation to grave markers, although there was one image of the hexagram on a Jewish tombstone as early as the third century, it did not begin to appear regularly on Jewish grave markers until the eighteenth century.[9] Jewish gravestones sometimes include also menorahs, books, hands, and other symbols but are most famous for the tradition wherein visitors place pebbles upon the grave. Many different explanations have been provided for this practice, ranging from the ancient use of cairns to the pagan urge to weigh down the soul. Most often, however, the explanations reference a desire to remind the deceased that they have not been forgotten.[10]

The Crescent Moon and Star as the religious symbol most associated with Islam seems to have originated with the Ottoman Empire and only in the nineteenth century.[11] Up until the twentieth century very few Islamic grave markers in the Balkans included the Crescent Moon and Star, but there was no particular reason for them to do so. Not only were cemeteries in the Balkans religiously segregated until the early twentieth century but all Muslim grave markers were nearly identical—white obelisk headstones and footstones— ensuring that passers-by could easily recognize a Muslim cemetery. Muslim graves also do not usually include many visual symbols, but in Bosnia after the eighteenth century grave markers were enhanced by religious elements through Qur'anic texts and greater use of Arabic script.[12]

Perhaps the most effective but by no means the most common means of describing the deceased on grave markers is with a visual image. By the thirteenth century effigies appeared, first in brass and then with life-size models directly on the sarcophagi. Initially the effigies were intended only to indicate social and occupational status through clothing and tools, but over time they became increasingly personalized. The deceased was often shown lying with hands crossed over the breast. There were also pairs of tombs with effigies of spouses lying side by side and some showing parents and children, indicating the important role played by the family after death. Others bore more distinctly religious themes, including the Virgin Mary and scenes from the Bible.[13]

Eventually, effigies were replaced with busts and then, in certain parts of the world and with changes in technology, photographs on grave markers. According to Aries, the tradition of placing a photograph on a gravestone is particularly widespread in Mediterranean countries and that is certainly true, but while some Catholic communities, including Italians, Croats, and even Mexicans, follow this tradition, the Orthodox are perhaps best known for it.[14] According to Nicholas Constas, painted grave portraits were found on Byzantine grave markers as early as the fifth century. He further describes a twelfth-century prince whose tomb included a large marble coffin inlaid with silver surrounded by a bronze railing, mosaic icons, and portraits of himself and his parents all properly lit and carefully maintained.[15] According to Olga Matich, the use of photographs among the elites in Russia was rare before the revolution as it was associated with the petty bourgeoisie and considered to be in bad taste. After the revolution, it came to dominate Soviet grave markers as it reflected their anti-Orthodox and anti-bourgeois attitudes.[16] Whatever its origins, photographs or etchings on grave markers are extremely widespread among Orthodox Slavs in the Balkans and are also common among Catholics there, dating as far back as the late nineteenth century. And while the use of graven images on Jewish and Muslim gravestones is theoretically forbidden, some Muslims and Jews in the region also adopted the practice.

One important development came about when many families first purchased small compact cameras and began taking spontaneous and unrehearsed photographs of relatives and friends in natural settings, engaged in everyday activities. From this point onward, the photographs on grave markers became far more personal, providing the viewer with a more intimate look at the deceased. Although such visual images are less common in the Netherlands than in Orthodox countries, they have begun to appear there also leading scholar Raf Vanderstraeten to remark that "many visual images on recent grave markers show something of the 'sensuality' of the body—in ways which would only a few decades ago have been regarded as entirely disrespectful if not blasphemous."[17]

Epitaphs are another and highly effective form of communication on grave markers. The earliest European epitaphs up to the fourteenth century paralleled the original goal of effigies to indicate social and occupational status. Along with the name, dates of birth and death, they offered words of praise for the occupation and skills of the deceased, and in some cases, prayers to God. By the fifteenth century, epitaphs began linking various deceased individuals together, and by the seventeenth century, they offered full biographical accounts focusing on lifetime merits and achievements.[18] A further development of epitaphs came after the Reformation thanks to its emphasis on the written word and a consequent rise in literacy rates. In accordance with Reformation beliefs that death rituals were mainly directed at those left behind, Protestant epitaphs eliminated all prayers and focused on preserving the memory of the deceased, bringing comfort to family and friends and reminding all of life's frailty.[19] Modern epitaphs have frequently taken poetic form and may be highly literary but are just as likely to be overtly sentimental.[20]

Epitaphs were common on pre-Islamic Arabic grave markers but began to show signs of Islamization through Qur'anic citations in the late eighth century intended to be read aloud by passers-by as additional prayers for the deceased. Although many traditionist scholars and jurists opposed the epitaphs, they persisted and promoted the spread of Islam.[21] Balkan Muslims have a strong heritage of modest but highly artistic tombstones, embellished with Qur'anic and poetic epitaphs. Medieval and early modern tombstones in Bosnia & Hercegovina developed a unique style both in their tombstones and epitaphs distinct from others in the Ottoman Empire and more clearly connected to regional forms of sepulchral art. Further evidence of their native style was the fact that the epitaphs in the earliest versions, from the fifteenth to sixteenth centuries, were written in Bosnian not Arabic.[22] While the earliest ones tended to be brief and austere, providing mainly warnings to passers-by that they too would die one day, by the eighteenth century, they also became more elaborate and poetic.[23]

Finally, many graves include small sculptures, figurines, or other personal items placed on the grave marker's footing or slab. Such paraphernalia is often religious in nature, including candles, lanterns, statues of the Virgin Mary, and cupids, but can also include objects relating to the decedent's personal interests such as miniature automobiles and motorcycles, soccer balls, musical instruments, or professional equipment. It is particularly common to find personal objects, including favorite toys, displayed on the graves of children or youth.

All of these developments indicate the growing personalization of grave markers that developed along with modernization and individualism. They represent, as Aries argued, "the discovery, at the hour or thought of death, of one's own identity, one's personal biography, in this world as in the next."[24] At the same time, they display efforts through multiple means to communicate that identity not only to the immediate family but among a broader social network. Even when constrained by social conventions and cemetery regulations, families and the deceased have been remarkably effective at telling the stories they want others to hear on grave markers.

Change over Time: 1945–91

An initial goal of this work was to consider the changing nature of stories etched on grave markers in Socialist Yugoslavia by documenting the evolution of their style and symbols over time. In practice, however, the complex interaction of private and public commemoration along with specific historical and contemporary practices in this region have made that a rather challenging enterprise. Grave markers straddle the boundary between private and public mourning. They are chosen and designed by the family of the deceased (if not the deceased themselves) but are intended also as a means of communication with friends and the broader community. Moreover, they are usually placed in an explicitly public (municipal cemetery) or semi-public (confessional cemetery) location where they can be seen not only by family, friends, and neighbors but sometimes also by complete strangers. To add to the complexity, the family is often limited in their choice of design first by the options provided by the monument industry and second by any regulations concerning size, style, and taste provided by the cemetery management, in this case either a religious community or the Communist regime. In that sense, the private and public elements of grave markers, far from being a dichotomy, more accurately represent Gal's "fractal distinction" as a recurring pattern of multiple nestings, and the family's final selection of a grave marker may not always represent their first choice but a compromise between what they wanted, what was available, what was considered socially acceptable, and what was permitted.[25]

One might reasonably assume that all monument firms would have been nationalized by the Communist regime along with all other industries in the years immediately following the Second World War. Yet no archival evidence supports this assumption, nor does any legal documentation even mention the existence of such enterprises.[26] In fact, very few laws restricted the style or design of grave markers during the Communist era. Only in the late 1960s and apparently only in Croatia did some of the municipalities begin to include articles in their local laws dealing specifically with the content displayed on grave markers. For example, Article 18 from the 1967 "Decree on Cemeteries" from the City of Zagreb stated, "It is forbidden to place an epitaph or picture on a gravestone that would insult anyone's national or religious feelings, or insult feelings of respect for the deceased or could provoke complaints among citizens." To a considerable extent, however, such articles in cemetery laws may have been considered unnecessary, as any "inappropriate" markers could be removed and prosecuted under criminal laws that banned the incitement of national, religious, or racial hatred.[27] In addition, the regime apparently relied on self-censorship among monument designers and producers as well as among their consumers to achieve the desired results.

Besides interpretive complexities relating to choice are those associated with historic practice. As Jeremy Walton has noted, "Temporal ambiguity is fundamental to the cemetery as a social and material space."[28] Accurate for all cemeteries, it is even more appropriate in those like the Balkans where a majority of grave markers among Christians and Jews are placed over family graves housing more than one and often multiple generations of one family. As such they bear not one but several sets of dates on them, some reaching back into the nineteenth century and continuing into the twenty-first. It is not uncommon therefore to find a marker with two names from the 1940s, one from the 1970s, and one from 1990s; or several from the pre-communist era, one from the 1940s, one from the 1960s, and one from the 1980s. If these grave markers were erected at the time of death of the first decedent, the style and symbols on them will not have changed over time as the family usually adds only the name, date of birth and death, and sometimes a photograph of each newly deceased family member (Figure 6.2).

Figure 6.2 Family grave markers
Titel, Serbia and Zagreb, Croatia.

At the same time, because the gravesites are leased, rather than owned, when a family moves away, dies out, or for any other reason ceases to pay the lease, the gravesite can be resold. The bones, if not yet entirely disintegrated, are moved to a mass grave and the headstone, if unclaimed, recycled and lost to memory.

Another challenging problem arises, however, when a family decides to renovate the grave marker, which can happen at any time, although the main turning point occurred in the late 1990s and early 2000s after the fall of communism and with the introduction of capitalism. Thus, one sees many obviously new grave markers, created in a new style and displaying new and very different postcommunist symbols but still bearing dates going back to the 1940s and even earlier. Accordingly, while it is still possible to discern certain patterns of continuity and change in the style and content of grave markers during the Communist era, they can be difficult to follow and have been interrupted by recent interjections bearing older dates. These patterns must also take into account inherent differences in the style and content of markers from the differing ethnoreligious communities and between grave markers in urban and rural settings.

While these challenges necessarily render the conclusions from this chapter somewhat tentative, certain changes in the form, style, and content of grave markers can be detected in the period from 1945 to 1991. These changes reflect evolving developments in the relationship between private consumers of grave markers and the framework of the socialist state that determined the consumer choices available to them, as well as changes in relationships between ethnoreligious communities.

Despite the absence of legal restrictions, the relative homogeneity of grave markers during the Communist era, in direct contrast to the changes that appeared immediately afterward, suggests the existence of effective informal constraints. In the first decades of its rule the Communist regime and the consequences of the war did apparently create a more egalitarian community of the dead through both economic austerity that limited the choices available to consumers selecting grave markers and a degree of self-censorship. While there were modest differences in the size of markers erected under communism, except for those created by the state to memorialize its leaders and heroes, very few were particularly large or extravagant. Nor were long epitaphs typical under communism, probably due to limitations of space. Religious symbols were certainly permitted, but they, too, were simple and modest. Similarly, the photographs and style of markers under communism remained relatively conservative.

The oldest markers from the communist period, from the 1940s and 1950s, are unsurprisingly the most conventional and, in most cases, the least ostentatious. The most common exceptions to the latter description for ordinary citizens were those already extant, beautifully sculpted, and lavish family graves and mausoleums in urban cemeteries like Novo Groblje and Mirogoj. While the Communists provided no model for civilian grave markers, ostentatious displays of wealth might draw attention to private citizens, but in any case, in the immediate years after the war, few of them had such wealth to display. By limiting options and discouraging outward displays of wealth, the regime hampered the ability of citizens to communicate by means of grave markers. Thus, most markers from all religious communities placed in the first two decades of communist rule tell us very little about the graves' inhabitants. Most appeared to be hewn from local stone or concrete. If they included images, they were clearly those taken by professional photographers and the subjects were usually formally posed and in their best attire, sometimes in national costume. Their demeanor was always serious. The inscriptions are simple and to the point—providing in most cases only the name and date of birth and death, though some had also begun to include the standard lines at the bottom explaining which family members had provided the marker. Most also include religious symbols, but they too are straightforward and unassuming (Figure 6.3).

With improvements to the Yugoslav economy in the 1960s and 1970s, many grave markers came to be fashioned from more expensive materials, often a polished gray or nearly black stone, probably granite or marble if Christian and white limestone or marble for Muslims. By the 1970s, we also begin to see increasing personalization of grave markers as evidenced in references and symbols referring to professions and hobbies of the deceased along with the inclusion of a few small figurines or sculptures representing their personal interests.[29] The photographs used on grave markers in the 1970s and beyond also changed in that they were less formal and often seemed to have been simply those that family members happened to have at home, probably personal identification photos. In these pictures, the deceased was now less formally dressed but still had clearly posed for the picture and was still very serious. Although many Yugoslav citizens certainly had small compact cameras by the 1980s, few individualized photos made their way onto grave markers until a decade later (Figure 6.4).

Figure 6.3 Typical rural grave marker from the 1940s to 1950s Vrebac, Croatia. For additional photographs on the theme of "Change Over Time" see https://yugcemeteries.omeka.net/exhibits/show/change-over-time

The number of epitaphs on graves also increased from the 1960s onward, although this was mainly (though not exclusively) a Serbian phenomenon that appealed mostly to the provincial and recently urbanized classes. In 1983, Ivan Čolović carried out an extensive study of epitaphs from Serbian cemeteries in which he specifically connected them to the tradition of laments, seeing them both as an important form of social communication between the grieving and the dead and a means of expressing emotion. Many premodern epitaphs on both Christian and Muslim gravestones had provided warnings from the deceased to the living about the transitory nature of life. By the Communist era, however, many epitaphs (like the laments on which they were modeled) spoke directly to the dead, always using the familiar form of address, and either reproaching them for leaving their loved ones behind or expressing love and sorrow at a time together on earth cut short and promising never to forget them. In other cases, the epitaphs represented a form of communication from the family to the broader community and focused more directly on the decedent's many virtues and talents.[30]

Figure 6.4 Grave markers from the 1970s
Besides indicating the professional and personal interests of the deceased, these Muslim markers show signs of acculturation. Sarajevo, Bosnia & Hercegovina

The evolution from sparse concrete grave markers toward those made of more expensive stone and with more highly personalized content indicates the growth of modernization. These are precisely the same trends in grave marker evolution that have been described in other modernizing states.[31] In the postcommunist period, as we will see later, grave markers changed far more dramatically, reflecting not only the introduction of capitalism and increased consumer choice but also the rise of ethnoreligious nationalism. Meanwhile, a closer look at several specific themes among grave markers in the socialist period reveals more complex social and political developments promoting both cultural adaptations and political polarization. Accepting Yugoslavia's ethnoreligious diversity and acknowledging the certain failure of any attempt to create an all-Yugoslav national identity, the Communist regime nonetheless encouraged social integration and unity within the broader community. Among the tools that it employed in this effort were language policy and the encouragement of mixed marriages. Both efforts had only moderate success and faced opposition, but their remnants are evident among grave markers from the Communist era.

Grave Markers and Language

It seems self-evident that an individual or family would design the grave marker in the native language of the deceased. Indeed, that was also most often the case in Croatia, Bosnia & Hercegovina, and Serbia under socialist rule. Yet the case of Yugoslavia entailed considerable linguistic complexity as it was a country of not only multiple languages but also two official alphabets. While most grave markers in the three republics were inscribed in some version of a language then generally referred to as Serbo-Croatian, some were in Latin script, while others were in Cyrillic. In addition, some stones were entirely or partially engraved in different languages and scripts such as Albanian, Arabic, Bulgarian, German, Hebrew, Hungarian, and Russian. Individuals frequently attach specific sociocultural significance to a particular language or script such that even if one is entirely bilingual or biscriptal, the choice of language or script is not completely arbitrary.[32] Each family's choice of language and script was a deliberate decision that may mainly have reflected the language of their daily use but could also communicate information regarding ethnoreligious or political identity.

The Yugoslav census of 1981 legally recognized eighteen different languages in Socialist Yugoslavia; nonetheless, approximately 73 percent of the population accepted some form of Serbo-Croatian as their native tongue. Serbo-Croatian was also used as the language of broader communication and in the military and diplomatic services.[33] The origins of Serbo-Croatian as a language reach back into the mid-nineteenth century when Croat Ljudevit Gaj founded the Illyrian movement seeking the unification of South Slavs. Although Gaj originally hoped for the creation of one united language among all South Slavs, his followers adopted a more pragmatic approach focused only on Croatian and Serbian. At the same time, Serbian linguist Vuk Stefanović Karadžić was engaged in a series of modernizing language reforms, and the historic accident of their overlapping agendas led to the 1850 Vienna Linguistic Agreement, which established a set of principles for a common language under the belief that they were one people.[34] The agreement had no practical consequences at that time and provided no common name for the language but set the stage for its later official codification as "Serbo-Croatian" within the interwar Kingdom of Serbs, Croats, and Slovenes. During the 1930s, the Dictatorship of King Alexander made efforts to impose Serbo-Croatian as a single unified language as part of its failed attempt to create a Yugoslav identity.[35]

Under the Communist regime, the 1948 Constitution provided full equality to the languages of Serbia, Croatia, Slovenia, and Macedonia without specifically naming them. Under the pressure of the Soviet-Yugoslav split, however, the regime promoted greater efforts at unity and came to see linguistic diversity as an obstacle. In December 1954, linguists from Serbia and Croatia signed the Novi Sad Agreement, which described Serbo-Croatian as a single language with two equal and official variants—Eastern and Western, along with other language idioms in various locations. In each republic, the language was defined as either Serbo-Croatian or Croato-Serbian; that is, both elements were always included.[36]

Over the next decade, however, language policy succumbed to growing forces of decentralization and nationalism. In 1967, a group of Croatian linguists rejected Croato-Serbian or any comparable name for their language, insisting that it be called the Croatian Literary Language. Although their "Declaration on the Name and Position of the Croatian Literary Language" was condemned at the time, the 1974 Constitution recognized official linguistic variants in Serbia, Croatia, Bosnia & Hercegovina, and Montenegro and again left their names up to the republic constitutions. According to Robert Greenberg, those variants became the nuclei of later successor languages.[37] As Yugoslavia disintegrated in the 1990s, so too did Serbo-Croatian as a common language and it is now referred to within each country by its own national moniker and by outsiders most often as BCS (Bosnian-Croatian-Serbian) or BCMS to include Montenegrin.

The linguistic variants of BCS exhibit some important differences in grammar, pronunciation, orthography, and lexicon, though almost none are so significant as to preclude mutual comprehension. However, one critical distinction between the Eastern and Western variant that can complicate understanding is the choice of the Cyrillic versus Latin alphabet. Versions of the Cyrillic script are traditionally associated only with East Slavic nations including the Russians, Ukrainians, Bulgarians, Macedonians, and Serbs, while the Western Slavs including Poles, Czechs, Slovaks, and Croats used the Latin script.[38] In much of the Balkan region that would eventually become Yugoslavia, centuries of ethnic migration resulted in more permeable borders between linguistic scripts. Accordingly, those who spoke some version of BCMS might use either Cyrillic or Latin or both. The 1850 Vienna Agreement did not mention script at all, but in 1867 the Croatian Parliament within the Austro-Hungarian Empire, basing its decision on that agreement, decreed that every citizen was allowed to use either the Croatian or Serbian language and the Latin or Cyrillic script. Both scripts were also legally equal in interwar Yugoslavia, although according to one informal study the vast majority of books published were in Cyrillic.[39] In Bosnia & Hercegovina, both scripts were commonly used but Cyrillic was banned twice—once by the Austro-Hungarian government during the First World War and then again under the Ustashe regime during the Second World War.[40]

In Socialist Yugoslavia, the Novi Sad Agreement also stated that both scripts were entirely equal and that both must be taught to schoolchildren whose native language was Serbo-Croatian/Croato-Serbian. Theoretically, both teachers and students had to write in each script on an alternating basis. Yet despite varieties in practice, many Croats equated the differing alphabets with national identity, and hence education in Cyrillic throughout Croatia was unreliable. Thus, up into the 1970s, the Cyrillic alphabet remained dominant in Serbia, while the Latin script was most common (though not exclusive) in Croatia. Only in Bosnia & Hercegovina where publications were printed in both scripts was usage nearly equal.[41] Nonetheless, to facilitate and ensure better communication, most legal and cross-republic communication was recorded in the Latin script. Moreover, from the mid-1970s up through Yugoslavia's official dissolution in 1991, Yugoslavia's increased ties to the West and its associated influences in the fields of education, culture, and entertainment promoted increased use of the Latin script in both public and private use even in Serbia proper. According to a 2002 survey in Serbia, 39.8 percent of Serbs used only Latin script, 21.9 percent only Cyrillic script, and 31.3 percent used both depending on circumstances.[42] Whether facilitated more by the regime's official communication or the forces of globalization, increased use of the Latin script at all levels facilitated a considerable degree of cultural pluralism. Serbs, Croats, Bosnians, and Montenegrins by the 1980s could and often did read one another's literature and media and participated in cross-republic forms of popular culture on a regular basis.

Nonetheless, the same forces of nationalism that led some Croats to resist educating their children in Cyrillic appeared in Serbia in the 1980s when nationalists began to complain of linguistic discrimination against Serb minorities. The 1986 *Memorandum* declared that Serbs in Croatia were subject to a deliberate policy of assimilation within which language policy represented a critical tool as it deprived them of "the right to use their own language and script."[43] From that point onward, both Serbian and Croatian nationalist elements gave a prominent role to the significance of script as a defining element of their national identity. Once Franjo Tudjman was elected president of Croatia in May 1990, he actively promoted a move toward Croatian national independence in part by privileging the Croatian version of the language and the Latin script above Cyrillic in ways that, according to Misha Glenny, were both provocative and senseless.

> According to moderate Knin Serbs I met in 1990, only about five percent of the local Serbs used the Cyrillic script, the rest not only spoke the Croatian variant, they used the Latin script. Eighteen months later, on my return, I witnessed the extraordinary spectacle of a Knin Serb attempting to write the address of his relations in Belgrade in Cyrillic—he could not do it. Half-way through the address, he gave up and wrote it in Latin.[44]

At the same time in Belgrade, signs in the Latin script were being torn down and replaced with Cyrillic. Glenny also recalled the attack on a participant at a demonstration for united Yugoslavia whose poster was destroyed because he had written "Yugoslavia" in Latin rather than Cyrillic script.[45]

The choice of script on grave markers is a complex matter and again involves their ambiguous and multiple roles within the public and private spheres. Many, though certainly not all, Partisan cemeteries, ossuaries, and memorials are in the Latin script. In the years immediately following the war, the choice of script for a local memorial could be extremely emotionally fraught, particularly in those areas of Bosnia & Hercegovina and Croatia where many of the worst atrocities took place between Yugoslavia's ethnoreligious groups. For families seeking to commemorate those victims, it would be essential to inscribe their names in their own language and script. Yet, as early as 1960 the Veterans'

Association was thinking about how the choice of language could affect a cemetery's function as a public site for education and tourism. Accordingly, instructions from SUBNOR in Bosnia & Hercegovina to all district and communal associations informed them that while they could use either the Latin or Cyrillic script, "our opinion is that it is better to use Latin, because others can read it more easily as a world script."[46] That same year, a conflict over the use of script on a Partisan monument took place in the village of Žagrović, near Knin, Croatia, where the local Orthodox population had raised a monument inscribed in Cyrillic to thirty-four Partisans killed during the war. When the monument needed repairs, however, the local government insisted that the inscription be in Latin script as it was located in Croatia and near a highway of international significance.[47] Although the outcome to this conflict is unknown, it exemplifies the private and public nature of the memorials as well as the role that scripts played in both worlds.

While it is possible to trace language policy through constitutions and political activity, it is more difficult to determine private motivations in the choice of script on grave markers. The chosen script may simply be the one with which the user was most comfortable. Yet grave markers often communicate ethnoreligious identity and epitaphs are meant to be read by passers-by. The choice of script may then be directed at a particular audience of mourners.[48] The use of Latin and Cyrillic script on grave markers in the cemeteries I visited was broadly representative of the patterns described earlier: most (though not all) grave markers in Serbia are in Cyrillic, most (but not all) in Croatia are in Latin script, while those in Bosnia & Hercegovina vary depending on the ethnoreligious and political background of the grave's inhabitant. Moreover, among the graves in Serbian cemeteries that use the Latin script, a majority are either on graves with a non-Orthodox cross, suggesting a different ethnic background, or without any religious symbol, sometimes also including a Partisan star. These grave markers fit the pattern described earlier of individuals secularized and globalized under socialism who have voluntarily replaced Cyrillic with the more "modern" and Westernized Latin script. Indeed, one strong (though not fully consistent) correlating factor in the use of Latin script among Serbs is the lack of any religious symbol.

A far more complex group to analyze is those Serbs living in Croatia who chose to use the Latin rather than the Cyrillic script on grave markers. Lacking any distinction in script or type of cross and in large municipal cemeteries without clear sections among Christians, it can be nearly impossible to determine if a given grave belongs to a Serb, a Croat, or some other Christian ethnic group.

Cyrillic markers certainly exist among the three municipal cemeteries in Zagreb but are increasingly rare after the 1970s.

Although the use of Latin script is more common on Serbian grave markers in large cities of Croatia, it also appeared in villages as exemplified by the cemetery in the tiny Serbian village of Vrebac, located in the District of Ličko-Senj, 13 kilometers east of Gospić, Croatia. In 1971, Vrebac had a population of 448, of whom 440 were Serbs, 1 Croat, and 7 undetermined. Following the end of the war in 2001, nearly all of the population had fled, and the census now lists it as nineteen, providing no nationality. I visited the Vrebac cemetery in 2015 and found six different grave markers belonging to the Narančić family. Of the six markers, four are in Cyrillic and two in Latin. All four of the Cyrillic markers included Orthodox crosses, while the two in Latin script did not. It is impossible to find a pattern based on dates for not only do most of them include multiple dates of death, in one case ranging from 1943 to 1991 and in another from 1967 to 2010, but it is evident that all but one or two had been recently renovated. For example, with death dates of 1943 and 1960, one marker noted that it had been erected by the grandchildren of the deceased. It is also possible that the two without crosses (both in Latin script, one clearly using the Western version of the language) were Partisan families, a case made more plausible by the large Partisan monument in this small cemetery. But if so, the Partisan stars had been left off their graves in the renovation, and in any case, the names on the Partisan monument were all in Cyrillic. In short, lacking more detailed information, the grave markers themselves can only tell us that even within one family of a small village, use of script varied considerably, but not why (Figure 6.5; see also Figure 6.3).

Grave markers are above all memorials to the deceased and while the choice of script undoubtedly reflected linguistic changes occurring in society over time, those making the choice may or may not have noticed or cared about them. Yet in biscriptal and highly politicized environments, the semiotic value of scripts will take on deeper meaning. Thus, some Serbs who chose Cyrillic over Latin may have done so deliberately to accentuate their national identity and allegiance to Serbian heritage, religion, and culture. Similarly, the use of Latin script particularly by those whose grave markers also included a Partisan star may have indicated an ideological preference for Yugoslavia over Serbia and pluralism over nationalism, or the desire to avoid conflict and blend in with the majority culture. In as much as grave markers represent forms of private/public communication, they provide individuals and families an opportunity to express their views on current issues through symbols and in this case the choice of script.

Grave Markers 167

Figure 6.5 Use of script
Markers for a Serbian family: the grave on the top uses Serbian Cyrillic script while that on the bottom is in Latin and uses word for "family" typical for the Western variant of the language (Figure 6.3 is from the same family and is also in Cyrillic). Vrebac, Croatia

Mixed Marriages

Perhaps the most poignant reflection of the ongoing tension between private and public forms of mourning in Socialist Yugoslavia concerned the placement of markers for those in mixed marriages. As we have seen, grave markers in the region of the former Yugoslavia are likely to include more than one decedent. Individual graves and grave markers do exist; they are perhaps most common among Muslims who follow a general rule of one grave per person. But Muslim married couples may also be buried side by side and thus share a marker. Otherwise, family graves are very common. The ethnoreligious diversity of the region may be reflected therefore not only in separate cemeteries or sections of cemeteries but even on grave markers when individuals from different ethnoreligious backgrounds unite in marriage.

The sometimes traumatic results of marriages forbidden by society, whether due to race, religion, or politics, are as old as time and have frequently been recorded in literature, if not history. It is somewhat less common to consider, within those tragic consequences, where the unfortunate couple will be buried, but traditionally, they have separated in death as in life. One vivid example is described in Chapter 1 with the grave marker of a Protestant/Catholic pair from the nineteenth century buried in separate cemeteries divided by a wall who erected a marker with hands clasped across that wall as a symbol of their eternal love (see Figure 1.1).

The Communist regime in postwar Yugoslavia encouraged mixed marriages seeing it as one way to moderate and eventually eliminate ethnoreligious conflict. Indeed, considerable literature both in the United States and Yugoslavia has been very hopeful about the long-term beneficial effects on society of mixed marriages. Perhaps the most positive argument has come from American political scientists Robert Putnam and David E. Campbell whose 2010 book *American Grace* argues that interfaith marriage in the United States has created a substantial increase in religious tolerance over the past fifty years. Describing what they refer to as the Aunt Susan effect, Putnam and Campbell claim that two out of three Americans have at least one extended family member of another religion with the result that a majority of Americans have a beloved "Aunt Susan" whom they cannot bear to believe is going to hell on the basis of her religion. Thus, according to one survey, some 89 percent of Americans claimed to believe that heaven was not reserved just for those who shared their religious faith even though their clergy usually disagreed.[49]

In Yugoslavia, the proportion of mixed marriages was certainly much lower, but some disagreement persists over the precise numbers and their significance. Ruža Petrović claimed that the proportion had increased gradually from the 1950s to 1980 from between 7 and 8 percent of the population to 13 percent. While Nikolai Botev accepted the overall figure of 13 percent, he disagreed with her figures and argument that the proportion had increased with time. Moreover, he focused more on the enormous regional differences (e.g., 18.4 percent in Vojvodina and 4.7 percent in Kosovo in 1989), insisting that, in fact, Yugoslavia had never been fully integrated, so its dissolution was really no surprise. Nonetheless, Robert Hayden, also using Petrović's numbers, points out that between 1953 and 1981, heterogeneity had increased in all regions of Yugoslavia except Vojvodina and Kosovo. In those two regions, he attributes the lack of increase to differing birth rates—that is, an exceptionally low birth rate among Hungarians in Vojvodina and exceptionally high birth rate among Albanians in Kosovo.[50]

Moreover, when Duško Sekulić, Garth Massey, and Randy Hobson analyzed the various factors contributing to a sense of Yugoslav identity they found that intermarriage was by far the most significant, and that children of mixed marriages were eleven times more likely than all others to identify as Yugoslav.[51] In other words, regardless of how successful the regime was in its attempts to encourage mixed marriages, those efforts were likely among its most important activities toward the integration of society and were critical to its ideological agenda. And yet, when it failed to create integrated cemeteries, the regime abandoned at death the very citizens who had supported its efforts and potentially represented its new community.

Individuals from a mixed marriage seeking to be buried together faced not only possible condemnation from within their own ethnoreligious communities but also bureaucratic complications in the public sphere as they negotiated a mutually acceptable resting spot. Mixed marriages among those from Christian denominations were certainly far more common and easier to accommodate, at least in municipal cemeteries. In many cases, we cannot determine which grave markers might involve mixed marriages between Catholic, Protestant, and Orthodox inhabitants as they may all use the same form of cross and script or, if they were secular or atheist, no religious symbol at all. Even so, some couples deliberately placed differing cross designs and even used different scripts on the left and right sides of the marker to indicate, for example, a marriage between Orthodox Serb and Catholic Croat inhabitants (Figure 6.6). The lack of visible

Figure 6.6 Mixed marriages among Christians. Note the differing crosses and scripts Zenica, Bosnia & Hercegovina. For more photographs on this theme see: https://yugcemeteries.omeka.net/exhibits/show/mixed-marriages

indicator, particularly in the earlier decades, does not necessarily imply that both parties to the burial were equally satisfied with the burial placement or marker.

Mixed marriages between Muslims and Christians (religious or otherwise) are simpler to detect since Muslim names are more easily distinguished even when the grave markers fail to include religious symbolism.[52] In most cases, the marriage took place between a Christian woman and a Muslim man as the social consequences for a Muslim woman leaving her family and faith were so extreme.[53] Here too, at least one member of the marriage (sometimes both) was often a communist and the grave marker in such cases was a rectangular gray or black stone, more typical of Christian markers. During the Communist era, religious symbols were rare for either spouse but if they existed were only for the still religious wife, and the marker often included a Partisan star as well for the husband.

The problem of placement for mixed marriages was particularly thorny in Bosnia & Hercegovina where many cemeteries remained confessional well into the 1980s, and even the municipal cemeteries were divided into multiple religious sections and an Atheist section. Those in mixed marriages were thus forced to choose between being buried separately in confessional cemeteries or sections, together in one of the religious sections of a municipal cemetery, or together in the Atheist section. Their children, though of mixed ethnic and/or religious heritage, also had to choose between burial in a specific ethnoreligious or Atheist location. As long as all those involved were and remained atheist, the choice was perhaps less difficult, but Yugoslavia's families (like those everywhere) were often complex. A husband might be atheist while the wife was devoutly religious; or both were communist atheists, but the parents remained pious and the family wished to be buried near one another; or the parents had been Communists but one or more of their children returned to religion, while rejecting its ethnic characterization.

Complexities of this kind could be more difficult to discern during the socialist era but were vividly revealed after the fall of communism when many markers increasingly included religious symbols for both the husband and wife. One striking marker was in Prašnica Municipal Cemetery of Zenica, which included a Muslim crescent moon and star on the husband's side and a Christian cross on the wife's, with the words: "We believe in God's Will." This marker, along with others like it displaying the religious faith and diversity of a united couple, was placed in the Atheist section of the cemetery. Integration remained out of reach (Figure 6.7).

Even so, over centuries and despite outbreaks of violence the peoples of the Balkans have often lived in peace and adapted their cultures in ways that allow them to share common space and resources. Despite their relatively small number, the determination of those in mixed marriages to communicate their love and choice on their grave marker represents a sign of hope for tolerance and integration. Through their grave markers, these individuals can be seen to be making a plea for a broader and more inclusive community of the dead, despite multiple public barriers placed before them. Another way that the burial practices of the Balkan peoples reveal their potential for cultural acceptance can be seen in the evolving styles of Muslim grave markers.

Muslim Grave Markers and Cultural Adaptation

Through centuries of migrations and cohabitation in the same geographic region, the peoples of the Balkan Peninsula have adopted many cultural practices from one another. Cultural similarities between them are evident in food, clothing, and life cycle rituals, including those related to burial. Even when clear differences

Figure 6.7 Mixed marriages: Muslims and Christians
The one on the top is Orthodox/Muslim, the one on the bottom is Christian/Muslim located in the "Atheist" section. Its epitaph reads, "We Believe in God's Will." Zenica, Bosnia & Hercegovina

existed, as between Muslims and Christians, there has been a tendency toward acculturation, though not assimilation, over time. Amila Buturović describes the many connections between Christian and Muslim burial cultures especially in the early Ottoman period, including the use of integrated cemeteries.[54] During the communist period, the tendency toward adaptation was most evident from the 1960s through the 1980s. The type of adaptation differed, however, depending on the Muslims' relative position in society and their form of cemetery.

Muslim grave markers in the Balkans are traditionally white obelisks with little external decoration or often even any religious symbolism. By far the most common adaption of Muslim gravestones to their neighbor's culture was in the use of photographs or other images on headstones. Theoretically, one would not expect to see photographs on Muslim grave markers given Islam's aniconistic policies. Nonetheless, beginning in the 1960s and increasing steadily thereafter, some Muslim grave markers began to include photographs of the deceased. Most often the photographs were on grave markers that showed other signs of acculturation, but a few traditional Ottoman post/pillar grave markers also bear photographs (Figure 6.8).[55]

Another version of adaptation was simply to accept the gray or black granite rectangular headstone (without a footstone) traditionally used by their Christian neighbors. It is not unreasonable to assume that some of those who adapted these elements of Christian burial culture had been secularized within the socialist state. Such individuals may have made a conscious choice to reject Islamic religious and cultural attributes and adopt those associated with the "modern" West. Yet, in other cases, the granite rectangular marker is adorned with an Islamic crescent moon and star and/or a short Qur'anic verse indicating the compatibility between modernity and Islam (Figure 6.9).

Finally, many Muslim grave markers should be described as hybrids, displaying elements of both traditional and modern design. For example, one frequent adaptation was to retain the white stone and elements of the traditional marker, such as one or more pillars, but then significantly rework it into different shapes. Some placed a white rectangular grave marker between the pillars, often bearing a photograph of the deceased. Others created entirely unique shapes based on floral images out of the white stone, either retaining the pillars as one element of the design or eliminating them altogether. While some of these redesigned grave markers are entirely secular, others include Islamic religious symbols (Figure 6.10; see also Figure 6.4).

Grave markers revealing elements of adaptation exist in all regions under examination but are least common in Novi Pazar and rural regions of Bosnia &

Figure 6.8 Traditional Muslim grave marker with photograph Sarajevo, Bosnia & Hercegovina. For more photographs on this theme see: https://yugcemeteries.omeka.net/exhibits/show/muslim-grave-markers

Hercegovina and most common in the large cities of Croatia, Serbia, and Bosnia & Hercegovina. Leor Halevi has argued that early Islamic funerary law was "partly 'adaptive' and partly 'reactive'" as it simultaneously opposed many existing practices and "worked to accommodate local customs."[56] While the context in Socialist Yugoslavia was obviously very different, I have adopted some of his concept and language to argue that in their private commemorative practices, Muslims in Bosnia & Hercegovina, Croatia, and Serbia were partly persistent and partly adaptive in their relations with non-Islamic religions and a new ideology. Rural Muslims and those who made up a large majority of the population (like the Bosnian Muslims and those in Novi Pazar) were those most likely to retain traditional designs in grave markers. In contrast, Muslims in urban centers and/ or who represented a small minority within larger non-Muslim populations (like those in Zagreb and Belgrade) were more likely to adapt to local circumstances by embracing nontraditional styles of grave markers.

Yet while Muslims made up the majority of the population in Kosovo, their municipal cemeteries undoubtedly contained the largest quantity of markers in strictly nontraditional shapes, many with no religious indicator whatsoever, and

Figure 6.9 Nontraditional Muslim grave markers with Islamic symbols Zagreb, Croatia and Travnik, Bosnia & Hercegovina

176 *Death and Burial in Socialist Yugoslavia*

Figure 6.10 Cultural adaptations on Muslim grave markers
Sarajevo, Bosnia & Hercegovina and Zagreb, Croatia

usually including a photograph of the deceased. This anomaly requires some explanation. Religion was never a dominant factor in the development of Albanian nationalism, and in Albania proper, Catholics and Orthodox together make up nearly 17 percent of the population. Moreover, Kosovar's Muslim Albanians had been successfully secularized by the socialist regime.[57] Accordingly, most grave markers in larger cities lost their Ottoman characteristics very early on and include no religious elements. Only in a few religious regions did the Ottoman post pillar markers persist into the 1970s.

The intent behind creating adaptive and hybrid grave markers was likely very different in these different locations. Muslims represented only small minorities of the population in Serbia and Croatia and were usually buried in separate sections of a municipal cemetery. Despite having their own sections, these Muslims could not reasonably consider the cemetery their own community of the dead. They knew that it represented instead the community of either Serbs or Croats within which Muslims were a minority. While that community might not be openly hostile to them and their religion, it also was not always entirely friendly—nor was the political community of the Communist regime, which, though guaranteeing freedom of religion, promoted atheism.

Lacking substantial oral histories, we cannot know how individual Muslim families living as minorities in Croatian or Serbian cities negotiated this relationship in the context of their burial culture or if they gave it any thought at all. Although grave markers are public monuments designed to be seen by an audience, we do not know how broad an audience the family imagined or how deeply that affected their choices. The secular and Westernized design of some Muslim markers may have been a personal cultural choice or reflected their acceptance of values promoted by the Communist regime. In other cases, however, the markers may have represented an attempt by Muslims to engage in what James Scott has called the "public transcript ... the open interaction between subordinates and those who dominate."[58] By conforming to the burial rituals and traditions of the dominant group, they may have sought to reassure neighbors and the regime that they were neither "backward" nor "outsiders" but "just like them." Whatever the intent, the difference between a traditional religious, modern secular, or hybrid grave marker for Muslim families in such cities had the potential to send a message that went well beyond the private commemoration of the deceased. Deliberate or not, the use of traditional religious forms might indicate a determination to remain outside the majority community (and the political system), whereas in contrast, the adoption of local customs and secularism could be read as a sign of integration and a desire to belong.

The hybridized grave markers evident in urban cemeteries throughout all three republics could have comparable impact but with more emphasis on synthesis than assimilation. Such markers were especially common in Bosnia & Hercegovina where the cemeteries were multiethnic and religious but had strictly segregated marked sections. In that case, Muslims who chose to retain their traditional values could do so with more confidence as they constituted, if not a majority, at least a plurality of the republic's citizenry. Yet, they were also in a stronger position to create a truly multicultural community, retaining aspects of their own culture if they chose and adopting any elements from Christian burial culture that suited them. Markers based on recognizable Ottoman traditions, while also including photographs and other Western motifs, resulted in syncretic gravestones that seemed to truly amalgamate diverse cultures. Meanwhile, fully secular and atheist Muslims (by nationality) could be buried in the Atheist section with or without the five-pointed star on their grave marker.

Finally, Muslim Albanians were a majority in AP Kosovo, but there too all cemeteries were separate or sectioned according to religion. According to Ger Duizings, Kosovar cities themselves were also largely segregated with quarters for each group and Orthodox Serbs living in downtown regions, while the Albanians populated most of the suburbs.[59] In that sense, most Kosovar cemeteries really were communities of the dead as only those of the same religious heritage were buried in and visited them. Muslim grave markers in Kosovo then were speaking to the community of Kosovar Muslim Albanians, not to the Serbs or Catholics who were buried in separate sections or even cemeteries. It is unlikely, therefore, that the secularism of Kosovar Muslim Albanian grave markers was intended as a message, though it may have been read as such by some pious Muslim Albanians. Only in the late 1980s and 1990s when the form, symbols, and inscriptions on their graves became overtly political can we presume that they were clearly intended to send a message.

Once again, it is difficult to accurately interpret what meanings Muslims throughout the former Yugoslavia attributed to their adaptive grave markers. Some may have felt pressure to adopt the cultural norms of the ethnoreligious majority. In other cases, however, the process of adaptation likely occurred more organically as individuals from different ethnoreligious groups interacted on a daily basis in school, at work, and in shared neighborhoods. Like countless citizens of all religions had done before them, they eschewed isolation (whether consciously or not) and broke the boundaries of their own burial culture to communicate more effectively or meaningfully with others. In all cases, while these were first and foremost private memorials, grave markers could also serve as powerful forms of communication to those both in and outside one's own ethnoreligious community. Although the cultural adaptions seen on some grave markers showed promise for greater integration, the Communist regime's policies of politicizing war dead and grave markers worked in the opposite direction.

Politicization of War Dead and Grave Markers

The secularization of states in Western Europe has been widely associated with nationalism and a modern political system.[60] The same cannot be said, however, about the secularization of cemeteries during the eighteenth to nineteenth centuries—that is, as cemeteries were secularized, they did not also become explicitly French, British, English, or German cemeteries. On the contrary, one important purpose of secularization was to promote pluralism within the cemetery on both religious and ethnic bases. Nor were cemeteries and grave markers in most of these countries overtly politicized. The closest form of cemetery politicization is usually found in military cemeteries. Indeed, as we have seen, the Communist regime's politicization of the dead in Yugoslavia began immediately following the Second World War when it made carefully crafted decisions about which victims deserved official commemoration in Partisan cemeteries.

Yet political forms of commemoration went beyond those public cemeteries and memorials, appearing also on individual grave markers. While religious symbols are normally placed on grave markers, it is far less common to see indicators of the deceased's political affiliation. There have been exceptions: a family's coat of arms was frequently included on the gravestone in many regions, the Freemasons have been known to etch their insignia on grave markers, and national heralds or those from a military regiment are sometimes displayed on the markers of fallen soldiers.[61] Some photographs from the early 1940s also show Nazi military cemeteries with swastikas on grave markers.[62] With the creation of the Soviet Union, however, it became common for the symbol of the Communist party, first the hammer and sickle and then more commonly the red five-pointed star, to be placed on the grave marker of its devout followers. The Soviets also created specific sections within cemeteries for its heroes, like "Communist Square" inside Moscow's Alexander Nevsky Monastery Cemetery whose markers were all adorned with Red Stars.⁶³ In Yugoslavia, the five-pointed star was introduced onto the caps of the Partisan military units as early as September 1941 shortly after Germany's invasion of the Soviet Union that year. Though always referred to as the "Partisan Star," it never lost its connection to Communism.⁶⁴

As we have seen, SUBNOR aspired to have the remains of all soldiers killed in the People's Liberation Struggle transferred into organized Partisan cemeteries or sections of cemeteries in the years and decades after the war. In fact, however, many families had already moved their relatives' bodies to local confessional or municipal cemeteries. In such cases, SUBNOR activists did not require their transfer but did urge that, regardless of location, all Partisans' graves be marked in the same way, with red five-pointed stars.

> In connection with the graves of fallen soldiers located in confessional cemeteries it is necessary to discuss the issue with the families or closest relatives of the fallen soldiers to determine if the remains can be moved to a new cemetery for soldiers. ... It would be desirable for the remains of the fallen soldiers to be in the newly constructed cemetery. However, if they do not agree, there is no need to make an issue out of it. Inasmuch as the remains of individual fallen soldiers remain in the confessional cemetery then it is necessary to arrange their graves in a similar way as the graves of the fallen soldiers in the newly constructed cemetery. It would be necessary to pay particular attention that the grave marker and inscriptions be the same.⁶⁵

SUBNOR also felt strongly that any soldiers buried in local cemeteries be in a separate location and not indiscriminately mixed in with ordinary civilians. Ideally, a separate section of the cemetery should be created for such soldiers, but even isolated graves should not be intermingled with the others as it reduced their educational effect. In many cases, those graves marked with partisan stars were indeed separated from the others buried in local confessional cemeteries but not necessarily for educational purposes. Rather, it often seemed that they had been deliberately placed at the farthest edge of the cemetery by the back wall because the religious administrators of the cemetery wished, but didn't quite dare, to refuse them burial altogether.

In any case, Yugoslavia's newly created Partisan cemeteries were open only to those soldiers who actually died during the war while those who survived to die later were buried in local civilian cemeteries. Their graves were also obligatorily marked with the Partisan star and/or hammer and sickle. Deceased members of the Communist party also placed the five-pointed star on their grave markers and eventually it seemed that the star could be placed on the grave of almost any citizen seeking to declare loyalty to the regime or whose family wished to do so in their name. For example, the graves of several children under the age of ten who died well after the war displayed the Partisan star, though it is difficult to imagine that they themselves were committed Communists (Figures 6.11 and 6.12).

At the same time, it was clear that alternative political symbols would not be tolerated in cemeteries just as they were not allowed in any part of the public sphere. Communists had the unique right and even duty to include a symbol of their political affiliation on their gravestones and memorials. In contrast, those who had fought for the wrong side during the war or who continued to oppose the regime had to remain invisible. Although their deaths might be privately mourned, any public recognition was intolerable and could lead to political consequences. Max Bergholz has described several such cases including one in Montenegro where veterans expressed outrage over the "public transfer of remains of obvious enemies of the people, the display of their photographs, and a gathering around them of what were ostensibly their closest relatives, which cannot be interpreted in any other way than a misunderstanding of our socialist reality." The Veterans' Association thus urged the local People's Council to take legal action to "forbid such clearly public manifestations much more than they have so far."[66]

The introduction of communist symbols and rejection of anti-communists marked cemeteries as public spaces that had also been taken over by the Communist regime. As a result, by the time communism and Yugoslavia fell, cemeteries had come to be seen as politicized arenas and fair ground in the approaching battle. Accordingly, they could be utilized as an area for performing ethnic violence on the dead, with devastating results for their living relatives.

Conclusion

Grave markers are a rich source of material culture that offer insights into changing social, economic, and political developments. The stories they tell are simultaneously private and public and create a complex narrative that enriches our understanding of the past. The multiple ethnoreligious cemeteries and/or sections of cemeteries within the republics of Croatia, Serbia, and Bosnia & Hercegovina are especially revealing. While every grave marker remains above all a testament to private grief, changes in the design and content of

Figure 6.11 Partisan grave markers
Belgrade, Serbia and Gjakova, Kosova. For more photographs on this theme see: https://yugcemeteries.omeka.net/exhibits/show/political-and-national-symbols

Figure 6.12 Partisan grave markers for children
Zenica, Bosnia & Hercegovina and Kačarevo, Serbia

those markers, though sometimes difficult to interpret, tell us a great deal about evolving relationships among and between ethnoreligious groups and their relationship with the socialist state. Changes in the use of script, evidence of mixed marriages, and the multiple styles adopted by the Muslim communities point to rich cultural interactions among ethnoreligious groups in the former Yugoslavia. At the same time, however, the one-sided imposition of communist symbolism within the cemetery created a new and destructive dynamic.

7

Ethnic Conflict and Politicization of the Dead

Yugoslavia's collapse into violence and war throughout the 1990s was accompanied by grave and cemetery desecrations that received local and international attention at levels rarely witnessed.[1] But in fact such desecrations were not unknown in Yugoslavia and had been increasing in certain regions prior to the wars of dissolution. Their escalation in the 1980s might be seen as a canary in the coal mine, suggesting that when communities of the dead are at war, those of the living should also be on guard. By the time Yugoslavia disintegrated, the politically regulated and ethnoreligiously segregated cemeteries had begun to serve as another performative site in the developing ethnic conflict.

As we have seen, nearly every aspect of burial culture—from cemetery structure to the funeral ceremony and symbols on grave markers—could be and often was politicized in Socialist Yugoslavia. Although the regime was willing to allow each religious community considerable leeway to provide funeral rituals and bury their dead according to religious traditions, it was implacably hostile toward any individual, organization, or ethnoreligious community that threatened its political hegemony. Religious leaders and activists critical of the Communist regime or who had openly promoted alternative political systems were frequently harassed, fined, and removed from their positions or even arrested and imprisoned. In the last years of Yugoslavia's existence, however, politicization of the dead moved from an activity of the Socialist regime to one instigated by its ethnoreligious opponents. This transition was manifested in three specific areas: the politicization of mass graves, political symbols on grave markers, and grave and cemetery desecrations.

We have already discussed how the Communist Party of Yugoslavia politicized dead bodies immediately following the Second World War and grave markers in the years to follow. The rise of nationalism in the 1980s led to the repoliticization of victims in mass graves from the Second World War and then, beginning in the 1990s, also those from the wars of Yugoslav dissolution but now from an entirely different perspective. Beginning in the late 1980s, hundreds and thousands of bodies from mass graves were exhumed and reburied in large public ceremonies with overtly political goals. The mass graves themselves became sites of pilgrimage, not only for families of the victims but also for nationalists stirring up public emotion and for political candidates seeking office. The fall of communism and the wars of Yugoslav dissolution also dramatically increased the number and changed the type of political symbols on grave markers in cemeteries. Whereas previously only communists could indicate any political affiliation on their grave markers, beginning in the mid- to late 1980s, but especially after the mid-1990s, nationalist symbols of varying types frequently appeared above graves among most ethnoreligious groups in the region. Simultaneously, many citizens began to renovate decedents' grave markers, often omitting previously displayed Partisan stars. Finally, grave and cemetery desecrations committed in the years just before, during, and after the wars of Yugoslav dissolution, whether for purposes of looting, vandalism, or as hate crimes, became increasingly common, or at least widely publicized, and reflected the ultimate failure of the Communist regime not only to create new communities of the dead but even to maintain civility among the old ones.

Mass Graves

Following the collapse of communism and outbreak of war in Yugoslavia, scholars analyzed the conflict and Yugoslavia's dissolution from multiple perspectives. Explanations for the break up and violence have ranged from primordial ethnic hatred to elite manipulation of the populace and many more nuanced theories that help bridge the gap between them by focusing on economics, media, gender, national security, and fear.[2] A particularly relevant element for this work that emerged in many of these arguments concerned the deliberate decision taken by some Serbs beginning in the late 1980s to employ a "narrative of bones and graves" to ethnicize the dead.[3] Ethnicizing the dead creates historical martyrs, appropriating and recasting the lives of individuals who may or may not have embraced the political orientations of those who employ their legacies. That decision and the rhetoric that followed reopened barely healed wounds from the Second World War, reminding Yugoslavia's citizens not only of the atrocities that had occurred but also how the regime had previously politicized their deaths through its decisions regarding which victims were worthy of commemoration and which were to be forgotten.

An early iteration of the "bones and graves" approach occurred in the 1960s with the memorialization by the Serbian Orthodox Church of one of its most important historical figures: fourteenth-century Serbian tsar Stefan Dušan. In May of 1968, the Serbian Republic's Commission for Religious Questions (CRQ) noted with dismay that the Serbian Orthodox Church had recently reported in its religious journal, *Pravoslavlje*, the relocation of Dušan's bones from a Belgrade museum to St. Mark's Church.[4] Apparently, the bones had been found in Prizren, Kosovo/Kosova, in 1926 by Professor Radoslav Grujić who had put them in an ordinary box and kept them with his books in his library in Skopje. After his death, the bones were found among his books and probably then taken first to the Skopje Museum and then in 1941 to Belgrade where they were placed in a museum of the Serbian Orthodox Church. In 1968, based on the decision of the Patriarch, they were to be buried in the Church of the Apostle and Evangelist St. Mark in Belgrade. According to *Pravoslavlje*, they would be placed on a recently built marble podium in a beautifully worked metal sarcophagus providing the first opportunity for Orthodox believers to see the relics of the Father of the Serbian church. The Church elaborated the program for May 19, 1968, with a holy liturgy and funeral service in memory of Tsar Dušan.

While agreeing that Dušan's bones likely should have been moved long ago, members of the CRQ were concerned by the staging of this event at a time of rising Albanian discontent in Kosovo, presuming that "the transfer of the bones in this way represents some kind of demonstration and certainly a call for the gathering of Serbs and so on." The likely goal, they concluded, was to present the leadership of the Orthodox church "as 'defenders' of Serbian history and Serbdom. Since the Church of St. Mark's is the most widely known and famous site in Belgrade, placing the sarcophagus of Tsar Dušan in such a location is sure to remind believers of Dušan's Empire and thus awaken Greater Serbian feelings." Ultimately, however, the committee concluded that the Orthodox Church had outplayed them and there was nothing they could do other than reprimand the Patriarch for taking such action without consulting members of the government in advance.[5] On May 19, 1968, the relics were indeed carried down the streets of Belgrade to St. Mark's where the Patriarch's statement appeared to support CRQ fears: "Now the people see their holy Tsar, who was a defender of our Orthodox Serbian faith and our national identity."[6]

By the mid-1980s, Serbian nationalist politics had begun its rapid rise. During these years, the Serbian Orthodox Church focused primarily on what it saw as the existential threat facing the Serbian population first in Kosovo but also in Croatia and Bosnia & Hercegovina. The most important and famous expression of Serbian nationalism at that time was the publication of the *Memorandum of the Serbian Academy of Arts and Sciences* in September 1986. The report outlined what it considered to be systemic economic and political discrimination against the Serbian nation that had reached catastrophic proportions in some regions. Claiming that the "physical, political, legal, and cultural genocide of the Serbian population of Kosovo and Metohija represents the most difficult defeat in the liberation struggles that Serbia has waged from 1804 to 1941," it concluded, "Except for the period of the NDH, Serbs in Croatia have never in the past been as threatened as they are today."[7]

Although the *Memorandum* considered Communist subservience to Slovene and Croat interests responsible for Serbia's endangered status, Slobodan Milošević skillfully manipulated the power of nationalism to eliminate his rivals and take control of the League of Communists of Serbia. His April 1987 speech at the site of the famous Battle of Kosovo Polje initiated the drive to restore Serbian control over its autonomous provinces of Kosovo and Vojvodina relying on the emotional power of Serbian history and traditions. Milošević continued to promote Serbian interests with his official support for the 1989 tour of King Lazar's relics commemorating the 600th anniversary of his death at the Battle of Kosovo Polje throughout all lands claimed by some nationalists as belonging to Serbia.

Growing Serbian nationalism also intersected with the politicization of dead bodies in the *Golubnjača* case. In 1980, Serbian intellectual Jovan Radulović published a collection of short stories, *Golubnjača* [The Dove Hole], that focused on interethnic relations in a small town after a group of children discovered a limestone pit where Croat Ustashe had murdered and disposed of their Serbian neighbors during the Second World War. The following year, the stories were presented in theatrical form both in Belgrade and Novi Sad but were quickly withdrawn after official criticism "citing its 'nationalist tone.'"[8] Although the event was not then publicized, the play and more importantly its banning, as an "incitement to ethnic hatred," marked an early round in the nationalist politics that would characterize the latter part of the decade.[9] By the late 1980s, the *Golubnjača* case was revived and fully publicized by the Serbian Writer's Association, which defended the play and condemned its censorship as evidence that the Communist regime was indifferent to or perhaps even supported a possible renewal of Serbian martyrdom. These examples indicate the continued ambivalence of Serbian nationalists and particularly the Serbian Orthodox Church toward Slobodan Milošević. Despite his willingness to support the grievances of Serbs in Kosovo and Croatia, as a communist he remained highly suspect.[10]

Both the Serbian Orthodox and Catholic Churches engaged in the processes of resurrecting and ethnicizing the wartime dead. In 1990, the Council of the Serbian Orthodox Church demanded that the Socialist government find, exhume, and properly bury the remains of all the Second World War dead still located in caves across Yugoslavia. Over the course of that year, news reports flooded in from Bosnia & Hercegovina and Croatia about the exhumation of bones and their reburial with elaborate masses, often providing detailed descriptions of their brutal murders and warnings about the revival of Ustashe ideology in Croatia.[11] As Michael Sells put it, the remains of Serb victims from the Second World War were disinterred among claims that Croats and Muslims were "genocidal by nature."[12]

Similar exhumations, reburials, and masses by the Catholic Church took place during the late 1980s and into the 1990s in Croatia, but in this case, while the victims were certainly described as ethnic Croats, the perpetrator was simply the Communist regime. The most famous case concerned those who died near Bleiburg, an Austrian town on the border of Croatia. At the end of the Second World War, some seventy to eighty thousand troops of the collaborationist NDH (Independent State of Croatia) surrendered at Bleiburg to the British. The British turned them over to the Partisans who summarily executed them. While no bodies are actually located at Bleiburg, it has been an unofficial gathering site for relatives of those killed and for supporters of the NDH for decades and, since the early 1990s, with the official support of the Croatian state and Catholic Church. It has also become a site of historical revisionism, which not only and reasonably critiques the previous Communist version of events but "has also been used as a platform to rehabilitate the Ustasha regime and NDH."[13] Michaela Schauble, for example, described the politicized speech of the former Franciscan provincial minister at a 2005 Catholic "Mass for the Victims of the Communist Regime" near Sinj on the border of Hercegovina where an unknown number of locals had been killed by Partisans during the Second World War. The minister's speech itemized the long list of injustices that the Croatian nation had suffered as a small nation, concluding that "the worst tragedy of all was the communist regime."[14]

Similar exhumations, reburials, and religious services were held for those of multiple ethnoreligious groups killed in the wars of Yugoslav dissolution. Among them, of course, were the more than 8,000 Bosnian Muslim men and boys slaughtered at Srebrenica between July 11 and 13, 1995, by Serbian forces who then buried and often reburied their remains several times in multiple mass graves in the surrounding regions. Within the first decade following the end of the war, survivors and the state had discovered forty-two mass graves. In 2003, the Srebrenica Genocide Memorial opened at Potočari, just outside Srebrenica, with the burial of the first 600 victims. Since then, people from throughout Bosnia & Hercegovina and the world gather in Srebrenica each year to commemorate the reburial of those victims of the massacre recovered in the past year. As of July 2023, 6,752 victims had been laid to rest at Potočari.

Postwar exhumations, reburials, and memorials like those provided by the German War Graves Commission after the Second World War and the Orthodox, Catholic, and Muslim religious communities in Yugoslavia serve multiple constituencies and cross the boundaries between private and public forms of mourning. As long as they remain hidden, mass graves entirely suppress both individual/private and public forms of mourning. Once discovered, however, they offer not only rich opportunities for communal and state commemoration but also a chance for the families to find comfort. Dr. Craig Evan Pollack addressed this issue in his interviews with Srebrenica survivors regarding the purpose and goal of the Genocide Memorial Center. The survivors who were not members of advocacy groups described the reburials as necessary so that they could visit, pray, and clean the graves. They just wanted to know where their loved ones were buried and be able to provide grave markers for them. Their goals were almost entirely private and only a very few spoke in terms of the Memorial's political significance. In contrast, those who were members of advocacy groups appeared unconcerned with questions of mourning and focused instead on reburial as a means of confronting the past. For some this meant that the Serbs must be forced to face their crimes while for others it was more about collective healing and allowing Muslims a way to return to their homes in Srebrenica.[15]

On a private level, for family members, friends, and neighbors of the victims, the reburials and rituals provide comfort for their loss and a place to mourn their loved ones, but the rituals may also be healing for communities. Both Michaela Schauble and Jelena Djureinović described the solace found by families of the deceased in the highly ritualized and politicized official masses and commemorations for recently exhumed dead from the Second World War. According to Schauble, the Mass she attended near Sinj in 2005 seemed to allow "for the release and revitalization of strong emotions related to painful personal memories, as people not only lit candles and strew flowers in the crevice but stayed behind long after the ceremony had ended to pray and mourn in silence."[16] These private expressions of grief were nested within the broader commemorations, which had usually been initiated and carried out by nonstate groups and individuals such as the relatives of the victims and leaders of anti-Communist political parties and religious communities but were often supported by official state entities.[17] But while the commemorations may have offered comfort to many, they also reopened old wounds and renewed or even created new forms of ethnic conflict, especially when they served implicit or explicit political purposes. As we have seen previously, grave markers were a more immediate form of private commemoration, even as they also communicated information to the broader public. As Yugoslavia disintegrated into ethnic violence, the messages on those grave markers became more explicitly political.

Politicized Grave Markers, 1991 to 1999

The decline of communism in the late 1980s and early 1990s led to the appearance on grave markers of new symbols indicating a resurgence of nationalist sentiments. These symbols had a variety of origins from religion to state flags and heralds, but up to this point their public display had been harshly suppressed as an incitement to racial, religious, or ethnic hatred. Their gradual appearance now signified not just the growth of national ideologies but also separatism. Perhaps unsurprisingly, the first nationalist symbols appeared in Muslim cemeteries of Kosovo where as early as 1986 and increasingly during the late 1980s, grave markers in municipal but entirely Muslim Kosovar cemeteries began to bear the symbol of the black double-headed eagle that has been associated with the Albanian nation since the fifteenth century.[18] As noted previously, both cemeteries and ethnoreligious communities in Kosovo were so strictly segregated that their appearance there was unlikely to be noticed by Serbian authorities. As the conflict between Serbia and Kosovo increased, so too did the frequency of such symbols on Albanian graves. By the late 1990s, during the war some also began to include etchings of a map of Kosovo separate from Serbia, and others yet, a map of Kosovo united with Albania, promoting a Greater Albania. By the 2000s, such nationalist symbols on Albanian grave markers were widespread throughout the region. Not surprisingly, many of these graves belonged to deceased soldiers and one also frequently found on them life-size etchings of fully armed soldiers in camouflage (Figures 7.1 and 7.2).

Similar nationalist symbols on graves in Croatia, Bosnia & Hercegovina, and Serbia also developed during the wars of Yugoslav dissolution. As in Kosovo, they appeared most commonly (though not exclusively) on the grave markers of soldiers. Such symbols began to appear on the grave markers of Croatian nationals in both Croatia and Bosnia & Hercegovina immediately after Croatia's

192   *Death and Burial in Socialist Yugoslavia*

Figure 7.1 Grave markers with Albanian national symbols
Prishtinë, Kosova For more photographs on this theme see: https://yugcemeteries.omeka.net/exhibits/show/political-and-national-symbols

Figure 7.2 Kosovar soldier's grave marker
Gjilan, Kosova

declaration of independence in 1991. One common symbol was the braided cross associated with the early medieval Kingdom of Croatia, while another was Croatia's checkerboard flag (šahovnica), which is prominently featured on its current state herald. Some Croatian nationals were also quick to replace old family grave markers with new ones often bearing these new symbols. Thus, many Croatian cemeteries have a very high proportion of shiny new gravestones with dates on them from the 1960s or even older but with braided crosses and/or šahovnicas in a posthumous reclamation of Croatian national identity (Figure 7.3).

Official symbols are a standard part of any military grave marker provided by the state. The Republic of Bosnia & Hercegovina was alone, however, in providing a standardized grave marker for those soldiers who died defending its state in the wars of Yugoslav dissolution. In cooperation with the Society of Veterans and the Muslim Religious Organization, it designed a marker that was the same for all regardless of class and rank but in contrast to the British in the First World War and, of course, the Partisans, did not seek to eliminate religious distinctions.[19] By 1997, all Muslim soldiers who died defending the Republic of Bosnia & Hercegovina (certainly the majority) were offered a gravestone in the traditional Ottoman Islamic style, consisting of a white obelisk headstone and footstone, inscribed with their name, date of birth and death, a Qur'anic verse in Bosnian and Arabic, and the fleur-de-lis.[20] The verse in Bosnian is from Surah Al-Baqarah 2:154, which has been translated as: "Do not say that those who are killed in God's cause are dead: they are alive, though you do not realize it."[21] The symbol of the fleur-de-lis was taken from the Coat of Arms of King Tvrtko I who ruled Bosnia from 1377 to 1463 and became a key element of the Bosnian flag from 1992 to 1998.[22] Accordingly, many grave markers in the Bosnian-Croat Federation dating from the war, whether those of soldiers or not, carry images of the fleur-de-lis; some graves were even designed in its image. In 1998, the herald was changed to a blue and gold shield bearing a row of diagonal white stars. Subsequently some soldiers' graves included that image, though others continued to display the fleur-de-lis (Figure 7.4; see also Figure 6.10).

Although the Serbian Republic of Yugoslavia was officially involved in the war in Croatia only until December 1991 and never in Bosnia & Hercegovina, many Serbs from all three Yugoslav republics fought and died in both wars for their national cause. Nonetheless, very few graves of Serbian soldiers or civilians, whether in Serbia, Croatia, or Bosnia & Hercegovina, bear any explicitly nationalist symbol. I had expected to find frequent images of the herald of the Serbian monarchy—the double-headed white eagle that also includes the

Ethnic Conflict and Politicization of the Dead 195

Figure 7.3 Grave markers with Croatian national symbols
Žepce Bistrica, Bosnia & Hercegovina and Zagreb, Croatia

Figure 7.4 Military markers in Bosnia & Hercegovina
Travnik and Sarajevo, Bosnia & Hercegovina

Serbian cross, or "ocilo," comprising four "c"s held within each section of the cross. In Serbian Cyrillic, the c's (the equivalent of Latin s's) stand for the famous nationalist slogan: *Samo Sloga Serbina Spasava*, meaning "Only the Unity of Serbs can Save Us." While the herald, and especially the ocilo, was widespread in Serbian nationalist propaganda throughout the 1980s and 1990s, they only rarely appeared on grave markers, even those of soldiers. Almost the only exceptions occurred in the municipal cemetery of the tiny Serbian village of Borovo Selo, Croatia, where the grave markers of several Serbian soldiers killed at the outbreak of war in the summer and early fall of 1991 bore etchings of the Serbian Cross and the inscription, "He perished for the freedom of the Serbian people" (*Poginuo za Slobodu Srpskog Naroda*). As an exception to the rule, Borovo Selo is perhaps unsurprising. Located just outside of Vukovar, Borovo Selo was the locus of one of the earliest outbreaks of violence in Croatia. It was also well known as a stronghold of Vojislav Šešelj's Chetnik organization.[23] I also found the ocilo on a Serbian civilian grave in the village of Bostan in Kosova and the herald on one elaborate soldier's grave in Banja Luka, capital of the Bosnian Serb Republic, and on the graves of two famous paramilitary soldiers in Serbia—the first was on the infamous paramilitary leader Arkan's grave in Novo Groblje and the other was on the grave of what was said to be the first Serbian soldier to die at Srebrenica, buried in Arandjelovac. Even so, these were exceptions rather than the rule (Figure 7.5).

It is somewhat difficult to interpret the lack of national imagery on Serbian grave markers. It is possible that because Serbian national ideology is so clearly associated with Orthodoxy, the fact that nearly all Serbian grave markers already include an Orthodox knobbed cross provides sufficient national designation. A more common explanation, however, is that for Serbs in all regions, grave markers remain exclusively in the private domain. While Serbia is as vulnerable to nationalist ideology as any of its neighbors, most individual Serbs have not thus far been moved to politicize their own grave markers by adding nationalist symbols to them.

One indication of the continuing private nature of even military graves among Serbs may be seen in their epitaphs, which, as noted previously, are reminiscent of traditional Serbian laments. Although the number and length of such epitaphs increased on the graves of Serbian soldiers from the wars of Yugoslav dissolution, in most cases the messages on them remained much the same. Serbian nationalist sentiments did appear in a few, hearkening back to the soldier's martial glory and noting that "our hero" had sacrificed "for the fatherland," but these too were the exception rather than the rule. Most of the

Figure 7.5 Markers with Serbian national symbols
Borovo Selo, Croatia and Arandjelovac, Serbia

Sad father, sad mother
We lost our son, Zlatko
We bore two sons
So we were happy with them
Until this damned war came
And Zoran lost his brother
Dear happy Alexandra
Doesn't remember her father
Gordana is a sad young girl
Because she no longer has her Zlatko
O' Evil Fate
That took away our Zlatko so early

Figure 7.6 Epitaphs on Serbian markers
Banja-Luka, Bosnia & Hercegovina. For more photographs on this theme see: https://yugcemeteries.omeka.net/exhibits/show/epitaphs-on-grave-markers

epitaphs, even on soldiers' graves, simply stated that their loved one's life had been "cut short" though now more specifically by "this damned war" or "the cursed enemy," while those left behind still bemoaned their loss, insisting that the deceased would live in their hearts forever (Figure 7.6).

One such typical epitaph read,

> Our dear only son. This eagle is the symbol of the flight of your youth, but this damned war ended your young life. Dear son, we will not get to see your wedding or our grandchildren, all that remains for us is grief, pain, bitterness, and tears. Our only son, everything that reminds us of you that we still have, we will preserve and cover with our tears. Dear son Peter. You are alive to us and will live forever. This plaque is all that we can give you. Love, Mama and Papa.

What was indisputable, however, alongside the increase in nationalist symbols, was a gradual decline of Partisan stars. While it is difficult to document this transition in the absence of oral histories, the visual pattern is evident. Markers with Partisan stars have always been a minority in cemeteries, but by the early 2010s, they had almost entirely disappeared from many cemeteries, particularly in Croatia, which were now filled with shiny new markers bearing religious or nationalist insignia. A local source in Zaprešić, Croatia, was the first to explain the phenomenon, assuring me that I was unlikely to find Partisan markers in that cemetery as local citizens had removed them when they renovated the markers.[24] This process developed most quickly and effectively in Croatia where the Communist party had been almost entirely replaced by Franjo Tudjman's nationalist HDZ. In Bosnia & Hercegovina, the old Partisan symbols were usually not erased as citizens there had the most to lose from the dissolution of Yugoslavia, but nonetheless, Croatian symbols appeared on the markers of Bosnian Croats and the new fleur-de-lis representing the Bosniak identity appeared on many grave markers. Serbia remains a bit of an enigma; certainly some Partisan stars were replaced, but many also remained. After all, the League of Socialists of Serbia did not actually lose power until 2000. Until then it was simply reengineered as a different version of itself. In Kosovo, there had likely been fewer Partisan stars on graves to begin with and many that did exist were likely on Serbian graves.[25] Some of those on Albanian graves still exist, while, as we shall see, many of those in Serbian cemeteries were subject to severe damage in the years following the war there.

Some new private grave markers bearing explicitly nationalist symbols also materialized to commemorate those soldiers whose activity during the Second World War had previously gone unmarked and officially unmourned. For nearly fifty years families of soldiers who fought on the opposite side of the Partisans had not been allowed to publicly memorialize their deaths, but they had not forgotten them and now did so openly and politically. For example, in the Catholic monastery of Guča Gora in Bosnia & Hercegovina, a simple cross with the date of death 1945 was covered over by a new marker bearing the Croatian šahovnica. A more explicit case may be found in the Gospić Municipal Cemetery in Croatia where a marker with a cross and šahovnica commemorates the 1970 death of Albin Hameršmitd who, according to his recently renovated marker, spent five years in prison after the Lika [Velebit] uprising organized by the Ustasha against the Interwar Regime in 1932 (Figure 7.7). While private mourning had finally triumphed over state restrictions, it had also clearly been politicized in the process.

Finally, several mass graves and memorials now commemorating the deaths of those killed by the Communist regime have appeared in many cemeteries. The Gospić Municipal Cemetery of St. Mary Magdalen now houses a mass grave bearing a cross and *šahovnica* with the bones of some 2,000 "Croatian Martyrs" killed by the Partisans in 1945. Dedicated in 2005 by the Patriots of Croatia and the Croatian Society of Political Prisoners, the inscription states, "The Communists denied us burial, they took away our right to a peaceful rest, they humiliated us once more in death—some of our bones were taken to the garbage dump, and public toilets, roads, parking lots and playgrounds were built atop our mass graves."[26] Zagreb's Mirogoj Cemetery includes not only a new section for Germany's war dead now in accordance with the Geneva Convention but also several massive monuments to soldiers who died fighting the Communists during the Second World War, including one for the victims of the Bleiburg massacre. These new monuments and symbols on grave markers diversify what had been strictly Communist politicization, by now adding nationalism. In doing so, Mirogoj has indeed incorporated, as Walton argues, "the material afterlives of multiple ideologies."[27] The process of politicization reaches its highest level of expression, however, with grave and cemetery desecrations.

Grave and Cemetery Desecrations

Grave and cemetery desecrations are likely as old as graves and cemeteries themselves, but the way that we think about that act has changed over time. The oldest form of grave desecration is usually associated with grave robbing. Wealthy citizens in many ancient civilizations placed belongings in the grave with the deceased on the assumption that they would need goods in the other world. Members of the royalty and elites were often buried with gold, weapons, pots, food, horses, slaves, and even wives, making their grave sites lucrative spots for local thieves.[28]

Figure 7.7 Renovated nationalist graves
Guča Gora, Bosnia & Hercegovina and Gospić, Croatia

In the modern era, two additional kinds of "grave robbing" developed, both associated with scientific discoveries and education. The first was the robbing of tombs to steal corpses for purposes of dissection and anatomy lectures in medical schools. Although the first human dissections were carried out in third century BCE, they were then banned in Rome during the second century CE and went through periods of legalization and bans in different countries from the Middle Ages up until the nineteenth century. But in no case was there any mechanism for the provision of bodies. The only legal supply was the bodies of those sentenced to death or condemned to dissection after death in jail by the courts.[29]

The Scientific Revolution of the seventeenth and eighteenth centuries resulted in an increasing demand for cadavers, the development of a black market in them, and the dubious profession of "body snatchers." Many of the body snatchers exploited the tradition of sitting with the body for up to three days before the funeral to steal the corpse before burial, while others simply dug up recently buried bodies. The problem encouraged an increase in fenced and gated cemeteries, guards, dogs, and "mortsafes"—a burial slab with bars and a lock explicitly designed to keep out the body snatchers. Despite such efforts, the burgeoning market for corpses even inspired murder until Britain passed the Anatomy Act of 1832, which allowed unclaimed bodies and those donated by relatives to be used for science and dissection.[30]

The second form of grave robbing associated with the modern era was carried out by archeologists for educational purposes but also as an expression of colonial power. The archaeological excavation of tombs remains a controversial subject when the culture being investigated is still viable or has living descendants as is the case not only with the Native American population of the United States but also with many Indigenous peoples of Latin and South America, Australia, South Asia, and Africa. A great deal of current literature available on grave desecrations addresses this last form of grave robbing and the conflict between archeology and indigenous rights. The central question is to what extent archeologists can excavate, examine, and remove from their original site the bones and other sepulchral artifacts that belong to a civilization's and people's heritage without their consent/consultation and when that counts as "grave desecration."[31]

Another form of grave desecration consists of simple vandalism, carried out most commonly by adolescents. It is common but largely unstudied. Most grave and cemetery desecrations that fall under this category are relatively random in scope and nature. The damaged markers are not targeted for any reason other than, perhaps, ease of access. In fact, however, many desecrations officially described and treated as vandalism may actually have had the more calculated goal of destroying the architectural works and landscapes devoted to the commemoration of a particular individual or group. It is precisely such acts with which this work is concerned and that I have termed grave and cemetery desecrations as a form of hate crime. There may be considerable overlap between desecrations as vandalism and as hate crimes since not only may those labeled vandalism often be more accurately categorized as hate crimes but also vice versa. Here too, there has been very little research, but those I describe as hate crimes are clearly directed and deliberate, with the explicit desire to cause emotional distress to the targeted individual or group.

Deliberate desecrations can be aimed strictly at one or more individual graves or they may be indifferent toward individual graves but specifically located within a particular section of a cemetery or only in a particular kind of cemetery. In any case, they clearly are targeted, whether on the basis of race, nation, religion, gender, sexual orientation, or some other distinguishing characteristic. The desecration itself can take a variety of forms with varying levels of destruction including defacing grave marker(s) by damaging or drawing on the stone, picture, or inscriptions; damaging the marker by knocking it down, removing, or destroying it in part or in whole; digging up the grave itself by removing the coffin and/or the body and throwing it out of the grave and/or the cemetery; and damaging or defacing other parts of the cemetery including the fence/wall, landscaping, paths, structures, or religious markers or buildings.[32]

The most familiar cases of grave desecrations as hate crimes have been those of Jews before, during, and after the Second World War. Most famously, the Nazis and their collaborators throughout Europe deliberately destroyed entire Jewish cemeteries using the gravestones for a variety of construction and infrastructural purposes. According to Nolan Menachemsen, Poland was the center of world Jewry in 1939: 84 percent of the world's Jewish population either lived in Poland or were of Polish Jewish descent, with three million Jews in both rural and urban areas. By the end of the Second World War, Poland's Jewish population had almost entirely disappeared and by 2007, Poland counted less than 20,000 Jews. In the course of the war, the Nazis had dismantled hundreds of the 1,000 prewar Jewish cemeteries in Poland using tombstones for paving stones and buildings with the result that 600 of them were damaged beyond repair. By 2007, only 400 Jewish cemeteries in Poland contained visible gravestones and only 116 could be considered relatively well preserved.[33] Although the Nazis were those most famous for the desecration of Jewish graves, they have not been the sole perpetrators. A recent excavation of Prague proved that the Communist regime of Czechoslovakia also used Jewish tombstones as paving stones, and desecrations of Jewish graves continue to take place throughout the world today.[34] In the United States, African American graves have also been desecrated in the past and are still today. Other historical cases have involved Catholic and Protestant cemeteries, while more recently Muslim and Roma graves have been under attack throughout Europe and the United States.

Despite the historical and continuing existence of clearly targeted destructions, almost no scholarly literature addresses the issue of cemetery or grave desecration as a hate crime. Several articles, chapters, or sections in books mention historical and modern cases of grave and/or cemetery desecration as part of the larger phenomenon of cultural warfare, but almost nothing addresses it in any detail as a phenomenon in its own right.[35] One partial exception is the work of Fred Vincent, who researched the topic in connection with his faith-based work and community activism in Northern Ireland and published a report for the Institute for Conflict Research and a shorter version in *Shared Space: A Research Journal on Peace, Conflict and Community Relations in Northern Ireland*.[36] But even Vincent's work, while explicitly on desecration, does not focus only on cemeteries and grave markers but addresses the desecration of all religious spaces. Accordingly, information for this section of the book, while drawing on these sources, is often based on descriptive reports from individuals in the region and my own observations.[37]

Fred Vincent defined desecration as "a planned and/or spontaneous attack on the religious and/or communal sacreds of an individual and/or community in order that their 'holy' might be violated and they might be disoriented and disempowered (if not destroyed)."[38] This definition is useful in that it allows for disparities in motivation (strategic vs. impulsive), target (individual vs. communal), and ultimate goal (to only weaken or entirely destroy one's opponent). It is also noteworthy for its inclusion of nonreligious objects within the definition of "sacred." While it is unlikely that every grave marker in Communist Yugoslavia was imbued with "religious" content, each was indeed "sacred" and had deep emotional and metaphysical meaning to the family as well as a larger communal meaning.

Vincent's team also sought explanations for why individuals and groups sometimes engage in desecrations. Although the reasons provided varied, "the most direct reason given for desecration is that by attacking the things that someone holds most dear to them, maximum hurt is able to be caused as 'the fundamental core of their belief of who they are and their existence has been attacked.'"[39] Grave and cemetery desecrations are most likely to occur under certain circumstances—or as Vincent put it: "It is evident that in situations of conflict, religio-cultural spaces and symbols are frequently targeted for attack."[40] More recently, the bombing of cemeteries has been documented as a deliberate strategy. Similarly, when militaries enter and occupy the territory of an enemy nation and/or religion, they may decide to desecrate cemeteries or graves in the region as an attack on the enemy's religion and culture.

The deliberate destruction of cultural property was long considered a legitimate wartime activity in customary law. By the mid-eighteenth century, some voices had begun to call for greater restraint, but despite several attempts at national and international treaties for the protection of cultural property from the mid-nineteenth century onward, they did not achieve fruition until the aftermath of the Second World War. It is briefly addressed in two Protocols Additional to the Geneva Convention of 1949 but more thoroughly in the 1954 Hague Convention supervised by the United Nations Educational, Scientific and Cultural Organization (UNESCO).[41] While the Hague Convention did not specifically mention cemeteries or grave markers, they were included in aspects of its broad definition of cultural property which included

> movable or immovable property of great importance to the cultural heritage of every people, such as monuments of architecture, art or history, whether religious or secular ... [and] centers containing a large amount of cultural property ... to be known as "centers containing monuments."[42]

In order to "safeguard" such cultural property against possible attacks, signatories to the Convention agreed

> to respect cultural property situated within their own territory as well as within the territory of other High Contracting Parties by refraining from any use of the property and its immediate surroundings or of the appliances in use for its protection for purposes which are likely to expose it to destruction or damage in the event of armed conflict; and by refraining from any act of hostility, directed against such property.[43]

Nonetheless, the wars of Yugoslav dissolution were especially characterized by extensive attacks on and the massive destruction of cultural property, including cemeteries.

Andrew Herscher has described such cultural destruction as part of a larger strategy termed "warchitecture"—an expression coined by Sarajevo's Association of Architects. Warchitecture includes attacks on not only famous architectural sites such as bridges and statues but also cultural institutions like museums, monuments, libraries, and universities and then religious sites such as churches, mosques, synagogues, and their accompanying cemeteries.[44] Robert Bevan described architecture and the cultural heritage of any society as a part of the "cache of historical memory, evidence that a given community's presence extends into the past and legitimizing it in the present and on into the future."[45] That historical legitimacy has provided architecture and material culture, including cemeteries, enormous national significance while also making it a prime target of attack by a nation's enemies, who hope that by destroying a nation's material culture they can also eradicate any memory of its very existence and assert their new authority.

Violence against architecture and culture is thus clearly intended as violence against those who use that culture. The goal is to drive them out and prevent them from returning by ensuring that they have no reason to return as there is nothing left for them to return to. That goal is even more obvious in the specific case of violence against cemeteries. If cemeteries are eradicated, then there is no one for whom the living must return. There is no one remaining to mourn or visit, no one to come back for. Indeed, in describing the consequences of desecration, Vincent's team agreed that it often resulted in intense grief, hopelessness, and despair. Vincent's subjects spoke of the extreme demoralization produced by desecrations of culture. Thus, even if the aggressor cannot eradicate an entire population, they may destroy their will to resist and return.

Yet Vincent's team also found that desecrations were just as likely to engender deep feelings of anger and a sense of resilience in the face of oppression. Very often, they concluded, although the desecrations were intended to weaken or destroy the opponent, they had the opposite effect of reinforcing a determination among minority communities to stay where they were. Most of all, acts of desecration were likely to exacerbate already existing conflicts, polarizing the two sides and possibly leading to the recruitment of new members in paramilitary groups. As one interviewee put it, "It's very difficult to love your enemy if he has desecrated you somehow."[46]

The political significance of grave and cemetery desecration is further highlighted in the work of a few scholars who have begun to discuss the destruction of shrines, mausoleums, and graves as well as the mutilation of dead bodies in the context of "necropolitics." Starting from Foucault's concept that sovereignty includes the right to determine who has the right to live and die, Achille Mbembe coined the term "necropolitics" to explain how the power of the state, particularly in colonial relationships, is used to create "new forms of social existence in which vast populations are subjected to conditions of life conferring on them the status of *living dead*."⁴⁷ Since Mbembe's 2008 publication, the term "necropolitics" has come into increasing academic use, mostly among scholars writing about marginalized populations. A few, however, have also begun to apply it in its most obvious form, regarding politics toward those already deceased.⁴⁸ Emily Jane O'Dell's 2012 analysis of the destruction of Sufi shrines in Timbuktu is particularly apt as she argued that the "ultimate expression of sovereignty may also reside in who condemns the *already dead* to death."⁴⁹ She further elaborated on the territorial significance of attacks on the dead and how victimizing and weaponizing them served also to terrorize those still living. Thus, in her view, necropolitics "might be conceptualized as the politics of waging war on the already dead and on landscapes of death to assert sovereignty over politics, land distribution and ritual commemorations of the past and to terrorize the local population in the present."⁵⁰

Such "necropolitics" in the former Yugoslav republics supported policies of ethnic cleansing, seeking to ensure a majority nation's ethnoreligious control not only by terrorizing and driving out the minority but also by convincing them that there was no reason to return. Though impossible to prove, anecdotal reports by both internal and external observers suggest that grave and cemetery desecrations during the wars of Yugoslav dissolution occurred in numbers far larger than during any previous conflict. There is less agreement among them about who was most responsible and whose graves and cemeteries suffered the most damage. Scholars have provided documentation that the wars of Yugoslav dissolution were especially characterized by the deliberate destruction of material culture. Robert Bevan argued that the amount of architectural heritage destroyed in the Bosnian Wars was far greater than that in the Second World War and while it can sometimes be difficult to determine the difference between targeted and collateral damage, the wanton destruction of the sixteenth-century Ottoman bridge in Mostar, the National Library in Sarajevo, and countless other sites left no room for doubt about intent.⁵¹

One might argue that the desecration of cemeteries was simply part of that larger destruction of cultural heritage and entirely unrelated to Communist party policies on cemeteries and in the case of wartime desecrations, that may be so. But while the destruction of churches, mosques, monuments, libraries, and museums began and ended only with the war, cemetery desecrations both preceded and continued after the wars of Yugoslav dissolution as is painfully evident in the case of the Mostar Partisan Memorial Cemetery. Some cases of desecrations took place in the years immediately following the Second World War, but reports of desecrations substantially increased in the years leading up to and following the wars of Yugoslav dissolution. While it remains difficult to provide anything like accurate statistics on their frequency, perhaps what matters most is the widespread perception among the population that they had indeed increased in the years leading up to, during, and right after the wars.

Cemetery Desecrations Following the Second World War

Most incidents of grave desecration in early postwar Yugoslavia were carried out by members or close associates of the new Communist regime as expressions of revolutionary radicalism in opposition to religion. In the late 1940s and early 1950s, the Commission for Religious Questions in both Croatia and Bosnia & Hercegovina fielded a number of complaints from various local religious communities—Catholic, Jewish, and Muslim—relating to desecrations of graves and cemeteries. Many reports came from the Catholic Archbishopric in Zagreb about attacks on and serious damage to Catholic cemeteries and grave markers as well as from the Jewish and Muslim communities about cemeteries that had been abused and damaged by actions of the Yugoslav People's Army. The degree of damage and seriousness of the crime varied considerably across the cases. In one case relating to damaged Jewish headstones, the report claimed that all those involved, including the Jewish community, agreed it was a matter of teenage vandalism and were content to let the school and parents deal with it.[52] In another case, however, the Bishop of Zagreb sent a very urgent request for intervention to the CRQ following the destruction of 96 crosses, 100 monuments, and 3 mausoleums in the cemetery, as well as broken windows, steps, and an altar in the Chapel at Virovitica.[53]

Two other serious cases in 1952 involved military violations of cemetery property, elucidating how lengthy can be the boundary between war and peace. The first, again, took place in Virovitica, Croatia, where members of the military engaged in considerable physical damage to a Jewish cemetery, breaking and digging out its pillars, fencing, and landscaping, so they could use cemetery land as a shortcut on its training route. In response to the caretaker's complaints, Svetozar Ritig and the Croatian CRQ immediately requested that the army protect the Jewish cemetery from harm and punish those responsible as it was important to maintain good relations with world Jewish organizations and the state of Israel. "Jews in our state and abroad pay a lot of attention to the care of their cemeteries, so it is important that we also pay attention to this!"[54]

The second complaint in 1952 from the head of the Muslim religious community in Sarajevo stated that military units were conducting their exercises atop an active Muslim cemetery on Grličić Hill and blasting holes in it with grenades. According to the report, Muslims were buried right where the damage was taking place. Sarajevo's Council for Communal Affairs asked the military to end the exercises but was told in no uncertain terms that this was outside their sphere of influence. Here, too, however, it seems that the CRQ acted decisively in favor of cemetery preservation and was able, over the course of a year, to successfully resolve the conflict. Although some new complaints occurred, the military eventually backed off and the cemetery at Grličić Hill is still in existence.[55]

In contrast, Max Bergholz has documented rare examples of early desecrations against Partisan graves and cemeteries. In some cases, Partisan cemeteries were simply not accorded appropriate respect, as when peasants allowed cattle to graze in them or teens appropriated them as local hangouts. Bergholz further cited some Croatian farmers plowing under the graves of Partisans, a phenomenon also noted by members of SUBNOR preparing the mass graves for commemoration at Jasenovac. The most serious cases of desecration involved deliberate damage to monuments for fallen soldiers in Belgrade and Novi Pazar.[56]

Essentially then, in the first two decades after the war, nearly all cases of desecration in Yugoslavia involved the Communist regime either as perpetrator or victim. By the late 1960s, however, the role of Communist ideology in society and its impact on religion was already declining, while signs of ethnic conflict between Serbs, Croats, and Albanians were on the rise. From that time until the late 1980s, the still relatively few references to grave and cemetery desecrations would nearly all have to do with attacks on Serbian Orthodox cemeteries.

In fact, there had been one early complaint against the Communist regime that foreshadowed the ethnoreligious desecrations to come. In his 1990 work seeking to document fifty years of crimes committed by Albanians against the Serbian population of Kosovo, retired bishop of the Serbian Orthodox Church Atanasije Jeftić cited a 1951 letter from Archpriest Steva Dimitrijević. In it, Dimitrijević blamed Albanians in the new Communist regime for substantial cultural desecrations in Prizren, claiming that Orthodox cemeteries in Prizren had been "destroyed and the gravestones are broken and also in the old military cemetery everything has been wiped out. Nor are there any crosses remaining in the cemeteries of any of the religiously mixed villages."[57]

By 1968 Serbian–Albanian relations in Kosovo had reached a boiling point in association with the student demonstrations of that year. At the same time, according to Andrew Herscher, the Holy Council of the Serbian Orthodox Church had made its personnel in Kosovo responsible for documenting all violations of church property by Albanians, including trespassing, unauthorized cattle grazing, and harvesting on church land and cemeteries, as well as damage to gravestones, cemeteries, churches, and monasteries. Over the next two decades, it collected these documents, providing reports about them to Yugoslav and eventually also international authorities.[58] According to Jeftić, the first serious wave of Albanian attacks on Orthodox churches, villages, and cemeteries occurred in response to the 1968 demonstrations. As evidence, Jeftić cited a report from the Bishop of Prizren, who described in detail a series of specific attacks on cemeteries of villages mostly in the region of Kosovska Mitrovica in the summer of 1972 resulting in the destruction of multiple grave markers.[59]

Meanwhile in Croatia, the CRQ fielded complaints about attacks on Orthodox cemeteries from the late 1960s and into the 1980s in Sisak, Graberje, Ostrovo, Vinkovci, Slavonski Brod, and Dubrovnik. From the perspective of the Serbian Orthodox Church, the situation had become so serious that in May 1969, Patriarch German sent a letter to Tito requesting his intervention.[60] In all cases, the CRQ and the police investigated the attacks but often with the clear hope of showing that they were unlikely to have been politically motivated.

One such case occurred in Sisak in late December of 1967. According to the initial reports, in an event widely interpreted as a deliberate Ustasha provocation, a large number of Serbian Orthodox graves and a few Catholic ones were destroyed on Christmas Eve. The official police report, however, insisted that there could be no political motive since of the forty-nine graves destroyed, nearly half (twenty-one) were Catholic, while twenty-eight were Orthodox. Moreover, the culprits were teenagers whose acts of vandalism were unrelated to Christmas as they took place on both the 21st and the 24th of December. In the following months, however, an Orthodox priest and several assistants filed a separate report, providing a complete list of all the names on the damaged gravestones, which included as many as ten mixed marriages, bringing the number of "pure" Catholic grave markers destroyed down to seven and increasing the likelihood that the graves were targeted and that the damage was indeed ethnoreligiously motivated.[61]

Another case occurred in 1971, when seven Orthodox graves were destroyed in the village cemetery of Graberje on March 22–23 and another six in the Orthodox cemetery of Kriz on May 19–20. While the report from the Orthodox priest makes it clear that the attack must have been deliberate, the police report notes that while the graves in Graberje were in Cyrillic, those in

Kriz were in Latin and the individuals targeted were entirely nonpolitical. As we have seen previously, use of script is not a reliable indicator of national or religious identity. Locals would likely have known which graves belonged to Serbs and which to Croats, though without additional information we cannot. Regardless, the local police concluded on the basis of script that the attacks seemed fairly random and apolitical. The report from the local CRQ agreed as there had been no previous desecrations and no atmosphere of intolerance between Croats and Serbs who made up only 2 percent of the population. Although the CRQ of Zagreb seemed more skeptical, no perpetrators were found, and the position stood until the Orthodox cemetery in Graberje was desecrated again three years later in November 1974. Although no final report was found, the Zagreb CRQ demanded a full accounting of the event from the local commission.

Despite the disturbing indications provided by such examples, a real increase in incidents of desecrations, or at least open discussion of such incidents, did not begin until the mid-1980s, and then they were nearly all associated with cemeteries and graves of the Serbian Orthodox Church in Kosovo. By then the Serbian Orthodox Church had gone on the offensive in a clear campaign to promote Serbian nationalism. That campaign was very closely linked to Serbia's religious, cultural, and architectural heritage, which had always been an integral part of Serbian national identity, particularly in Kosovo. The Medieval Serbian Nemanjić Dynasty had established a significant number of monasteries and churches in Kosovo/Kosova, including most prominently those in Gračanica, Dečani, and the Patriarchate of Peć. For Serbs, who have a highly developed cult of the dead, the symbolic significance of cemeteries was always strong, but it was ever more closely associated with national identity during the 1980s.

According to Jeftić, the Albanian protests of 1981 led not only to greater incidents of grave and cemetery desecrations, but now they were very often perpetrated on fresh graves and especially on the eve of Orthodox Day of the Dead (Zadušnice) holidays in order, he said, to increase the pain and sadness of those Serbian families coming to mourn their loved ones.[62] In April of 1982, following a mysterious fire at the Patriarchate of Peć, twenty-one priests associated with the Serbian Orthodox Church signed and sent a document entitled "Appeal for the Protection of the Serbian Population and their Sacred Monuments in Kosovo" to the highest state organs of Serbia and Yugoslavia. That document was the first step in the Church's increasingly vocal defense of what it described as "the spiritual and biological existence of the Serbian people of Kosovo and

Metohija" through speeches, publications, petitions, and organized protests. Church publications from the early 1980s on regularly included information and material from or about what it called "Old Serbia." Toward the end of 1983, Jevtić began to publish a supplement to the official bulletin of the Serbian Orthodox Church, which described and documented crimes said to have been perpetrated against the Serbian people over the past decades in Kosovo and throughout Yugoslavia. All these publications and documents included the desecration of graves and cemeteries among the crimes the Church felt were being perpetrated against Serbia and Serbs on a daily basis in Kosovo.

The most elaborate story described in Jeftić's 1990 book and one that has been repeated in the Serbian press multiple times in the years since, took place in 1988 on the night of Krstovdan [Holy Cross Day]. According to his description, on July 4–5, 1988, Serbian twin infant boys were buried in the village cemetery of Grace outside of Vučitrn/Vushtrri.[63] Nearly three months later, on September 27, Krstovdan, their grandfather went to visit the grave and found it had been dug up, the infants' bodies removed, dismembered, and hastily reburied, though remnants of bones, diaper, and paper money were strewn around the gravesite. The police and medical commissioner investigated the site the next day and quickly arrested five Albanian teens, aged eleven to fifteen, from the neighboring village of Donje Stanovce/Stanovc i Ulet, who claimed they had committed the act because they had heard that Serbs often bury money along with bodies. The trial lasted seven days after which two of the boys were sentenced to six months of juvenile detention and the other three to house arrest.[64]

Even with more than thirty years distance, it is difficult to know how one should interpret this horrific act. In the immediate aftermath, local Serbs gathered first at the cemetery and then in the village with placards reading, "Kosovo is Serbia," "We Want Freedom," and "Emigrants Out!" clearly perceiving the brutal behavior of the preteens and teens as a political attack and hate crime, likely instigated by their parents. Within a week, 10,000 Serbs from all over Kosovo and students from Belgrade had gathered in the region to protest the desecration. In the words of one speaker, "Kosovo is the new Serbian Golgotha [the site of Jesus' crucifixion] which has now lasted a full eight years. Is there any other country where one can see such brutal persecution of people and terror over the dead."[65] Clearly their assumption was either that the teenagers had been inspired to act as they did by the adults around them or that, young as they were, they knew exactly what they were doing. Either way, there was no room in their interpretation for the desecration as either vandalism, however brutally applied, or even grave robbing. These Serbs simply had no doubt that this was a hate crime. When interviewed about the events some fifteen years later, the twins' father said, "My children were dug up here. That has not happened to any nation except the Serbs. I guarantee it. For them, [the Albanians] even dead Serbian children are enemies."[66]

It is plausible that the Kosovar Albanian teens had learned over their short lifespan that Serbs were "others" and "enemies," yet it seems less likely that a group of children, two of whom were aged eleven, and the others twelve, thirteen, and fifteen, could be capable of committing a hate crime or devising a political act with the goal of driving the Serbian nation from Kosovo.

Andrew Herscher has argued that the Serbian Orthodox Church helped create a public discourse of ethnic conflict, relating both to the past and present, precisely "by scripting vandalism as a component of 'genocide' and 'ethnic purification.'"[67] Likewise, Bergholz contends that, rather than ethnic conflict leading to violence, the violence itself, often motivated by economic gain, creates and sustains ethnicization, leading to further conflict and violence.[68]

In Kosovo/Kosova, of course, where both violence and ethnic conflict have coexisted for a sustained period, it can become a question of the chicken and the egg. But this case seems perfectly designed to support Bergholz' argument, while it also shows the symbolic power of the dead over the living. While the Albanian adolescents may have had no other motivation than money for candy and cigarettes, their indifference to burial practices considered sacred in nearly all cultures left their acts open to interpretation as part of a nationalist conspiracy. The mutilation of the infants's bodies might suggest their complete dehumanization in the consciousness of the teens.[69] Or perhaps their bodies had simply decayed to the extent that what seemed deliberate mutilation was only accidental disintegration. At the same time, Jeftić claimed that the entire month of September that year had been filled in Kosovo-Metohija, Serbia, and Montenegro with protests and demonstrations "in solidarity and support of the disenfranchised Serbian people in their centuries old hearth of Historic Old Serbia."[70] If Fred Vincent is correct that the most direct motivation for desecration is to attack those things that the enemy holds most dear in order to cause maximum pain, these Serb nationalists may unwittingly have provided them with an ideal target. According to one Serbian novelist, "The Albanians knew what graves meant to the Serbs; that's why they were destroying them."[71]

On May 22, 2019, I visited the village of Grace with my Albanian guide and translator, Mrika Limani, hoping to find a memorial that had been erected in memory of the twins in 1989. After driving around lost for a while, we asked for an Orthodox cemetery and were given directions by another adolescent Albanian boy who sent us to the "field of Serbs," using a pejorative term for Serbs (Skija). Finding no cemetery (but some Serbian nationalist graffiti), we knocked on the door of a nearby house whose owner, a local Serb, invited us in for coffee and conversation. When we asked him about the memorial and event, he recalled it as having all been blown out of proportion, but he knew about the plaque and offered to take us there. We followed him to a spot perhaps a mile away to find the plaque broken and entirely covered with grass and debris. As we worked to unearth it, another car approached whose Albanian driver emerged from his car with fury and shouted at us to leave it be and depart, which we did in some haste. It was a tense moment, revealing the strong feelings still engendered by the event over thirty years later (Figure 7.8).

Jeftić documented sixteen other cases involving the desecration of Serbian graves and cemeteries by Albanians in a twenty-six-month period from March 1988 through June 1990.[72] Although some of the desecrations almost certainly did represent hate crimes and must not be minimized, as with this particular instance, a compelling case for them as hate crimes cannot be made for all. Three of them, for example, involved the Albanian cultivation of land that had been used as a Serbian cemetery. While to do so was certainly impious, unacceptable, and illegal, one may reasonably question whether the perpetrators were motivated more by hate or profit, or perhaps both. In these cases, the Albanian authorities supported the Serbian complainants, as the perpetrators were punished for their crimes, in two cases with jail sentences, suggesting at least that they had not been encouraged by local Albanian authorities. Four other cases are also questionable—one in which the perpetrator was determined to be mentally deranged and three cases of fires in cemeteries that broke out during drought seasons. That leaves only nine likely hate crime desecrations during the twenty-six-month period, or just one every three months for the entire country. Obviously, no number is acceptable but that begins to look less like a wave of epidemic proportions and more like the deliberate use of a few violent and hostile acts to promote policies based on ethnic and cultural identity. Nonetheless, the publicity surrounding these desecrations spread far beyond Kosovo throughout the rest of the Yugoslav republics. By the time the wars of Yugoslav dissolution broke out three years later, the concept of cemeteries as sites of ethnic conflict was well established. In the years from 1991 to 1995, grave and cemetery desecrations would take place in both Croatia and Bosnia & Hercegovina in all religious communities and were perpetrated from all sides, though certainly not with equal fervor or success.

Figure 7.8 Krstovdan incident at Grace, Kosova
Serbian nationalist graffiti near Grace and the buried plaque commemorating the infants' death in 1988

Grave and Cemetery Desecrations During the Wars of Yugoslav Dissolution: 1991 to 1995–

Grave and cemetery desecrations took place in all areas of military and civilian conflict in Croatia and Bosnia & Hercegovina in the years from 1991 to 1995. Both Partisan and civilian cemeteries were targeted as both by now represented politicized spaces. While some of those desecrations were carefully documented, many others likely went unreported given wartime conditions. Moreover, as long as family members were on-site and able to repair the damage, it is difficult to find evidence of previous desecration. As a result, photographs of damaged graves and cemeteries that I took some fifteen years after the war's end may say more about changing demographics than the actual balance of desecrations that occurred in the cemeteries of each ethnoreligious community.

Desecrations in Croatia

In 1992, Croatian architect Vesna Jureško Hermann collected data for an exhibit on the destruction of Croatia's cultural heritage during the war with Serbia. Altogether she claimed that 583 cultural monuments had been destroyed, of which almost 62 percent were religious in character, including eight mausoleums, tombs, and cemeteries.[73] In Vukovar, archeological gravesites were destroyed, and the tomb and interred bodies belonging to the family of an interwar nobleman recently turned politician were brutally desecrated, while in Dubrovnik and Osijek old Jewish cemeteries, dating to the mid-seventeenth and mid-nineteenth centuries, respectively, were badly damaged by mortar shells.[74]

Twenty years later, in the summer of 2015, I spent several weeks in Croatia, visiting and photographing cemeteries in Zagreb, eastern Croatia, and the region formerly known as Krajina. Although there certainly had been damage to Croatia's Catholic cultural heritage, it had by this time been almost entirely repaired. In contrast, signs of damage to the Jewish cemetery in Osijek and especially to Serbian Orthodox graves remain to this day. They were visible in Orthodox cemeteries in the eastern towns of Nova Gradiška and Vukovar, though, interestingly, not in the small military cemetery that commemorates Serbian members of the former JNA from Vukovar who died in battle there in 1991–2. The continued state of destruction was most evident, however, in the district of Lika-Senj in the former Krajina. Along several roads I saw markers warning of landmines in the region and entire cemeteries or significant sections of them had been simply abandoned while their grave markers, if undamaged, were badly neglected.

In Jasikovac Orthodox Cemetery in Gospić, a town that saw violent Croat-Serb conflicts in the early 1990s, I found the cemetery grounds well-tended and mown, yet many headstones and memorials with Orthodox crosses and Partisan stars remained broken and lying on the ground just as they surely had been right after the war.[75] The local caretaker explained that only the graves of those whose relatives still lived in the area had been repaired. Since the demographic structure of the region had changed from 64 percent Croat and 31 percent Serb in 1991 to 93 percent Croat and 5 percent Serb by 2001, it was clear why so few graves had been repaired.[76] I was even more taken aback, however, by what he told me next. Pointing to one of multiple empty grave sites, he explained that many of the Serbs who had fled the region had taken their relatives' remains with them. I had read of similar cases in the suburbs of Sarajevo, but it felt very different seeing the empty holes in the ground.[77] Although the exhumation of bodies is not unusual among the Orthodox, this act surprised me most as it stood in direct contrast to nationalist notions that connect blood and territory. Not only had Serbian nationalist politician Vuk Drašković claimed that Serbia was wherever Serbs were buried, but the Serbian poet Matije Bećković called the tomb "the largest shrine and the oldest church of the Serbian people. The tomb is our longest and most persistent faith."[78] Here Serbian individuals and families were tearing down those shrines, pulling up roots, moving out, and taking the dead with them. And in doing so, they were tacitly giving up the territory where their dead had been buried. They had not abandoned their ancestors but in the face of overwhelming force and desecration had decided that private forms of mourning superseded the demands of either the community or the state (Figure 7.9).

Desecrations in the Bosnian Wars

In Bosnia & Hercegovina, damage to cemeteries and grave markers also occurred on all sides, but some ethnoreligious groups suffered more than others. According to Andras Riedelmayer, who has conducted extensive research on cultural destruction for The Hague in both Bosnia & Hercegovina and Kosova, 48.89 percent (forty-four of ninety) of Muslim mausolea or shrines in Bosnia & Hercegovina were damaged or destroyed during the war between 1992 and 1995, forty of them by Serb extremists and four by Croat extremists.[79] Meanwhile,

Figure 7.9 Damaged and empty graves after the wars of Yugoslav dissolution Gospić, Croatia For more photographs on this theme see: https://yugcemeteries.omeka.net/exhibits/show/damaged-graves-and-cemeteries

author and former director of the Gazi Husrev-Beg library in Sarajevo, Muharem Omerdić, claims that of the 8,000 Muslim cemeteries in Bosnia & Hercegovina, 2,000 were completely destroyed and 1,800 were damaged.[80] Anecdotally, most sources blamed Bosnian Serb military forces and Serbian and Croatian paramilitaries that flattened mosques and cemeteries, reusing the space for buildings, parking, garbage, or, most insultingly to Muslims, to house pigs. More disturbing yet is the June 1995 report from Dr. Marian Wenzel of the Bosnia & Hercegovina Heritage Rescue Association (BHHR), which claimed that the Bosnian Serbs had systematically planted landmines in old Bosnian cemeteries.

> The most prevalent mines in Bosnia are small green plastic cylinders, surmounted by a plunger resembling a star-form on a stem, manufactured in the former Yugoslavia and with a shelf life of 50 years. When buried, the star resembles a weed; if it is stepped on, it explodes to maim or kill. It is estimated there are around six million unexploded mines in the ground of Bosnia and Croatia. There is an incomplete record of where they have been all put, but they can be expected around the perimeter areas of confrontation lines, as they were cheaper than guard dogs. In East Bosnia, they are certainly attested to have been planted in graveyards, whereas in other regions, this is thought highly probable to have occurred.

Dr. Wenzel recommended professional mine clearing, aided by locals who might know where the mines were located, though she noted that "a rudimentary method is to send in herds of sheep, but this method does not precision-check the total endangered territory."[81]

Since Serbs held most of the territory in Bosnia & Hercegovina during the war, Orthodox cemeteries were less likely to have been desecrated. Nonetheless, a 1995 report from the Committee on Culture and Education described some damaged and destroyed Orthodox cemeteries, though certainly fewer than the Muslim ones.[82] In the fall of 2013, I visited an Orthodox cemetery that may have been mined. Located in central Bosnia in the village of Karaula near Kakanj, it was directly across the street from what was by then a well-kept and mown Muslim cemetery. The Orthodox one, in contrast, had a very different feel to it. While the graves themselves were largely, though not entirely, undamaged, only narrow paths between and directly around the graves had been mown, while all else was entirely unkempt. My Bosnian guide and assistant, Selma Hadžihalilović, immediately recognized the danger of possible landmines and strictly warned me to walk only on the mown paths. I was also told in interviews that both Jewish and Catholic cemeteries had been destroyed by Muslims during the war.⁸³ As the war ended, following NATO bombings of Serbian positions and driven by ideological disinformation from Belgrade and the Serbian Orthodox Church, many Serbs throughout Bosnia & Hercegovina were clearly convinced that the graves of their ancestors were in great danger of desecration from their Muslim and Croat enemies. It was under these conditions that Serbs in the enclaves around Sarajevo began to exhume their deceased relatives, packing them into wagons with their other luggage as they themselves fled to Serbia proper.⁸⁴ While there is no evidence that large-scale desecration of Orthodox graves or cemeteries occurred in the Federation of Bosnia & Hercegovina after the war, Serbian newspapers recorded sporadic incidents for some time.⁸⁵

Desecrations in and after the War in Kosovo/Kosova

Shortly after the wars ended in Croatia and Bosnia & Hercegovina, violence erupted in Kosovo when Serbian military forces invaded in March 1998 to suppress the insurrectionist activities of the Kosovo Liberation Army. Compared to the conflicts in Croatia and Bosnia & Hercegovina, which lasted approximately four years, the war in Kosovo ended relatively quickly with the NATO bombing of Serbia in March 1999. The rapidity of the Serbian invasion and equally quick withdrawal may help explain the almost complete absence of Muslim grave and cemetery desecrations in that war. The invading Serbian forces certainly engaged in massive and deliberate cultural destruction, damaging or destroying one-third of the mosques in the country.⁸⁶ But to the extent that Muslim cemeteries were also destroyed, it appeared to occur only as "collateral damage." Neither in the extensive research carried out by Herscher and Riedelmayer on the destruction of historic and religious monuments during the war nor in my own interviews with Kosovar Muslim religious clerics is there evidence of deliberate large-scale desecration by Serbs of Muslim tombs, mausoleums, or cemeteries. According to Imam Ahmed Hoxha at the Office of the Islamic Union in the Hadam Mosque in Gjakovo, "During the war, there was a great deal of damage to religious objects—218 religious objects in Gjakovo were damaged or destroyed. ... Cemeteries were also damaged in that process but were not specifically targeted."⁸⁷

As soon as Serbian forces withdrew under NATO and UN occupation, however, some Albanian Kosovars took brutal revenge for a war that had resulted in the deaths of some 13,500 Kosovar Albanians and the displacement of 1.2–1.45 million more. In the war's aftermath, approximately 200,000 Serbs,

Montenegrins, and Roma fled the region, while those remaining often suffered serious human rights violations. The Serbian cultural heritage also came under heavy attack, leading to the destruction and severe damage of many medieval churches and monasteries. As communities of the dead that had been politicized first by the communists, but even more so during the 1980s, Orthodox cemeteries also suffered attacks and desecrations. Initially, these attacks and reprisals took place without interference from the occupying NATO forces but eventually the international community intervened and stationed guards to ensure the safety of several Orthodox historic landmarks, including some cemeteries. Actions then gradually began in Kosovo/Kosova, as they had earlier in Croatia and Bosnia & Hercegovina, to restore many important cultural and historic monuments.

In June and July of 2010, the Organization for Security and Cooperation in Europe, Mission in Kosovo, conducted a survey of 392 Orthodox graveyards in Kosova. While attempting to visit all known Orthodox graveyards, those compiling and carrying it out admitted that they could not claim that the resulting report was comprehensive since some graveyards simply could not be found.[88] Further, the survey did not include graveyards in areas north of the Ibar River, which were shown to have no cases of cemetery damage. The report evaluated graveyards on a scale of one to five with those rated one being in very good condition with mown grass, no garbage, and no damage to grave markers and five being in very bad condition with substantial vegetation, garbage, and damage to most or all grave markers if indeed they were visible. As of 2010, 51 percent of the graveyards surveyed were in very bad condition, 7 percent in bad condition, 9 percent in decent condition, 21 percent in good condition, and 12 percent in very good condition. Of those in good or very good condition, all but two were located in or near villages inhabited by Kosovar Serbs. The two exceptions were attached to the Dević Monastery under KFOR protection and maintained by resident nuns. In contrast, 82 percent of those in bad or very bad condition were located near villages without any resident Kosovar Serbs. According to the report, most municipalities were at least theoretically legally responsible for cemetery maintenance, but very few had dedicated a specific budgetary line for that purpose. Several other state and nonstate actors, both local and international, including the Ministry of Communities and Return, the Reconstruction Implementation Commission for Serbian Orthodox Religious Sites in Kosovo, the Serbian Ministry for Kosovo and Metohija, and the OSCE itself, had also engaged in reconstruction and repair efforts at various graveyards. Nonetheless, it was clear that much more needed to be done, and the report provided specific administrative and financial recommendations to Kosovar municipalities, the government of Kosovo, and the OSCE.[89]

Yet, by the time I visited Kosova for research in May 2019, twenty years after the war, and ten years after this report, I found the situation to be remarkably similar. Then, as a decade earlier, the restoration of cemeteries seemed to rely mainly on the existence and strength of communities of the living. In those areas where a Serbian community was extant and functioning, many Orthodox cemeteries had been largely, if not entirely, restored. Where there were few or no Serbs, the cemeteries remained largely devastated. During my trip, I visited Orthodox cemeteries in three larger cities (Priština/Prishtinë, Prizren, and Pejë/Peć) as well as in four smaller towns or villages (Gračanica/Graçanicë, Vučitrn/Vushtrria, Bostane/Bostani, and Berivojce). The two cemeteries within the walls of monastery grounds at Gračanica and Peć showed no damage. The monasteries of Gračanica and Peć had both sustained indirect damage from NATO bombing in 1999, but if the cemeteries themselves were damaged, they were since repaired.[90] The municipal Orthodox cemetery in the almost entirely Serbian town of Gračanica/Graçanicë was also well maintained, though a few of the older graves still showed minor signs of damage. The Serbian cemetery in Bostan/Bostanë was in excellent shape and showed no damage; at least one grave there included the Serbian ocilo and several of the men portrayed on the graves wore šajkačas, the famous Serbian military cap from the First World War. The Serbian Orthodox cemetery in Berivojce near Kamenica/Kamenicë, a mixed town in eastern Kosova nearly untouched by the war and well known for its ethnic toleration, was also undamaged though less well kept.

In contrast, the remainder of the Orthodox cemeteries I visited in Kosova still showed significant signs of the postwar desecrations, though some are in the process of being restored. What is referred to as the Orthodox cemetery in Priština/Prishtinë is really a mixed cemetery for the city's non-Muslim residents and includes not only Orthodox but Catholic and Jewish sections also. In 2019 only the Catholic section of the cemetery could be said to be truly well maintained, but there were indications that the rest of the cemetery was in the process of renewal, apparently by the Ministry of Communities and Return.[91] "Before and After" photographs posted at the entrance showed the progress already made in repairing the Orthodox Chapel, removing debris, and clearing pathways. Nonetheless, much work remains to be done. The Jewish section seemed mainly to be neglected, but while some graves in the Orthodox section were well maintained and either untouched or repaired, many were broken, damaged, or entirely destroyed and entire parts of that cemetery, particularly those including large numbers of Partisan stars, were overgrown and impassable. Similar conditions prevailed in the Orthodox cemetery in Vučitrn/Vushtrri and in the Orthodox section of the municipal Christian cemetery in Prizren. There again the Catholic section was in perfect condition, while the Orthodox section was entirely overgrown, and although many of the Orthodox graves in Prizren were in good condition, broken or damaged ones were clearly visible among them, apparently just as they had been a decade earlier.[92]

None of this, however, had prepared me for what I saw in Peć/Pejë, a town that experienced extreme levels of interethnic violence both before, during, and after the war. According to Matthew McAllester, one of the few Western journalists to spend time there during the war, Serbs were determined to completely destroy all Albanian homes and regions of Peć/Pejë due to a combination of factors that included the strength of the KLA in the region that had enabled them to carry out several successful attacks, the unusual wealth of Albanians in the region, and the location there of the Serbian Patriarchate. In addition, Slobodan Milošević may have targeted the region for extreme destruction, driving the Albanian population of 70,000 into Montenegro within a few days, in order make an example of the town and fully destabilize the Balkans early on in the war.[93]

In May 2019, my Kosovar Albanian guide and I visited the Patriarchate of Peć, the thirteenth-century monastery, seat of the Serbian Patriarchs and burial site for many. Nestled at the entrance to the Rugova Canyon it is an idyllic spot, particularly in late May. Surrounded by orchards with a stream that runs nearby, it seems a perfect place for the meditative life of monks. In 2006 it was placed on UNESCO's World Heritage List (Figure 7.10). After leaving the monastery, we returned to town in search of the municipal cemeteries and following the often problematic instructions on our GPS eventually found that we had "arrived" at our destination—the Orthodox Municipal Cemetery. At first, there seemed to be nothing there, but eventually we walked across an empty lot to a concrete and wire wall, finding the old and now very decrepit-looking entrance to the cemetery, entirely locked up. Peering inside, I could see only a pile of trash and some broken graves. I was about to give up but walked around the side only to discover that one could, in fact, get in through the back. Once inside, the impression of destruction only increased. All of the chapels had been entirely demolished, tree branches and debris lay all about, and broken and destroyed graves were everywhere you looked. Clearly this was what the OSCE report had meant by a graveyard in "very bad" condition. The atmosphere in the place was not just sad, though it was, but also a bit frightening. While not every grave was broken, one could not look in any direction without seeing broken graves and

Figure 7.10 Patriarchate of Peć

imagining the pain deliberately inflicted on their families. It had been a large cemetery and though I wanted to investigate it further to see the extent of the damage, I wished even more desperately to get out of there. However justified the anger that had sparked this act, it was unquestionably both a desecration and a hate crime (Figure 7.11).

It is not my place or intention here to draw lines equating the evil done between individuals of ethnoreligious communities whether out of revenge or fear. How many rapes count for a murder? Or is it the other way around? And is cemetery desecration really "worse than murder" as has been suggested to me on more than one occasion? That anyone should seek to find a balance between the multiple acts of violence committed by and against individuals, communities, and their cultural heritage in times of conflict and war is frankly incomprehensible. My purpose in drawing attention to these acts is not to make such comparisons, even less so to further inflame hatred between ethnoreligious groups. Yet it does seem worth asking, as did Father Vincent, why and under what conditions do the bodies of the dead become cannon fodder in the wars of the living? Over and over throughout my research Croats, Serbs, Bosniaks, and Albanians asserted that, although ethnic conflict among them had always existed, never in the past had there been grave desecrations on such a scale.

Figure 7.11 Grave desecrations
Pejë, Kosova

It is difficult to either confirm or deny their claims since so little research on this topic exists, but perhaps there has been so little research on it precisely because they are right. Or perhaps all that matters is their perception and fear that a sense of respect for the dead that once crossed all ethnoreligious boundaries has been lost. Some may be tempted to find blame in the growth of secularism, but as Laqueur and Vincent both made clear, human belief that the dead are sacred is unrelated to religious belief or a lack thereof. I would argue, therefore, that at least some part of that loss of respect must be laid at the feet of the Yugoslav Communist party, not because it secularized cemeteries (which it did only partially) but rather because it reinvented them as political spaces, thus making them fair game in any political battlefield. At the same time, those spaces remained segregated along ethnoreligious and/or national lines, allowing what had been, at least theoretically, a politics of class identity to become one of ethnoreligious and national identity. Thus, as Yugoslavia disintegrated, it was both logistically possible (indeed easy) and within acceptable political boundaries to attack the cemeteries of one's ethnoreligious or national enemies. Orthodox Serbs could destroy the graves and cemeteries or cemetery sections of their Muslim and Catholic enemies without harming their own graves and vice versa. Many did so, moreover, in accordance with a nationalist ideology that now claimed a direct connection between land ownership and the location of a nation's dead.

Those who desecrated the graves of their ethnoreligious enemies were often inclined also to violate Partisan graves, cemeteries, ossuaries, and mausoleums, especially those marked with the five-pointed star but even many of those with more abstract symbolism. Some of the new nationalist forces associated Communist rule and Yugoslavia itself with "Serbian hegemony" and were thus inclined to consider Partisan graves and cemeteries as the functional equivalent to those of Serbs. Moreover, Yugoslavia's nationalist successor states explicitly or implicitly rejected many or all of the ideals and values of the collective identity that the Partisan cemeteries had helped to create: a united Yugoslav state, brotherhood and unity, and Socialist construction.

Under these conditions, it is hardly surprising that during and after Yugoslavia's dissolution, many of these cemeteries and memorials suffered neglect, abandonment, and in some cases repeated desecration. This then brings us back full circle to the Partisan Cemetery in Mostar. In his exemplary work on that cemetery, Andrew Lawler created a ranking system to evaluate its status relative to the postwar protection and condition of Bogdan Bogdanović's other twenty-one monuments to the People's Liberation Struggle located throughout

Yugoslavia. Although the level of official protection among them varied considerably, it was not necessarily the most important criteria, particularly as Lawler could not evaluate enforcement, and issues such as location and the memorial's value to the community were equally relevant.[94] The Partisan Memorial Cemetery served as the location not only for regular and well-attended commemorative events but was also an extremely popular site for leisure-time activities among the city's population. Its verdant landscaping, fountain, and rivulets created a cool oasis within Mostar's often-scorching urban environment. In addition, Bogdanović's remarkable architecture was widely promoted among tourists and was one of the city's and republic's prime attractions.[95]

More importantly, there is some evidence that the cemetery indeed helped create that collective identity. In 2013, Kristin Ilić and Nevena Škrbić Alempijević interviewed younger Mostar residents about their perceptions of the Partisan Cemetery. Some expressed a sense of nostalgia reflecting the views of their parents who "really really miss it." According to the authors, expressions often emerged in the interviews advocating "the return of the cohesive dimension of the memorial complex as a potential place that connects different groups within the city."[96] It may be precisely that potential to connect different groups that makes the Mostar Partisan Cemetery such a threat to those nationalist/fascist forces so determined to destroy it and any hope of reconciliation. Had the cemetery also included the remains of soldiers from the opposing side, perhaps they might have left it alone, allowing it to create once again that "cohesive dimension."

The politicization of cemeteries in Socialist Yugoslavia reached its apex during the late 1980s and throughout the 1990s. The selective commemoration of soldiers and victims that had followed the Second World War culminated in their overt politicization with the "narrative of bones and graves" deliberately designed to ethnicize dead bodies in late 1980s and 1990s. Meanwhile, grave markers were gradually transformed into visual and representational emblems, displaying the political affiliation of the dead, initially only for supporters of the regime, but then they were turned against the regime by supporters of nationalist parties seeking autonomy and separation. Ultimately, the constant and multifarious means by which the regime had insinuated politics into burial culture reached their logical conclusion with the desecration of graves and cemeteries, both private and public, leading up to, during, and after the wars of Yugoslav dissolution. None of this was inevitable—not the dissolution, not the violence, and certainly not the grave and cemetery desecrations. Yet in all cases, the party's policies and actions made the final outcomes more likely than not.

Conclusion: Death after Communism

Yugoslavia failed twice: once in 1941 with the onset of the Second World War and concurrent civil war and once in 1991 when the wars of Yugoslav dissolution ended the Communist regime. Although both attempts at South Slavic unity ended in civil war and nationalist atrocities, one cannot draw parallel lines of repeated policies leading to a predictably disastrous outcome. In direct contrast to the first interwar regime, the communists never really tried to create a Yugoslav nation, recognizing its abject failure in the country's first iteration. Rather, while seeking to prevent overt nationalist expressions, particularly among Serbs and Croats, it also explicitly avoided any intimation that national cultures or identities would be subsumed or oppressed within the new Yugoslav Federation. That was precisely the point of the slogan "brotherhood and unity." All nations were to be equal and fully capable of self-realization under the broad umbrella of the federal system, while united by their loyalty to the state and Marxist-Leninist ideology.

An important element of that ideology was respect for pluralism and secularism. Although religious freedom was guaranteed by law, so too was the strict separation of church and state. Moreover, the Communist regime sought to reduce religion's influence on society by means of science, technology, and education. The Yugoslav Communist party was also especially anxious to disentangle what had often been an integral connection between national and religious identity. Thus, while the Communist regime could not wish to create Yugoslav cemeteries in which all citizens renounced their original national identity, nor could it reasonably wish to maintain ethnoreligiously segregated ones. Such cemeteries in the first Yugoslavia were owned, managed, and controlled by the religious communities and were explicitly exclusive as they frequently denied burial rights to individuals outside their community. In order to support and promote its own ideological program, the Communist regime would need to create a society, communities, and even cemeteries based neither on religion nor Yugoslavism but concepts it promoted for its Partisan cemeteries: a united Yugoslav state and brotherhood and unity.

Those Partisan cemeteries and other memorials dedicated to soldiers and victims of fascism may be favorably judged for their ability both to help alleviate grief and create a new collective identity. Alongside the concepts of a united Yugoslav state and brotherhood and unity was also the construction of socialism. While all three values were evident, Partisan cemeteries created in the first fifteen years after the war were often hastily conceived and constructed. They often followed stereotypical Soviet-style designs heavily reliant on Communist symbols like the five-pointed star and formulaic inscriptions about "occupiers and domestic collaborators," "sacrificed youth," and "eternal glory." Nonetheless, they represented the genuine efforts and desire for remembrance by families, friends, and comrades who visited them regularly as legitimate spaces of mourning.

Over time, the main purpose and character of the Partisan cemeteries evolved to better suit the needs of the state in its desire to create a collective identity. A critical aspect of that process was the development of a more sophisticated and tolerant form of socialism, along with the abandonment of many Soviet ideological dogmas and symbols. Although Yugoslav communists never dropped their attachment to the five-pointed Partisan star, or even the Marxist hammer and sickle, they opened the door for Yugoslavia's artists and designers to create alternate and more abstract symbolic forms, which proved to be more flexible in helping the state promote its collective identity. The secular, integrated, and more egalitarian design of Partisan cemeteries was also more conducive to a new Yugoslav identity. Nonetheless, by remaining politically exclusive, and refusing entrance to those who had fought against the Communist regime, the Partisan cemetery and its form of collective identity was also clearly limited.

Moreover, when it came to civilian cemeteries, the regime did not even try to integrate them and use them as a source for collective identity. In Croatia and Serbia, it effectively removed cemetery ownership and management from the hands of the religious communities by the mid-1960s. It did not, however, change the essential structure of either the already existing cemeteries or even, in most cases, newly created ones, reconfirming their ethnoreligious segregation. In Bosnia & Hercegovina, the republic with the greatest degree of ethnoreligious pluralism, the regime did not even seriously try to assume ownership and management of the cemeteries until the 1980s when the country itself was on the verge of destruction. The new municipal cemeteries in that republic not only maintained the ethnoreligious segregation but sometimes even accentuated it with visual markers.

Similarly, in order to support and confirm its own ideological program, the regime might logically have worked to create new secular burial rituals that could eventually supplement if not entirely supplant the old religious ones. But again, it did not, or only to a very limited degree. The party's general reluctance to interfere with national and cultural autonomy meant that it tolerated many religious traditions and rituals but particularly those related to burial culture, properly understood to be an area of exceptional sensitivity. The Communist regime's forbearance in this regard could be fortunate and even admirable. The remarks and analyses of CRQ, state, and party officials regarding the cultural significance and sensitivity of burial rites and traditions were often a tribute, however unexpected, to their insight and perception. Many European countries have fared well with similar approaches to cemetery management and design in the twentieth and twenty-first centuries. Certainly, none of Yugoslavia's religious communities would have complained about a consistent policy of benign neglect. Had it been left at that, those in charge of Yugoslavia's burial policies might only be blamed for being insufficiently vigilant communists—faint damnation.

Along with maintaining cemetery segregation, however, Communist policies regarding the burial of its adherents and enemies made cemeteries into spaces of political discourse in ways that opened them up to weaponization in the late 1980s and 1990s. Immediately following the Second World War, the Communist party focused attention mainly on the sacrifices made by Partisans and to a lesser degree victims of fascist terror, while generally avoiding discussions and commemorations of interethnic atrocities. Only funerals of its own supporters were prioritized after the war, and specific burial rituals were created only for them. Those rituals sometimes caused conflict with families who also wished to include religious rites at their funerals. The political credentials of Partisans and those loyal to the regime in civilian cemeteries were celebrated and commemorated with the placement of five-pointed stars on their graves. Meanwhile, the sacrifices of countless others who died in the war were neglected and those who died on the opposing side of the war were left officially unmourned, often in deliberately unmarked or even eradicated graves.

The nationalist narrative of "bones and graves" that arose in the 1980s sought to remind families and religious communities of those whose sacrifices had gone unmarked by the Communist regime. By the time those nationalist policies intensified into violence by the late 1980s and 1990s, cemeteries and grave markers had become well known throughout the region as sites and symbols of not only one's own beloved ancestors but also one's national and political enemies. Their graves were clearly marked and set aside for anyone to find and defile. The desecrations that took place in the years leading up to, during, and following the wars of Yugoslav dissolution reveal the role that the dead had come to play in battles of the living.

Epilogue

I began conducting research for this topic in 2011 and made regular research trips every few years up through 2022. By then each of the three former Yugoslav republics as well as the former Autonomous Province of Kosovo were functioning as fully independent states. In Croatia, the Serbian population had been largely driven out in the final stages of the war and reduced from 12 percent to 4.4 percent of the population. Similarly, the Serbian population of Kosova was reduced from 10 percent in 1991 to 1.5 percent in 2011. Serbia, still united with Vojvodina, remained somewhat multiethnic, but Serbs certainly made up the vast majority with 83.3 percent of the population. Only Bosnia & Hercegovina could really claim to still be seriously multiethnic, but even that country was less pluralistic than it had been in 1991. In 1981 Muslims made up 39.5 percent of the population, Serbs 32 percent, Croats 18.4 percent, Yugoslavs 7.9 percent, and various others 2.3 percent. According to the 2013 census, Bosniaks made up 50.11 percent, Serbs 30.78 percent, Croats 15.4 percent, others 2.3 percent, and undeclared or no answer 0.89 percent. More significantly, the ethnic groups were less mixed and more likely to have established clear majorities within specific territorial regions.

More important than altered demographics for purposes of burial culture was the transformed political and economic culture of each country, which was clearly reflected in grave markers. All three states were characterized by increasingly religious political cultures, sometimes combined with virulent anti-communism. This trend was unsurprisingly marked by a significant increase in the number and style of religious symbols on grave markers. While the Communist regime had legally allowed the inclusion on grave markers of all regular religious symbols (such as Crosses, the Crescent Moon and Star, and the Star of David), very few graves during the Communist period bore conspicuous additional religious symbols. Although no written laws prevented an individual from doing so, one can only assume that such symbols were simply not made available by those creating the monuments who understood that they might be held responsible.

Many citizens also likely engaged in a degree of self-censorship appropriate in a state well known for its persecution of prominent religious figures.

It is perhaps unsurprising, therefore, that the fall of communism resulted in an enormous increase in the religious content of many grave markers. This change was most obvious on the graves of Catholic Croats, though it could be seen to a lesser degree elsewhere as well. On Catholic graves, along with the cross, many markers came also to include etchings of a crucifix and/or an angel. Just as often, however, these symbols were included as figurines placed on the slab, including statuettes of the Virgin Mary, cupids, doves, and multiple candles and lanterns. Muslim religious indicators also increased, particularly in Bosnia & Hercegovina during and after the war, when Arabic inscriptions were increasingly evident on grave markers. The one significant exception here occurred in Kosova where grave markers remain largely secular. Given the long-standing tension between private and public attention to mourning, it is difficult to ascertain whether the increase in religious iconography most reflects piety, nationalism, or anti-communism. What is clear, however, is that the balance of power in that relationship has shifted away from the state and back into the hands of the private citizen though clearly influenced by ethnoreligious communities (Figure C.1).

In many ways the most striking distinction between grave markers before and after the fall of communism was a function of economics. Regardless of their religiosity or ideological response to communism, all four regions reflected the strong influence of global capitalism. Although the monument industry was never officially nationalized under communism, it has become far more consumer-oriented in the new capitalist era providing many greater options in grave marker selection. Meanwhile the rapid rise of conspicuous consumption and its display as a means of establishing status has contributed to the creation of enormous and ostentatious funeral monuments, commemorating the lives of murdered Mafiosi or the nouveaux riche.

The great majority of new grave markers erected after 1991 were made of shiny black marble; many were also larger than those in the past. It has become common to see on them not so much the photographs described earlier but now life-sized etchings of the deceased in various attire and poses, surrounded by images or figurines representing their most important possessions, including automobiles. Some even include shelves to hold the growing number of figurines (Figures C.2 and C.3). In a few cases, full-color hologram-like images allow the visitor to see the deceased from all sides.

By far the most unusual grave I encountered is located in the Banja Luka municipal cemetery. Towering over a shiny black marble slab is the life-size

Figure C.1 Increased religious elements on grave markers
Zaprešić, Croatia for more photos on this theme see: https://yugcemeteries.omeka.net/exhibits/show/change-over-time

holographic image of a middle-aged deceased male in glass—a different image on each side, one in a blue suit, one in red. Although the marker includes a crescent moon and star and the deceased was evidently Muslim (possibly Roma), the epitaphs and paraphernalia reveal his worldly attitudes and interests. One small plaque bears an image of the deceased in a Muslim head scarf but wearing a suit jacket, tie, and sunglasses, above pictures of a wine glass, ashtray, and the Versace logo. The epitaph reads, "I raised this memorial to myself in honor of my life." Another plaque in the shape of a heart reads: "Here lies X, who left behind

Figure C.2 Capitalism and grave markers
Belgrade, Serbia

ten children, two wives, and thirty-three grandchildren. And when I put on my glasses, I see naked women" (Figure C.4).

While these new styles indicate the greater options now available to consumers, they have elicited negative reactions among many local observers. Although I neglected to photograph the grave markers to the left and right of this monument they are far more traditional and I could not help but wonder how the owners feel about their neighbor and how this addition is contributing to a new kind of community of the dead. Nonetheless, freed from the constraints of the Communist regime, cemetery administrators, and even apparently social norms, many citizens, dead and still living, are publicly displaying for all, elements of their individuality and status in a way previously unimaginable.

Roma Burial Customs

Many of the most interesting new grave markers to appear in the post-Communist era belong to the Roma community. Roma graves and cemeteries represent an entirely separate topic that I cannot begin to address properly but will only touch

236 *Death and Burial in Socialist Yugoslavia*

Figure C.3 Capitalism and grave markers
Zagreb, Croatia and Sarajevo, Bosnia & Hercegovina

Figure C.4 Mehmed

on as a stimulus for further research.¹ As a rule, the Roma community adopts the religion of the nation within which they reside. Thus, Roma in much of Serbia are Orthodox Christians, many in Croatia are Catholic, and most Roma in Bosnia & Hercegovina, Novi Pazar, and Kosovo/Kosova adopted Islam, but many of those Roma moved elsewhere while retaining their Muslim faith. In 1998, scholars at the Niš Romological School carried out a survey of Roma burial practices in Serbia. They expected to find that where Roma share the religion with the majority nation, they would be buried side by side with them in the same cemeteries. Indeed, nearly 52 percent of Orthodox Roma buried their deceased alongside other Orthodox non-Roma and 22.6 percent in the same cemetery, but in a different section, while 25.3 percent buried them in a different cemetery. Among the Muslim Roma, however, only 8.3 percent buried them in the same cemetery alongside non-Roma, 34.7 percent in the same cemetery but in a different section, and nearly 57 percent in a separate cemetery.²

Since the fall of Communism, separate Roma cemeteries currently exist in all three republics. Although a few are now publicly accessible, it is unclear if they are under municipal administration. I visited two Roma cemeteries in Serbia—an Orthodox one in Mali Crljen and a Muslim one in Leskovac—both of which, however, apparently dated only from the fall of Communism. I also visited a Muslim Roma cemetery in Vitez, Bosnia & Hercegovina, with markers dating back at least to the 1950s.³ Another Roma cemetery apparently existed in Novi Pazar, but I was unable to gain directions or access to it lacking the necessary contacts. The suspicion evident among those I asked was certainly justified. The very existence of separate Roma cemeteries despite their common religious connections to the local population indicates the strength of their isolation and the very real discrimination and persecution that many experience in some areas of the country. The Niš survey asked various non-Roma how comfortable they would be with deceased Roma being buried in their cemeteries. While the responses varied considerably depending on religion, nationality, and location, a substantial proportion, and in most cases a majority, preferred them to be buried in either separate sections or cemeteries.⁴ That this view is not unique to Serbia or the Balkan Peninsula may be seen in the 2015 decision of a French mayor to refuse burial to a Roma infant in a local municipal cemetery.⁵ The long-standing persecution of Roma has also often included gravestone and cemetery desecration. In 2013 the Ombudsman for the Institution of Human Rights ordered the Municipality of Lukavac, Bosnia & Hercegovina, to prevent repeated vandalism of its small local Roma cemetery but as late as October 2016, the town still had not done so.⁶

A common feature within Roma cemeteries, though one not unique to them, is the construction of fences around the gravesites or even entire buildings. Every gravesite at the Leskovac Roma cemetery was a fenced-in area approximately 15' × 15' square. Although the cemetery itself did not appear to be maintained by the municipality, each individual gravesite was meticulously cleaned and cared for. Many had benches and flowers and while some appeared to have been constructed with "leftover" materials, others were quite luxurious. Among the Roma and Serbian communities in Eastern Serbia and in the Serbian Republic of Bosnia & Hercegovina, families have also created for their decedents fully furnished houses rather than grave markers.[7] Made of brick or wood, they have doors and curtained windows. Looking inside, the visitor can see in each a table and chairs bearing flowers and fruit and sometimes also a small loveseat. Paintings and memorials hang on the walls dedicated to the deceased.

Nonetheless, most Roma are still buried in municipal cemeteries and during the Communist era their grave markers were often indistinguishable from those of non-Roma with only the photographs and names offering any indication of the ethnicity of their inhabitants. Since the fall of Communism, however, many Roma grave markers, both Orthodox and Muslim, have begun to develop a distinctive style. They have tended toward a much larger size, made of shiny marble, with highly personalized etchings of the inhabitants often on both sides of the stone. The etchings often portray the individual in typical Roma clothing engaged in everyday activities such as drinking coffee or alcohol, playing cards, or participating in favorite hobbies. Some also include images of beloved vehicles or musical instruments. They are dramatic, sometimes colorful, and instantly recognizable. By the 2010s, a few Roma graves had also begun to include the Roma national symbol of the wagon wheel and epitaphs in the Roma language. Otherwise, they were always in BCS, using Cyrillic or the Latin script depending on their location (Figure C.5).

Figure C.5 Roma grave markers
Sarajevo and Banja Luka, Bosnia & Hercegovina and Leskovac, Serbia. For more photographs on this theme see: https://yugcemeteries.omeka.net/exhibits/show/roma-graves-and-cemeteries.

I end this monograph with a tribute to my all-time favorite grave marker located close to the front gate in the Municipal Cemetery of Banja Luka. This remarkable gravestone is exceptional for its evident determination to maintain private forms of inclusive mourning, in protest against nationalist demands for exclusionary politics. A family marker with five surnames and nine individuals born between 1918 and 1940, of whom only three were then deceased (in 2007 and 2013). The stone displays four symbols: a Catholic/or Protestant cross, a knobbed Orthodox cross, the Islamic Crescent Moon and Star, and a Partisan Star, unconnected to specific names but reflecting multiple mixed marriages and creating diversity evident in the names which, though not entirely reliable,

Conclusion 241

Figure C.6 Hope for the future
Banja Luka, Bosnia & Hercegovina

suggest Serbian (Milijana, Aleksandar), Croatian (Krunoslav, Vlasta), and Muslim (Muharem) heritage. Designed and erected after the bloody wars of Yugoslav dissolution and in the capital of the deeply nationalist Bosnian Serb Republic, this grave marker stands out as a plea for ethnoreligious tolerance and peace. As I see it, this grave marker is very close to what the Yugoslav Communist regime should have been aiming for from the beginning. The future residents of this grave, while still specifying their ethnoreligious affiliation, do so with complete tolerance for one another on one grave marker. It provides hope for a better future, even as they have come from one failed state and live in another that is still struggling (Figure C.6).

Glossary

Bosniak—term for Bosnian citizens who based their identity on Islam.

Bošnjaštvo—beginnings of Bosnian national identity, developed during the period of the Austro-Hungarian administration (1907–14) by Bosnian Muslim nobles.

Chetnik (četnik)—although technically the term could simply mean any member of a Serbian military unit (četa), it is normally used in reference to those who sided with the Serbian nationalist Dragoljub-Draža Mihailović during the Second World War. Although officially operating also in resistance to the occupiers, Mihailović's Chetniks sometimes collaborated with the Germans considering the Partisans a greater threat to the postwar order.

Columbarium—a building or wall containing niches to hold urns for cremated remains.

Dvoeverie—Russian term for "dual belief" that refers to the merging of Christian beliefs and rituals with those already extant from pre-Christian pagan religions.

Gemeinschaft—community, individuals bound together by common values.

Gesellschaft—society, associations formed on the basis of self-interest.

Hevra Kadisha—Jewish funeral society.

Koheni—Jewish priests

Krajina—officially known as "Vojska Krajina" meaning "Military Frontier." Formerly a region of Croatia along what had been the border between the Austrian Empire and the Ottoman Empire. In the sixteenth century, the Habsburg Dynasty invited Orthodox Serbs to colonize the region, offering them free land and religious rights in return for which they would fight the invading Turks. Though expected to be temporary, the arrangement became permanent. As a result, by 1948 Serbs made up some 14.5 percent of Croatia's population.

Matična knjiga—registry book for birth, marriage, and death.

Millet system—Ottoman administrative system that provided religious communities considerable economic and educational autonomy. The system strengthened the connection between religious and national identity in the region.

Ocilo—part of the Serbian herald and flag consisting of four Cyrillic "c"s (s's in the Latin alphabet) separated by a cross. Each "c represents the first letter of the slogan: "Samo Sloga Srbina Spasava" (Only the Unity of Serbs Can Save Us).

Općina/Opština—township.

Opštejugoslovenski—general Yugoslav.

Ossuary—a mausoleum or monument containing bones of the dead.

Reis-ul-ulema—title of the highest cleric of Bosnian Muslims, with authority over other Muslims in Socialist Yugoslavia.

Šahovnica—term for the red and white checkerboard flag of Croatia. Although its origins are said to date back to the tenth century, it became known as the state symbol in the nineteenth century. Because it was also used by the fascist Ustashe regime, its revival in the 1990s was highly controversial.

Shiva—week-long period of mourning among Jews.

Stećci (stećak singular)—medieval tombstones in Bosnia & Hercegovina.

Tabut—flat wooden board, covered with cloth (usually green) used in place of a coffin for Muslim burials.

Tehvid—Muslim communal mourning ritual in Bosnia & Hercegovina, usually held at the home of a relative of the deceased. During these meetings, women read prayers for the deceased while also engaging in various social networking activities.

Ustasha (ustaša)—Croatian fascist organization founded during the interwar period that came to power during the Second World War. Working in collaboration with the Nazi occupiers, the Ustasha sought to exterminate not only the region's Jewish and Roma but also its Serbian population.

Vakuf/waqf—Muslim inalienable charitable endowment.

Vojska Krajina—see Krajina.

Zadušnica—Serbian holiday to commemorate the dead. Comparable to the Catholic Day of the Dead/All Souls' Day, but there are four throughout the year.

Notes

Introduction

1 Azem Kurtić, "Vandals Wreck Yugoslav Partisans' Necropolis in Bosnia's Mostar," *Balkan Transitional Justice*, BIRN, June 15, 2022. Accessed October 20, 2022, https://balkaninsight.com/2022/06/15/vandals-wreck-yugoslav-partisans-necropolis-in-bosnias-mostar.

2 A considerable literature on the Mostar Partisan Memorial Cemetery has developed in the past decade. Andrew Lawler, "The Partisan's Cemetery in Mostar, Bosnia & Herzegovina: Implications of the Deterioration of a Monument and Site," MA Thesis, Faculty of Engineering, Catholic University Leuven, Belgium (September 2013); Kristina Ilić and Nevena Škrbić Alempijević, "Cultures of Memory, Landscapes of Forgetting: The Case Study of the Partisan Memorial Cemetery in Mostar," *Studia ethnologica Croatica*, 29 (2017): 73–101; Mateo Gospić, "The Partisan Memorial Cemetery in Mostar," *Pro Tempore*, 15 (2020): 185–91; Marija Ivanović, "Of (Anti)fascists and (Anti)communists: Constructing the People and Its Enemies at the Partisan Memorial Cemetery in Mostar," in Jody Jensen, ed., *Memory Politics and Populism in Southeastern Europe* (New York: Taylor and Francis, 2021), 64–77. Also see the remarkable Spomenik Database created by Donald Niebyl, https://www.spomenikdatabase.org/home.

3 I am grateful to Andrew Lawler who elaborated on the complex relationship between the memorial cemetery, stones, and ossuary based on his extensive research on this topic. According to Lawler, as the relationship between the memorial cemetery, gravestones, and ossuary has become blurred with time, this question of if and where actual remains are located in the cemetery has become a touchstone issue between those who want to preserve the site and those who negate its historic value. Personal email correspondence, December 28, 2022.

4 Terri Williams, "Jim Crow and African-American Cemeteries and Burial Practices," *Higher Ground: Honoring Washington Park Cemetery, Its People and Place*. Accessed June 17, 2020, http://omeka.wustl.edu/omeka/exhibits/show/washington-park/about-cemetery/jimcrow; Tess Pantoja Perez and Josie Mendez-Negrete, "Burial Practices Expose Identity Formation: Muerte y figura hasta la sepultura," *Association of Mexican American Educators (AMAE) Journal*, 13, 1 (2019): 79–101. Accessed January 31, 2021, https://journals.coehd.utsa.edu/index.php/AMAE/article/view/226/217; Sue Fawn Chung, "An Ocean Apart: Chinese American Segregated

Burials," in Allan Amanik and Kami Fletcher, eds., *Til Death Do Us Part: American Ethnic Cemeteries as Borders Uncrossed*, (Jackson: University Press of Mississippi, 2020), 85–120.

5. Charles Van Onselen, "Dead But Not Quite Buried," *London Review of Books*, 20, 21 (October 29, 1998). Accessed January 29, 2021, Charles van Onselen Dead But Not Quite Buried: The Desecration Industry in South Africa · LRB 29 October 1998, https://www.lrb.co.uk/the-paper/v20/n21/charles-van-onselen/dead-but-not-quite-buried.

6. Mehrdad Amanat, "Set in Stone: Homeless Corpses and Desecrated Graves in Modern Iran," *International Journal of Middle East Studies*, 44, 2 (May 2012): 257–83.

7. Editorial Staff, "The Destruction of Sufi Shrines," *The Muslim 500*. Accessed February 3, 2021, https://themuslim500.com/destruction-of-sufi-shrines/.

8. I have chosen to focus on those republics in part because I am fluent in Bosnian-Croatian-Serbian (BCS). Moreover, these three republics make for an excellent comparison given their ethnoreligious diversity. According to the 1948 census, which counted national rather than religious affiliation, Croatia's population was largely made up of Croats who are mostly Catholic but included a substantial Serbian Orthodox minority (14.4 percent); Serbia was largely inhabited by Serbs but had far more ethnoreligious diversity in Vojvodina, which included substantial numbers of Croats, Hungarians, and Slovaks (many of whom are Catholic), and in Novi Pazar and Kosovo where Muslims made up a large proportion of the population. Bosnia & Hercegovina was the most diverse republic with Serbs accounting for 44 percent of the population, Bosnian Muslims 31 percent, and Croats 24 percent. All three republics also included citizens belonging to various Protestant denominations and the Jewish faith. Likely as a result of this ethnoreligious diversity, the greatest amount of conflict and violence took place precisely in those regions during the wars of Yugoslav dissolution. *Stanovništvo po narodnosti po popisu od 15. marta 1948 godine*, Beograd, 1954. http://pod2.stat.gov.rs/ObjavljenePublikacije/G1948/Pdf/G19484001.pdf.

9. Phillip Aries, *The Hour of Our Death* (New York: Vintage Books, 1982).

10. Thomas Laqueur, *The Work of the Dead* (Princeton, NJ: Princeton University Press, 2015).

11. Ralph Houlbrook, *Death, Religion, and the Family in England, 1480–1750* (Oxford: Clarendon Press, 1998); Thomas Kselman, *Death and the Afterlife in Modern France* (Princeton, NJ: Princeton University Press, 1993); John R. Gillis, ed., *Commemorations: The Politics of National Identity*, (Princeton, NJ: Princeton University Press, 1994); Clodagh Tait, *Death, Burial and Commemoration in Ireland, 1550–1650* (New York: Palgrave McMillan, 2002); Richard Meyer, ed., *Ethnicity*

and the American Cemetery (Bowling Green, OH: Bowling Green State University Popular Press, 1993).
12 Julie Rugg, *Churchyard and Cemetery: Tradition and Modernity in Rural North Yorkshire* (Manchester: Manchester University Press, 2013).
13 Rugg; Monica Black, *Death in Berlin: From Weimar to Divided Germany* (Cambridge: Cambridge University Press, 2010); Felix Robin Schulz, *Death in East Germany, 1945–1990* (New York: Berghan Books, 2013).
14 Schulz, 4.
15 Schulz, 35.
16 Black; Schulz; L. M. Danforth, *The Death Rituals of Rural Greece* (Princeton, NJ: Princeton University Press, 1982).
17 Leor Halevi, *Muhammad's Grave: Death Rites and the Making of Islamic Society* (New York: Columbia University Press, 2007); Nicholas Constas, *Death and Dying in Byzantium* (Minneapolis, MN: Fortress, 2006); Amila Buturović, *Carved in Stone, Etched in Memory: Death, Tombstones and Commemoration in Bosnian Islam since c. 1500* (Farnham: Ashgate, 2015); Tone Bringa, *Being Muslim the Bosnian Way: Identity and Community in a Central Bosnian Village* (Princeton, NJ: Princeton University Press, 1995); Nolan Menachemson, *A Practical Guide to Jewish Cemeteries* (Bergenfield, NJ: Avotaynu, 2007); Rabbi Elyokim Schlesinger, *The Sacred Obligation of Burial and Life after Death in Jewish Belief* (Antwerp: European Agudas Yisroel, 2008).
18 Christel Lane, *The Rites of Rulers: Ritual in Industrial Society—the Soviet Case* (Cambridge: Cambridge University Press, 1981); Catherine Merridale, *Night of Stone: Death and Memory in Twentieth Century Russia* (New York: Viking Penguin, 2002); Catriona Kelly, *St. Petersburg: Shadows of the Past* (New Haven, CT: Yale University Press, 2014); Victoria Smolkin, *A Sacred Space Is Never Empty: A History of Soviet Atheism* (Princeton, NJ: Princeton University Press, 2018); Katherine Verdery, *The Political Lives of Dead Bodies: Reburial and Postsocialist Change* (New York: Columbia University Press, 1999); Gail Kligman, *The Wedding of the Dead* (Berkeley: University of California Press, 1988).
19 Penny Roberts, "Contesting Sacred Space: Burial Disputes in Sixteenth Century France," in Bruce Gordon and Peter Marshall, eds., *The Place of the Dead: Death and Remembrance in Late Medieval and Early Modern Europe* (Cambridge: Cambridge University Press, 2000), 131–48; Tait; Keith Luria, "Separated by Death: Cemeteries, Burials and Confessional Boundaries in Seventeenth Century France," *French Historical Studies*, 24, 2 (Spring 2001): 185–221; Banu Barga, "Another Necropolitics," *Theory and Politics*, 19, 1 (January 2016): 1–18.
20 Allan Amanik and Kami Fletcher, eds., *Till Death Do Us Part: American Ethnic Cemeteries as Borders Uncrossed* (Jackson: University of Mississippi Press, 2020).

21 Fred Vincent, "From Desecration to Reconciliation: Considering Attacks on the Sacred During the Troubles and Proposing a Framework Response, *Shared Space: A Research Journal on Peace, Conflict and Community Relations in Northern Ireland*, Institute for Conflict Research, 8 (July 2009): 67–84; Robert Bevan, *The Destruction of Memory: Architecture at War* (London: Reaktion Books, 2006); Andrew Herscher and Andras Riedelmayer, "Monument and Crime: The Destruction of Historic Architecture in Kosovo," *The Grey Room*, 1 (Autumn 2000): 108–22; R. Ravindran, *Religious Desecration and Ethnic Violence*, Unpublished Master's Thesis, Monterey, California, Naval Post-Graduate School (2006); Emily Jane O'Dell, "Waging War on the Dead: The Necropolitics of Sufi Shrine Destruction in Mali," *Archaeologies: Journal of the World Archeological Congress*, 9, 3 (December 2013): 506–24; Barga.

22 Andrew Herscher, *Violence Taking Place* (Stanford, CA: Stanford University Press, 2010) 51.

23 Laqueur, 4.

24 Radmila Radić, *Verom protiv vere: Država i verske zajednice u Srbiji 1945–1953* (Beograd: INIS, 1995); Miroslav Akmadža, *Katolička crkva u komunističkoj Hrvatskoj, 1945–1985* (Zagreb: Hrvatska Povijest, 2013); Buturović; Stjepan Sršan, *Osječka Groblja* (Osijek: Povijesni Arhiv, 1996); Ivan Trčak, ed., *Mirogoj: Kulturno-povijesni vodič* (Zagreb: Kršćanska Sadašnjost i Rektorat Crkve Krista Kralja, Mirogoj, 1987); Bratislava Kostić, *Novo groblje u Beogradu* (Beograd: JKP: Pogrebne Usluge, 1999); Mehmed Mujezinović, *Islamska Epigrafika Bosne i Hercegovine*, 2 vols. (Sarajevo: Sarajevo Publishing, 1998).

25 Ivan Čolović, *Književnost na Groblju: Zbirka novih epitafa* (Beograd: Narodna Knjiga, 1983); Bojan Jovanović, *Srpska knjiga mrtvih* (Novi Sad: Prometej, 1992); Edit Petrović, "Posmrtni običaji kod ateista: na primeru crnogorskih kolonista u Bačkoj," *Etnološke sveske*, VIII (1987): 179–86; Dunja Rihtman-Augustin, "Novinske osmrtnice," *Narodna umjetnost*, 15 (1978): 119–74.

26 Pierre Nora, ed., *Les liex de memoire*, 7 vols. (Paris: Gallimard, 1984–92); Jay Winter, *Sites of Memory, Sites of Mourning: The Great War in European Cultural History* (Cambridge: Cambridge University Press, 1995).

27 Jelena Djureinović, *The Politics of Memory of the Second World War in Contemporary Serbia* (London: Routledge Press, 2020); Heike Karge, *Sećanje u Kamenu—Okamenjeno Sećanje*, translated by Aleksandra Kostić (Belgrade: Biblioteka XX Vek, 2014); Donald Niebyl, *Spomenik Monument Database* (London: Fuel Publishing, 2018); Lawler, "The Partisan's Cemetery in Mostar"; Jelena Subotić, *Red Star, Yellow Star: Holocaust Remembrance after Communism* (Cornell, NY: Cornell University Press, 2019).

28 Jay Winter's extraordinary work also crosses this boundary but does so still by focusing mainly on public memorials, rather than cemeteries. Jay Winter,

Remembering War: *The Great War Between Memory and History in the Twentieth Century*, (New Haven: Yale University Press, 2008).

29 Jürgen Habermas, *The Structural Transformation of the Political Sphere* (Cambridge: MIT Press, 1998), 27–30.

30 Hannah Arendt, *The Human Condition*, 2nd ed. (Chicago, IL: University of Chicago Press, 1998), 62–3, 72.

31 Susan Gal, "A Semiotics of the Public/Private Distinction," *differences: A Journal of Feminist Cultural Studies*, 13, 1 (Spring 2002): 77.

32 Habermas, 122–9.

33 Gal, 86.

34 Habermas, 2.

35 Craig Calhoun, "Secularism, Citizenship and the Public Sphere," *Hedgehog Review*, 10, 3 (2008): 11.

36 Under the Ottoman Empire religious faiths (Orthodox, Armenian, Jews, and eventually also Catholics) were organized into communities referred to as "millets," which were then permitted a degree of indirect self-governance.

37 Habermas's framework included three categories, two described as private and one public, but one of the ostensibly "private" categories was "an unnamed intermediary realm as part of the Private realm that includes the Public sphere in the political realm, the public sphere in the world of letters (clubs, press) and 'Town' (the market of culture products)." Habermas, 30.

38 Tone Bringa, *Being Muslim the Bosnian Way: Identity and Community in a Central Bosnian Village* (Princeton, NJ: Princeton University Press, 1995): 54–5, 70–3, 194–5.

39 Gal, 82.

40 Many thanks to Max Garvue and Laurinda Weisse for their invaluable assistance with the creation and proper placement of this map. I could not have done it without them! https://openspaces.unk.edu/data/1/. doi: 10.32873/unk.data.01

41 In this work, I will generally use the term *Kosovo* for the period from 1945 to 2008, *Kosova* after its official independence in 2008, and *Kosovo/Kosova* for other general use. I realize that this is not an entirely satisfactory compromise and likely to result in inconsistencies for which I apologize in advance.

42 Much of this chapter has been previously published as "Communities of the Dead: Secularizing Cemeteries in Communist Yugoslavia," *Slavonic and East European Review*, 97, 4 (2019): 676–710.

43 I use the term "mixed marriages" as a generalized term for both interfaith and interethnic marriages in the former Yugoslavia. While most individuals in marriages that fall under that term were of both differing religious and ethnic backgrounds, many considered themselves atheists (i.e., without religion) and thus the term "interfaith" does not properly apply. In other cases, while the husband and

wife clearly belong to differing religious communities, their ethnic origin cannot be determined from the grave marker.

44 Laqueur, 8.
45 Caitlin Doughty, *From Here to Eternity: Traveling the World to Find the Good Death* (London: W. W. Norton, 2017), 7–12.

1 Burial Cultures of the Region

1 Jaoa Zilhao, "Lower and Middle Paleolithic Mortuary Behaviors and the Origins of Ritual Burial," in Colin Renfrew, Micheal Boyd, and Iain Morley, eds., *Death Rituals, Social Order and the Archeology of Immortality in the Ancient World* (Cambridge: Cambridge University Press, 2016), 27–45.
2 See Thomas Laqueur's lovely chapter on this topic, "Do the Dead Matter?" in *The Work of the Dead* (Princeton, NJ: Princeton University Press), 35–54.
3 Michel Ragon, *Space of Death: Study of Funerary Architecture, Decoration and Urbanism* (Charlottesville: University of Virginia Press, 1983), 14; Philippe Aries, *The Hour of Our Death* (New York: Vintage Books, 1982), 29–42; Frederick Paxton, *Christianizing Death: The Creation of a Ritual Process in Early Medieval Europe* (Ithaca, NY: Cornell University Press, 1990), 18.
4 Aries, 46–51; Ralph Houlbrooke, *Death, Religion and the Family in England, 1480–1750* (Oxford: Clarendon Press, 1998), 331.
5 Aries, 56–60; Houlbrooke, 332–3; J. Goody and C. Poppi, "Flowers and Bones: Approaches to the Dead in Anglo-American and Italian Cemeteries," *Comparative Studies in Society and History*, 36, I (1994): 159.
6 Richard Etlin, *The Architecture of Death: The Transformation of the Cemetery in Eighteenth Century Paris* (Cambridge: MIT Press, 1984), 10; Harold Mytum, *Recording and Analysing Graveyards*, vol. 15 of series: *Practical Handbooks in Archaeology* (York: Council for British Archaeology in Association with English Heritage, 2000), 44; Houlbrooke, 332–3.
7 Etlin, 10; Houlbrooke, 332.
8 Harold Mytum, *Mortuary Monuments and Burial Grounds of the Historic Period* (New York: Kluwer Academic, 2000), 17.
9 Ragon, 50–1; Rosemary Horrox, "Purgatory, Prayer and Plague: 1150–1380," in Peter C. Jupp, ed., *Death in England: An Illustrated History* (New Brunswick, NJ: Rutgers University Press, 2000), 103–5.
10 Paxton, 32–3; Horrox, 96–8; Thomas A. Kselman, *Death and the Afterlife in Modern France* (Princeton, NJ: Princeton University Press, 1993), 69.
11 Kselman, 90–4; Asmir Hodžić and Rodoljub Tansaić, *Funkcije pogrebne djelatnosti* (Sarajevo: JKP "Gradsko groblje" k.o.o. Visoko, 2007) 45–9; Odbor za pogrebne

delatnosti, *Kodeks Pogrebnih Usluga* (Beograd: Privredna komora Jugoslavije, Savet za zanatstvo, komunalnu i stambenu privredu, 1974), 31; Nikola Buconjić, *Život i obijčaji Hrvata katoličke vjere u Bosni i Hercegovini* (Sarajevo: Daniel A. Kajona, 1908), 137–44.

12 Clare Gitting, "Sacred and Secular: 1558–1660," in Peter C. Jupp and Clare Gitting eds., *Death in England: An Illustrated History* (New Brunswick, NJ: Rutgers University Press, 2000), 153; Penny Roberts, "Contesting Sacred Space: Burial Disputes in Sixteenth Century France," in Bruce Gordon and Peter Marshall, eds., *The Place of the Dead: Death and Remembrance in Late Medieval and Early Modern Europe* (Cambridge: Cambridge University Press, 2000), 134; Glennys Howarth, "Professionalizing the Funeral Industry in England, 1700–1960," in Peter C. Jupp and Glennys Howarth, eds., *The Changing Face of Death: Historical Accounts of Death and Disposal* (New York: St. Martin's Press, 1997), 121.

13 Roberts, 134–5; Houlbrook, 334; Howarth, 121–3; Goody and Poppi, 164.

14 Roberts, 132–9; Aries, 315–17; Tait, 79–81.

15 Roberts, 132; Tait, 83. See also Ragon, 52–3.

16 Peter Jupp and Glennys Howarth, "Introduction," in Jupp and Howarth, *The Changing Face of Death*, 4; Julie Rugg, *Churchyard and Cemetery: Tradition and Modernity in Rural North Yorkshire* (Manchester: Manchester University Press, 2013), 27–8.

17 Roberts, 140–3; Aries, 351; Ragon, 53.

18 Rosemarie van den Breemer and Marcel Maussen, "On the Viability of State-Church Models: Muslim Burial and Mosque Building in France and the Netherlands," *Journal of Immigrant and Refugee Studies*, 10, 3 (2012): 283.

19 Van den Breemer and Maussen, 283. On cemetery ownership in Britain, Germany, and Sweden, see Rugg, *Churchyard and Cemetery*; Felix Robin Schulz, *Death in East Germany: 1945–1990* (New York: Bergahn Books, 2013), 17–24; and Eva Reimers, "Death and Identity: Graves and Funerals as Cultural Communication," *Mortality*, 4, 2 (199): 154.

20 Etlin, 12–14.

21 Howard Colvin, *Architecture and the Afterlife* (New Haven, CT: Yale University Press, 1991), 368; Schulz, 17–24.

22 Aries, 506–9; Etlin, 229–39.

23 Aries, 495–8, 504–5; Etlin, 229, 248. Some of these conditions were not unique to France. When Mozart died in 1791, burials were also no longer permitted within Vienna's city limits. By the time his modest funeral ceremony ended, it was getting dark, so his body was stored overnight and taken to the cemetery out of town on the following day. Many have since expressed outrage that no one accompanied the wagon, but it was not customary for relatives to do so at the time. He was not placed in a common grave, but after ten years the lease on his grave was not

renewed and his bones were removed with the result that there is now no marker commemorating the site. James Steven Curl, *The Victorian Celebration of Death* (England: Sutton, 2000), 39.

24 Aries, 519; Etlin, 273–80.
25 Etlin, 295.
26 Aries 516–18; Etlin 295–300.
27 Colvin, 367.
28 Houlbrooke, 334–6; Curl, 37.
29 Houlbrooke, 338–41; Mytum, *Mortuary Monuments*, 20–2.
30 Julie Rugg, "The Origins and Progress of Cemetery Establishment in Britain," in Jupp and Howarth, *The Changing Face of Death*, 105–6; Curl, 111–12.
31 Curl, 113–19; Julie Rugg, "From Reason to Regulation: 1760–1850," in Jupp and Gitting, *Death in England*, 220–1.
32 Rugg, *Churchyard and Cemetery*.
33 Colvin, 373.
34 Goody and Poppi, 154, 164; Kodo Matsunami, *Funeral Customs of the World: A Comprehensive Guide to Practices and Traditions* (Tochigi: Buddhist Searchlight Center, 1998). The lessees were invited to claim the grave markers, but if they did not, they were usually recycled.
35 Colvin, 101; Etlin, 281–2; Curl, 181; Jalland, 249; Ragon, 284–5.
36 Curl, 182–5; Ragon, 272; Rugg, *Churchyard and Cemetery*, 289; Peter C. Jupp and Tony Walter, "The Healthy Society," in Peter C. Jupp and Clare Gitting, eds., *Death in England: An Illustrated Text* (New Brunswick: Rutgers University Press, 2000), 264.
37 A more radical and self-consciously egalitarian approach to the treatment of cremated remains developed in interwar Germany and continues to this day in many areas of Northern and Central Europe. These are, in German, *Urnengemeinschaftsanlage*, quite awkwardly translated as "anonymous communal areas for the internment of urns." They differ from more typical burial spaces for urns in that the precise burial space of each urn is unknown to the family since there are no names or other markers on them. It is perhaps unsurprising that these anonymous burial sites were particularly popular with the Socialist regimes of North Central Europe as they were seen to reject the individualistic approaches to burial associated with capitalism. Nonetheless, they were not unique to them, as they exist also in West Germany, the Scandinavian countries, the Netherlands, and even Great Britain. Schulz, 143, 159–67; Rugg, *Churchyard and Cemetery*, 346–8; Ragon, 287.
38 Nicholas Constas, "Death and Dying in Byzantium," in Derek Krueger, ed., *Byzantine Christianity*, Vol. 3 of *A People's History of Christianity* (Minneapolis, MN: Fortress, 2006), 134–5; Catherine Merridale, *Night of Stone: Death and*

Memory in Twentieth Century Russia (New York: Penguin, 2000), 44; Katya Vladimirov, "Dead Men Walking: Soviet Elite Cemeteries and Social Control," *Forum on Public Policy*, 8, 2 (2008): 2.
39 Constas, 144.
40 See, e.g., Bojan Jovanović, *Srpska knjiga mrtvih* (Novi Sad: Prometej, 1992).
41 See Jovanović, 21-3; Maria Bucur-Deckard, *Heroes and Victims: Remembering War in Twentieth Century Romania* (Bloomington: Indiana University Press, 2009), 19-21; Robert W. Habenstein and William M. Lamers, *Funeral Customs the World Over* (Milwaukee, WI: Bulfin Printers Inc., National Funeral Directors Association of the United States, 1960), 428-9; Monica Black, *Death in Berlin: From Weimar to Divided Germany*, (Cambridge: Cambridge University Press, 2010), 26-8.
42 Merridale, 24-6.
43 Merridale, 30-46; Matsunami, 256; Jovanović, 21-25; Maria Carlson, "Death and Funeral Meats, Moscow Style (An Investigation into the Soviet Way of Death)" (Unpublished Manuscript, Cited with Permission of the Author), 13; Edit Petrović, "Posmrtni običaji kod ateista: na primeru crnogorskih kolonista u Bačkoj," *Etnološke sveske*, VIII (1987): 179-86; Maja Bosić, "Arhaični elementi u pogrebnim običajima u Vojvodini," *Etnološke sveske*, VI (1985): 89-94; Bucur-Deckard, 41-2.
44 Habenstein and Lamers, *Funeral Customs the World Over*, 428-9, 432; Merridale, 24-6, 37-40; Marian Wenzel, "Graveside Feasts and Dances in Yugoslavia," *Folkore*, 73, 1 (Spring 1962): 1-3; Jovanović, 109-10; Gail Kligman, *The Wedding of the Dead* (Berkeley: University of California Press, 1988), 166-79; Petrović, 183; Bucur-Deckard, 41-2; Constas, 128-9; Melissa Bokovoy, "Gendering Grief: Lamenting and Photographing the Dead in Serbia, 1914-1941," *Aspasia*, 5 (June 2011): 46-69.
45 Carlson, 2.
46 Constas, 138; Bojanović, 131; L. M. Danforth, *The Death Rituals of Rural Greece* (Princeton, NJ: Princeton University Press, 1982), 19-22.
47 Nolan Menachemson, *A Practical Guide to Jewish Cemeteries* (Bergenfield, NJ: Avotaynu, 2007), 1-2, 206.
48 There were exceptions as in Prague, which suffered from severe shortages of space, where the cemetery was placed directly behind the synagogue, but then they built a high wall around it to establish a barrier between the two. Menachemson, 3-4, 185.
49 Rabbi Elyokim Schlesinger, "The Sacred Obligation of Burial and Life after Death in Jewish Belief," in *Jewish Cemeteries and Mass Graves in Europe: Protection and Preservation* (Antwerp: European Agudas Yisroel, 2008) 7. Menachemson also noted that the tradition of saint visitation had evolved within European Jewish burial culture by the nineteenth century. Menachemson, 6.
50 Menachemsen, 193.

51 Rebecca Golbert, "Judaism and Death: Finding Meaning in Ritual," in Kathleen Garces-Foley, ed., *Death and Religion in a Changing World* (New York: M. E. Sharpe, 2006), 51–2; Schlesinger, 6.
52 Julia Barrow, "Urban Cemetery Location in the High Middle Ages," in Steve Bassett, ed., *Death in Towns: Urban Responses to Dying and the Dead, 100–1600* (Leicester: Leicester University Press, 1992), 94.
53 Schlesinger, 6; Piet de Bruyn, "Jewish Cemeteries Report," Document # 12930, published by the Committee on Science, Culture, Education and Media, Council of Europe, May 10, 2012. Accessed December 2, 2014, http://assembly.coe.int/ASP/XRef/X2H-DW-XSL.asp?fileid=18710&lang=EN, 6.
54 Menachemson, 5, 184–5; Schlesinger, 13
55 Menachemson, 190.
56 Van den Breemer and Maussen, 283; De Bruyn, 8.
57 De Bruyn, 8–9.
58 Menachemson, 192; Black, 43–4.
59 Menachemson, 190.
60 Black, 30.
61 Dr. Eli Tauber, Interview with the Author, November 11, 2013, Sarajevo.
62 Menachemson, 3.
63 Black, 88–91.
64 Black, 158, 265.
65 Golbert, 45–68; Ellen Levine, "Jewish Views and Customs on Death," in Colin Murray Parkes, Pittu Laungani, and Bill Young, eds., *Death and Bereavement across Cultures* (London: Routledge, 1997), 98–130.
66 Golbert, 59–63; Habenstein, 194–200; Levine, 112–20.
67 Juan Eduard Campo, "Muslim Ways of Death: Between the Prescribed and the Performed," in *Death and Religion in a Changing World* (New York: Sharpe, 2006), 149; Leor Halevi, *Muhammad's Grave: Death Rites and the Making of Islamic Society* (New York: Cambridge University Press, 2007), 10–12.
68 For more on the stećci see, Amila Buturović, *Carved in Stone, Etched in Memory: Death, Tombstones and Commemoration in Bosnian Islam Since c. 1500.* (Farnham: Ashgate, 2015); Mehmed Mujezinović, *Islamska Epigrafika Bosne i Hercegovine* (Sarajevo: Sarajevo Publishing, 1998).
69 Perhaps the best examples may be found in the epic poem *Mountain Wreath* by the Montenegrin Bishop/King Petar II Petrović Njegoš. Accessed August 19, 2018. https://www.rastko.rs/knjizevnost/umetnicka/njegos/mountain_wreath.html.
70 *Report of the International Commission to Inquire into the Causes and Conduct of the Balkan Wars* (Washington, DC: Carnegie Endowment for International Peace, 1914).
71 Noel Malcolm, *Kosovo* (New York: New York University Press, 1998), 131–3; Buturović, 144.

72 Mustafa Sušić, 'Naš odnos prema natkaburskim obilježima', in Muharem Omerdić and Aziz Kadribegović, eds., *Takvim za 2011* (Sarajevo: El-Kalem--Izdavački centar Rijaseta, 2010), 171; Halevi, 205–6; For additional views on this topic see Buturović, 1–11; Enver Mulahalilović, *Vjerski običaji muslimana/bošnjaka*, 3rd ed. (Sarajevo: El-Kalem--Izdavački centar Rijaseta, 2005).
73 Halevi, 206.
74 Halevi, 205–7.
75 Halevi, 218–28.
76 Halevi, 207; Mulahalilović, 302; Buturović, 70–5.
77 Halevi, 206; Buturović, 36–8; Bringa, 185; Mulahalilović, 284–9.
78 See Halevi, 114–42.
79 Mulahalilović, 270–28; Bringa 187–94.
80 Buturović, 35–6.
81 English language exceptions to this rule are the monographs by Monica Black *Death in Berlin: From Weimar to Divided Germany* (Cambridge: Cambridge University Press, 2010)) and Felix Schulz (*Death in East Germany, 1945–1990* (New York: Bergahn Books, 2013), dealing with burial culture in East Germany both of which are extremely valuable. There are also two important works that touch on burial culture in Socialist Romania: Gail Kligman's *The Wedding of the Dead* (Berkeley: University of California Press, 1988) and Maria Bucur's *Heroes and Victims: Remembering War in Twentieth-Century Romania* (Bloomington: University of Indiana Press, 2009).
82 Merridale, 81–5; Vladimirov, 1–11.
83 Merridale, 131–3.
84 Vladimirov, 3; Catriona Kelly, *St. Petersburg: Shadows of the Past* (New Haven, CT: Yale University Press, 2014), 316.
85 Victoria Smolkin, *A Sacred Space Is Never Empty: A History of Soviet Atheism* (Princeton, NJ: Princeton University Press, 2018), 167.
86 Merridale, 139–40; Habenstein and Lamers, 432.
87 Yaacov Ro'i, *Islam in the Soviet Union from the Second World War to Gorbachev* (New York: Columbia University Press, 2000), 9–19.
88 Smolkin, 165–93.
89 Kelly, 313.
90 Merridale, 141; Habenstein, 433; Carlson, 10–12; Vladimirov, 8.
91 Merridale, 133–6, 201–4, 279–82; Matsunami, 256–7; Carlson, 4.
92 Kelly, 329–31.
93 Nathaniel Davis, *A Long Walk to Church: A Contemporary History of Russian Orthodoxy* (Boulder, CO: Westview Press, 1995), 209; William C. Fletcher, *The Russian Orthodox Church Underground, 1917–1970* (London: Oxford University Press, 1971), 93.

94 Merridale, 141.
95 Paul Bergne, "Some Thoughts on Grave Symbolism in Tashkent Cemeteries," *Durham Middle East Papers*, 76 (April 2004), 6, 13.

2 Religion, Nationalism, and the State in Socialist Yugoslavia

1 Dennison Rusinow, *The Yugoslav Experiment, 1948–1974* (Berkeley, CA: Cambridge University Press, 1977).
2 The terminology associated with nationalism can be extremely obstruse. In the Yugoslav context, *nations* (narodi) were the original five major South Slavic ethnic groups that constituted the Yugoslav state (Serbs, Croats, Slovenes, Macedonians, and Montenegrins). Only in 1968, did the Bosnian Muslims also gain legal recognition as an ethnic nation. All of the original five nations had their own republics, while the Bosnian Muslims shared the republic of Bosnia & Hercegovina with Serbs and Croats. All other ethnic groups within the state were referred to as national minorities or *nationalities* (narodnosti) and included Albanians, Bulgarians, Czechs, Germans, Greeks, Hungarians, Italians, Jews, Roma, Romanians, Ruthenians, Slovaks, Turks, and Vlahs. While 1974 Constitution of the Socialist Federal Republic of Yugoslavia provided significant cultural, linguistic, and educational rights to all nations and nationalities in Yugoslavia, only nations had the right to self-determination, including the right to secession.
3 Paul Shoup, *Communism and the Yugoslav National Question* (New York: Columbia University Press, 1968), 113, 110, fn. 27.
4 See, e.g., "Presidents Apologise over Croatian War," *BBC*, September 10, 2003. Accessed July 26, 2020, http://news.bbc.co.uk/2/hi/europe/3095774.stm; Marie-Janine Calic, "Ethnic Cleansing and War Crimes," in Charles Ingrao and Thomas Emmert eds., *Confronting the Yugoslav Controversies*, 2nd ed. (West Lafayette, IN: Purdue University Press, 2013), 140; Milka Domanović, "List of Kosovo War Victims Published," *Balkan Transitional Justice*, December 10, 2014. Accessed July 26, 2020, https://balkaninsight.com/2014/12/10/kosovo-war-victims-list-published/.
5 *Stanovništvo po narodnosti po popisu od 15. marta 1948 godine*, Beograd, 1954. Accessed online June 13, 2016, http://pod2.stat.gov.rs/ObjavljenePublikacije/G1948/Pdf/G19484001.pdf.
6 Stella Alexander, *Church and State in Yugoslavia Since 1945* (London: Cambridge University Press, 1979), 26–40; Rada Radić, *Vera protiv verom* (Belgrade: INIS, 1995), 74–82.
7 Alexander, 57–9; Radić, 104–6.
8 Alexander, 68.
9 Alexander, 95–120; Radić, 226–34.

10 Alexander, 133–5.
11 Aleksandar Ranković, "Pretsedniku Izvršnu Vijeću NR BiH," July 18, 1959, Arhiv BiH; Mitja Velikonja, *Religious Separation and Political Intolerance in Bosnia-Herzegovina*, (College Station: Texas A&M University Press, 2003), 188, 204.
12 Vjekoslav Perica, *Balkan Idols: Religion and Nationalism in the Yugoslav States* (Oxford: Oxford University Press, 2002), 56–61.
13 Perica, 60–73.
14 Marcus Tanner, *Croatia: A Nation Forged by War* (New Haven, CT: New Haven Press, 1997), 230; Perica, 176.
15 See http://www.tudjman.hr/govori/. Accessed March 25, 2020.
16 While the origins of the šahovnica are said to date back to the tenth century, it became known as the state symbol for Croatia only in the mid-19th century under the Habsburg regime. It was also, however, widely used by the fascist Ustasha regime during the Second World War.
17 Tanner, 230.
18 Branka Magaš, *The Destruction of Yugoslavia* (London: Verso, 1993), 283.
19 Mile Bjelajac and Ozren Zunec, "The War in Croatia, 1991–1995," in Charles Ingrao and Thomas A. Emmert, eds., *Confronting the Yugoslav Controversies*, 2nd ed. (West Lafayette, IN: Purdue University Press, 2015), 247.
20 Bjelac and Zunec, 258–60.
21 Population of Croatia, 1931–2001. Accessed July 27, 2020, http://www.vojska.net/eng/armed-forces/croatia/about/population/.
22 Alexander, 173.
23 Perica, 43–5.
24 The most important nationalists in Serbia were Vuk Drašković and Vojislav Šešelj. In Croatia, the main Serb nationalists were Jovan Rašković, Milan Babić, and Milan Martić. In Bosnia & Hercegovina, they were Radovan Karadžić, Ratko Mladić, Milorad Dodik, and Biljana Plavšić.
25 Maria Vivod, "Stronger than the State," *Etnofor*, 23, 2, State/Violence (2011): 101; On women's participation in the military see: Carol S. Lilly and Jill A. Irvine, "Negotiating Interests: Women and Nationalism in Serbia and Croatia, 1990-1997," *East European Politics and Societies,* 16 (1) (February 2002) 109-144.
26 Gezim Krasniqi, "The 'Forbidden Fruit': Islam and Politics of Identity in Kosovo and Macedonia," *Southeast European and Black Sea Studies*, 11, 2 (June 2011): 192.
27 Noel Malcolm, *Kosovo* (New York: New York University Press, 1998), 265–88.
28 Malcolm, 313.
29 "Stanovništvo po narodnosti," March 15, 1948, Belgrade, 1954.
30 Malcolm, 323–6.
31 Malcolm, 331.

32 Socialist Yugoslavia's modernization policies, at least in urban areas, achieved considerable success not only in marginalizing the Muslim clergy but also in creating an atheistic political and intellectual elite, perhaps thanks to Albanian-language education policies. Although a large majority of Albanians are Muslim, their practice of Islam has been restricted to the private sphere and attendance at Muslim worship services and religious instruction is low. See Robert Donia, "Nationalism and Religious Extremism in Bosnia-Herzegovina and Kosovo Since 1990," *Miscellany IFIMES* (2007), International Institute for Middle East and Balkan Studies Series, 5–6; Jeton Mehmeti, "Faith and Politics in Kosovo: The Status of Religious Communities in a Secular Country," in Arolda Elbasani and Olivier Roy, eds., *The Revival of Islam in the Balkans: From Identity to Religiosity* (Basingstoke: Palgrave MacMillan, 2017), 66–8; Perica, 145.

33 Aydin Babuna, "The Albanians of Kosovo and Macedonia: Ethnic Identity Superseding Religion," *Nationalities Papers*, 28, 1 (2000): 72.

34 Krasniqi, 195.

35 Tim Judah, *Kosovo: War and Revenge* (New Haven, CT: Yale University Press, 2002), 60–73.

36 Judah, 99–140.

37 Robert Donia and John Fine Jr., *Bosnia and Hercegovina: A Tradition Betrayed* (New York: Columbia University Press, 1994), 18–23.

38 Ivo Banac, *The National Question in Yugoslavia: Origins, History, Politics* (Ithaca, NY: Cornell University Press, 1984), 39–40.

39 "Stanovništvo po narodnosti," March 15, 1948, Belgrade, 1954.

40 Banac, 361.

41 Emily Greble, *Sarajevo, 1941–1945: Muslims, Christians, and Jews in Hitler's Europe* (Ithaca, NY: Cornell University Press, 2011), 163–77.

42 Donia and Fine, 163. For much more on this topic see Amir Duranović, *Islamska Zajednica u Jugoslavenskom Socijalizmu* (Sarajevo: Udruženje za modernu istoriju, 2021).

43 Velikonja, 223.

44 Xavier Bougarel, "Bosnian Muslims and the Yugoslav Idea," in Dejan Djokić, ed., *Yugoslavism: Histories of a Failed Idea, 1918–1992* (Madison: University of Wisconsin Press, 2003), 100.

45 Robert Hayden, "Imagined Communities and Real Victims—Self-Determination and Ethnic Cleansing in Yugoslavia," *American Ethnologist*, 23, 4 (November 1996): 778; Donia and Fine, 186.

46 Perica, 74–88; Donia and Fine, 200–1.

47 See, e.g., Donia and Fine, 262–5; Lenard J. Cohen, *Broken Bonds: Yugoslavia's Disintegration and Balkan Politics in Transition* (Boulder, CO: Westview Press, 1995), 144.

48 Alija Izetbegović, *Izetbegović: Odabrani govori, pisma, izjavie, intervjui* (Zagreb: Prvo muslimansko dioničko društvo, 1995).
49 See Cohen, 281.
50 Xavier Bougarel, "Bosnian Islam Since 1990: Cultural Identity or Political Ideology," Convention annuelle de l'Association for the Study of Nationalities (ASN), April 1999, New York. <halshs-00220516>, 9.
51 Hayden; Marko Milanović, "Sejdi & Finci v. Bosnia and Herzegovina," *American Journal of International Law*, 104, 4 (2010): 636–41; "U.S. Secretary of State Blinken Calls for Changes to Bosnia's Constitution," *Reuters World News*, April 1, 2021. Accessed September 4, 2021, https://www.reuters.com/article/uk-bosnia-usa-blinken/u-s-secretary-of-state-blinken-calls-for-changes-to-bosnias-constitution-idUKKBN2BO6CI.
52 "Stanovništvo prema etničko/nacionalnoj pripadnosti," *Popis 2013*. Accessed July 26, 2020, https://popis.gov.ba/popis2013/knjige.php?id=2; Census of Population, Households and Dwellings in Republika Srpska, 2013. Accessed July 26, 2020, https://www.rzs.rs.ba/static/uploads/bilteni/popis/rezultati_popisa/Results_of_the_Census_2013.pdf. For information on the political background to the census see Ionnis Armakolas and Maja Maksimović, "Memory and the Uses of Wartime Past in Contemporary Bosnia and Herzegovina: The Case of the Bosniak Campaign for the October 2013 Population Census," *Science and Society: Journal of Political and Moral Theory*, 32 (October 2014): 59–93.
53 Though originally named the Savez Boraca Narodnooslobodilačkog Rata, this work will refer to it as SUBNOR for the entire period.
54 "Article 11," *Statut Savez Udruzenja Boraca Narodnooslobodilačkog Rata Jugoslavija*, Beograd, 1963, 9; see also Ajdin Muhedinović, *Uloga SUBNOR-a u Obilježavanju Narodnooslobodilačkog Rata tokom 1970—ih godina*, Završni Magisterski Rad, University of Sarajevo (Sarajevo, 1981), 8.
55 No author, Beograd, "Uputstvo o uredjenju groblja boraca Narodno-oslobodilačkog Rata i Žrtava Fašističkog Terora," May 30, 1953, HDA, 179/1241, 2.
56 Muhedinović, 9. "Article 4," *Statut SUBNOR*, 1963, 5–6; For example, Marko Belinić, the president of SUBNOR Croatia from 1961 to 1969, had joined the CPY in 1934 and became member of the Politbureau of the Communist Party of Croatia by 1943. Vera Humski, "Marko Belinić," *Hrvatski Biografski Leksikon*, 2009. Accessed September 9, 2022, https://hbl.lzmk.hr/clanak.aspx?id=1648.
57 For example, the first Federal Council for the Cultivation of Traditions of the People's Liberation Struggle, created in 1964, consisted of seventeen members plus an additional representative from the Commission for the Cultivation of Traditions from each republic. Besides its own president and secretary, its members included the director of the Military Publishing Institute *Vojno delo*; the state undersecretary in the Secretariate of the Federal Executive Council for Industry; two writers

(Čeda Minderović and Milorad Surep-Panić); a film worker (Stole Janković); a journalist from *Komunist*; and one representative each from the Federal Parliament; the Yugoslav Institute for the Study of Pedagogical and Educational Issues; the Administration for the Moral-Political Education of the Yugoslav People's Army; the Federal Institute for the Defense of Monuments of Culture; the Institute for the Study of the Worker's Movement; the Military Historical Institute; the Commission for Education, Culture, and Ideological Problems of the Central Council of the Unions; and the Presidency of the Central Committee of the Youth Organization of Serbia. Savet za negovanje tradicija NOB, "Stenografske beleške," February 18, 1964, Arhiv Jugoslavija, 313, 1962–4, 1966–7.

58 Klaus Buchenau has argued that until the 1960s the CRQs "had been de facto agencies of the UDBA (Uprava Državne Bezbednosti, Administration of State Security)." While it is indeed likely that in cases relating to political activity the CRQs worked closely with UDBa, that is a serious oversimplification of their work, even in the earliest years after the war. Klaus Buchenau, "What Went Wrong? Church-State Relations in Socialist Yugoslavia," *Nationalities Papers*, 33, 4 (December 2005): 550.

59 Alexander, 68.

60 Specifically, the CRQ most often sent its recommendations not only to the Local and District People's Councils, to the Executive Committees of the Republic Parliaments, and the Presidencies of the Republic Governments but also to a variety of ministries and secretariats including those for legislation and administration, construction, urbanism and communal affairs, health, and internal affairs.

61 Radić, 20–1.

62 The relationship between Communist regimes and religious communities has generated a large body of literature focused on the efforts of state-socialist governments to reduce or eradicate the power and institutions of organized religion while instilling secular scientific values and beliefs in the population. See, e.g., Daniel Peris, *Storming the Heavens: The Soviet League of the Militant Godless* (Ithaca, NY: Cornell University Press, 1998); and William B. Husband, *Godless Communists: Atheism and Society in Soviet Russia, 1917–1931* (DeKalb: Northern Illinois University Press, 2000). Recent scholars have begun to pay more attention to significant accommodations negotiated between those regimes and religious communities in the face of domestic and international challenges. Defining state-sponsored atheism as a form of secularism, these scholars see it more as a process rather than completed project and note important differences in the kinds of challenges and opportunities presented by non-Western religions like Eastern Orthodoxy, Buddhism, and Islam. See Catherine Wanner, "Introduction," in Catherine Wanner, ed., *State Secularism and Lived Religion in Soviet Russia and Ukraine* (New York: Oxford University Press, 2012); Tam T. T. Ngo and Justine

B. Quijada, "Introduction," in Tam T. T. Ngo and Justine B. Quijada, eds., *Atheist Secularism and Its Discontents: A Comparative Study of Religion and Communism in Eurasia* (London: Palgrave MacMillan, 2015).
63 The actual relationship between religious and national identity in Yugoslavia is far more complex and lies beyond the bounds of this work. What matters here is that Communist party leaders believed them closely connected if not identical. See Rogers Brubaker, "Religion and Nationalism: Four Approaches," *Nations and Nationalism*, 18, 1 (2012): 2–20; Pieter Troch, "The Intertwining of Religion and Nationhood in Interwar Yugoslavia: The School Celebrations of St. Sava's Day, *Slavonic and East European Review*, 91, 2 (April 2013): 235–61.
64 Radić, 85–111.
65 See Alexander; Radić.
66 Radić, 306.
67 Radić, 85–111; Perica, 21–4; Buchenau, 2.
68 Radić, 162–6.
69 Radić, 147–55.
70 "Osnovni zakon o eksproprijaciji," *Službeni list FNRJ*, 28, April 4, 1947. Accessed online September 23, 2021, Codex projuris, www.projuris.org.
71 "Zakon o pravnom položaju verskih zajednica," *Službeni list FNRJ*, 22, May 27, 1953, 209–10.
72 Radmila Radić and Momcilo Mitrović, eds., *Zapisnici sa sednica Komicije za verska pitanja NR/SR Srbije 1945–1978. Godine* (Beograd: Institut za noviju istoriju Srbije, 2012), 164, n. 240.

3 Partisan Communities of the Dead

1 Jay Winter, *Sites of Memory, Sites of Mourning: The Great War in European Cultural History* (Cambridge: Cambridge, University Press, 1995), 94.
2 https://www.facebook.com/spomenicinob.info, accessed November 28, 2022. The goal of Lawler's website https://www.spomenicinob.info/ is to document all monuments and memorials in BiH but may eventually be extended to all the former Yugoslav republics. The website is self-funded and structured so that volunteers can also contribute to it.
3 Phillipe Aries, *The Hour of Our Death* (New York: Vintage Books, 1982), 550.
4 Susan-Mary Grant, "Patriot Graves: American National Identity and the Civil War Dead," *American Nineteenth Century History*, 5, 3 (Fall 2004): 77–83.
5 George Mosse, *Fallen Soldiers: Reshaping the Memory of the World Wars* (New York: Oxford University Press, 1990) 80–1; Thomas Laqueur, *The Work of the Dead* (Princeton, NJ: Princeton University Press, 2015), 366–487.

6 Jeremy F. Walton, "The Dead Wait: Material Afterlives in Sepulchral Spaces," *Journal of Material Culture*, 27, 4 (2022): 386.
7 Benedict Anderson, *Imagined Communities: Reflections on the Origin and Spread of Nationalism*, revised ed. (London: Verso, 2006), 10.
8 Grant, 83, 96–7.
9 Grant, 88–91. Over 1,000 enemy POWs from the First and Second World Wars are also buried in US military cemeteries in accordance with the requirements of the Geneva Convention. *Facts: National Cemetery Administration History and Development*, Veteran's Administration, United States. Department of Veteran's Affairs, 3, accessed September 8, 2022, https://www.cem.va.gov/facts/NCA_History_and_Development_1.asp; Kelly Merrifield, "From Necessity to Honor: The Evolution of National Cemeteries in the United States," National Park Service, US Department of the Interior. Accessed September 8, 2022, https://www.nps.gov/nr/travel/national_cemeteries/development.html.
10 Mosse, 82.
11 Anna Petrig, "The War Dead and Their Gravesites," *International Review of the Red Cross*, 91, 874 (June 2009): 342. "Convention for the Amelioration of the Condition of the Wounded and Sick in Armies in the Field," Geneva, Article 4, 1929, Treaties, State Parties, and Commentaries, International Committee of the Red Cross. Accessed November 3, 2021, Treaties, States Parties, and Commentaries—Geneva Convention Wounded and Sick, 1929 - 4 - (icrc.org).
12 Monica Black, *Death in Berlin* (Cambridge: Cambridge University Press, 2010), 93.
13 The German War Graves Commission was founded as a private charity in 1919. It currently cares for 832 cemeteries in 46 countries, including Croatia, Montenegro, Macedonia, and Kosova but not any of the other former Yugoslav republics. Accessed December 20, 2021, https://www.volksbund.de/en/together-for-peace.
14 "Official Exhumation of Greek Soldiers Killed in Albania During WWII to Begin on Monday," *The National Herald*, January 22, 2018. Accessed February 9, 2019, https://www.thenationalherald.com/188129/official-exhumation-greek-soldiers-killed-albania-wwii-begin-monday/.
15 Goran Miloradović, "Prah prahu: Staljinistički pogrebni rituali u socialističkoj Yugoslaviji," *Godišnjak za društvenu istoriju*, 1–2 (2007): 95–100.
16 Sekretarijat SIV za Socijalnu, političku i komunalna pitanju, Glavnom Odboru SBNORH, predsedniku drugu Beliniću, March 24, 1962, HDA, 179/1241, SUBNOR; Emil Ivanec, "Zapisnik sa prvog sastanka Republičke komisije za ekshumaciju posmrtnih ostataka poginulih crvenoarmejaca na teritoriju NRH," April 13, 1962, HDA, 179/1241, SUBNOR.
17 Vladimir Geiger and Sladjana Josipović Batorek, "O provodjenju odluke komunističkih vlasti iz 1945. o uklanjanju groblja i grobova 'okupatora' i 'narodnih neprijatelja' u Slavoniji i Srijemu," *Scrinia Slavonica*, 15 (2015): 291–4; Vladimir

Geiger, "O provodjenju odluke komunističkih vlasti iz 1945. o uklanjanju grobalja i grobova 'okupatora' i 'narodnih neprijatelja' u Bosni i Hercegovini," *Časopis za kulturno i povijesno naslijedje*, 2 (2016): 287–317; Vladimir Huzjan and Jazmin Medved, "O pokopanim vojnicima Sila Osovine Na Varaždinskom Groblju," *Radovi*, Zavod za znanstveni rad HAZU Varaždin, June 19, 2015, 195–266.

18 Bratislava Kostić, *Novo Groblje u Beogradu* (Beograd: JKP "Pogrebne Usluge", 1999), 18–23.

19 Gvozden Otašević, "Pronašla očev grob posle 63 godine," *Politika*, October 10, 2007. Accessed June 29, 2020, Pronašla očev grob posle 63 godine (politika.rs).

20 Geiger, "O provodjenju odluke komunističkih vlasti iz 1945. o uklanjanju grobalja i grobova 'okupatora' i 'narodnih neprijatelja' u Bosni i Hercegovini," 305.

21 Max Bergholz, "When All Could No Longer Be Equal in Death," *The Carl Beck Papers in Russian and East European Studies*, XIV, 2008 (November 2010), 10–16, 25.

22 "Zapisnik prve redovne sjednice Odbora za izgradnju Spomen-parka na Vracama," December 18, 1965, Arhiv BiH, SUBNOR, 152, 1960–5; Documents about marking of "Ljubin Grob" at Sutjeska, 1968 to May 15, 1969, Arhiv BiH, SUBNOR, 115.

23 According to Jan Assman, the "concretization of identity" through objective manifestations of cultural memory is how a group develops an awareness of its "unity and peculiarity." Information included within that cultural memory sharply defines "those who belong and those who do not." Jan Assman and John Czaplicka, "Collective Memory and Cultural Identity," *New German Critique*, 65 (Spring–Summer 1995): 130.

24 Heike Karge, *Sećanje u kamenu-okamenjeno sećanje?*, translated from original German by Aleksandra Kostić (Beograd: Biblioteka XX Vek, 2014), 17–18.

25 Wolfgang Höpken, "Between Memory Politics and Mourning: Remembering World War II in Yugoslavia," in C. Sighele and F. Vanoni, eds., *Bad Memories: Sites, Symbols and Narrations of the Wars in the Balkans*, Contributions to the Conference "Bad Memories" held in Rovereto, November 9, 2007 (Rovereto: Osservatorio Balcani e Caucaso, 2010), 27–8.

26 Karge, *Sećanje*, 51. It is nearly impossible to accurately translate that figure into today's dollars. My nearest estimate is somewhere around $35,000, which might seem low but would have been an impossible amount to cover for most rural villages.

27 For a thorough discussion of the Tjentište site see Karge, *Sećanje*, 97–135.

28 Statut Savez Udruženja Boraca Narodnooslobodilačkog Borba Jugoslavije, Beograd, 1963, 27.

29 Savezni Odbor SUBNOR, "Stenografske beleške sa sastanka Komisije za obeležavanje istoriskih mesta i uredjivanje grobova Saveza boraca," 42–4, October 5, 1954, Arhiv Jugoslavije, 297, F81, 1954–71.

30 "Zakon o Grobljima Boraca," *Službeni List FNRJ*, Broj 52, December 30, 1961, 1053–4.
31 Savet za negovanje tradicija NOB, Savezni Odbor SUBNOR, "Stenografske Beleške," February 18, 1964, Arhiv Jugoslavije and Arhiv BiH, 313, 1962–4, 1966–7, and 154, 1959–63.
32 See Andrew Lawler, *The Partisan's Cemetery in Mostar, Bosnia & Herzegovina: Implications of the Deterioration of a Monument and Site*, MA thesis, Faculty of Engineering, Catholic University Leuven, Belgium (September 2013).
33 A total of 35,286 belonged to fallen soldiers, 90,144 to victims of fascism, and 6,699 to others—not including those at Donja Gradina associated with Jasenovac. SR BiH Republički Sekretarijat za Zdravstvo i Socijalnu Politiku, "Informacija o sprovodjenju Zakon o grobljima i grobovima jugoslovenskih boraca," nd [1967], Arhiv BiH, SUBNOR, 21.
34 Savjet za njegovanje tradicija NOB-e, "Izvještaj o izvršenju program rada za 1967 godina," nd [1967], Arhiv BiH, SUBNOR, 114; Republički Odbor SBNOR BiH, Savjet za njegovanje tradicije NOB-e, "Informacija o problemima izgradnje i uredjivanje grobalja jugoslovenskih boraca i ŽFT: Radni material," April 1970, Arhiv BiH, SUBNOR, 21.
35 Republički Odbor SUBNOR BiH Komisija za njegovanje tradicije NOB, "Neki problemi obilježavanja i utvrdjivanja masovnih stratišta i grobalja žft u Bosni i Hercegovini," March 20, 1975, Arhiv BiH, SUBNOR, 168.
36 Republički Savet za boračka i invalidska pitanja, "Izveštaj o sprovodjenju Zakona o uredjivanju i održavanju grobalja boraca," October 1974, Arhiv Jugoslavije, 134, 1974.
37 Republički Savet za boračka i invalidska pitanja, "Informacija o grobljima i grobovima boraca NOR i grobljima savezničkih i drugih stranih armija na teritoriju SR Hrvatske," June 1979, HDA, 179/1241.
38 Savezni Odbor SUBNOR, "Preporuka o uredjenju i održavanju grobalja i grobova boraca NOR i ŽFT," February 11, 1964, HDA, 179/1241 and Arhiv BiH, SUBNOR, 116; UBNOR Općine Zabok, "Skupštine Općine Odjelu na komunalne poslove Zabok," October 23, 1964, HDA, 179/1241; Odbor SUBNORa BiH, Savjet za njegovanje tradicija NOB-e, "Orijentacioni Program Angažovanja Organizacija Savez Udruženja Boraca u Proslavi 50-godišnjica Saveza Komunista Jugoslavije," February 5, 1968, Arhiv BiH, SUBNOR, 115; Dr. Zvonko Petrinović, Republički Zavod za urbanizam, stambene i komunalne poslove, SR Hrvatske, "Predmet: Groblje i grobovi boraca—uredjenje i održavanje," March 30, 1971, HDA, 179/1241.
39 Organizacioni odbor Simpozium "Spomenici NOR i revolucije u BiH—stanje i problem," "Preporuke za dalju aktivnost na podizanju, održavanju i prezentovanju spomenika NOR i revolucije," December 1975, Arhiv BiH, SUBNOR, 220; Općinska

Skupština Slavonska Požega, "Samoupravni Sporazum o održavanju i utvrdjivanju spomenika revolucije" and "Popis Spomenik Revolucije," February 21, 1980, HDA, 179/1241.

40 Općinski Odbor Orahovića, Memo to Republičkom Odbor SUBNOR-a SR Hrvatske, June 7, 1976, HDA, 179/1241.

41 For example, once the Cemetery at Gettysburg was established, many families who had originally intended to take the bodies of their loved ones home reconsidered and chose to leave them in the National Cemetery. Grant, 88.

42 Karge, *Sjećanje*, 247.

43 Zemaljski Odbor SBNOR Hrvatske, "Svim Oblasnim i Kotarskim i gradskim odborima SBNOR," August 2, 1949, HDA, 179/1241.

44 Glavni Odbor NOR Beograd, Memo to Zemaljski odbor SBNOR Zagreb, February 9, 1949, HDA, 179/1241; Beograd, "Uputstvo O Uredjenju Groblja Boraca NOR i Žrtava Fašističkog Terora," May 30, 1953, HDA, 179/1241 SUBNOR.

45 Winter, 29–54.

46 Karge, *Sećanje*, 47; Lawler, https://www.facebook.com/spomenicinob.info, accessed November 29, 2022.

47 Ajdin Muhedinović, "Uloga SUBNOR-a u Obilježavanju Narodnooslobodilačkog Rata Tokom 1970-ih godina," Master's Thesis, University of Sarajevo, 2018, 17; Max Bergholz, "Medju rodoljubima, kupusom, svinjama i varvarima: Spomenici i grobovi NOR 1947–1965. Godine," *Godišnjak za društvenu istoriju*, 1–3 (2007): 66–7; Lawler, *The Partisan's Cemetery*.

48 According to Lawler, not all ŽFT burial sites or memorials were funded or authorized by the SUBNOR, including some that were quite impressive. Personal email correspondence, December 28, 2022.

49 Höpken, 30; Heike Karge, "Sajmište, Jasenovac i društveni okviri sećanja i zaborava," *Filozofija i društvo*, 4 (2012): 106–18.

50 Based on Donald Niebyl's impressive but far from complete Spomenik Database, it would appear that somewhere between one-quarter and one-third of those created in Serbia, Croatia, and Bosnia & Hercegovina in the 1960s were dedicated to civilian victims who died at the hands of Nazis and/or Ustashe. Among them were monuments in Belgrade, Dragutinac, Kragujevac, Niš, and Sremska Mitrovica in Serbia, Dotrščina and Zagreb in Croatia, and Jasenovac/Donja Gradina in Croatia/Bosnia & Hercegovina (accessed November 3, 2022), Spomenik Database | A Map of Yugoslavia's Historic Spomenik.

51 See Karge's detailed discussion of the creation of Jasenovac in "Sajmište," 111–16; and *Sećanje*, chapter 6.

52 "Koncentracioni logor Jasenovac," *Naša starina*, XII/1969, 119–25; "Koncentracioni logor Jasenovac 1941–1945," Feljton, *Oslobodjenje*, XXII/1966, #6489–92, June 28–July 1, 1968; and "Velike groblje," *4. Jul*, January 20, 1968.

53 Dušan Misirača, Sreskom-Opštinskom Odboru SBNOR, May, 5, 1960, Arhiv BiH, SUBNOR, 116 and HDA, 179/1241.
54 Andrew Lawler, Personal email correspondence, November 30, 2022.
55 Republička Komisija za spomen-obilježavanja istorijskih dogadjaja i ličnosti, "Izvještaj o radu Komisije i problemima u vezi spomen-obilježavanja istorijskih dogadjaja i ličnosti," December 1969, Arhiv BiH, SUBNOR, 21.
56 See, e.g., Max Bergholz, *Violence as a Generative Force: Identity, Nationalism, and Memory in a Balkan Community* (Ithaca, NY: Cornell University Press); Bette Denich, "Nationalist Ideologies and the Symbolic Revival of Genocide," *American Ethnologist*, 21, 2 (May 1994): 367–90; Jelena Djureinović, *The Politics of Memory of the Second World War in Contemporary Serbia* (London: Routledge, 2020); Vjeran Pavlaković, Dario Brentin, and Davor Pauković, "The Controversial Commemoration: Transnational Approaches to Remembering Bleiburg," *Croatian Political Science Review*, 55, 2 (2018): 7–32.
57 Bergholz, *Violence*, 297–9.
58 Karge, *Sećanje*, 23, 29.
59 Tihić was originally employed by the Institute for the Protection of Monuments in Bosnia & Hercegovina in the area of medieval heritage but in the mid-1960s moved into the preservation of monuments from the People's Liberation Struggle where he personally wrote a long series of reports, most of which unfortunately have not survived. Andrew Lawler, personal email correspondence, December 28, 2022.
60 Dr. Smail Tihić, "Neki problemi izgradnje, održavanja i reprezentacije spomenika NOR i revolucije na području Bosne i Hercegovine," April 1969, Arhiv BiH, SUBNOR, 162, 1963–9, 6.
61 Ibid., 8.
62 "Neki problemi izgradnje, održavanja i presentacije spomenika NOR-a i revolucije na području BiH--Poseban prilog," nd [late 1960s], Arhiv BiH, SUBNOR, 162, 1963–9; Razumenka Petrović, "Stanje i problem zaštite i uredjivanje spomenika NOR," 1970, Arhiv Jugoslavije, SUBNOR, F81, 1954–71.
63 "Zakon o spomen-obilježavanju istaknutih ličnosti i dogadjaja iz revolucije i radničkog pokreta," nd [June 1964], Arhiv BiH, SUBNOR, 154, 1959–63; In 1966, the SUBNOR Council of the AP Vojvodina requested a copy of that law for use in preparing its own. Pokrajinski odbor SUBNOR AP Novi Sad, Memo to RO SUBNOR BiH, May 20, 1966, Arhiv BiH, SUBNOR, 122, 1967–72.
64 Republička Komisija za spomen-obilježavanja istorijskih dogadjaja i ličnosti, "Izvještaj o radu Komisije i problemima u vezi spomen-obilježavanja istorijskih dogadjaja i ličnosti," December 1969, Arhiv BiH, SUBNOR, 21.
65 SUBNOR Sreski Odbor Sarajevo, "Izvještaj o izvršenom pregledu spomen ploča na terenu grada Sarajeva," nd [August 1959], Arhiv BiH, SUBNOR, 154, 1959–63.

66 Zapisnik sa proširenog sastanka Sekretarijata Sreskog komiteta SK Sarajevo, May 23, 1963, Arhiv BiH, SUBNOR, 152, 1960-15; Report about Spomen-Park Vraca, nd [1965], Arhiv BiH, SUBNOR, 152, 1960-5.
67 Zapisnik sa II sjednice Ocjenjivačkog suda sa sprovodjenje konkursa za idejno rješenje spomen-parka i partizanskog groblja "Vraca," November 13, 1964, Arhiv BiH, SUBNOR, 152, 1960-5; Zapisnik prve redovne sjednice Odbora za izgradnju Spomen-parka na Vracama, December 18, 1965, Arhiv BiH, SUBNOR, 152, 1960-5; Zapisnik sa sastanka grupe za organizaciju i pripremu sjednica Odbora za izgradnju Spomen-parka Na Vracama, January 20, 1966, Arhiv BiH, SUBNOR, 152, 1960-5; Odbor za izgradnju "spomen-parka" Vraca, Memo to SUBNORa SR BiH, October 14, 1967, Arhiv BiH, SUBNOR, 114.
68 Zapisnik sa proširenog sastanka Sekretarijata Sreskog komiteta SK Sarajevo, May 23, 1963, Arhiv BiH, SUBNOR, 152, 1960-5; Izgradnja partizanskog spomen groblja u Sarajevu—materijal za diskusiju, nd [1964], Arhiv BiH, SUBNOR, 152, 1960-5.
69 SR BiH Fond za izgradnju objekata od zajedničkog interesa za grad pri gradskom vijeću grada Sarajeva, Rješenje, July 29, 1964, Arhiv BiH, SUBNOR, 152, 1960-5; Zapisnik prve redovne sjednice Odbora za izgradnju Spomen-parka na Vracama, December 18, 1965, Arhiv BiH, SUBNOR, 152, 1960-5; Odbor za izgradnju "spomen-parka" Vraca, Memo to SUBNORa SR BiH about Vraca, October 14, 1967, Arhiv BiH, SUBNOR, 114. His collaborators were Alija Kučukalić and Aleksandar Maltarić. One debate also concerned whether to allow alcohol to be sold at the Park.
70 Niebyl, accessed October 4, 2022, https://www.spomenikdatabase.org/sarajevo.
71 The Memorial Park did also include a museum within the fortress, and the information there was also certainly imbued with references to communism.
72 See Vladimir Kulić, "Building Brotherhood and Unity: Architecture and Federalism in Socialist Yugoslavia"; and Sanja Horvatinčić, "Memorial Sculpture and Architecture in Socialist Yugoslavia," both in Martino Stierli and Vladimir Kulić, eds., *Toward a Concrete Utopia: Architecture in Yugoslavia 1948-1980* (New York: Museum of Modern Art, 2017), 26-40, 104-12. Donald Niebyl, *Spomenik Monument Database* (London: Fuel, 2018).
73 Gavin Stamp, *The Memorial to the Missing of the Somme* (London: Profile Books, 2006).
74 Initially it held only the remains of Ivo Lola Ribar and Ivan Milutinović, but in 1949 and 1957 the remains of Djuro Djaković and Moša Pijade were added. Perhaps because he died so much later, and long after Yugoslavia had left the Soviet orbit, the body of Josip Broz Tito was not embalmed to lie in state forever in a monstrous mausoleum as were those of Lenin, Mao, and Ho Chi Minh. His remains are in the "House of Flowers" in the courtyard of the president's Belgrade residence under a slab of white marble inscribed only with his name and dates of birth and death, surrounded by flowers and greenery. Apparently, Tito designed the grave himself

after seeing Franklin D. Roosevelt's tomb in New York. Its setting in a glass house, however, does evoke the mausolea of his predecessors. Miloradović, 91–3, 99.

4 The Secularization of Cemeteries

1. Thomas Laqueur, *The Work of the Dead* (Princeton, NJ: Princeton University Press, 2015), 17.
2. Laqueur, 112–13.
3. Penny Roberts, "Contesting Sacred Space: Burial Disputes in Sixteenth Century France," in Bruce Gordon and Peter Marshall, eds., *The Place of the Dead: Death and Remembrance in Late Medieval and Early Modern Europe* (Cambridge: Cambridge University Press, 2000), 131–48; Keith Luria, "Separated by Death: Cemeteries, Burials and Confessional Boundaries in Seventeenth Century France," *French Historical Studies*, 24, 2 (Spring 2001): 185–221; Clodagh Tait, *Death, Burial, and Commemoration in Ireland 1550–1650* (Basingstoke: Palgrave MacMillan, 2002); Philippe Aries, *The Hour of Our Death* (New York: Vintage Books, 1981), 315–20.
4. See, e.g., Julie Rugg, *Churchyard and Cemetery: Tradition and Modernity in Rural North Yorkshire* (Manchester: Manchester University Press, 2013).
5. While civil marriages were legally established in the 1946 Constitution, the civil registration of births and deaths was a more complex affair as it required the state to take control over the *matične knjige* held by religious communities throughout the state. Efforts began in 1946 but were not completed until 1949. Rada Radić, *Vera Protiv Verom* (Beograd: INIS, 1995), 164–9.
6. "Opći Zakon o Narodnim Odborima," *Službeni list FNRJ*, 43 (May 28, 1946): 482–90.
7. "Uredbu o službi pregleda mrtvaca," *Narodne Novine*, 6, 50 (September 30, 1950); "Rešenja," *Službeni glasnik Narodnog odbora grada Zagreba*, VII, 5–8 (March 15, 1953); "Odluka o grobljima," *Beogradske novine*, 16, 1–3 (1956).
8. Bratislava Kostić, *Novo groblje u Beogradu* (Beograd: JKP "Pogrebne Usluge", 1999), 21, fn. 37.
9. Although recent experts, including the World Health Organization, insist that dead bodies pose no health threat under normal conditions, by the end of the nineteenth century and continuing to this day, promoters of modernization have strongly discouraged home funerals.
10. Jeremy Walton describes tombstones in the now overgrown Orthodox section as often "chipped and rusted," their minority having been "consigned to a 'subaltern past'." Jeremy Walton, "The Dead Wait: Material Afterlives in Sepulchral Spaces, *Journal of Material Culture*, 7, 4 (2022) 382.

11 Statut za opće skupno groblje Grada Zagreba u Mirogoju (Zagreb: Tiskarski i Litografički Zavod C. Albrechta, 1878), Opće Skpupno Groblje Grada Zagreba na Mirogoju, Sign. 196; Ivan Trčak, *Mirogoj: Kulturno-povijesni vodić* (Zagreb: Krščanska Sadašnjost i Rektorat Crkve Krista Kralja, Mirogoj, 1987), 126-7; Naredbenik Obću Mrtvačnicu u Mirogoju: Pogrebni Red (Zagreb: Tiskarski i Litografički Zavod C. Albrechta, 1888).
12 "Hrvatsko-Slavonski Zakon o Zdravstvu," March 25, 1906, cited in "O grobljima na području NR Hrvatske s pravnog gledišta," HDA, 310/134, n.d.
13 *Zbornik*, 1906, cited in "O grobljima na području NR Hrvatske s pravnog gledišta," HDA, 310/134, n.d.
14 "O grobljima na području NR Hrvatske s pravnog gledišta," HDA, 310/134, n.d.
15 KVP, June 30, 1947, HDA, 310/134.
16 Nadbiskupski Duhovni Stol u Zagrebu, August 6, 1948, HDA, 310/134; KVP, August 9, 1948, HDA, 310/134.
17 No author, February 16, 1949, HDA, 310/134.
18 *Uredba o Grobljima*, November 1, 1949, HDA, 310/134.
19 NRH Narodni Odbor Grada Osijeka Povjereništvo komunalnih poslova, November 8, 1949, HDA, 310/134.
20 Biskupski Ordinarijat Djakovo, November 25–December 7, 1949, HDA, 310/134; Biskupski Ordinarijat Djakovo, November 17, 1949, HDA, 310/134; Mgr Dr. Antun Aksamović Biskup Djakovo, November 21, 1949, HDA, 310/134.
21 Svetozar M. Ritig, January 1–4, 1950, HDA, 310/134. See also Ministar bez portfelja Svetozar Ritig, 1950, HDA, 310/136.
22 Ministar bez portfelja Svetozar Ritig, March 22, 1950, HDA, 310/136.
23 NRH Narodni Odbor Oblasti Osijek, Tajništvo, February 27, 1950, HDA, 310/136; NRH Ministarstvo komunalnih poslova, Sekretarijat, April 5, 1950, HDA, 310/136.
24 According to Stjepan Sršan, all cemeteries in the city were finally taken over in 1957 by the Communal Enterprise Vrt (Garden) founded in 1952. According to the organization's 1958 report, it had appropriated seventeen cemeteries of various religious denominations, which it claimed were "in a dilapidated state, disorderly and overfull." That explanation, while perhaps partially true, may also have been manufactured to correspond to the conditions established in Serbia that cemeteries would be taken over only if abandoned or in serious disrepair. Stjepan Sršan, *Osječka groblja* (Osijek: Povijesni Arhiv, 1996), 28.
25 It is perhaps no surprise that within the CRQ, Roko Rogošić supported the position of the Catholic Church. Having completed degrees in theology in Croatia and his doctorate at the Oriental Institute in Rome, he was a professor of Church history and law both before and after the Second World War. He served on the CRQ as the expert on Roman Catholic religious history from 1945 to 1960. Vjekoslav Štefanić,

"Nekrolog. **Roko Rogošić** In memoriam," *Slovo: Časopis Staroslavenskoga instituta u Zagrebu*, 14 (September 1964): 131–2.

26 Roko Rogošić, KVP, May 29, 1952, HDA, 310/139.

27 "Izvadak iz zapisnik sastavljenog na sednici prezviterija reformatske crkvene općine u Feketiću," December 6, 1949, Arhiv Srbije, G21, F10; "Zapisnik sa sednice Komisije RIVa za verska pitanja koja je održana," November 4, 1968, in Radmila Radić and Momcilo Mitrović, eds., *Zapisnici sa sednica Komisije za verska pitanja NR/SR Srbije 1945–1978. godine* (Beograd: Institut za noviju istoriju Srbije, 2012), 527; "Izveštaj o stanju verskih organizacija i sekti u NR Srbiji, 13. VI. 1955," in Radić and Mitrović, eds., 671; "Tromesečeni izveštaj o radu Komisije," October 28, 1950, Arhiv Jugoslavije, Fond 1944, fasc. 2.

28 Alji Sukrija, "Predmet: Opšteg Zakona o Narodnim Odborima," May 22, 1951, Agjencia Shtetërore e Arkivave të Kosovës (ASHAK); Pretsednik vakufskog odbora. Islamskom Stareštinstvo IVZ Priština, February 1956, Bashkesia e Fes Islame IVZ ZURA e Vakufit Prishtine, Agjencia Shtetërore e Arkivave të Kosovës (ASHAK), K-55, 1956 (translated by Mrika Limani Myrtaj).

29 "Izveštaj o radu Zemaljske komisije za verske poslove NR Srbije u četvrtome tromesečju 1949 godine," January 15, 1950, Arhiv Jugoslavije, Fond 1944, fasc. 2; "Tromesečni izveštaj Državnoj KVP pri Pretsedništvu Vlade FNRJ from Zemaljska KVP NR Srbija 10. X. 1949," in Radić and Mitrović, eds., 616.

30 Tromesečni izveštaj o radu Komisije," October 28, 1950, Arhiv Jugoslavije, Fond 144, fasc. 2.

31 Izveštaj o rad Saborskog odbora IVZ za NRS u Prištini u vremenu od 10 aprila do 15 decembra 1956 godine, December 15, 1956, Bashkesia e Fes Islame IVZ ZURA e Vakufit Prishtine, Agjencia Shtetërore e Arkivave të Kosovës (ASHAK), K-53, 1956.

32 Izveštaj o radu Zemaljske KVP NR Srbije u 1951 godini, January 15, 1952, in Radić and Mitrović, eds., 629.

33 Roko Rogošić, KVP, December 1, 1952, HDA, 310/139. See also Roko Rogošić, KVP, January 28, 1953, HDA, 310/139.

34 Approximately five years later, these laws were amended in each republic to incorporate bureaucratic changes resulting from institutional and economic reforms. The Law on the Legal Status of Religious Questions underwent similar minor revisions in the 1960s.

35 "Ukaz o proglašenju Zakon o grobljima," *Narodne Novine: Službeni list Narodne Republike Hrvatske*, XVI, June 29, 1960, 26, 269–70; "Zakon o grobljima," *Narodne Novine*, 32, July 30, 1965, 409–11.

36 Dr. Ante Matković, "Izvod iz *Vjesnika* Biskupije splitske i makarske, br III," April 19, 1969, HDA, 310/186.

37 "Zakon o sahranjivanju i grobljama," *Službeni glasnik NRS*, 20 (May 13, 1961): 325.

38 Vendim mbi vorrezat, December 21, 1961, Fletorja zyrtare KAKM, Agjencia Shtetërore e Arkivave të Kosovës (ASHAK), 42/1193 (translated by Mrika Limani Myrtaj).
39 All documents relating to the survey are from: HDA 310/174 opći spisi, 106–60, 1966.
40 In many cases, the reports claimed that they had passed into the hands of the Local Communities—"Mjesni Zajednici"—only within the last year or two, but that does not necessarily mean that these districts had not taken cemeteries out of the hands of the religious communities only in the required two years after the passage of the 1960 Law of Cemeteries. Rather, the reports seem to have been referring explicitly to a set of administrative changes that took place throughout the governing system of Yugoslavia in connection with the Economic Reforms of 1965 and which resulted in a change of name from Local Councils (Mjesni Odbori), previously responsible for cemetery management, to Local Communities (Mjesni Zajednici). There were a few exceptions to the rule, and rare documents referring to the conflict between ownership and management of cemeteries still appeared during the late 1960s. "Razgovor sa svećenicima Arhijerijskog namjesništva baranjskog Srpske pravoslavne crkve—izvještaj," KVP IV Sabora SR Hrvatske Zagreb and KVP Skupštine Kotara Osijek, December 29, 1966, HDA, 310/178, 1–50; Ivan Lasić, "Republički zavod za Urbanizam, stambene, i komunalne poslove, Zagreb," June 3, 1968, HDA, 310/186.
41 KVP Dubrovnik, "Izvještaj," May 24, 1966, HDA, 310/174.
42 NRJ VIII Stanica Narodne Milicije Kotar Zagreb, 29 June 1956, HDA, 310/143.
43 NRJ VIII Stanica Narodne Milicije Kotar Zagreb, 24 June 1956, HDA, 310/143; "Rimokatolička župa u Granešini, kotar Zagreb, predlog za ulaganje zahtjeva za zaštitu zakonitosti," June 21, 1957, HDA, 310/141.
44 NRJ VIII Stanica Narodne Milicije Kotar Zagreb, 27 August 1956, HDA, 310/143.
45 Ksenija Basić, "Decentralization of the Zagreb Urban Region," *Dela*, 21 (2004): 520–1.
46 "Izvadak iz zapisnika," March 3, 1914, Opće Skupno Groblje Grada Zagreba na Mirogoju, Sign. 196; "Prijedlog," July 1, 1941, Opće Skupno Groblje Grada Zagreba na Mirogoju, Sign. 196.
47 Gradska groblja Zagreb, Zagrebački Holding. Accessed June 9, 2017, http://www.gradskagroblja.hr/default.aspx?id=256.
48 Sršan, 30, 63; Report from KVP Osijek, June 11, 1966, HDA, 310/174.
49 "Stanje i problem sahranjivanja u Beograd," December 1971, Istorijski Arhiv Beograd, Narodni Odbor grada Beograda, 1971. For more on cremation, see Chapter 5.
50 Ivan Petrović and Branko Amanović, *Informacija o stanju gradskih groblja i o realizacija programa izgradnje gradskih groblja* (Beograd: Zavod za komunalnu i stambenu delatnost grada, June 1973), Istorijski Arhiv Beograd.

51 Petrović and Amanović.
52 Laqueur, 112–13.
53 Since I have not visited every cemetery in all three republics, there may be a few others like Nova Bežanija and Lešče but they would still have represented a small minority.
54 For example, the municipal cemeteries in Knin and Nova Gradiška have separate sections for Orthodox and Catholics.
55 "Muslimanska vjerska zajednica Gunja, uredjenje groblja," June 9, 1962, HDA, 310/155.
56 Professor Šefedin Šehović, University of Novi Pazar, Interview with the Author, September 20, 2013.
57 For more information on this issue see Amir Duranović, *Islamska Zajednica u Jugoslavenskom Socijalizmu* (Sarajevo: Udruženje za Modernu Historiju, 2021).
58 Zapisnik sa sjednice Komisije za razmatranje odnosa izmedju države i vjerskih zajednicu sa Vrhovnim islamskim starješinstvom, April 14, 1953, AJ, Fond 144, fasc. 8. As Tito's close confidant, Bijedić is also said to have played a prominent role in the legal creation of a Muslim ethnic nation in the late 1960s. Mitja Velikonja, *Religious Separation and Political Intolerance in Bosnia-Herzegovina* (College Station, TX: Texas A&M Press, 2003), 223. The Reis-ul-Ulema from 1947 to 1957 was Ibrahim Fejić who had joined the Partisans during the war, denounced wartime persecutions of Jews, Serbs, and Roma, and joined the Communist campaign against the veiling of women. https://www.islamskazajednica.ba/index.php/dosadasnje-reisu-l-uleme, accessed October 8, 2021.
59 Vakufskoj Direkciji, April 17, 1952, Arhiv BiH, 71/51; Eksproprijacije vak. Zemljišta, May 14, 1952, Arhiv BiH, 93/52; Eksproprijacija zemljišta za podizanje Dome kulture u Goraždu and Potraživanja suglasnosti za expropriaciju vakufskog zemljišta u Goraždi, April 9 and May 15, 1953, Arhiv BiH, 1818/53.
60 KVP pri Pretsjedništvu vlade NR BiH, June 2, 1952, Arhiv BiH, 1306/52; KVP pri Izvršnom vijeću NR BiH, Žalba vakufska direkcija za nepravilno oduzimanje vakufskih zemljišta u Bos. Krup. and Narodnom odboru Sreza Bos. Krupskog, Pretstavka Vakufske direkcije KVP, April 1–May 21, 1954, Arhiv BiH, 1357/54, 2963/54, 2963/54; KVP pri Izvršnom vijeću NR BiH, October 6, 1954, Arhiv BiH, 2008/54.
61 "Zemljoknjižni izvadak"; "Dostava Podataka po Dopisu Broj 04/1-47-1/91," Opštinksi komisije za urbanizma, gradjivinarstvo, komunalne i imovinske pravne poslove, Socijalistička Republika BiH, Zenica, February 22, 1991, Archives of Parish Church of St. Ilija, Zenica, BiH. Accessed November 5, 2013.
62 Aleksandar Ranković, "Pretsedniku Izvršnu Vijeću NR BiH," July 18, 1959, Arhiv BiH.
63 https://en.wikipedia.org/wiki/Stup_Interchange, accessed December 4, 2021.
64 "Zakon o grobljima," *Službeni list Narodne Republike Bosne-Hercegovine*, XVI, 10 (March 15, 1960): 88–91.

65 Analiza vjerskih objekata, Islamska vjerska zajednica, January 8, 1965, Arhiv BiH, 13/65.
66 "Izvještaj o radu republičke komisije za vjerska pitanja SR BiH i stanju odnosa sa vjerskim zajednicama u SR BiH za 1974 godinu," February 24, 1975, Arhiv BiH, 011, 11/75; "Izvršno Vijeća Skupštine SR BiH Komisija za vjerska pitanja," May 29, 1975, Arhiv BiH.
67 "Zapisnik Komisije za odnose sa vjerskim zajednicima," November 1, 1975, Arhiv BiH.
68 "Djelatnosti komisija za odnose sa vjerskim zajednicama u SR BiH—Iskustva i problemi u radu," December 1984, Arhiv BiH.
69 "Informacija o realizaciji Zaključaka Skupština SRBiH i Ocjena i stavova Predsjedništva SRBiH o provodjenju Zakona o pravnom položaju vjerskih zajednica u SRBiH," August 1985, Arhiv BiH, 14–16.
70 "Informacija o nekim problemima provodjenja Zakona o pravnom položaju vjerskih zajednica i aktuelnim aspektima njihovog djelovanja u SRBiH," October 1989, Arhiv BiH.
71 Friar Zdravka Anđić, Interview with the Author, Zenica, November 5, 2013.
72 Robert Donia, *Sarajevo: A Biography* (Ann Arbor: University of Michigan Press, 2006), 234.
73 "Informacija," July 3, 1963, Arhiv BiH, 332/63.
74 "Stenografske zabilješke: proširene zajednice komisije za vjerska pitanja SR BiH," June 30, 1964, Arhiv BiH.
75 Dr. Eli Tauber, Interview with the author, Sarajevo, November 11, 2013.
76 "Regulacioni plan Groblje 'Vlakovo,'" Zavod za planiranje razvoja grada Sarajeva, Sarajevo, November 1989, at Javno Komunalno Preduzeće Pokupno Društvo Sarajevo, Summer 2012. In 2005, the Burial Society published a revision based on postwar demographic predictions, allotting 55 percent of the space to Muslims, 18 percent to Orthodox, 15 percent to Catholics, and 12 percent to Atheists and Others. The crematorium has yet to be constructed. "Korekcija Regulacionog plana Groblja Vlakovo," Zavod za Planiranje Razvoja Kantona Sarjevo, Sarajevo, June 2005.

5 Burial Rituals

1 Fred Paxton, *Christianizing Death: The Creation of a Ritual Process in Early Medieval Europe* (Ithaca, NY: Cornell University Press, 1990); Nicholas Constas, *Death and Dying in Byzantium* (Minneapolis, MN: Fortress, 2006).
2 Pat Jalland, "Victorian Death and Its Decline: 1850–1918," in Peter C. Jupp and Clare Gittings, eds., *Death in England: An Illustrated History* (New Brunswick, NJ: Rutgers University Press, 2000), 254–67; Elizabeth Hallam and Jenny Hockey,

Death, Memory, and Material Culture (Oxford: Berg, 2001), 82–3; Clare Gittings, *Death, Burial, and the Individual in Early Modern England* (London: Croom Helms, 1984), 159.

3 Katherine Verdery, *The Political Lives of Dead Bodies: Reburial and Postsocialist Change* (New York: Columbia University Press, 1999), 107–10; Eva Reimers, "Death and Identity: Graves and Funerals as Cultural Communication," *Mortality*, 4, 2 (1999): 147–8; Bojan Jovanović, *Srpska knjiga mrtvih* (Novi Sad: Prometej, 1992), 24.

4 Carol S. Lilly, *Power and Persuasion: Ideology and Rhetoric in Communist Yugoslavia, 1944–1953* (Boulder, CO: Westview Press, 2001), 102. Pijade was also of Jewish heritage.

5 Radmila Radić, *Verom protiv vere: Država i verske zajednice u Srbiji 1945–1953* (Beograd: Inis, 1995), 166.

6 "Pravilnik o organizaciji i poslovanju gradskog pogrebnog zavoda," *Službeni glasnik Beograda*, 9 (March 1, 1947): 94–6; "Rešenje o saglasnosti na odluku Komunalnog preduzeća 'pogrebni zavod' i Uprave za gradskog groblja o spajanju," *Službeni list grada Beograda*, 2 (February 1, 1971): 44; "Rješenje," *Službeni glasnik Narodnog odbora grada Zagreba*, VII, 5–8 (March 15, 1953).

7 Zora Hendija, "Prvo hrvatsko gradjansko kaptolsko društvo za sjajne pogrebe u Zagrebu (1835–1948)," *Arhivski Vjesnik*, 37 (1994): 272.

8 "Zabrana djelovanja Hevre Kadishe u Čakovcu, odnosno konfiskacija imovine," May 6, 1946–November 17, 1948, HDA, 310/opći spisi, 139.

9 Historijat—Bakije. Accessed September 14, 2021. http://www.bakije.com/historijat.html.

10 Florijan Brodić, Srećko Katavić, Mato Matijić, and Karlo Škec eds., *Hrvatsko Pogrebno Društvo u Sarajevo, 1921–1991* (Sarajevo: Hrvatsko Pogrebno Društvo, 1991).

11 Brodić et al, eds., 38–9.

12 "Zapisnik Komisije za odnose sa vjerskim zajednicama," November 1, 1975, Arhiv BiH.

13 https://bakije.ba/, accessed September 14, 2021; Brodić et al., eds., 54–9; Nelo Veljača, Interview with the author, November 5, 2013, Zenica; Željko Kocaj, ed., *Katoličko pokopno društvo "Sveti Anto" Zenica, 1932–2010* (Zenica: KPD "Sveti Anto" Zenica, 2010).

14 See, e.g., Janko Balorda, "Običaji oko smrti i pogreba u okolini Visokog," *Etnografska gradja: Akademija nauka i umjetnosti bosne i hercegovine*, 20, 16 (1976): 77–86; Dušan Bandić, "Koncept posrmtnog umiranja u religiji Srba," *Etnološki pregled*, 19 (1983): 39–47; Maja Bosić, "Arhaični elementi u pogrebnim običajima u Vojvodini," *Etnološke sveske*, VI (1985): 89–94, Nikolaj Buconjić, *Život i obijčaji Hrvata katoličke vjere u Bosni i Hercegovini* (Sarajevo: Danijela A. Kajona,

1908); L. M. Danforth, *The Death Rituals of Rural Greece* (Princeton, NJ: Princeton University Press, 1982).

15 Edit Petrović, "Posmrtni običaji kod ateista: na primeru crnogorskih kolonista u Bačkoj," *Etnološke sveske*, VIII (1987): 179–86.

16 Milka Jovanović, "Sastanak sa 'Pokojnikom,'" *Glasnik Etnografskog Instituta SANU*, 39 (1990): 80–93.

17 Jovanović, "Sastanak sa 'Pokojnikom,'"; Bojan Jovanović, *Srpska Knjiga Mrtva* (Prometej: Novi Sad, 1992), 131; see also Danforth. Louis de Bernières includes an exquisite fictionalized description of this ritual in his novel of life in Turkey's diverse religious communities of the early 20th century. Louis de Bernieres, *Birds Without Wings*, (Vintage Books: New York, 2005) 63-72.

18 Tone Bringa, *Being Muslim the Bosnian Way* (Princeton, NJ: Princeton University Press, 1995), 194.

19 Aleksandra Pavičević, *From Mystery to Spectacle: Essays on Death in Serbia from the 19th-21st Century* (Belgrade: Serbian Academy of Sciences: Ethnographic Institute, 2015), 9–13.

20 "Zapisnik sa sednice republičke KVP održane 15 XII 1960", in Radmila Radić and Momcilo Mitrović, eds., *Zapisnici sa sednica Komicije za verska pitanja NR/SR Srbije 1945–1978 godine* (Beograd: Institut za noviju istoriju Srbije, 2012), 322.

21 Sladjana Rajković, Museum Advisor, National Museum of Leskovac, Interview with the author, September 25, 2013.

22 Professor Šefedin Šehović, Pedagogical Faculty, Interview with the author, Novi Pazar, September 20, 2013.

23 "Tromesečni izveštaj Državnoj KVP pri Pretsedništvu Vlade FNRJ from Zemaljska KVP NR Srbija 10. X. 1949," in Radić and Mitrović, eds., 609.

24 "Zapisnik sa sednice Republicke KVP održane 17 XII. 1963," in Radić and Mitrović, eds., 429.

25 "Informacija," July 3, 1963, Arhiv BiH, 332/63.

26 "Informacija," July 3, 1963, Arhiv BiH, 332/63.

27 "Pokupno društvo 'Bakije'—Narodnom odboru Srezu—na ruke Pretsjednika," March 7, 1971, Arhiv BiH; "Zapisnik sa sjednice KVP Narodnog odbora sreza Sarajevo," June 7, 1962 and December 23, 1964, Arhiv BiH.

28 "KVP pri Predsjedništvu Vlade NRH," January 18, 1947, HDA, 310/129; "Popovaca dozvola služenja mise i dijeljenje sv. Sakramenata," March 21–May 9, 1947, HDA, 310/131; "Pro-Memorata za P.N. Mons. Dra Svetozara Ritig-a," April 14, 1947, HDA, 310/131; "Bolnica u Puli, slobodan ulaz dušobriznika u bolnicu," October 23, 1948–February 9, 1949, HDA, 310/133; "Virovitca-bolnica-pristup svećenika bolesnicima," July 21 and October 21, 1950, HDA, 310/137. There was also one case in Belgrade in 1949 addressed in the same way. "Izveštaj o radu Zemaljske komisije

za verske poslove NR Srbije u četvrome tromesečju 1949 godine," January 15, 1950, Arhiv Jugoslavija, F144, f2.
29 "Pristup svećenika u bolnica," January 15–February 2 1952, HDA, 310/139.
30 "Zakon o pravnom položaju verskih zajednica," *Službeni list FRNJ*, May 22, 27, 1953, 209–10.
31 "Sprečavanje pohoda svećenika bolesnicima u Domu Staraca u Bjelovaru," February 15, 1957, HDA, 310/141; "Svećenika pohadjanje u bolnicu radi ispovjedanja na zahtijev stranaka, objašnjenje moli," May 15, 1957, HDA, 310/145; "Sprečavanje bolesnika na primanje sakramenata u senjskoj Bolnici—predstavka," December 31, 1960, HDA, 310/151.
32 "Pravilo o izmena pravila službe Jugoslavenske Narodne Armije," May 15, 1967, HDA, 310/197.
33 "KVP pri Predsjedništvu Vlade NRH," January 18, 1947, HDA, 310/129.
34 "Izvještaj o sprečavanju sprovoda," November 9, 1956, HDA, 310/141.
35 "Nadbiskupski Duhovni Stol u Zagrebu," July 26, 1956, HDA, 310/143. The reference to Ranković's comments is a bit confusing since his internal memo on relations with the religious community was not sent for another three years. Apparently, these ideas were already in circulation.
36 Ivan Krajcar, Župnik, Request for intervention to the Office of the President of the Republic, Belgrade, February 25, 1969, HDA, 310/189.
37 Aleksandar Ranković, "Pretsedniku Izvršnu Vijeću NR BiH," July 18, 1959, Arhiv BiH.
38 Okružni Sud u Karlovac, "Presuda u ime naroda," March 10, 1972, HDA, 310/207; Mije Liković, "Predmet: Predstavka u povodu sudkse presude," April 15, 1972, HDA, 310/207.
39 Ivan Koprčina, "Republičkom Sekretarijatu za Unutrašnje Poslove SRH-e," June 28, 1974, HDA, 310/219; Ivan Koprčina "Općinski Javni Tužiocu Split," June 26, 1974, HDA, 310/219; Tajništvo Izvršno Vijeće SRH, "Informacija," July 2, 1974, HDA, 310/219.
40 KVP NR Hrvatske, "Godišnji izvještaj Republičke KVP," 1961, Arhiv Jugoslavija, F144, f57.
41 KVP NR Hrvatske, "Godišnji izvještaj Republičke KVP," 1961, Arhiv Jugoslavija, F144, f57; "Zapisnik za nastavljene sjednice KVP," September 10 and 25, 1964, HDA, 310 Zapisnici 2.
42 Susan Woodward, *Socialist Unemployment: The Political Economy of Yugoslavia 1945–1990* (Princeton, NJ: Princeton University Press, 1995), 272. Thus, the state's most serious conflict with the 7th-Day Adventists was their refusal to work and send their children to school on Saturdays.
43 "Zapisnik za nastavljene sjednice KVP," September 10 and 25, 1964, HDA, 310/Zapisnici 2.

44 "Zapisnik sa sednice Republičke KVP održane 26. V. 1962," in Radić and Mitrović, eds., 382–3; "Zapisnik sa sednice KVP NR Srbije održane 19 oktobra 1962," in Radić and Mitrović, eds., 385.
45 "Zapisnik sa sednice Komisije RIVa za verska pitanja održane 6. V. 1970," in Radić and Mitrović, eds., 534. See also "Zapisnik sa sednice Komisije RIVa sa verska pitanja održane 22. X. 1970," in Radić and Mitrović, eds., 551.
46 "Zapisnik sa sednice Komisije IV Skupštine SR Srbije za odnose sa verskim zajednicama održane 21. maja 1976; Informacija o delatnost verskih zajednica na području opštine Niš," in Radić and Mitrović, eds., 567–9.
47 Odbor za pogrebne delatnosti, *Kodeks Pogrebne Usluge* (Beograd: Privredna komora Jugoslavije, Savet za zanatstvo, komunalnu i stambenu prevredu, 1974). Of the thirteen authors, four were from Serbia (two from AP Vojvodina and none from AP Kosovo), three were from Croatia, three from Slovenia, and one each from Bosnia & Hercegovina, Montenegro, and Macedonia. While it is risky to try to guess the national origin based on names, it seems likely that Stjepan Bartolić from Bosnia & Hercegovina was Croatian.
48 See, e.g., Victoria Smolkin, *A Sacred Space Is Never Empty* (Princeton, NJ: Princeton University Press, 2019), 165–93; Christel Lane, *The Rites of Rulers: Ritual in Industrial Society—the Soviet Case* (Cambridge: Cambridge University Press, 1981), 83–6.
49 *Kodeks*, 32.
50 *Kodeks*, 28.
51 Smolkin, 193.
52 Catherine Merridale, *Night of Stone: Death and Memory in Twentieth Century Russia* (New York: Penguin Books, 2000), 25; Aleksandra Pavičević, "Cremation as an Urban Phenomenon of the New Age: From Ecology to Ideology: The Serbian Case," *Ethnologica Balkanica*, 10 (2006): 254–5; Marius Rotar," Attitudes toward Cremation in Contemporary Romania," *Mortality*, 20, 2 (2015): 148–50.
53 "Instruction *Ad resurgendum cum Christo* Regarding the Burial of the Deceased and the Conservation of the Ashes in the Case of Cremation," Congregation of the Doctrine for the Faith. Accessed September 20, 2021, https://www.vatican.va/roman_curia/congregations/cfaith/documents/rc_con_cfaith_doc_20160815_ad-resurgendum-cum-christo_en.html.
54 "Zakon o sahranjivanju i grobljama," *Službeni glasnik NRS*, 20 (May 13, 1961): 325.
55 "Odluka o sahranjivanju i grobljima," September 26, 1963, Istorijski Arhiv Beograd, 1346; "Zakon o sahranijivanju i grobljima," July 17, 1965, *Službeni glasnik SRS*, 30, 716–18.
56 Pavičević, 255.
57 Pavičević, 256.

58 Ivan Petrović and Branko Amanović, *Informacija o stanju gradskih groblja i o realizacija programa izgradnje gradskih groblja* (Beograd: Zavod za komunalnu i stambenu delatnost grada, June 1973), Istorijski Arhiv Beograd, 22, 29; "Stanje i problem sahranjivanja u Beograd," December 1971, Istorijski Arhiv Beograd, Komunalno preduzeće za pogrebne usluge, Narodni Odbor Grada Beograda, 1971.

59 Petrović and Amanović.

60 Pavičević, 258-9.

61 "Regulacioni Plan Groblje 'Vlakovo,'" Zavod za Planiranje Razvoja Grada Sarajeva, Sarajevo, November 1989, Jugoslovensko Komunalno Poduzeće Pokupno Društvo Sarajevo.

62 Pavičević, 257, fn. 7; Marius Rotar, "Attitudes toward Cremation in Contemporary Romania," *Mortality*, 20, 2 (2015): 148; Kelly, 320-1.

63 Pavičević, 256.

64 Petrović and Amanović, 21.

65 Goran Miloradović, "Prah prahu: Staljinistički pogrebni rituali u socialističkoj Yugoslaviji," *Godišnjak za društvenu istoriju*, 1-3 (2007): 87.

66 One is, reminded of Catriona Kelly's comment that the standard Soviet funeral "always boiled down to two elements: wreaths and speeches." Catriona Kelly, *St. Petersburg: Shadows of the Past* (New Haven, CT: Yale University Press, 2014), 316.

67 "Pravilnik o odavanju počasti prilikom sahrane pomrlog učesnika Narodnooslobodilačkog Rata Jugoslavije," May 19, 1976, HDA, 310/244; SUBNOR SR Hrvatske, June 24, 1976, HDA, 310/244.

68 Uprava Parohije Velika Bršljanica, "Savezu Udruženja Pravoslavnog Sveštenstva SR Hrvatske," April 13, 1976, HDA, 310/228; Episkop Gornokarlovački, Documents about funerals of members of SUBNOR in Glina, Vrginmost, and Vojinić, July 8-22, 1977, HDA, 310/235; Documents about burial of member of SUBNOR, July 7-16, 1986, HDA, 310/264.

69 Documents about funerals of veterans, June 14-November 2, 1977, HDA, 310/234; Nadbiskupski Ordinarijat Split, Komisiji za odnose s vjerskim zajednicama, January 19, 1980, HDA, 310/244; Documents about military burial in Bjelovar, November 2, 1983-March 3, 1984, HDA, 310/256.

6 Grave Markers: Messages in Stone

1 Harold Mytum, *Mortuary Monuments and Burial Grounds of the Historic Period* (New York: Kluwer Academic, 2004), 160.

2 Mytum, *Mortuary Monuments*, 23-5.

3 Leor Halevi, *Muhammad's Grave: Death Rites and the Making of Islamic Society* (New York: Columbia University Press, 2007), 32-3, 188; Kodo Matsunami,

Funeral Customs of the World: A Comprehensive Guide to Practices and Traditions (Tochigi: Buddhist Searchlight Center 1998), 155–7, 162, 164–7.

4 Mehdmed Mujezinović, *Islamska Epigrafika Bosne i Hercegovine* (Sarajevo: Sarajevo Publishing, 1998), 14–15.

5 William Oliver Stevens, *The Cross in the Life and Literature of the Anglo-Saxons* (New York: Henry Holt, 1904), 56, Ebook edition. Crosses were sometimes placed on tombstones throughout Europe earlier than the tenth century to positively identify the deceased as Christians at Resurrection. Bonnie Effros, *Merovingian Mortuary Archaeology and the Making of the Middle Ages* (Berkeley: University Press of California, 2003), 182; Celtic crosses also have been dated as early as the sixth century, and there is some evidence linking them and the later use of the plain cross in England.

6 Thomas Kselman, *Death and the Afterlife in Modern France* (Princeton, NJ: Princeton University Press, 1993), 69.

7 John Morley, *Death, Heaven and the Victorians* (London: Studio Vista Blue Star House, 1971), 52; Julie Rugg, "From Reason to Regulation: 1760–1850," in Peter Jupp and Clare Gittings, eds., *Death in England: An Illustrated Text* (New Brunswick, NJ: Rutgers University Press, 2000), 226.

8 Howard Colvin, *Architecture and the Afterlife* (New Haven, CT: Yale University Press, 1991), 373; Harold Mytum, *Recording and Analysing Graveyards*, vol. 15 of Practical Handbooks in Archaeology (York: Council for British Archaeology in Association with English Heritage, 2000), 29–38.

9 Noel Menachemson, *A Practical Guide to Jewish Cemeteries* (Bergenfield, NJ: Avotaynu, 2007), 45; Roberta Halporn, "American Jewish Cemeteries: A Mirror of History," in Richard Meyer, ed. *Ethnicity and the American Cemetery* (Bowling Green, OH: Bowling Green State University), 132.

10 Menachemson, 27–47, 199.

11 Thomas Arnold, "Symbolism and Islam," *Burlington Magazine for Connoisseurs*, 53, 307 (1928): 155–6.

12 Amila Buturović, *Carved in Stone, Etched in Memory: Death, Tombstones and Commemoration in Bosnian Islam Since c. 1500* (Farnham: Ashgate, 2015), 166–84.

13 Clare Gitting, "Sacred and Secular: 1558–1660," in Peter C. Jupp and Clare Gittings, eds., *Death in England: An Illustrated History* (New Brunswick, NJ: Rutgers University Press, 2000), 166–9; Rosemary Horrox, "Purgatory, Prayer and Plague: 1150–1380," in Peter C. Jupp and Clare Gitting, eds., *Death in England: An Illustrated History* (New Brunswick, NJ: Rutgers University Press, 2000), 108; Ralph Houlbrooke, *Death, Religion and the Family in England, 100–1600* (Oxford: Clarendon Press, 1998), 345–9.

14 Phillip Aries, *The Hour of Our Death* (New York: Vintage Books, 1982), 538.

15 Nicholas Constas, "Death and Dying in Byzantium," in Derek Krueger, ed., *Byzantine Christianity*, from A People's History of Christianity, vol. 3 (Minneapolis, MN: Fortress, 2006), 137.
16 Olga Matich, "'Whacked But Not Forgotten': Burying the Mob." Accessed February 27, 2015, http://www.stanford.edu/group/Russia20/volume.
17 Raf Vanderstraeten, "Burying and Remembering the Dead," *Memory Studies*, 7, 4 (2014), 8, https://doi.org/10.1177/1750698013519122.
18 Elizabeth Hallam and Jenny Hockey, *Death, Memory, and Material Culture* (Oxford: Berg, 2001), 169.
19 Houlbrook, 351–60.
20 Mytum, *Recording and Analysing*, 53–4.
21 Halevi, 21–42.
22 According to Mehmed Mujezinović, they were not only often similar to but were also located near ancient Bosnian *stećaks*—medieval pre-Ottoman tombstones usually associated with the Bosnian Church. Mujezinović, 13.
23 Buturović, 190–9.
24 Aries, 293.
25 Susan Gal, "A Semiotics of the Public/Private Distinction," *differences: A Journal of Feminist Cultural Studies*, 13, 1 (Spring 2002): 81.
26 My best guess, in consultation with local experts in all regions, is that it was a craft considered sufficiently small scale to be ignored. In fact, that still often appeared to be the case when I was conducting research in all three republics in the 2010s. Moreover, despite consistent efforts, I was never able to gain interviews with individuals involved in the industry, though based on my interviews with individuals from contemporary funeral enterprises, it is possible that had I succeeded, they would not have had any information about (or interest in) the Communist period.
27 *Službeni glasnik Narodnog odbora grada Zagreba*, XXI, 18 (November 18, 1967), Hrvatski Institut za Povijest; Paul Shoup, *Communism and the Yugoslav National Question* (New York: Columbia University Press, 1968), 110, fn. 27.
28 Jeremy F. Walton, "The Dead Wait: Material Afterlives in Sepulchral Spaces," *Journal of Material Culture*, 7, 4 (2022): 377.
29 Soviet graves also began to include such depictions in the 1970s, particularly those referring to the profession of the deceased. In that case, however, according to Victoria Smolkin, the impetus came more clearly from Soviet leaders seeking to promote heroic labor through ritual. There is no evidence that either Yugoslav citizens or monument designers were even aware of the Soviet policies, to say nothing of emulating them. Victoria Smolkin, *A Sacred Space Is Never Empty* (Princeton, NJ: Princeton University Press, 2018), 184.

30 Ivan Čolović, *Književnost na Groblju: Zbirka novih epitafa* (Beograd: Narodna Knjiga, 1983), 29–45, 78–91.
31 Aries, 520–40; Houlbrooke, 380; Vanderstraeten, 4–6.
32 Daniel Bunčić, "Bigrafism: Serbo-Croatian/Serbian: Cyrillic and Latin," in Daniel Bunčić, Sandra L. Lippert, and Achim Rabus, eds., *Biscriptality: A Sociolinguistic Typology* (Heidelberg: Universitätsverlag Winter, 2016), 234.
33 Vesna Požgaj Hadži, "Language Policy and Linguistic Reality in Former Yugoslavia and Its Successor States," *Inter Faculty*, 5 (2014): 58; Dubravko Škiljan, *Jezična Politika* (Zagreb: Naprijed, 1988), 65; Robert Greenberg, *Language and Identity in the Balkans* (Oxford: Oxford University Press, 2004), 11.
34 Požgaj Hadži, 53–4; Greenberg, 9.
35 Greenberg, 21–2, 27.
36 Greenberg, 31–2; Vinko Grubišić, "The Croatian Language in the Constitutional Development of the SFRY," *Journal of Croatian Studies*, 30 (1989): 140–1.
37 Grubišić, 144; Greenberg, 11, 57.
38 Cyrillic was also used in Croatia but only between twelfth and fourteenth centuries along with Glagolitic. Greenberg, 42, 29.
39 Vasilije Kleftakis, "Zatiranje Srpske ćirilice—plan ili slučaj," *Nova Srpska Politička Misao*. Accessed November 2, 2021, Zatiranje srpske ćirilice—plan ili slučaj | Kulturna politika (nspm.rs).
40 Bunčić, 232.
41 Sarajevo's main daily, *Oslobodjenje*, printed one page in Latin and the next in Cyrillic. Bunčić, 231; Požgaj Hadži, 57; Greenberg, 43–4.
42 Požgaj Hadži, 77; Ranko Bugarski, "Jezička politika i jezička stvarnost u Srbiji posle 1991. godine," in Vesna Požgaj Hadži, ed., *Jezik Izmedju Lingvistike i Politike* (Belgrade: Biblioteke XX Vek, 2013), 96.
43 "Memorandum SANU," 25. Accessed January 1, 2022, https://pescanik.net/wp-content/PDF/memorandum_sanu.pdf; Greenberg, 11.
44 Misha Glenny, *The Fall of Yugoslavia: The Third Balkan War* (London: Penguin, 1992), 12.
45 Glenny, 43.
46 Glavni Odbor SBNOR-a BiH, "Sreskom-Opstinskom Odboru Saveza Boraca," April 12, 1960, Arhiv BiH SUBNOR, 155.
47 Potpukovnik Jovo Nonković, "Spor oko pisanja slova na spomeniku palim borcima," September 20, 1960, HDA, 179/1241.
48 Monica Huțanu and Annemarie Sorescu-Marinković, "Novi nadgrobni natpisi na vlaškom u istočnoj Srbiji," *Folkloristika*, 1, 2 (2016): 29; Biljana Sikmić and Motoki Nomachi, "Jezički pejsaž memorijalnih prostora višejezičnih zajednica, banatski Bugari/Palčanci u Srbiji," *Južnoslovenski filolog*, 72 (2016): 8.

49 Robert Putnam and David E. Campbell, *American Grace: How Religion Divides and Unites Us* (New York: Simon and Schuster, 2010), 494–540.

50 Ruža Petrović, *Etnički mešoviti brakovi u Jugoslaviji* (Beograd: Institut za sociološka istraživanja, Filozofskog fakulteta u Beogradu, 1985), 57; Nikolai Botev, "Where East Meets West: Ethnic Intermarriage in the Former Yugoslavia, 1962 to 1989," *American Sociological Association*, 59, 3 (June 1994): 461–80; Robert Hayden, "Imagined Communities and Real Victims—Self-Determination and Ethnic Cleansing in Yugoslavia," *American Ethnologist*, 23, 4 (November 1996): 788.

51 Duško Sekulić, Garth Massey, and Randy Hobson, "Who Were the Yugoslavs? Failed Sources of a Common Identity in the Former Yugoslavia," *American Sociological Review*, 59, 1 (February 1994): 83–97.

52 Although some of those in these mixed marriages may have become fully secularized, I use the term "Christian" and "Muslim" here since their burial cultures and traditions still reflect that heritage.

53 Haris Korkut, *Mješoviti brakovi po islamskom pravu: teološko-pravna rasprava* Bejrut, 1965); Tone Bringa, *Being Muslim the Bosnian Way* (Princeton, NJ: Princeton University Press, 1995), 143–53.

54 Buturović, 109–64.

55 The same is true for many Jewish grave markers, though many of them began including photographs even in the interwar period.

56 Halevi, 11.

57 Aydin Babuna, "The Albanians of Kosovo and Macedonia: Ethnic Identity Superseding Religion," *Nationalities Papers*, 28, 1 (2000): 67–92; Duizings, 30–1; Arolda Elbasani, "Introduction: Nation, State and Faith in the Post-Communist Era," in Arolda Elbasani and Olivier Roy, eds., *The Revival of Islam in the Balkans: From Identity to Religiosity* (Basingstoke: Palgrave McMillan, 2015), 11.

58 James Scott, *Domination and the Arts of Resistance: Hidden Transcripts* (New Haven, CT: Yale University Press, 1990), 2.

59 Duizings, 10.

60 See, e.g., Benedict Anderson, *Imagined Communities* (London: Verso, 1983); Eugen Weber, *Peasants into Frenchmen* (Stanford, CA: Stanford University Press, 1976). To be clear, neither Anderson nor Weber describes a causal relationship between secularism and nationalism. The relationship is more correlational based on common economic and cultural forces that developed in the eighteenth and nineteenth centuries.

61 Thomas A. Zaniello, "The Keystone of Neoclassicism: Fremasonry and Gravestone Iconography," *Journal of American Culture*, 3, 4 (Winter 1980): 581–94.

62 Alamy Stock photos, category "Nazi Graves", ID #s B9NYXN (RM) and 2D5JMTC (RF). Accessed October 26, 2021, https://www.alamy.com/search/imageresults.aspx?imgt=0&qt=Nazi+graves.

63 Catriona Kelly, *St. Petersburg: Shadows of the Past* (New Haven, CT: Yale University Press), 316
64 Gaj Trifković, *Sea of Blood: A Military History of the Partisan Movement in Yugoslavia, 1941–1945* (Warwick: Helion, 2022), 46; Milija Stanišić, *KPJ u izgradnji oružanih snaga revolucije 1941–1945* (Beograd: Vojnoizdavački zavod, 1973), 66.
65 Dušan Misirača, Sreskom-Opštinskom Odboru SBNOR, May 5, 1960, Arhiv BiH SUBNOR 116 and HDA 179/1241.
66 Cited in Max Bergholz, "Medju rodoljubima, kupusom, svinjama i varvarima: Spomenici i grobovi NOR 1947-1965. godine," *Godišnjak za društvenu istoriju*, XIV, 1–3 (2007): 72.

7 Ethnic Conflict and Politicization of the Dead

1 Due to a lack of documentation and scholarly research on this topic, it is impossible to establish relative levels of cemetery desecration in wartime. Only the desecration of Jewish graves during the Second World War eventually received comparable amounts of international concern.
2 See, e.g., such works as Robert Kaplan, *Balkan Ghosts* (New York: St. Martin's Press, 1993); Lenard Cohen, *Broken Bonds: Yugoslavia's Disintegration and Balkan Politics in Transition* (Boulder, Co: Westview Press, 1993); Susan Woodward, *Socialist Unemployment: The Political Economy of Yugoslavia, 1945–1990* (Princeton, NJ: Princeton University Press, 1995); Branka Magaš, *The Destruction of Yugoslavia: Tracking the Break-Up 1980–1992* (London: Verso, 1993); Mark Thompson, *Forging War: The Media in Serbia, Croatia, Bosnia and Herzegovina* (London: University of Luton Press, 1999); Dubravka Žarkov, *The Body of War: Media, Ethnicity and Gender in the Break-Up of Yugoslavia* (Durham, NC: Duke University Press, 2007).
3 See, e.g., Bette Denich, "Nationalist Ideologies and the Symbolic Revival of Genocide," *American Ethnologist*, 21, 2 (May 1994): 372; Ana Dević, "Waking the Dead (Who May Never Die): Ethnonationalist Politics of Dead Bodies and Graves in the War- and Post-War Serbia," 2009, 7–8, http://chdr-ns.com/pdf/documents/opatija2009_ana_devic.pdf, accessed February 15, 2019.
4 St. Mark's Church was built during the interwar period but on the site of an earlier church built in 1835–6 where several members of the Serbian royal family were buried. In 1968, it was the largest church in Serbia.
5 "Informacija u vezi prenosa kostiju cara Dušana 16. V. 1968" and "Zapisnik sa sednice Komisije Republičkog izvršnog veća za verska pitanja održane 29. V. 1968," in Radmila Radić and Momčilo Mitrović, eds., *Zapisnici sa sednica Komicije za*

verska pitanja NR/SR Srbije 1945–1978. godine (Beograd: Institut za noviju istoriju Srbije, 2012), 520–2, 855–6.
6 Vjekoslav Perica, *Balkan Idols: Religion and Nationalism in Yugoslav States* (Oxford: Oxford University Press, 2002), 44–5.
7 "Memorandum_SANU"—memorandum_sanu.pdf, Fall 1986. Accessed July 12, 2016, https://pescanik.net/wp-content/PDF/memorandum_sanu.pdf. For additional analysis of the memorandum see Nick Miller, *The Nonconformists: Culture, Politics, and Nationalism in a Serbian Intellectual Circle, 1944–1991* (Budapest: CEU Press, 2007), 267–77.
8 David A. Norris, "Jovan Radulović's *Golubnjača* (Dove Hole): Analysis and Context of the Stories and Play Which Was Banned in Yugoslavia (1980–1984)," *Slavonic and East European Review*, 90, 2 (2012): 202.
9 Denich, 367; Dević, 10.
10 Denich, 382.
11 Rada Radić, "Crkva i 'Srpsko Pitanje,'" in Nebojša Popov, ed., *Srpska Strana Rata: Trauma i katarza u istorijskom pamčenju* (Beograd: Republika, 1996), 287; Michael Sells, "Crosses of Blood: Sacred Spaces, Religion, and Violence in Bosnia-Hercegovina," *Sociology of Religion*, 64, 3 (Autumn 2003): 313.
12 Sells, 313.
13 Vjeran Pavlaković, Dario Brentin, and Davor Pauković, "The Controversial Commemoration: Transnational Approaches to Remembering Bleiburg," *Croatian Political Science Review*, 55, 2 (2018): 20; See also Michaela Schauble, "How History Takes Place: Sacralized Landscapes in the Croatian-Bosnian Border Region," *History and Memory*, 23, 1 (Spring/Summer 2011): 23–61.
14 Schauble, 36.
15 Craig Evan Pollack, "Intentions of Burial: Mourning, Politics, and Memorials Following the Massacre at Srebrenica," *Death Studies*, 27, 2 (February 1, 2003): 130–3.
16 Schauble, 29; see also Jelena Djureinović, *The Politics of Memory of the Second World War in Contemporary Serbia* (London: Routledge, 2020).
17 See Djureinović, 108–29. Although Djureinović's book and sources mainly focus on the post-Milošević era, it includes references to the 1990s and much of the argument applies also to commemorations that took place during the last years of Yugoslavia and the wars of Yugoslav dissolution.
18 The black double-headed eagle on a red background has served as the Albanian national flag from its independence in 1912 to the present. That flag is essentially the same as one flown by the Albanian Kastrioti family when it led a revolt against the Ottoman Empire in the fifteenth century leading to a brief period of Albanian independence from 1443 to 1479. Although it is often presumed that the double-headed eagle seen on many flags in the region originated with the

Byzantine Empire, its origins go as far back as the Sumerians and Hittites around 1650 BCE.

19 Gavin Stamp, *The Memorial to the Missing of the Somme* (London: Profile Books, 2006), 72–8; Xavier Bougarel, "Death and the Nationalist: Martyrdom, War Memory and Veteran Identity Among Bosnian Muslims," in Elisa Helms, Xavier Bougarel, and Gerhard Duizings, eds, *The New Bosnian Mosaic: Identities, Memories and Moral Claims in a Post-War Society* (Burlington, VT: Ashgate, 2007), 167–91.

20 Non-Muslim soldiers were offered a rectangular headstone with just the fleur-de-lis.

21 Abdul Haleem, "Al-Baqarah, 2–154." Accessed November 7, 2021, https://quran.com/2:154?font=v1&translations=85%2C101.

22 Tvrtko himself was raised Catholic but was of partial Serbian descent and married a Bulgarian Orthodox princess. He was known for maintaining good relations with all the religious communities in his realm, though, of course, they did not at that time include Muslims.

23 Marcus Tanner, *Croatia: A Nation Forged in War* (New Haven, CT: Yale University Press, 1997), 246.

24 Lela Baća, Interview with the author, Zaprešić, July 22, 2012.

25 In 1946 the Communist party in Kosovo had only 5,505 members in total, of which approximately one-third were Albanian, while the rest were Serbian and Montenegrin. Those figures may have shifted in the 1970s when Serbian domination of society diminished considerably, but those communists are somewhat less likely to be deceased. Aleksandar Petrović and Djordje Stefanović, "Kosovo 1944–1981: The Rise and Fall of a Communist 'Nested Homeland,'" *Europe-Asia Studies*, 62, 7 (September 2010): 1073–1106.

26 Ivan Markesić, "Gospićka groblja," *Gospić: grad, ljudi, identitet*, 1 (2013): 551, 555.

27 Jeremy F. Walton, "The Dead Wait: Material Afterlives in Sepulchral Spaces," *Journal of Material Culture*, 7, 4 (2022): 382.

28 See, e.g., Jess Beck and Katherine M. Kinkopf, "Bioarcheological Approaches to Looting: A Case Study from Sudan," *Journal of Archeological Science: Reports*, 10 (2016): 263–71.

29 Neville M. Goodman, MD, "The Supply of Bodies for Dissection: A Historical Review," *British Medical Journal*, 2, 4381 (December 23, 1944): 807.

30 See M. J. Durey, "Bodysnatchers and Benthamites: The Implications of the Dead Body Bill for the London Schools of Anatomy, 1820–42," *The London School*, 2, 2 (1976): 200–25.

31 A key development occurred in the United States in 1990 with the passage of the Native American Graves Protection and Repatriation Act (NAGPRA), which requires all agencies and institutions that receive federal funding to establish procedures for the discovery and excavation of cultural sites on federal or tribal

lands and makes it a criminal offense to traffic in Native American human remains without right of possession or any cultural items obtained in violation of the act.

32 This categorization is based on my own personal examination of multiple desecrated graves and cemeteries in the former Yugoslavia and photographs of desecrated graves and cemeteries elsewhere.

33 Nolan Menachemsen, *A Practical Guide to Jewish Cemeteries* (Bergenfield, NJ: Avotaynu, 2007), 231–3.

34 "Prague Revamp Reveals Jewish Gravestones Used to Pave Streets," *The Guardian*, May 5, 2020. Accessed May 13, 2020, https://www.theguardian.com/world/2020/may/05/prague-revamp-reveals-jewish-gravestones-used-to-pave-streets.

35 See, e.g., Penny Roberts, "Contesting Sacred Space: Burial Disputes in Sixteenth Century France," in Bruce Gordon and Peter Marshall, eds., *The Place of the Dead: Death and Remembrance in Late Medieval and Early Modern Europe* (Cambridge: Cambridge University Press, 2000), 131–48; Monica Black, *Death in Berlin: From Weimar to Divided Germany* (Cambridge: Cambridge University Press, 2010); Andrew Herscher, *Violence Taking Place* (Stanford, CA: Stanford University Press, 2010); Robert Bevan: *The Destruction of Memory: Architecture at War*, 2nd ed. (London: Reaktion Books, 2016); Dacia Viejo Rose, "Conflict and the Deliberate Destruction of Cultural Heritage," in Helmut K. Anheier and Yudhishthir Raj Isar, eds., *Cultures and Globalization: Conflicts and Tensions* (London: Sage, 2007), 102–21.

36 Fred Vincent, "From Desecration to Reconciliation: Considering Attacks on the Sacred During the Troubles and Proposing a Framework Response," *Shared Space*, 8 (2009): 67–84; Fred Vincent, *Everybody Got a Hug That Morning … from Desecration to Reconciliation* (Belfast: Institute for Conflict Research, 2009).

37 Police reports would be another valuable source but have not been available for most of this region in the period under consideration.

38 Vincent, *Everybody Got a Hug That Morning*, 36.

39 Vincent, *Everybody Got a Hug That Morning*, 41.

40 Vincent, "From desecration to reconciliation," 67.

41 Karen J. Detling, "Eternal Silence: The Destruction of Cultural Property in Yugoslavia," *Maryland Journal of International Law*, 17, 1 (1993): 53–8.

42 "Convention for the Protection of Cultural Property in the Event of Armed Conflict with Regulations for the Execution of the Convention 1954," Article 4, The Hague, May 14, 1954. Accessed November 27, 2021, http://portal.unesco.org/en/ev.php-URL_ID=13637&URL_DO=DO_TOPIC&URL_SECTION=201.html.

43 Ibid.

44 Herscher, 82–97.

45 Bevan, 18.

46 Vincent, *Everybody Got a Hug*, 70–92.

47 Achille Mbembe, "Necropolitics," in S. Morton and S. Bygrave, eds., *Foucault in an Age of Terror: Essays on Biopolitics and the Defence of Society* (New York: Palgrave MacMillan, 2008), 176.
48 See Anya Bernstein, "The Post-Soviet Treasure Hunt: Time, Space and Necropolitics in Siberian Buddhism," *Comparative Studies in Society and History*, 53, 3 (July 2011): 623–53; Emily Jane O'Dell, "Waging War on the Dead: The Necropolitics of Sufi Shrine Destruction in Mali," *Archaeologies: Journal of the World Archeological Congress*, 9, 3 (December 2013): 506–24; Banu Barga, "Another Necropolitics," *Theory and Event*, 19, 1 (Supplement) (January 2016): 1–18.
49 O'Dell, 508
50 O'Dell, 509.
51 Bevan, 61.
52 Memos to KVP, February 28 to June 11, 1959, HDZ, 310/opći spisi kutija 146.
53 Memo to KVP from Archbishop of Zagreb, May 12, 1950, HDZ, 310/opći spisi kutija 136.
54 Memos regarding desecration of Jewish cemetery, March 7–11, 1952, HDZ, 310/opći spisi kutija 139. According to the president of the Jewish Religious Community, in 1951, the entire population of the Jewish community in postwar Yugoslavia was 6,105. Of that number, 2,564 resided in Serbia and its autonomous regions, 2,078 in Croatia, 1,261 in Bosnia & Hercegovina, 100 in Slovenia, 99 in Macedonia, and 3 in Montenegro. Albert Vajs, Savez Jevrejski Veroispovednih Opština FNRJ, "Predmet: Brojno stanje Jevreje u FNRJ," November 21, 1951, HDA, 310/opći spisi kutija 138.
55 Ulema Medžliš u Sarajevu, KVP pri Pretsjedništvu Vlade NR BiH, January 8, 1952, Arhiv BiH, 2/52–54/52.
56 Max Bergholz, "Medju rodoljubima, kupusom, svinjama i varvarima: Spomenici i grobovi NOR 1947–1965 godine," *Godišnjak za društvenu istoriju*, 1–3 (2007): 72–7; Dušan Misirača, SUBNORa BiH Predsjedništvo, Predsjedništvu UBNORa Bosanska Dubica, September 15, 1964, Arhiv BiH SUBNOR 221.
57 While Jeftić's book includes multiple crimes, including murder, assaults, rape, theft, damage to property, and threats of violence, he also specifically includes cases of cemetery and grave desecrations going back as far as 1945 but focusing especially on a two-year period from 1988 to 1990. Jeftić includes many descriptions of violence in his book from other sources, including newspapers, political parties, and individuals, that lack detail or specific information. I have largely excluded those from my analysis, addressing only those for which he is able to provide names, villages, and dates. While these cases seem to represent actual incidents of desecration, Jeftić's interpretation of them is much less reliable. Atanasije Jeftić, "Stradanje u prvoj posle ratnoj deceniji (1945–1955)," *Stradanja Srba na Kosovu i Metohiji od 1941. do 1990. Godine*, in Projekat Rastko Gračanica-Peć. Accessed

May 16, 2019, http://www.rastko.rs/kosovo/istorija/stradanje_srba/atanasije_1deo.html#_Toc485531489.
58 Herscher, 57.
59 Jeftić, "Četvrt veka golgote Kosovskih Srba (1956–1981)."
60 Sveti Arhijerejski Sabor SPC, "Predsedniku SFRJ Josipu Brozu Titu," May 19, 1969, in Radić and Mitrović, eds., 876–7.
61 Documents from Sisak about cemetery desecration, December 27, 1967–March 20, 1968, HDA, 310/183.
62 Jeftić, "Kratka hronika stradanja Srba na Kosovu i Metohiju (1941–1988)."
63 According to a later interview with the infants' parents, the children were not actually buried in the cemetery but on their own property because as unbaptized babies, they could not be buried on sanctified ground. Ivan Maksimović, "Република Српска: ŠIPTARSKI ZLOČIN: Raskopali grob srpskih beba i raskomadali njihova tela," June 27, 2014. Accessed May 19, 2020, Република Српска: ŠIPTARSKI ZLOČIN: Raskopali grob srpskih beba i raskomadali njihova tela (rep-srpska.blogspot.com).
64 Jeftić, "Krstovdan Srba na Kosovo"; Maksimović.
65 Jeftić, "1988" Entry for October 4, 1988.
66 Maksimović.
67 Herscher, 65
68 Bergholz, 311–21.
69 For information on the political goals and significance of postmortem mutilations, see Thomas Gregory, "Dismembering the Dead: Violence, Vulnerability and the Body in War," *European Journal of International Relations*, 22, 4 (2014): 944–65. Again, however, it is somewhat difficult to imagine the mutilations in this case as politically premeditated.
70 Jeftić, "1988" Entry for September 20, 1988.
71 Danko Popović, cited in Herscher, 69.
72 Jeftić, "Opširnija hronika stradanja Srba za poslednje dve i po godine (Januar 1988. - Vidovdan 1990)."
73 Vesna Jureško Herman, "Destruction of Art and Architecture in Croatia," *Journal of Croatian Studies*, 32/33 (1991/1992): 232–3.
74 Detling, 67, fn. 166. The tomb belonged to the family of Jakov Grof Eltz, a prewar politician who had emigrated to West Germany after the Communist regime expropriated his lands but returned to take up politics again under Franjo Tudjman in 1991.
75 For more information on this cemetery, see Markesić, "Gospićka groblja."
76 See Vjeran Pavlaković, "Blowing Up Brotherhood and Unity: The Fate of World War Two Cultural Heritage in Lika," in Petra Jurlina, ed., *The Politics of Heritage and Memory* (Zagreb: University of Zagreb Press, 2014), 400; Državni Zavod za

Statistitku—Republika Hrvatska, Statistitka prema narodnosti po gradovima/ općinama, Popis 2011, Ličko-senjska županja, Grad Gospić.

77 See Katherine Verdery, *The Political Lives of Dead Bodies: Reburial and Postsocialist Change* (New York: Columbia University Press, 1999), 109; Robert Donia, *Sarajevo: A Biography* (Ann Arbor: University of Michigan Press, 2006), 338–9.

78 Vuk Drašković, cited by Verdery, 98; Matije Bečković, cited by Radić, "Crvka i 'Srpsko Pitanje," 276.

79 Andras Riedelmayer, "From the Ashes: The Past and Future of Bosnia's Cultural Heritage," in Maya Shatzmiller, ed. *Islam and Bosnia: Conflict Resolution and Foreign Policy in MultiEthnic States* (Montreal: McGillQueens University Press, 2002), 2–3.

80 Muharem Omerdić, *Prilozi izučavanjanu genocida nad bošnjacima (1992–1995)* (Sarajevo: Rijašet islamske zajednice u Bosni i Hercegovini, 1999), 24. Omerdić's statistics regarding the number of mosques destroyed are roughly consistent with Riedelmayer's.

81 Dr. Marian Wenzel, "Bullets at Butterflies—Bosnia's Heritage Attacked," in *War Damage to the Cultural Heritage in Croatia and Bosnia-Herzegovina*, Eighth Information Report, Doc. 7341, June 28, 1995, presented by the Committee on Culture and Education. Accessed May 26, 2020, http://assembly.coe.int/nw/xml/XRef/X2H-Xref-ViewHTML.asp?FileID=6989&lang=EN.

82 European Community Monitoring Mission, "Cultural Heritage Report," April 2, 1995, in *War Damage to the Cultural Heritage in Croatia and Bosnia-Herzegovina*.

83 Father Drago, Interview with author, Guča Gora Monastery, November 19, 2013; Dr. Eli Tauber, Interview with author, Sarajevo, November 11, 2013.

84 Verdery, 109–10; Jasminka Udovicki and Ejub Štitkovac, "Bosnia-Hercegovina: The Second War," in Jasminka Udovicki and James Ridgeway, eds., *Burn This House: The Making and Unmaking of Yugoslavia* (Durham, NC: Duke University Press, 2000), 200.

85 Suzana Radjen-Todorić, "Pravoslavno groblje na meti vandala," *Politika*, February 25, 2008. Accessed June 29, 2020, Pravoslavna groblja na meti vandala (politika.rs); D. Stanišić, "Na udaru vandala i crkve i sveštenice," *Politika*, June 2, 2011. Accessed June 29, 2020, На удару вандала и цркве и свештеници (politika.rs).

86 Andrew Herscher and Andras Riedelmayer, "Monument and Crime: The Destruction of Historic Architecture in Kosovo," *Grey Room*, 1 (Autumn 2000): 112.

87 Imam Ahmed Hoxha, Interview with the author, Office of the Islamic Union, Gjakovo, May, 20, 2019.

88 "Maintenance of Orthodox Graveyards in Kosovo," Organization for Security and Cooperation in Europe, Mission in Kosovo, September 2011. Accessed August 2, 2020, OSCE— https://www.ecoi.net/en/document/1305060.html. "Photo Catalogue: Orthodox Graveyards in Kosovo," Organization for Security and

Cooperation in Europe, Mission in Kosovo, September 2011. Accessed June 15, 2020, https://www.osce.org/kosovo/84413.
89 "Maintenance of Orthodox Graveyards in Kosovo."
90 Slobodan Čurčić, "The Destruction of Serbian Cultural Patrimony in Kosovo: A Worldwide Precedent?" Accessed on DocPlayer, May 28, 2020, http://docplayer.net/45699705-Destruction-of-serbian-cultural-patrimony-in-kosovo-a-world-wide-precedent.html.
91 "Maintenance of Orthodox Graveyards in Kosovo."
92 "Photo Catalogue: Orthodox Graveyards in Kosovo."
93 Matthew McAllister, *Beyond the Mountains of the Damned: The War Inside Kosovo*, Kindle ed. (New York: New York University Press, 2003), 132–5.
94 Altogether Bogdanović created eleven in Serbia, four in Croatia, three in Bosnia & Hercegovina, two in Macedonia, and one each in Montenegro and Kosova. Andrew Lawler, *The Partisan's Cemetery in Mostar, Bosnia & Herzegovina: Implications of the Deterioration of a Monument and Site*, MA thesis, Faculty of Engineering, Catholic University Leuven, Belgium (September 2013), 243–9.
95 Lawler, 222.
96 Kristina Ilić and Nevena Škrbić Alempijević, "Cultures of Memory, Landscapes of Forgetting: The Case Study of the Partisan Memorial Cemetery in Mostar," *Studia ethnologica Croatica*, 29 (2017): 91.

Conclusion: Death after Communism

1 It is generally very difficult to find specific information regarding Roma burial rituals, grave markers, and cemeteries. Certainly, Roma were never included in discussions of the CRQ or other archival documents. Anecdotally, when in the course of my research I asked ordinary people (and even some experts), "Where are the Roma buried?" a disturbingly common response was an astonished look, followed by "Nowhere!!" Published secondary sources are more helpful as the Serbian Academy of Sciences initiated the study of Roma history and culture already in the 1970s as part of the regime's broader commitment to pluralism and the equality of all national and ethnic communities. Scholars at the Niš Romological School have also begun to publish valuable work on Roma burial customs and Roma cemeteries.
2 Dragoljub B. Djordjević, "Burying of Roma: A Test of Ethnic and Religious Tolerance," in Dragoljub B. Djordjević, Dragan Todorović, and Lela Milošević, *Romas and Others—Others and Romas: Social Distance* (Sofia: "Ivan Hadjiyski" Institute for Social Values and Studies, 2004), 41.

3 Interestingly, however, that cemetery while mostly Muslim also included two Catholic grave markers, one the wife of a Muslim Roma and the other a young man who died in the war bearing a Croatian šahovnica. His connection to others in the cemetery was unclear.
4 Djordević, 37–9.
5 Aurelien Breeden, "A Furor in France over the Final Resting Place for a Roma Child," *New York Times*, January 5, 2015. Accessed July 18, 2018, https://www.nytimes.com/2015/01/06/world/europe/a-french-mayor-is-accused-of-refusing-cemetery-plot-to-a-roma-child.html?action=click&module=RelatedCoverage&pgtype=Article&region=Footer.
6 "Lukovac Case (Skrnavljene Mezarje Lukavac)," https://www.youtube.com/watch?v=ms6twsJ7xx0&feature=share. Accessed August 15, 2018.
7 Apparently, a few of those in Serbia were built before the fall of communism by guest workers bringing home cash from Austria and Germany. Aleksandar Vasović, "Serbia's Bungalow Cemeteries," *Reuters, The Wider Image*, November 11, 2016. Accessed August 2, 2018, https://widerimage.reuters.com/story/serbias-bungalow-cemeteries.

Bibliography

Archival and Primary Sources

Archives, Fonds, and Abbreviations

Agjencia Shtetërore e Arkivave të Kosovës—Bashkesia e Fes Islame IVZ ZURA e Vakufit Prishtinë; Fletorja zyrtare KAKM (ASHAK).
Archives of Parish Church of St. Ilija, Zenica, Bosnia & Hercegovina.
Arhiv Bosne i Hercegovine (BiH)—Komisija za verska pitanja (KVP), Savez Udruženje Boraca Narodnooslobodilačkog Rata (SUBNOR)
Arhiv Jugoslavije—(AJ) Komisija za verska pitanja (KVP). Savez Udruženje Boraca Narodnooslobodilačkog Rata (SUBNOR)
Arhiv Srbije—Komisija za verska pitanja (KVP).
Hrvatski Državni Arhiv—(HDA) Komisija za vjerska pitanja (KVP). Savez Udruženje Boraca Narodnooslobodilačkog Rata (SUBNOR)
Hrvatski Institut za Povijest.
Istorijski Arhiv Beograd—Komunalno preduzeće za pogrebne usluge, Narodni Odbor grada Beograda.
Jugoslovensko Komunalno Poduzeće Pokupno Društvo Sarajevo.
Opće Skupno Groblje Grada Zagreba na Mirogoju.

Newspapers

Beogradske novine.
Narodne Novine: Službeni list Narodne Republike Hrvatske (NRH).
Službeni glasnik Beograda.
Službeni glasnik Narodne Republike Srbije (NRS).
Službeni glasnik Narodnog odbora grada Zagreba.
Službeni glasnik Sociajalističke Republike Srbije (SRS).
Službeni list Federativne Narodne Republike Jugoslavije (FNRJ).
Službeni list grada Beograda.
Službeni list Narodne Republike Bosne i Hercegovine (NRBiH).

Published Primary Sources

Bošnjaković, Fra Josip Zvonimir. *Svjedok Jednog Vremena: Moja Usputna Sjećanja.* Zagreb, 2005.

Hadžišehović, Munevera, Thomas (translator) Butler, and Sab (translator) Risaluddin. *A Muslim Woman in Tito's Yugoslavia.* College Station: Texas A&M University Press, 2003.

Izetbegović, Alija. *Izetbegović: Odabrani Govori, Pisma, Izjave, Intervjui.* Zagreb: Prvo muslimansko dioničko društvo, 1995.

Odbor za pogrebne delatnosti. *Kodeks Pogrebnih Usluga.* Beograd: Privredna komora Jugoslavije, Savet za zanatstvo, komunalnu i stambenu privredu, 1974.

Report of the International Commission to Inquire into the Causes and Conduct of the Balkan Wars. Washington, DC: Carnegie Endowment for International Peace, 1914.

Radić, Radmila, and Momčilo Mitrović, eds. *Zapisnici sa Sednica Komisije za Verska Pitanja NR/SR Srbije 1945–1978. Godine.* Beograd: Institut za noviju istoriju Srbije, 2012.

Online Primary Sources

"Census of Population, Households and Dwellings in Republika Srpska," 2013, https://www.rzs.rs.ba/static/uploads/bilteni/popis/rezultati_popisa/Results_of_the_Census_2013.pdf.

"Convention for the Protection of Cultural Property in the Event of Armed Conflict with Regulations for the Execution of the Convention," Article 4, The Hague, May 14, 1954, unesco.org.

"Maintenance of Orthodox Graveyards in Kosovo," Organization for Security and Cooperation in Europe, Mission in Kosovo, September 2011, https://www.ecoi.net/en/document/1305060.html Accessed August 2, 2020.

"Memorandum SANU," https://pescanik.net/wp-content/PDF/memorandum_sanu.pdf. Accessed June 30, 2016.

"Photo Catalogue: Orthodox Graveyards in Kosovo," Organization for Security and Cooperation in Europe, Mission in Kosovo, September 2011, https://www.osce.org/kosovo/84413.Population of Croatia, 1931–2001, http://www.vojska.net/eng/armed-forces/croatia/about/population/. Accessed April 10, 2020.

Stanovništvo po narodnosti po popisu od 15. marta 1948 godine, Beograd, 1954, http://pod2.stat.gov.rs/ObjavljenePublikacije/G1948/Pdf/G19484001.pdf.

"Stanovništvo prema etničko/nacionalnoj pripadnosti," *Popis*, 2013, https://popis.gov.ba/popis2013/knjige.php?id=2.

Udin, Zack, Keely Bakken, Niala Mohammada, Kurt Werthmuller, Madeline Vellturo, and John Lechner. "Fact Sheet: Destruction of Cemeteries," Factsheet: Destruction of Cemeteries, September 2021, uscirf.gov.

War Damage to the Cultural Heritage in Croatia and Bosnia-Herzegovina, Eighth Information Report, Doc. 7341, June 28, 1995, presented by the Committee on Culture and Education. http://assembly.coe.int/nw/xml/XRef/X2H-Xref-ViewHTML.asp?FileID=6989&lang=EN. Accessed May 26, 2020.

Značajniji intervuji i govori dr. Franje Tudjmana, http://www.tudjman.hr/govori/. Accessed March 25, 2020.

Interviews

Andjić, Friar Zdravka. St. Ilija District. Zenica, November 5, 2013.
Baća, Lela. Zaprešić, July 22, 2012.
Bondžić, Dragomir. Institute of Contemporary History, Belgrade, September 14, 2013.
Bušatlić, Prof. Dr. Ismet. Faculty of Islamic Studies, Sarajevo, November 11, 2013.
Čupina, Mirad. Mostar, July 3, 2022.
Hoxha, Imam Ahmed. Office of the Islamic Union, Hadam Mosque, Gjakova, May 20, 2019.
Ikonov, Svetozar. Tourist Guide, Titel, September 14, 2013.
Jacanović, Miodrag. Curator of the National Museum Požarevac, September 24, 2013.
Janjušić, Miro. Representative of Prosveta. Zenica, November 6, 2013.
Jašarević, Adnadin, Director of the Museum of Zenica. Zenica, November 6, 2013.
Omerdjić, Efendia Muharem. Rijaset, Sarajevo, November 20, 2013.
Pranjec, Father Drago. Guča Gora Monastery, November 19, 2013.
Rajković, Sladjana. Museum Advisor. National Museum of Leskovac, September 25, 2013.
Šećibović, Prof. Dr. Sc. Refik. The Higher School for Tourism and Management, Konjić, November 12, 2013.
Šehović, Professor Šefedin. University of Novi Pazar, Novi Pazar, September 20, 2013.
Shkodra, Ramadan. Professor at the Faculty of Islamic Studies, Islamic Union of Kosova. Prishtinë, May 14, 2019.
Spahić Atif. Assistant Director, "Gradsko Groblje" Funeral Enterprise. Zenica, November, 6, 2013.
Tauber, Dr Eli. Sarajevo, November 11, 2013.
Veljača, Nelo. Secretary, St. Anto Funeral Society. Zenica, November 5, 2013.

Secondary Sources

Akmadža, Miroslav. *Katolička Crkva u Komunističkoj Hrvatskoj 1945–1980.* Zagreb: Hrvatski Institute za povijest, 2013.
Alexander, Stella. *Church and State in Yugoslavia Since 1945.* Cambridge: Cambridge University Press, 1979.

Amanat, Mehrdad. "Set in Stone: Homeless Corpses and Desecrated Graves in Modern Iran." *International Journal of Middle East Studies*, 44, no. 2 (May 2012): 257–83.

Amanik, Allan. "'A Beautiful Garden Consecrated to the Lord': Marriage, Death, and Local Constructions of Citizenship in New York's Nineteenth-Century Jewish Rural Cemeteries." In *Till Death Do Us Part*, Allan Amanik and Kami Fletcher, eds., 15–33. Jackson: University Press of Mississippi, 2020.

Amanik, Allan, and Kami Fletcher. *Till Death Do Us Part: American Ethnic Cemeteries as Borders Uncrossed*. Jackson: University Press of Mississippi, 2020.

Anastasijević, Dejan, with Anthony Borden, ed. *Out of Time: Drašković, Djindjić and Serbian Opposition Against Milošević*. London: Institute for War and Peace Reporting and Beta News Agency, 2000.

Anderson, Benedict. *Imagined Communities*. 2nd ed. London: Verso, 1983.

Ansari, Humayan. "'Burying the Dead': Making Muslim Space in Britain." *Historical Research*, 80, no. 210 (November 2007): 545–66.

Arendt, Hannah. *The Origins of Totalitarianism*. 2nd enlarged ed. Cleveland, OH: Meridian, 1951.

Arendt, Hannah. *The Human Condition*. 2nd ed. Chicago: University of Chicago Press, 1958.

Aries, Philippe. *The Hour of Our Death*. New York: Vintage Books, 1982.

Arnold, Thomas "Symbolism and Islam." *Burlington Magazine for Connoisseurs*, 53, no. 307 (1928): 154–6.

Asad, Talal. *Formations of the Secular: Christianity, Islam, Modernity*. Stanford, CA: Stanford University Press, 2003.

Babuna, Aydin. "The Albanians of Kosovo and Macedonia: Ethnic Identity Superseding Religion." *Nationalities Papers*, 28, no. 1 (2000): 67–92.

Balkan, Osman. "Not in My Graveyard: Citizenship, Memory and Identity in the Wake of the Boston Marathon Bombing." In *The Democratic Arts of Mourning: Political Theory and Loss*, Alexander Keller Hirsch and David W. McIvor, eds., 83–101. Lanham, MD: Lexington Books, 2019.

Ballinger, Pamela. *History in Exile: Memory and Identity at the Borders of the Balkans*. Princeton, NJ: Princeton University Press, 2002.

Banac, Ivo. *The National Question in Yugoslavia: Origins, History, Politics*. Ithaca, NY: Cornell University Press, 1984.

Bandić, Dušan. "Koncept Posrmtnog Umiranja u Religiji Srba." *Etnološki Pregled*, 19 (1983): 39–47.

Banjeglav, Tamara. "Conflicting Memories, Competing Narratives, and Contested Histories in Croatia's Post-War Commemorative Practices." *Politička Misao*, 49, no. 5 (2012): 7–31.

Barga, Banu. "Another Necropolitics." *Theory and Event*, 19, no. 1, Supplement (January 2016): 1–18.

Barrow, Julia. "Urban Cemetery Location in the High Middle Ages." In *Death in Towns: Urban Responses to Dying and the Dead, 100–1600*, Steve Bassett, ed., 78–100. Leicester: Leicester University Press, 1992.

Basch, Gabor. "Settlers, Natives, and Refugees: Classificatory Systems and the Construction of Autochthony in Vojvodina." In *Us and Them: Symbolic Divisions in Western Balkan Societies*, Ivana Spasić and Predrag Cvetičanin, eds. Niš: Center for Empirical Cultural Studies of Southeast Europe, 2013.

Basić, Ksenija. "Decentralization of the Zagreb Urban Region." *Dela*, 21 (2004): 519–30.

Basu, Ranu. "Multiethnic Neighbourhoods as Sites of Social Capital Formation: Examining Social to Political 'Integration' in Schools." *Education, Citizenship and Social Justice*, 1, no. 1 (March 1, 2006): 59–82. https://doi.org/10.1177/1746197906060713.

Bax, Mart. "Mass Graves, Stagnating Identification, and Violence: A Case Study in the Local Sources of 'The War' in Bosnia Hercegovina." *Anthropological Quarterly*, 70, no. 1 (January 1997): 11–19.

Beck, Jess, and Katherine M. Kinkopf, "Bioarcheological Approaches to Looting: A Case Study from Sudan," *Journal of Archeological Science: Reports*, 10 (2016): 263–71.

Ben-Amos, Avner. *Funerals, Politics, and Memory in Modern France, 1789–1996*. Oxford: Oxford University Press, 2000.

Bergholz, Max. "Medju rodoljubima, kupusom, svinjama i varvarima: Spomenici i grobovi NOR 1947-1965. Godine." *Godišnjak za društvenu istoriju*, XIV, 1-3, (2007): 61-82.

Bergholz, Max. *Violence as a Generative Force: Identity, Nationalism, and Memory in a Balkan Community*. Ithaca, NY: Cornell University Press, 2016.

Bergholz, Max. "When All Could No Longer Be Equal in Death: A Local Community's Struggle to Remember Its Fallen Soldiers in the Shadow of Serbia's Civil War, 1955–1956." *The Carl Beck Papers in Russian and East European Studies*, no. 2008, November 2010.

Bergne, Paul. "Some Thoughts on Grave Symbolism in Tashkent Cemeteries." *Durham Middle East Papers*, 76 (April 2004): 1–24.

Bernstein, Anya. "The Post-Soviet Treasure Hunt: Time, Space and Necropolitics in Siberian Buddhism." *Comparative Studies in Society and History*, 53, no. 3 (July 2011): 623–53.

Bevan, Robert. *The Destruction of Memory: Architecture at War*. London: Reaktion Books, 2006.

Bjelajac, Mirko, and Ozren Zunec. "The War in Croatia, 1991–1995." In *Confronting the Yugoslav Controversies: A Scholars' Initiative*, Charles Ingrao and Thomas A. Emmert, eds., 233–72. West Lafayette, IN: Purdue University Press, 2013.

Black, Monica. *Death in Berlin: From Weimar to Divided Germany*. Cambridge: Cambridge University Press, 2010.

Blanchard, Pierre. "Communities and Cultural Heritage in Times of Conflict: Case Studies of Contemporary and Historic Destruction to Sacred Sites and Places of Worship." The Centre for Academic Shi'a Studies, December 23, 2014.

Boase, T. S. R. *Death in the Middle Ages: Mortality, Judgment and Remembrance*. New York: McGraw Hill, 1972.

Bokovoy, Melissa. "Gendering Grief: Lamenting and Photographing the Dead in Serbia, 1914–1941." *Aspasia*, 5 (June 2011): 46–69.

Bokovoy, Melissa. "Scattered Graves, Ordered Cemeteries: Commemorating Serbia's Wars of National Liberation, 1912–1918." In *Staging the Past: The Politics of Commemoration in Habsburg Central Europe: 1848 to the Present*, Maria Bucur and Nancy Wingfield, eds., 236–54. Ashland, OH: Purdue University Press, 2001.

Bosić, Maja. "Arhaični Elementi u Pogrebnim Običajima u Vojvodini." *Etnološke Sveske*, VI (1985): 89–94.

Botev, Nikolai. "Where East Meets West: Ethnic Intermarriage in the Former Yugoslavia, 1962 to 1989." *American Sociological Association*, 59, no. 3 (June 1994): 461–80.

Bougarel, Xavier. "Bosnian Islam Since 1990: Cultural Identity or Political Ideology," Convention annuelle de l'Association for the Study of Nationalities (ASN), April 1999, New York. <halshs-00220516>.

Bougarel, Xavier. "Bosnian Muslims and the Yugoslav Idea." In *Yugoslavism: Histories of a Failed Idea, 1918–1992*, Dejan Djokić, ed., 100–15. Madison: University of Wisconsin Press, 2003.

Bougarel, Xavier. "Death and the Nationalist: Martyrdom, War Memory and Veteran Identity among Bosnian Muslims." In *The New Bosnian Mosaic: Identities, Memories and Moral Claims in a Post-War Society*, Elissa Helms, Xavier Bougarel, and Ger Duizings, eds., 167–91. Burlington, VT: Ashgate, 2007.

Bringa, Tone. *Being Muslim the Bosnian Way*. Princeton, NJ: Princeton University Press, 1995.

Brodić, Florijan, Srećko Katavić, Mato Matijić, and Karlo Škec. *Hrvatsko Pogrebno Društvo u Sarajevo, 1921–1991*. Sarajevo: Hrvatkso Pogrebno Društvo, 1991.

Brubaker, Rogers. "Religion and Nationalism: Four Approaches." *Nations and Nationalism*, 18, no. 1 (2012): 2–20.

Buchenau, Klaus. "What Went Wrong? Church-State Relations in Socialist Yugoslavia." *Nationalities Papers*, 33, no. 4 (December 2005): 547–67.

Buckley, Chris, and Austin Ramzy. "China Is Erasing Mosques and Precious Shrines in Xinjiang." *New York Times*, September 25, 2020. https://www.nytimes.com/interactive/2020/09/25/world/asia/xinjiang-china-religious-site.html.

Buconjić, Nikola. *Život i obijčaji Hrvata katoličke vjere u Bosni i Hercegovini*. Sarajevo: Danijela A. Kajona, 1908.

Bucur-Deckard, Maria. *Heroes and Victims: Remembering War in Twentieth Century Romania*. Bloomington: Indiana University Press, 2009.

Bugarski, Ranko. "Jezička Politika i Jezička Stvarnost u Srbiji Posle 1991. Godine." In *Jezik Izmedju Lingvistike i Politike*, Vesna Požgaj Hadži, ed., 91–111. Beograd: Biblioteka XX Vek, 2013.

Bugarski, Ranko. "Language and Boundaries in the Yugoslav Context." In *Language, Discourse and Borders in the Yugoslav Successor States*, Brigitta Busch and Helen Kelly-Holmes, eds., 21–37. Clevedon: Multilingual Matters, 2004.

Bunčić, Daniel. "Bigrafism: Serbo-Croatian/Serbian: Cyrillic and Latin." In *Biscriptality: A Sociolinguistic Typology*, Daniel Bunčić, Sandra L. Lippert, and Achim Rabus, eds. Heidelberg: Universitätsverlag Winter, 2016.

Butler, Judith. *Precarious Life: The Powers of Mourning and Justice*. London: Verso, 2004.

Buturović, Amila. *Carved in Stone, Etched in Memory: Death, Tombstones and Commemoration in Bosnian Islam Since c. 1500*. Farnham: Ashgate, 2015.

Calhoun, Craig. "Secularism, Citizenship and the Public Sphere." *Hedgehog Review*, 10, no. 3 (2008): 7–21.

Calic, Marie-Janine. "Ethnic Cleansing and War Crimes." In *Confronting the Yugoslav Controversies*, Charles Ingrao and Thomas Emmert, eds., 114–53. 2nd ed. West Lafayette, IN: Purdue University Press, 2013.

Campo, Juan Eduardo. "Muslim Ways of Death: Between the Prescribed and the Performed." In *Death and Religion in a Changing World*, Kathleen Garces-Foley, ed., 147–77. New York: M. E. Sharpe, 2006.

Carlson, Maria. "Death and Funeral Meats, Moscow Style (An Investigation into the Soviet Way of Death)." *Unpublished Manuscript*. Cited with Permission of Author, 1989.

Casperson, Nina. "Contingent Nationalist Dominance: Intra-Serb Challenges to the Serb Democratic Party." *Nationalities Papers*, 34, no. 1 (March 2006): 51–69.

Chumachenko, Tatiana. *Church and State in Soviet Russia: Russian Orthodoxy from World War II to the Khrushchev Years*. Edited and translated by Edward Roslof. Armonk, NY: M. E. Sharpe, 2002.

Chung, Sue Fawn. "An Ocean Apart: Chinese American Segregated Burials." In *Till Death Do Us Part*, Allan Amarik and Kami Fletcher, eds., 85–128. Jackson: University Press of Mississippi, 2020.

Clark, Janine Natalya. "Reconciliation Through Remembrance? War Memorials and the Victims of Vukovar." *International Journal of Transitional Justice*, 7 (2013): 116–35. https://doi.org/10.1093/ijtj/ijs031.

Cohen, Lenard J. *Broken Bonds: Yugoslavia's Disintegration and Balkan Politics in Transition*. 2nd ed. Boulder, CO: Westview Press, 1995.

Cohen, Lenard J. "Prelates and Politicians in Bosnia: The Role of Religion in Nationalist Mobilisation." *Nationalities Papers*, 25, no. 3 (1997): 481–99.

Cohen, Lenard J. *Serpent in the Bosom: The Rise and Fall of Slobodan Milošević*. Boulder, CO: Westview Press, 2001.

Čolović, Ivan. *Književnost Na Groblju: Zbirka Novih Epitafa*. Beograd: Narodna Knjiga, 1983.

Čolović, Ivan. "Preobražaj Novinske Tužbalice." *Etnološke Sveske*, IX (1988): 59–64.

Colvin, Howard. *Architecture and the Afterlife*. New Haven, CT: Yale University Press, 1991.

Confino, Alon, ed. *Between Mass Death and Individual Loss: The Place of the Dead in Twentieth-Century Germany*. Oxford: Berghahn Books, 2011.

Constas, Nicholas. "Death and Dying in Byzantium." In *Byzantine Christianity*, Derek Krueger, ed. Vol. 3. A People's History of Christianity. Minneapolis, MN: Fortress, 2006.

Cooper, Helene. "They Helped Erase Ebola in Liberia. Now Liberia Is Erasing Them." *New York Times*, December 9, 2015. http://www.nytimes.com/2015/12/10/world/afr ica/they-helped-erase-ebola-in-liberia-now-liberia-is-erasing-them.html.

Curl, James Stevens. *The Victorian Celebration of Death*. Thrupp: Sutton, 2000.

Danforth, L. M. *The Death Rituals of Rural Greece*. Princeton, NJ: Princeton University Press, 1982.

Davies, Jon. "Introduction: Ancestors—Living and Dead." In *Ritual and Remembrance: Responses to Death in Human Societies*, Jon Davies, ed., 11–24. Sheffield: Sheffield Academic Press, 1994.

Davis, Nathaniel. *A Long Walk to Church: A Contemporary History of Russian Orthodoxy*. Boulder, CO: Westview Press, 1995.

de Bernieres, Louis. *Birds without Wings*. New York: Vintage Books, 2005.

de Bruyn, Piet. "Jewish Cemeteries Report." Committee on Science, Culture, Education and Media, Council of Europe, May 10, 2012. http://assembly.coe.int/ASP/XRef/X2H-DW-XSL.asp?fileid=18710&lang=EN.

Denich, Bette. "Nationalist Ideologies and the Symbolic Revival of Genocide." *American Ethnologist*, 21, no. 2 (May 1994): 367–90.

Detling, Karen J. "Eternal Silence: The Destruction of Cultural Property in Yugoslavia." *Maryland Journal of International Law*, 17, no. 1 (1993): 41–75.

Dević, Ana. "Waking the Dead (Who May Never Die): Ethnonationalist Politics of Dead Bodies and Graves in the War- and Post-War Serbia," 2009. http://chdr-ns.com/pdf/documents/opatija2009_ana_devic.pdf.

Di Lellio Anna, and Stephanie Schwandner-Sievers. "Sacred Journey to a Nation: The Construction of a Shrine in Postwar Kosovo." *Journeys*, 7, no. 1 (May 2006): 27–49.

Djokić, Dejan, ed. *Yugoslavism: Histories of a Failed Idea, 1918–1992*. Madison: University of Wisconsin Press, 2003.

Djordjević, Dragoljub B. "Burying of Roma: A Test of Ethnic and Religious Tolerance." In *Romas and Others—Others and Romas: Social Distance*, 35–43. Sofia: "Ivan Hadjiyski" Institute for Social Values and Studies, 2004.

Djordjević, Dragoljub B., Dragan Todorović, and Danijela Gavrilović. *Cemeteries and Burial Customs on the Border*. Niš: Punta, 2015.

Djordjević, Dragoljub B., Dragan Todorović, Lela Milošević, and Ilona Tomova. *Romas and Others, Others and Romas: Social Distance*. Sofia: Institute for social values and structures "Ivan Hadjiyski," 2004.

Djumrukčić, Mustafa. "Izrada Generalnog Urbanističkog Plana." *Sarajevo u Socijalističkoj Jugoslaviji*, 2 (1990): 387–407.

Djurdjević, Goran. *Povijest i Običaji Autohtonih Hrvatskih Roma-Lovara*. Bjelovar: Centar savjetovanja edukacije s kulture Roma, 2009.

Djureinović, Jelena. *The Politics of Memory of the Second World War in Contemporary Serbia*. London: Routledge, 2020.

Djurica, Marko. "Serbia's Bungalow Cemeteries." The Wider Image. Accessed August 2, 2018. https://widerimage.reuters.com/story/serbias-bungalow-cemeteries.

Domanović, Milka, "List of Kosovo War Victims Published." *Balkan Transitional Justice*, December 10, 2014. https://balkaninsight.com/2014/12/10/kosovo-war-victims-list-published/.

Donia, Robert J. "Nationalism and Religious Extremism in Bosnia-Herzegovina and Kosovo Since 1990." *Miscellany IFIMES*, International Institute for Middle East and Balkan Studies, 2007.

Donia, Robert J., and John Fine. *Bosnia and Hercegovina: A Tradition Betrayed*. New York: Columbia University Press, 1994.

Donia, Robert J. *Sarajevo: A Biography*. Ann Arbor: University of Michigan Press, 2006.

Doughty, Caitlin. *From Here to Eternity: Traveling the World to Find the Good Death*. New York: W.W. Norton, 2017.

Dubisch, Jill. "Death and Social Change in Greece." *Anthropological Quarterly*, 62, no. 4 (1989): 189–200.

Duizings, Gerhard. *Religion and the Politics of Identity in Kosovo*. London: Hurst, 2000.

Durey, M. J. "Bodysnatchers and Benthamites: The Implications of the Dead Body Bill for the London Schools of Anatomy, 1820–42." *The London School*, 2, no. 2 (1976): 200–25.

Editorial Staff, "The Destruction of Sufi Shrines." *The Muslim 500*. Accessed February 3, 2021, https://themuslim500.com/destruction-of-sufi-shrines/.

Effros, Bonnie. *Merovingian Mortuary Archaeology and the Making of the Middle Ages*. Berkeley: University Press of California, 2003.

Ejdus, Filip, and Jelena Subotić. "Kosovo as Serbia's Sacred Space: Governmentality, Pastoral Power, and Sacralization of Territories." In *Politicization of Religion, the Power of Symbolism: The Case of Former Yugoslavia and Its Successor States*, Gorana Ognjenović and Jasna Jozelić eds., 159–84. New York: Palgrave MacMillan, 2014. http://ebookcentral.proquest.com/lib/unomaha.

Elbasani, Arolda. "Introduction: Nation, State and Faith in the Post-Communist Era." In *The Revival of Islam in the Balkans: From Identity to Religiosity*, Arolda Elbasani and Olivier Roy, eds., 1–19. London: Palgrave MacMillan, 2015.

Etlin, Richard. *The Architecture of Death: The Transformation of the Cemetery in Eighteenth Century Paris*. Cambridge: MIT Press, 1984.

Farrell, James J. *Inventing the American Way of Death, 1830–1920*. Philadelphia, PA: Temple University Press, 1980.

Flere, Sergej. "The Broken Covenant of Tito's People: The Problem of Civil Religion in Communist Yugoslavia." *East European Politics and Societies*, 21, no. 4 (2007): 681–703.

Fletcher, William C. *The Russian Orthodox Church Underground, 1917–1970*. London: Oxford University Press, 1971.

Fortescue, Adrian. *The Orthodox Eastern Church*. Freeport, NY: Books for Libraries Press, 1920.

Foster, Gary S., and Richard L. Hummel. "The Adkins-Woodson Cemetery: A Sociological Examination of Cemeteries as Communities." *Markers*, 11 (1995): 93–117.

Gal, Susan. "A Semiotics of the Public/Private Distinction," *differences: A Journal of Feminist Cultural Studies*, 13, no. 1 (Spring 2002): 77-95.

Gal, Susan, and Judith Irvine. "The Boundaries of Languages and Disciplines: How Ideologies Construct Difference." *Social Research*, 62, no. 4 (Winter 1995): 967–1001.

Garces-Foley, Kathleen, ed. *Death and Religion in a Changing World*. New York: M. E. Sharpe, 2006.

Gasinski, Thaddeus. "The National Minority Policy of Today's Yugoslavia." *Nationalities Papers*, VIII, no. 1 (Spring 1980): 29–51.

Gatrad, A. R. "Muslim Customs Surrounding Death, Bereavement, Postmortem Examinations, and Organ Transplants." *BMJ*, 309, no. 6953 (August 20, 1994): 521–23. https://doi.org/10.1136/bmj.309.6953.521.

Geiger, Vladimir. "O Provodjenju Odluke Komunističkih Vlasti iz 1945. O Uklanjanju Grobalja i Grobova 'Okupatora' i 'Narodnih Neprijatelja' u Bosni i Hercegovini." *Časopis za kulturno i povijesno naslijedje* 2 (2016) 287–317.

Geiger, Vladimir, and Sladjana Josipović Batorek. "O Provodjenju Odluke Komunističkih Vlasti Iz 1945. O Uklanjanju Grobalja i Grobova 'Okupatora' i 'Narodnih Neprijatelja' u Slavoniji i Srijemu." *Scrinia Slavonica* 15 (2015): 291–316.

Gillis, John R. "Memory and Identity: The History of a Relationship." In *Commemorations: The Politics of National Identity*, John R. Gillis, ed., 3–24. Princeton, NJ: Princeton University Press, 1994.

Gillis, John R., ed. *Commemorations: The Politics of National Identity*. Princeton, NJ: Princeton University Press, 1994.

Gittings, Clare. *Death, Burial and the Individual in Early Modern England*. London: Croom Helm, 1984.

Gittings, Clare. "Expressions of Loss in Early Seventeenth Century England." In *The Changing Face of Death: Historical Accounts of Death and Disposal*, Peter C. Jupp and Glennys Howarth, eds., 19–33. New York: St. Martin's Press, 1997.

Gittings, Clare. "Sacred and Secular: 1558–1660." In *Death in England: An Illustrated History*, Peter C. Jupp and Clare Gittings eds., 147–73. New Brunswick, NJ: Rutgers University Press, 2000.

Glenny, Misha. *The Fall of Yugoslavia: The Third Balkan War*. London: Penguin, 1992.

Golbert, Rebecca. "Judaism and Death: Finding Meaning in Ritual." In *Death and Religion in a Changing World*, Kathleen Garces-Foley, ed., 45–68. New York: M. E. Sharpe, 2006.

Goodman, Neville M. "The Supply of Bodies for Dissection: A Historical Review." *British Medical Journal*, 2, no. 4381 (December 23, 1944): 807–11.

Goody, J., and C. Poppi. "Flowers and Bones: Approaches to the Dead in Anglo-American and Italian Cemeteries." *Comparative Studies in Society and History*, 36, no. 1 (1994): 146–75.

Gordon, Bruce, and Peter Marshal. *The Place of the Dead: Death and Remembrance in Late Medieval and Early Modern Europe*. Cambridge: Cambridge University Press, 2000.

Gramsci, Antonio, and Lynne Lawner. *Letters From Prison, Selected*. New York: Harper and Row, 1973.

Grandits, Hannes, and Christian Promitzer. "'Former Comrades' at War: Historical Perspectives on 'Ethnic Cleansing' in Croatia." In *Neighbors at War: Anthropological Perspectives on Yugoslav Ethnicity, Culture and History*, Joel Halpern and David Kideckl, eds., 125–42. State Park: Pennsylvania State University Press, 2000.

Greble, Emily. *Sarajevo, 1941–1945: Muslims, Christians, and Jews in Hitler's Europe*. Ithaca, NY: Cornell University Press, 2011.

Greenberg, Robert. *Language and Identity in the Balkans*. Oxford: Oxford University Press, 2004.

Greenberg, Robert. "When Is Language a Language? The Case of Former Yugoslavia." *Harvard Ukrainian Studies*, 35, no. 1/4 (2017–18): 431–42.

Gregory, Thomas. "Dismembering the Dead: Violence, Vulnerability and the Body in War." *European Journal of International Relations*, 22, no. 4 (2015): 944–65.

Grubišić, Vinko. "The Croatian Language in the Constitutional Development of the SFRY." *Journal of Croatian Studies*, 30 (1989): 139–52.

Habenstein, Robert W., and William M. Lamers. *Funeral Customs the World Over*. Milwaukee, WI: Bulfin Printers Inc., National Funeral Directors Association of the United States, 1960.

Habermas, Jurgen. *The Structural Transformation of the Public Sphere*. Cambridge: MIT Press, 1989.

Halevi, Leor. *Muhammad's Grave: Death Rites and the Making of Islamic Society*. New York: Columbia University Press, 2007.

Hallam, Elizabeth, and Jenny Hockey. *Death, Memory, and Material Culture*. Oxford: Berg, 2001.

Halporn, Roberta. "American Jewish Cemeteries: A Mirror of History." In *Ethnicity and the American Cemetery*, Richard E. Meyer, ed., 131–55. Bowling Green, OH: Bowling Green State University Popular Press, 1993.

Hayden, Robert. "Imagined Communities and Real Victims—Self-Determination and Ethnic Cleansing in Yugoslavia." *American Ethnologist*, 23, no. 4 (November 1996): 783–801.

Hayden, Robert. "Muslims as 'Others' in Serbian and Croatian Politics." In *Neighbors at War: Anthropological Perspectives on Yugoslav Ethnicity, Culture and History*, Joel Halpern and David Kideckl, eds., 116–24. State Park: Pennsylvania State University Press, 2000.

Helms, Elissa. *Innocence and Victimhood: Gender, Nation, and Women's Activism in Postwar Bosnia-Hercegovina*. Madison: University of Wisconsin Press, 2013.
Helms, Elissa, Xavier Bougarel, and Ger Duijzings. *The New Bosnian Mosaic: Identities, Memories and Moral Claims in a Post-War Society*. Ebsco Publishing: Ebook Academic Collection. Burlington, VT: Ashgate, 2007.
Hendija, Zora. "Prvo Hrvatsko Gradjansko Kaptolsko Društvo Za Sjajne Pogrebe u Zagrebu (1835–1948)." *Arhivski Vjesnik*, 37 (1994): 263–81.
Herman, Vesna Jureško. "Destruction of Art and Architecture in Croatia." *Journal of Croatian Studies*, 32, no. 33 (1991–2): 231–74.
Herscher, Andrew. *Violence Taking Place*. Stanford, CA: Stanford University Press, 2010.
Herscher, Andrew, and Andras Riedlmayer. "Monument and Crime: The Destruction of Historic Architecture in Kosovo." *Grey Room*, 1 (Autumn 2000): 108–22.
Hockey, Jenny, Carol Komaromy, and Kate Woodthorpe eds. *The Matter of Death: Space, Place and Materiality*. Basingstoke: Palgrave MacMillan, 2010.
Hodson, Randy, Dušan Sekulić, and Garth Massey. "National Tolerance in the Former Yugoslavia." *American Journal of Sociology*, 99, no. 6 (May 1994): 1534–58.
Hodžić, Asmir, and Rodoljub Tansaić. *Funkcije pogrebne djelatnosti*. Sarajevo: JKP "Gradsko groblje" k.o.o. Visoko, 2007.
Horrox, Rosemary. "Purgatory, Prayer and Plague: 1150–1380." In *Death in England: An Illustrated History*, Peter C. Jupp and Clare Gittings, eds., 90–118. New Brunswick, NJ: Rutgers University Press, 2000.
Houlbrooke, Ralph. "The Age of Decency: 1660–1760." In *Death in England: An Illustrated History*, Peter C. Jupp and Clare Gittings, eds., 174–201. New Brunswick, NJ: Rutgers University Press, 2000.
Houlbrooke, Ralph. *Death, Religion, and the Family in England, 1480–1750*. Oxford: Clarendon Press, 1998.
Howarth, Glennys. "Professionalizing the Funeral Industry in England, 1700–1960." In *The Changing Face of Death: Historical Accounts of Death and Disposal*, Peter C. Jupp and Glennys Howarth, eds., 120–34. New York: St. Martin's Press, 1997.
Husband, William B. *Godless Communists: Atheism and Society in Soviet Russia, 1917–1931*. DeKalb: Northern Illinois University Press, 2000.
Huțanu, Monica, and Annemarie Sorescu-Marinković. "Novi nadgrobni natpisi na vlaškom u istočnoj Srbiji." *Folkloristika*, 1, no. 2 (2016): 27–42.
Huzjan, Vladimir, and Jasmin Medved. "O Pokopanim Vojnicima Sila Osovine Na Varaždinskom Groblju." *Radovi*, Zavod za znanstveni rad HAZU Varaždin, June 19, 2015, 195–266.
Ingimundarson, Valur. "The Politics of Memory and the Reconstruction of Albanian National Identity in Postwar Kosovo." *History and Memory*, 19, no. 1 (Spring/Summer 2007): 95–123.
Ingrao, Charles, and Thomas A. Emmert, eds., *Confronting the Yugoslav Controversies*. 2nd ed. West Lafayette, IN: Purdue University Press, 2015.

Irvine, Jill A. "Ultranationalist Ideology and State-Building in Croatia, 1990–1996." *Problems of Post-Communism*, 44, no. 4 (August 1997): 30–43.

Jalimam, Salih. *Prošlost Zenice Do 1941 Godine: Glavni Tokovi Društvenog Razvoja*. Zenica, BiH: Muzej grada Zenica, 1996.

Jalland, Pat. "Victorian Death and Its Decline: 1850–1918." In *Death in England: An Illustrated History*, Peter C. Jupp and Clare Gittings eds., 230–55. New Brunswick, NJ: Rutgers University Press, 2000.

Janine de Giovanni. *Madness Visible: A Memoir of War*. New York: Knopf, 2003.

Janković, Ljubica S. "Dancing for the Dead in Yugoslavia." *Folk Music Journal*, 1, no. 4 (1968): 223–7.

Jareb, Mario. *Hrvatski Nacionalni Symboli*. 1st ed. Zagreb: Hrvatski Institute za povijest, 2010.

Jeffries, Ian. *The Former Yugoslavia at the Turn of the Twenty-First Century: A Guide to the Economies in Transition*. London: Routledge Press, 2002.

Jeftić, Atanasije. "Od Kosova Do Jadovna," 1984. http://www.kosovo.net/sk/rastko-kosovo/istorija/kosovo-jadovno.html.

Jeftić, Atanasije. "[Projekat Rastko Gračanica-Peć] Vladika Atanasije Jeftić: Stradanja Srba Na Kosovu i Metohiji Od 1941. Do 1990. Godine," 1990. http://www.rastko.rs/kosovo/istorija/stradanje_srba/atanasije_1deo.html#_Toc485531489.

Jovanović, Bojan. *Srpska Knjiga Mrtvih*. Novi Sad: Prometej, 1992.

Jovanović, Milka. "Sastanak Sa 'Pokojnikom.'" *Glasnik Etnografskog Instituta SANU*, 39 (1990): 89–93.

Jupp, Peter C. "Enon Chapel: No Way for the Dead." In *The Changing Face of Death: Historical Accounts of Death and Disposal*, Peter C. Jupp and Glennys Howarth, eds., 90–104. New York: St. Martin's Press, 1997.

Jupp, Peter C. "Introduction: Death as a Social and Historical Actor." In *The Changing Face of Death: Historical Accounts of Death and Disposal*, Peter Jupp and Glennys Howarth, eds., 1–17. New York: St. Martin's Press, 1997.

Jupp, Peter C., and Tony Walter. "The Healthy Society: 1918–98." In *Death in England: An Illustrated History*, Peter C. Jupp and Clare Gittings, eds, 256–78. New Brunswick, NJ: Rutgers University Press, 2000.

Jupp, Peter C., and Clare Gittings, eds. *Death in England: An Illustrated History*. New Brunswick, NJ: Rutgers University Press, 2000.

Kadare, Ismail. *The General of the Dead Army*. New York: Arcade, 1971.

Kallen, Jeffrey L. "Changing Landscapes: Language, Space and Policy in the Dublin Linguistic Landscape." In *Semiotic Landscapes: Language, Image, Space*, Adam Jaworksi, Crispin Thurlow and Tommaso M. Milani eds., London: Continuum, 2010.

Kardov, Kruno. "Remember Vukovar: Memory, Sense of Place, and the National Tradition in Croatia." In *Democratic Transition in Croatia: Value Transformation, Education & Media*, Sabrina P. Ramet and Davorka Matić, eds. EBSCO Publishing: eBook Academic Collection (EBSCOhost), n.d. Accessed October 7, 2014.

Katsikas, S. "European Modernity and Islamic Reformism among Muslims of the Balkans in the Late-Ottoman and Post-Ottoman Period (1830s–1945)." *Journal of Muslim Minority Affairs*, 29, no. 4 (2009): 537–43.

Kelly, Catriona. *St. Petersburg: Shadows of the Past*. New Haven, CT: Yale University Press, 2014.

Kelly, Jon. "Osama Bin Laden: The Power of Shrines." *BBC News Magazine*, May 4, 2011, online World Edition. http://www.bbc.co.uk/news/magazine-13264959.

Kenna, Margaret. "The Power of the Dead: Changes in the Construction and Care of Graves and Family Vaults on a Small Greek Island." *Journal of Mediterranean Studies*, 1, no. 1 (1991): 101–19.

Kinzer, Stephen. "Ousted Croats Go to Seized Towns." *New York Times*, October 28, 1992, sec. World. https://www.nytimes.com/1992/10/28/world/ousted-croats-go-to-seized-towns.html.

Klapetek, Martin. "Muslim Areas at Municipal Cemeteries in Germany and Austria." *Studia Religiologica*, 50, no. 3 (2017): 203–20.

Kleftakis, Vasilije. "Василије Клефтакис: Затирање српске ћирилице—план или случај." Нова српска политичка мисао. Accessed November 2, 2021. http://www.nspm.rs/kulturna-politika/zatiranje-srpske-cirilice-%E2%80%93-plan-ili-slucaj.html?alphabet=l.

Kligman, Gail. *The Wedding of the Dead*. Berkeley: University of California Press, 1988.

Kocaj, Željko, ed. *Katoličko Pokupno Društvo "Sveti Anto" Zenica, 1932–2010*. Zenica, BiH: KPD "Sveti Anto" Zenica, 2010.

Korkut, Haris. *Mješoviti Brakovi po Islamskom Pravu: Teološko-Pravna Rasprava*. Bejrut, 1965.

Korošec, Josip and Snežana Mutapčić. *Sanacija, rekonstrukcija i restauracija skulpture umirući lav*. Sarajevo: Akademija likovnih umjetnosti Sarajevo, n.d.

Kostić, Bratislava. *Novo Groblje u Beogradu*. Beograd: JKP "Pogrebne Usluge," 1999.

Kovačević, Ivan. "Socijalno-Emfatička Funkcija Monumentalnih Grobnica." *Etnološke Sveske*, VI (1985): 81–7.

Krasniqi, Gezim. "The 'Forbidden Fruit': Islam and Politics of Identity in Kosovo and Macedonia." *Southeast European and Black Sea Studies*, 11, no. 2 (June 2011): 191–207.

Krasniqi, Vjollca. "Cultures of History Forum: Between History and Memory: The Jashari Family Memorial in Prekaz (Kosovo)." Accessed May 23, 2019. http://www.cultures-of-history.uni-jena.de/debates/kosovo/between-history-and-memory-the-jashari-family-memorial-in-prekaz-kosovo/.

Kselman, Thomas A. *Death and the Afterlife in Modern France*. Princeton, NJ: Princeton University Press, 1993.

Lane, Christel. *The Rites of Rulers: Ritual in Industrial Society—the Soviet Case*. Cambridge: Cambridge University Press, 1981.

Laqueur, Thomas. "Memory and Naming in the Great War." In *Commemorations: The Politics of National Identity*, John R. Gillis, ed., 150–67. Princeton, NJ: Princeton University Press, 1994.

Laqueur, Thomas. *The Work of the Dead*. Princeton, NJ: Princeton University Press, 2015.
Le Goff, J. *History and Memory*. New York: Columbia University Press, 1992.
Le Normand, Brigitte. *Designing Tito's Capital: Urban Planning, Modernism, and Socialism in Belgrade*. Pittsburgh, PA: University of Pittsburgh Press, 2014.
LeBor, Adam. *Milošević: A Biography*. New Haven, CT: Yale University Press, 2002.
Levenger, Matthew, and Paula Franklin Lytle. "Myth and Mobilisation: The Triadic Structure of Nationalist Rhetoric." *Nations and Nationalities*, 7, no. 2 (2001): 175–94.
Levine, Ellen. "Jewish Views and Customs on Death." In *Death and Bereavement Across Cultures*, Colin Murray Parkes, Pittu Laungani, and Bill Young, eds., 98–130. London: Routledge Press, 1997.
Lilly, Carol S. "Communities of the Dead: Secularizing Cemeteries in Communist Yugoslavia." *Slavonic and East European Review* 97, 4 (2019): 676–710.
Lilly, Carol S. *Power and Persuasion: Ideology and Rhetoric in Communist Yugoslavia, 1944–1953*. Boulder, CO: Westview Press, 2001.
Lilly, Carol S. and Jill A. Irvine. "Negotiating Interests: Women and Nationalism in Serbia and Croatia, 1990-1997." *East European Politics, Societies, and Cultures*. 16 (1) (2002): 109-44.
Litten, Julian. "The Funeral Trade in Hanoverian England, 1714–1760." In *The Changing Face of Death: Historical Accounts of Death and Disposal*, Peter C. Jupp and Glennys Howarth, eds., 48–61. New York: St. Martin's Press, 1997.
Ljubojević, Julij Liebald. *Groblje i Pokop: Poleg Poviesti i Prava*. Osijek: Vatroslav Medersičko, 1869.
Luria, Keith. "Separated by Death: Cemeteries, Burials and Confessional Boundaries in Seventeenth Century France." *French Historical Studies*, 24, no. 2 (Spring 2001): 185–221.
Magaš, Branka. *The Destruction of Yugoslavia*. London: Verso, 1993.
Maksimović, Bogdan. "Stadion, 'Koševo.'" In *Sarajevo u Socijalističkoj Jugoslaviji: od Oslobodjena do Samoupravljanja (1945–1950)*, 1, 584–90. Sarajevo: Istorijski Arhiv Sarajevo, 1988.
Maksimović, Mirko, ed. *Spomenica Srpskog-Pravoslavnog Pogrebnog Društva Svetog Marka u Sarajevo Prilikom Desetogodišnjice 1922–1932*. Sarajevo, Upravni Odbor Srpska-Pravoslavnog Pogrebnog Društva Sv. Marka, 1933.
Malcolm, Noel. *Kosovo*. New York: New York University Press, 1998.
Manojlović-Pintar, Olga. "'Široka Strana Moja Rodnaja,': Spomenici Sovjetskim Vojnicima Podizani u Srbiji 1944-1954." *Tokovi Istorije*, 1–2 (2005): 134–45.
Manojlović-Pintar, Olga. "'Tito je Stena': (Dis)kontinuitet vladarskih predstavljanja u Jugoslaviji i Srbiji XX veka." *Godišnjak na društvenu istoriju*, 2–3 (2004): 85–100.
Manojlović-Pintar, Olga. "Uprostoravanje ideologije: Spomenici Drugoga svetskog rata i kreiranje kolektivnih identiteta." *Dijalog povjesničara*, 10, no. 1 (July 2005): 287–307.
Mant, Madeleine, and Nancy Lovell. "Individual and Group Identity in WWII Commemorative Sites." *Mortality*, 17, no. 1 (2012): 18–35.

Matić-Bošković, Milica. "Novija etnološka ispitivanja pogrebnih običaja Srba u Sremu." *Radovi XI Savjetovanja etnologa Jugoslavije*, izdanja Muzeja grada Zenica, 1970, 267–83.

Matich, Olga. "'Whacked But Not Forgotten': Burying the Mob." Accessed February 27, 2015. http://www.stanford.edu/group/Russia20/volume.

Matsunami, Kodo. *Funeral Customs of the World: A Comprehensive Guide to Practices and Traditions*. Tochigi: Buddhist Searchlight Center, 1998.

Matturri, John. "Windows in the Garden: Italian-American Memorialization and the American Cemetery." In *Ethnicity and the American Cemetery*, Richard E. Meyer, ed., 14–35. Bowling Green, OH: Bowling Green State University Popular Press, 1993.

Mbembe, Achille. "Necropolitics." In *Foucault in an Age of Terror: Essays on Biopolitics and the Defence of Society*, S. Morton and S. Bygrave, eds., 152–82. New York: Palgrave MacMillan, 2008.

McAllister, Matthew. *Beyond the Mountains of the Damned: The War Inside Kosovo*. Kindle ed. New York: New York University Press, 2003.

Mehmeti, Jeton. "Faith and Politics in Kosovo: The Status of Religious Communities in a Secular Country." In *The Revival of Islam in the Balkans: From Identity to Religiosity*, Arolda Elbasani and Olivier Roy, eds., 62–79. New York: Palgrave MacMillan, 2015.

Mekić, Sejad. *A Muslim Reformist in Communist Yugoslavia: The Life and Thought of Husein Đozo*. London: Routledge, 2016.

Menachemson, Nolan. *A Practical Guide to Jewish Cemeteries*. Bergenfield, NJ: Avotaynu, 2007.

Merridale, Catherine. *Night of Stone: Death and Memory in Twentieth Century Russia*. New York: Viking Penguin, 2002.

Meyer, Richard E. "Strangers in a Strange Land: Ethnic Cemeteries in America." In *Ethnicity and the American Cemetery*, Richard E. Meyer, ed., 1–13. Bowling Green, OH: Bowling Green State University Popular Press, 1993.

Meyer, Richard E., ed. *Ethnicity and the American Cemetery*. Bowling Green, OH: Bowling Green State University Popular Press, 1993.

Milanović, Marko "Sejdi & Finci v. Bosnia and Herzegovina." *American Journal of International Law*, 104, 4 (2010): 636–41.

Miller, Nicholas J. *Between Nation and State: Serbian Politics in Croatia before the First World War*. 1st ed. Pittsburgh, PA: University of Pittsburgh Press, 1998.

Miller, Nick. *The Nonconformists*. Budapest: CEU Press, 2007.

Miloradović, Goran. "Prah Prahu: Staljinistički Pogrebni Rituali u Socialističkoj Yugoslaviji." *Godišnjak za Društvenu Istoriju*, 1–3 (2007): 83–106.

Minority Rights Group International. *Lukovac Case (Skrnavljenje Mezarja Lukavac)*. Accessed July 18, 2018. https://www.youtube.com/watch?v=ms6twsJ7xx0&feature=share.

Mittford, Jessica. *The American Way of Death*. New York: Simon and Schuster, 1963.

Morel, Anne-Francoise. "Identity and Conflict: Cultural Heritage, Reconstruction, and National Identity in Kosovo." *Architecture, Media, Politics, Society*, 3, no. 1 (May 2013): 1–20.
Morley, John. *Death, Heaven and the Victorians*. London: Studio Vista, Blue Star House, 1971.
Mosse, George. *Fallen Soldiers: Reshaping the Memory of the World Wars*. New York: Oxford University Press, 1990.
Mujezinović, Mehmed. *Islamska Epigrafika Bosne i Hercegovine*. Vols. 1 and 2. 2 vols. Sarajevo: Sarajevo Publishing, 1998.
Mulahalilović, Enver. *Vjerski Običaji Muslimana/Bošnjaka*. 3rd ed. Sarajevo: El-Kalem—Izdavački centar Rijaseta, 2005.
Muller-Wille, Michael. "The Cross as a Symbol of Personal Christian Belief in a Changing Religious World." In *The World View of Prehistoric Man*, Lars Larsson and Berta Stjernquist, eds. Vol. Konferenser 40. Papers Presented at a Symposium in Lund, Sweden, Kungl Vitterhets Historie och Antikvitets Akademien, 1997.
Mytum, Harold. *Mortuary Monuments and Burial Grounds of the Historic Period*. New York: Kluwer Academic, 2004.
Mytum, Harold. *Recording and Analysing Graveyards*. 1st ed. Vol. 15. Practical Handbooks in Archaeology. York: Council for British Archaeology in Association with English Heritage, 2000.
Niebyul, Donald. *Spomenik Monument Database*. London: Fuel Publishing, 2018.
Ngo, Tam T. T., and Justine B. Quijada. "Introduction: Atheist Secularism and Its Discontents." In *Atheist Secularism and Its Discontents: A Comparative Study of Religion and Communism in Eurasia*, Tam T. T. Ngo and Justine B. Quijada, eds., 1–26. London: Palgrave MacMillan, 2015.
Norris, David A. "Jovan Radulović's *Golubnjača* (Dove Hole): Analysis and Context of the Stories and Play Which Was Banned in Yugoslavia (1980–1984)." *Slavonic and East European Review*, 90, 2 (2012): 201–28.
O'Dell, Emily Jane. "Waging War on the Dead: The Necropolitics of Sufi Shrine Destruction in Mali." *Archaeologies: Journal of the World Archeological Congress*, 9, no. 3 (December 2013): 506–24.
Oberschall, Anthony. "The Manipulation of Ethnicity: From Ethnic Cooperation to Violence and War in Yugoslavia." *Ethnic and Racial Studies*, 23, no. 6 (2000): 982–1001.
Omerdić, Muharem. *Prilozi Izučavanju Genocida Nad Bošnjacima (1992–1995)*. Sarajevo: Rijaset islamske zajednice u Bosni i Hercegovini, 1999.
OO SDS Sokolac. *Srpsko Vojničko Groblje, "Mali Zejminlik"—Sokolac*, 2012. https://www.youtube.com/watch?v=R8dINVEjEgM. Accessed August 10, 2016.
Oran, Baskin. "Religious and National Identity among the Balkan Muslims: A Comparative Study on Greece, Bulgaria, Macedonia and Kosovo." *Cahiers d'etude Sur La Mediterranee Orientale et Le Mode Turco-Iranien* 18, 1 (December 1994): 307–24.

Organization for Security and Co-operation in Europe and Office for Democratic Institutions and Human Rights. *Hate Crimes in the OSCE Region: Incidents and Responses: Annual Report for 2006*. Warsaw: OSCE Office for Democratic Institutions and Human Rights, 2007.

Otašević, Gvozden. "Pronašla očev grob posle 63 godine." *Politika Online*. Accessed June 29, 2020. Pronašla očev grob posle 63 godine (politika.rs).

Pavičević, Aleksandra. "Cremation as an Urban Phenomenon of the New Age: From Ecology to Ideology: The Serbian Case." *Ethnologica Balkanica*, 10 (2006): 251–62.

Pavičević, Aleksandra. "Dan Žalosti i Vreme Uspomena: Smrt, Sahrana i Sećanje/Pamčenje Javnih Ličnosti u Srbiji u Vreme Socijalizma i Posle Njega." *Glasnik Etnografskog Instituta SANU*, LVI, no. I (2009): 223–38.

Pavičević, Aleksandra. *From Mystery to Spectacle: Essays on Death in Serbia from the 19th–21st Century*. Belgrade: Serbian Academy of Sciences: Ethnographic Institute, 2015.

Pavičević, Aleksandra. "Spomenici i/Ili Grobovi--Sećanje Na Mrt i/Ili Dekoracija." *Spomen Mesta—Istorija—Sećanja*, Collection of Papers, 26 (2009): 46–60.

Pavičević, Aleksandra. "'Sveta Smrt' Slobodana Miloševića, Antropološki Esej." *Kulturne Paralele: Svakodnevna Kultura u Postsocijalističkom Periodu*, Collection of papers, 25 (2008): 147–56.

Pavičević, Aleksandra. *Vreme (Bez) Smrti: Predstavi o Smrti u Srbiji 19–21. Veka*. Special Editions, Vol. 73. Vol. Bulletin of the Institute of Ethnography. Beograd: Serbian Academy of Sciences: Ethnographic Institute, 2011. www.etno-institut.co.rs.

Pavlaković, Vjeran, "Blowing Up Brotherhood and Unity: The Fate of World War Two Cultural Heritage in Lika." In *The Politics of Heritage and Memory*, Petra Jurlina, ed., 351–426. Zagreb: University of Zagreb Press, 2014.

Pavlaković, Vjeran. "Symbols and the Culture of Memory in Republika Srpska Krajina." *Nationalities Papers*, 41, no. 6 (2013): 893–909.

Pavlaković, Vjeran, Dario Brentin, and Davor Pauković. "The Controversial Commemoration: Transnational Approaches to Remembering Bleiburg." *Croatian Political Science Review*, 55, no. 2 (2018): 7–32.

Paxton, Frederick S. *Christianizing Death: The Creation of a Ritual Process in Early Medieval Europe*. Ithaca, NY: Cornell University Press, 1990.

Peklić, Ivan. "Komunalno Poduzeće Križevci." *Cris*, VIII, no. I (2006): 79–99.

Perez, Tess Pantoja, and Josie Mendez-Negrete. "Burial Practices Expose Identity Formation: Muerte y figura hasta la sepultura." *Association of Mexican American Educators (AMAE) Journal*, 13, no. 1 (2019): 79–101. https://journals.coehd.utsa.edu/index.php/AMAE/article/view/226/217.

Perica, Vjekoslav. *Balkan Idols: Religion and Nationalism in Yugoslav States*. Oxford: Oxford University Press, 2002.

Peris, Daniel. *Storming the Heavens: The Soviet League of the Militant Godless*. Ithaca, NY: Cornell University Press, 1998.

Petrig, Anna. "The War Dead and Their Gravesites." *International Review of the Red Cross*, 91, no. 874 (June 2009): 341–69.

Petrović, Aleksander, and Djordje Stefanović. "Kosovo 1944–1981: The Rise and Fall of a Communist 'Nested Homeland.'" *Europe-Asia Studies*, 62, no. 7 (September 2010): 1073–1106.

Petrović, Edit. "Posmrtni Običaji Kod Ateista: Na Primeru Crnogorskih Kolonista u Bačkoj." *Etnološke Sveske*, VIII (1987): 179–86.

Petrović, Ruža. *Etnički Mešoviti Brakovi u Jugoslaviji*. Beograd: Institut za sociološka istraživanja, Filozofskog fakulteta u Beogradu, 1985.

Pinfold, John. "The Green Ground." In *The Changing Face of Death: Historical Accounts of Death and Disposal*, Peter C. Jupp and Howarth, Glennys, eds., 76–89. New York: St. Martin's Press, 1997.

Pollack, Craig Evan. "Burial at Srebrenica: Linking Place and Trauma." *Social Science & Medicine*, 56, no. 4 (February 2003): 793–801. https://doi.org/10.1016/S0277-9536(02)00078-3.

Pollack, Craig Evan. "Intentions of Burial: Mourning, Politics, and Memorials Following the Massacre at Srebrenica." *Death Studies*, 27, no. 2 (February 1, 2003): 125–42. https://doi.org/10.1080/07481180302893.

Posavec, Koroljka. "Sociokulturna Obilježja i Položaj Roma u Europi—Od Izgona do Integracije." *Društvena Istraživanja*, 9, nos. 2–3, 46–7 (2000): 229–49.

Poulton, Hugh, and S. Taji-Farouki. *Muslim Identity and the Balkan State*. London: Hurst, 1997.

Požgaj Hadži, Vesna. "Language Policy and Linguistic Reality in Former Yugoslavia and Its Successor States." *Inter Faculty*, 5 (2014): 49–91. https://doi.org/10.15068/00143222.

Pula, James S. "'Death Is Not a Wedding': The Cemetery as a Polish American Communal Experience." In *Till Death Do Us Part*, Allan Amanik and Kami Fletcher, eds., 35–83. Jackson: University Press of Mississippi, 2020.

Putnam, Robert D., and David E. Campbell. *American Grace: How Religion Divides and Unites Us*. New York: Simon and Schuster, 2010.

Radić, Radmila. "Crkva i 'Srpsko Pitanje.'" In *Srpska Strana Rata: Trauma i Katarza u Istorijskom Pamćenju*, Nebojša Popov, ed., 267–304. Beograd: Republika, 1996.

Radić, Radmila. *Verom Protiv Vere: Država i Verske Zajednice u Srbiji 1945–1953*. Belgrade: INIS, 1995.

Ragon, Michel, and translated by Alan Sheridan. *Space of Death: Study of Funerary Architecture, Decoration and Urbanism*. Charlottesville, VA: University Press of Virginia, 1983.

Rajković, Zorica. "Obilježavanje Mjesta Smrti u Predajama." *Etnološki Pregled*, 20–21 (1984–5): 11–24.

Ramazani, Jahan. "Nationalism, Transnationalism, and the Poetry of Mourning." In *The Oxford Handbook of the Elegy*, Karen Weisman, ed., 601–19. Oxford: Oxford University Press, 2010.

Reimers, Eva. "Death and Identity: Graves and Funerals as Cultural Communication." *Mortality*, 4, no. 2 (1999): 147–66.

Reljić, Mitra. "Zatiranje Srpske Jezičke Baštine Na Grobljima Kosova i Metohije." *Slavistika*, 11 (2007): 151–7.

Rev, Istvan. "Parallel Autopsies." *Representations* 49, Identifying Histories: Eastern Europe before and after 1989 (Winter 1995): 15–39.

Riedelmayer, Andras. "From the Ashes: The Past and Future of Bosnia's Cultural Heritage." In *Islam and Bosnia: Conflict Resolution and Foreign Policy in Multi-Ethnic States*, Maya Shatzmiller, ed. 98–135. Montreal: McGillQueens University Press, 2002.

Rihtman-Augustin, Dunja. "Novinske Osmrtince." *Narodna Umjetnost*, 15 (1978): 119–74.

Riley, Naomi Schaefer. *'Til Faith Do Us Part: How Interfaith Marriage Is Transforming America*. Oxford: Oxford University Press, 2013.

Ro'i, Yaacov. *Islam in the Soviet Union from the Second World War to Gorbachev*. New York: Columbia University Press, 2000.

Roberts, Penny. "Contesting Sacred Space: Burial Disputes in Sixteenth Century France." In *The Place of the Dead: Death and Remembrance in Late Medieval and Early Modern Europe*, Bruce Gordon and Peter Marshall, eds., 131–48. Cambridge: Cambridge University Press, 2000.

Rogel, Carole. *The Breakup of Yugoslavia and Its Aftermath*. Westport, CT: Greenwood Press, 2004.

Rose, Dacia Viejo. "Conflict and the Deliberate Destruction of Cultural Heritage." In *Cultures and Globalization: Conflicts and Tensions*, H. K. Anheier and Y. R. Isar, eds., 102–21, 2008. http://ebookcentral.proquest.com.

Roslof, Edward. *Red Priests: Renovationism, Russian Orthodoxy, and Revolution, 1905–1946*. Bloomington: Indiana University Press, 2002.

Rotar, Marius. "Attitudes toward Cremation in Contemporary Romania." *Mortality*, 20, no. 2 (2015): 145–62.

Roy, Olivier. *Secularism Confronts Islam*. New York: Columbia University Press, 2007.

Rugg, Julie. *Churchyard and Cemetery: Tradition and Modernity in Rural North Yorkshire*. Manchester: Manchester University Press, 2013.

Rugg, Julie. "From Reason to Regulation: 1760–1850." In *Death in England: An Illustrated History*, Peter C. Jupp and Clare Gittings, eds., 202–29. New Brunswick, NJ: Rutgers University Press, 2000.

Rugg, Julie, "The Origins and Progress of Cemetery Establishment in Britain." In *The Changing Face of Death: Historical Accounts of Death and Disposal*, Peter C. Jupp and Glennys Howarth, eds., 105–19. New York: St. Martin's Press, 1997.

Rusinow, Dennison. *The Yugoslav Experiment, 1948–1974*. Berkeley: Cambridge University Press, 1977.

Said, Edward W. *Orientalism*. 2nd ed. New York: Random House, 1979.

Salamurović, Aleksandra. "Script in Public Space: Example of Bosnia-Hercegovina." Unpublished Manuscript, n.d. Cited with Permission of the Author.

Salamurović, Aleksandra, and Marija Mandić. "Latin Script in Serbian Society Today: Denying Authenticity." Unpublished manuscript, March 11, 2021. Cited with Permission of the Authors.

Savić, Savo. "Etnografska Gradja Iz Donjeg Birca." *Etnografska Gradja: Akademija Nauka i Umjetnosti Bosne i Hercegovine*, 20 (1976): 89–133.

Schauble, Michaela. "How History Takes Place: Sacralized Landscapes in the Croatian-Bosnian Border Region." *History and Memory*, 23, no. 1 (Spring/Summer 2011): 23–61.

Schlesinger, Rabbi Elyokim. *The Sacred Obligation of Burial and Life after Death in Jewish Belief.* Jewish Cemeteries and Mass Graves in Europe: Protection and Preservation. Antwerp: European Agudas Yisroel, 2008.

Schulz, Felix Robin. *Death in East Germany, 1945–1990.* New York: Bergahn Books, 2013.

Scott, James C. *Domination and the Arts of Resistance: Hidden Transcripts.* New Haven, CT: Yale University Press, 1990.

Sekulić, Duško, Garth Massey, and Randy Hodson. "Who Were the Yugoslavs? Failed Sources of a Common Identity in the Former Yugoslavia." *American Sociological Review*, 59, no. 1 (February 1994): 83–97.

Sells, Michael. "Crosses of Blood: Sacred Spaces, Religion, and Violence in Bosnia-Hercegovina." *Sociology of Religion*, 64, no. 3 (Autumn 2003): 309–31.

Sells, Michael. "Kosovo Mythology and the Bosnian Genocide." In *In God's Name: Genocide and Religion in the Twentieth Century*, Omer Bartov and Phyllis Mack, eds., New York: Bergahn Books, 2001.

Serbia, RTS, "Radio televizija Srbije, Radio Television 'Nagazna mina na groblju.'" Accessed December 2, 2018. http://www.rts.rs/page/stories/sr/story/135/hronika/881770/nagazna-mina-na-groblju.html.

Shoup, Paul. *Communism and the National Question.* New York: Columbia University Press, 1968.

Sikmić, Biljana, and Motoki Nomachi. "Jezički pejsaž memorijalnih prostora višejezičnih zajednica, banatski Bugari/Palčanci u Srbiji." *Južnoslovenski filolog*, 72 (2016): 7–31.

Silber, Laura, and Allan Little. *Yugoslavia: Death of a Nation.* First Revised and Updated. New York: Penguin, 1997.

Silberberg, Naftali Rabbi. "Why Does Jewish Law Forbid Cremation? Death and Mourning." Chabad.org. Accessed December 5, 2014. http://www.chabad.org/library/article_cdo/aid/510874/jewish/Why-Does-Jewish-Law-Forbid-Cremation.htm.

Škiljan, Dubravko. *Jezična Politika.* Zagreb: Naprijed, 1988.

Slijepčević, Miloš. *Samobor: Selo u Gornjoj Hercegovini.* Vol. 11. Gradja—Odjeljenje društvenih nauka, XV. Sarajevo: Akademija nauka i umjetnosti Bosne i Hercegovine, 1969.

Smith, Michael G. "The Russian Revolution as National Revolution: Tragic Deaths and Rituals of Remembrance in Muslim Azerbaijan, (1907–1920)." *Jahrbücher Für Geschichte Osteuropas*, 49, no. 3 (2001): 363–88.

Smolkin, Victoria. *A Sacred Space Is Never Empty: A History of Soviet Atheism*. Princeton, NJ: Princeton University Press, 2018.

Sørensen, Marie Louise Stig, and Dacia Viejo Rose. *War and Cultural Heritage*. Cambridge: Cambridge University Press, 2015.

Sršan, Stjepan. *Osječka Groblja*. Osijek: Povijesni Arhiv, 1996.

Stamp, Gavin. *The Memorial to the Missing of the Somme*. London: Profile Books, 2006.

Stanišić, D. "На удару вандала и цркве и свештеници." *Politika Online*. Accessed June 29, 2020. На удару вандала и цркве и свештеници (politika.rs).

Stevens, William Oliver. *The Cross in the Life and Literature of the Anglo-Saxons*. Ebook, Google. New York: Henry Holt, 1904. https://play.google.com/books/reader?id=AWALAAAAIAAJ&printsec=frontcover&output=reader&authuser=0&hl=en.

Stević, Miroslav. *Bratunačko Groblje17.04.1999*, 2011. https://www.youtube.com/watch?v=liwDn_cD5VY. Accessed 10, 2016.

Stierli, Martino, and Vladimir Kulić. *Toward a Concrete Utopia: Architecture in Yugoslavia 1948–1980*. New York: Museum of Modern Art, 2017.

Sušić, Mustafa. "Naš odnos prema natkaburskim obilježima." In *Takvim za 2011*, Muharem Omerdić and Aziz Kadribegović, eds., 171–81. Sarajevo: El-Kalem—Izdavački centar Rijaseta, 2010.

Tait, Clodagh. *Death, Burial and Commemoration in Ireland, 1550–1650*. Great Basingstoke: Palgrave MacMillan, 2002.

Tanner, Marcus. *Croatia: A Nation Forged in War*. New Haven, CT: Yale University Press, 1997.

Taylor, Lawrence. "Introduction: The Uses of Death in Europe." *Anthropological Quarterly*, 62, no. 4 (1989a): 149–54.

Thomas, Robert. *Serbia under Milošević: Politics in the 1990s*. London: Hurst, 1999.

Thompson, Mark. *Forging War: The Media in Serbia, Croatia, Bosnia and Herzegovina*. London: University of Luton Press, 1999.

Tolvaisis, Leonas. "Historical Memories of Kosovo Serbs in the Postwar Period and Conflicting Serbian National Narratives About Kosovo." *Darbai Ir Dienos*, 60 (2013): 205–35.

Trčak, Ivan, ed. *Mirogoj: Kulturno-povijesni vodič*. Zagreb: Kršćanska Sadašnjost i Rektorat Crkve Krista Kralja, Mirogoj, 1987.

Tritton, A. S. "Muslim Funeral Customs." *Bulletin of the School of Oriental Studies*, 9, no. 3 (1938): 653–61.

Troch, Pieter. "The Intertwining of Religion and Nationhood in Interwar Yugoslavia: The School Celebrations of St. Sava's Day." *Slavonic and East European Review*, 91, no. 2 (April 2013): 235–61.

Udovicki, Jasminka, and Štitkovac, Ejub. "Bosnia-Hercegovina: The Second War." In *Burn This House: The Making and Unmaking of Yugoslavia*, Jasminka Udovicki and James Ridgeway, eds., 174–214. Durham, NC: Duke University Press, 1997.

Unknown. "Република Српска: ŠIPTARSKI ZLOČIN: Raskopali Grob Srpskih Beba i Raskomadali Njihova Tela." *Република Српска* (blog), June 27, 2014. http://rep-srp ska.blogspot.com/2014/06/siptarski-zlocin-raskopali-grob-srpskih.html.

Uzelak, Gordana. "Franjo Tudjman's Nationalist Ideology." *East European Quarterly* XXXI, no. 4 (1998): 449–72.

Valjan, Fra Velimir, and Ivan Lovrenčić, eds. *Franjevački Samostan Guča Gora: Mala Monografija*. Guča Gora: Franjevački Samostan Guča Gora, Kulturno-povijesni institut Bosne Srebrene, 2009.

van den Breemer, Rosemarie, and Marcel Maussen. "On the Viability of State-Church Models: Muslim Burial and Mosque Building in France and the Netherlands." *Journal of Immigrant and Refugee Studies*, 10, no. 3 (2012): 279–98.

Van Onselen, Charles. "Dead But Not Quite Buried." *London Review of Books*, 20, no. 21 (October 29, 1998).

Vanderstraeten, Raf. "Burying and Remembering the Dead." *Memory Studies*, February 3, 2014. https://doi.org/10.1177/1750698013519122.

Vasović, Aleksandar. "Serbia's Bungalow Cemeteries." *Reuters, The Wider Image*, November 11, 2016. https://widerimage.reuters.com/story/serbias-bungalow-cem eteries.

Velikonja, Mitja. *Religious Separation and Political Intolerance in Bosnia-Herzegovina*. College Station: Texas A & M University Press, 2003.

Venbrux, Eric, Thomas Quartier, Claudia Venhorst, and Brenda Mathijssen. *Changing European Death Ways*. Münster: LIT Verlag, 2013.

Verdery, Katherine. *National Ideology under Socialism: Identity and Cultural Politics in Ceausescu's Romania*. Berkeley: University of California Press, 1991.

Verdery, Katherine. *The Political Lives of Dead Bodies: Reburial and Postsocialist Change*. New York: Columbia University Press, 1999.

Vincent, Fred. *Everybody Got a Hug That Morning ... from Desecration to Reconciliation*. Belfast: Institute for Conflict Research, 2009.

Vincent, Fred. "From Desecration to Reconciliation: Considering Attacks on the Sacred During the Troubles and Proposing a Framework Response." *Shared Space*, 8 (2009): 67–84.

Vivod, Maria "Stronger than the State." *Etnofor*, 23, no. 2, State/Violence (2011): 99–114.

Vladimirov, Katya. "Dead Men Walking: Soviet Elite Cemeteries and Social Control." *Forum on Public Policy* 8, (2008): 1–11.

Walasek, Helen. *Bosnia and the Destruction of Cultural Heritage*. New ed. Farnham: Ashgate, 2015.

Wanner, Catherine. "Introduction." In *State Secularism and Lived Religion in Soviet Russia and Ukraine*, Catherine Wanner, ed., 1–26. New York: Oxford University Press, 2012.

Warner, W. Lloyd. *The Living and the Dead: A Study of the Symbolic Life of Americans.* Yankee City Series 5. New Haven, CT: Yale University Press, 1959.

Weber, Eugen. *Peasants into Frenchmen.* Stanford, CA: Stanford University Press, 1976.

Wegren, Stephen K. "Civil Society in Rural Russia." In *Russian Civil Society: A Critical Assessment*, Alfred B. Evans, Jr., Laura A. Henry, and Lisa McIntosh Sundstrom, eds., 126–46. London: Routledge, 2006.

Welch, Alfred T. "Death and Dying in the Qur'an." In *Religious Encounters with Death*, Frank E. Reynolds and Earle H. Waugh, eds., 183–99. University Park: Pennsylvania State University Press, 1977.

Wenzel, Marian. "Graveside Feasts and Dances in Yugoslavia." *Folklore*, 73, no. 1 (Spring 1962): 1–12.

Williams, Howard. "Death Warmed Up: The Agency of Bodies and Bones in Early Anglo-Saxon Cremation Rites." *Journal of Material Culture*, 9, no. 3 (2004): 263–91.

Williams, Terri. "Jim Crow and African-American Cemeteries and Burial Practices." *Higher Ground: Honoring Washington Park Cemetery, Its People and Place.* http://omeka.wustl.edu/omeka/exhibits/show/washington-park/about-cemetery/jimcrow. Accessed February 21, 2020.

Winter, Jay. *Remembering War: The Great War between Memory and History in the Twentieth Century.* New Haven, CT: Yale University Press, 2008.

Winter, Jay. *Sites of Memory, Sites of Mourning: The Great War in European Cultural History.* Cambridge: Cambridge University Press, 1995.

Woodthorpe, Kate. "Private Grief in Public Spaces: Interpreting Memorialization in the Contemporary Cemetery." In *The Matter of Death: Space, Place and Materiality*, Jenny Hockey, Carol Komaromy, and Kate Woodthorpe, eds., 117–32. Basingstoke: Palgrave MacMillan, 2010.

Woodward, Susan. *Socialist Unemployment: The Political Economy of Yugoslavia 1945–1990.* Princeton, NJ: Princeton University Press, 1995.

Zaniello, Thomas A. "The Keystone of Neoclassicism: Fremasonry and Gravestone Iconography." *Journal of American Culture*, 3, no. 4 (Winter 1980): 581–94.

Zaretsky, Eli. "Hannah Arendt and the Meaning of the Public/Private Distinction." In *Hannah Arendt and the Meaning of Politics*, Craig Calhoun and John McGowan, eds., 207–31. Minneapolis: University of Minnesota Press, 1997.

Žarkov, Dubravka. *The Body of War: Media, Ethnicity and Gender in the Break-Up of Yugoslavia.* Durham, NC: Duke University Press, 2007.

Zilhao, Jaoa. "Lower and Middle Paleolithic Mortuary Behaviors and the Origins of Ritual Burial," In *Death Rituals, Social Order and the Archeology of Immortality in the Ancient World*, Colin Renfrew, Micheal Boyd, and Iain Morley, eds., 27–45. Cambridge: Cambridge University Press, 2016.

Index

Alexander, King 58, 162
Amanat, M. 4
Anderson, B. 75
Andjić, Friar 12, 120
Appeal for Protection of the Serbian Population and their Sacred Monuments 212
archaeological excavation and indigenous rights 203
Arendt, H. 11, 12
Arkan's grave, Novo Groblje 197
Arkan's Tigers 59
Association for Fighters from the People's Liberation War archives 15
Association of Architects 206
Atheism 45, 133, 177
Austro-Hungarian Empire 50, 58, 61, 64, 100, 115, 163

Barić, D. 118
Bečković, M. 218
Belgrade Municipal Council for Communal Services 140–1
Bergholz, M. 77, 88, 181, 210, 214
Bešanić, Father M. 108–9
Bešić, M. 118, 127
Bevan, R. 207, 208
Bijedić, D. 115
Black, M. 8, 9, 76
Bleiburg massacre, Austria 189, 201
Boards of Health, National and Municipal, Britain 30
Bogdanović, B. 1, 92, 227–8
bones and graves narrative 186–7, 228, 231
Bosnia & Hercegovina Heritage Rescue Association (BHHR) 220
Bosnia & Hercegovina
 historical context 63–8
 League of Communists of Bosnia & Hercegovina 65
 Social Political Council and Presidency of the Parliament of Bosnia & Hercegovina 119
 Socialist Alliance of Bosnia & Hercegovina 118
Bosnian Muslim SS Division (Waffen Handžar Division) 65
Bosnian Serb Republic 67, 68, 197, 241
Botev, N. 169
Bougarel X. 65
Bringa, T. 13, 129
British Red Cross 74
brotherhood and unity 5, 10, 17, 50, 55, 62, 65, 68, 78, 86, 88–9, 93, 102, 124, 227, 229–30
burial culture
 background 4–11
 benign neglect 126–31, 231
 burial policies 12
 Catholic 23, 102, 108
 civilian 5, 17, 69
 Communist 12, 43, 49
 cremation culture 138
 cult of the dead/death 32–3, 41, 115, 140, 212
 early 23
 influences 115–23
 institutions 70, 99
 Jewish 35–39
 mixed marriage 15, 169–71
 Muslim 40–2, 130, 173–8
 nationalist 18
 Orthodox 32–5
 Protestant Reformation 23–6
 religious minority 108–9
 rituals 40, 126, 138, 142, 231
 secularization 100
 Socialist Yugoslavia 6–7, 14–16, 43–6, 49, 72, 99, 126, 138, 142, 185, 228, 232
 Soviet Union 9, 16, 43, 46, 49

Sunni and Shi'a 40
burial rituals
  conflicts over 24–5, 132–6, 142–4
  creation of new rituals 17, 44, 126,
    136–9, 141–9
  cremation 141
  ethnoreligious 129
  exclusion of women 42, 129
  local 8, 10, 128
  military honors 142
  Niš, Serbia 138
  non-Partisans 231
  private 14, 128, 177
  religious 23–4, 26, 42–3, 103, 125, 128,
    130–1, 135–6
  separation of church and state 104
  State (communist and socialist) 17,
    125–6, 131, 135–6, 138, 144,
    231
  traditional 11, 128–9
  veterans 87, 142–4
Buturović, A. 41, 173
Byzantine 32, 34, 40, 141, 152

Campbell, D. 168
Catherine II, Empress of Russia 34
Catholic Church 140, 148, 151
  in Bosnia & Hercegovina 116
  in Croatia 51, 54–6, 58, 101, 108–9, 115,
    123, 126, 131, 133, 135, 137, 189
Catholicism and Protestantism in Western
    and Central Europe 21–32
cemeteries
  Bosnia & Hercegovina
    Banja Luka 95, 237, 241
    Bare Cemetery, Central Cemetery,
      Sarajevo 121–2, 130
    Guča Gora Monastery 200, 202
    Karaula, Orthodox cemetery 220
    Mostar Partisan Memorial
      Cemetery, 228
    Ossuary to the People's Heroes in
      Veliki Park, Sarajevo 91
    Stup Cemetery, Sarajevo 117
    Travnik 175
    Vlakovo cemetery, Sarajevo 121
    Vraca Partisan Cemetery and
      Memorial Park, Sarajevo 91–3
    Zenica 170, 172, 183

  Croatia
    Gospić Municipal Cemetery of St.
      Mary Magdalen 201–2
    Graberje 211–12
    Granešina, Zagreb 108–9
    Gunja 112–13
    Jasikovac Orthodox Cemetery,
      Gospić 94, 218–19
    Markovo Polje, Zagreb 109
    Mirogoj, Zagreb 101, 141, 201
    Miroševac, Zagreb 109
    Nova Gradiška 217
    Osijek 57, 104, 109, 112, 217
    Šestine, Zagreb 102
    Vrebac 85, 159, 166–7
    Zaprešić 234
  France
    Les Innocents, Paris 28
    Père Lachaise, Paris 29, 31
  Germany
    Heerstrasse 38
    Weissensee, Berlin 37–9
  Kosovo/Kosova
    Berivojce 223
    Bostan/Bostanë 223
    Devič Monastery 222
    Gjakovo 182
    Gračanica 212, 223
    Pejë, Orthodox Cemetery 226
    Patriarchate of Peć 225
    Prizren 224
    Vučitrn/Vushtrri 224
  Netherlands, Roermond 27
  Serbia
    Kačarevo 183
    Kostolac 111
    Lešče, Belgrade 110, 112
    Novo Bežanija, Belgrade 110–12,
      114, 124, 141
    Novo Groblje, Belgrade 76, 77, 100,
      110, 140–2, 158, 197
    Titelj 111
    Zemun 113
  Soviet Union, Alexander Nevsky
    Monastery, Moscow 179
cemetery
  administration vs. ownership 70, 101–6
  appropriation (see also nationalization of
    church properties) 104

British urban 30, 179, 194
as communities of the dead 3
confessional 25, 26, 90, 101–5, 107, 111, 124, 154, 171, 180
to create collective identity 230–1
creation of new 109–14, 120–4
Decree on Cemeteries 1949 102–3, 155
integration 124, 230
Jewish cemetery segregation 100, 113
maintenance and care 82, 111, 118, 209, 239
nationalization 119–20
overcrowding 23, 30–1, 34, 109, 124, 141
as part of ethnoreligious community 120
as places for political discourse 5
politicization 228, 231
property ownership 12–13, 70, 102, 104–6, 111, 115–16, 120, 227, 230
Red Square graves 44
revenue 104–5
secular cemeteries 17, 25, 97–8, 121, 124, 227
secularization 6, 100–20, 123
as sites of education 83, 89, 92, 120, 165, 180
as sites of ethnic conflict, 1991–5 215
as sites of tourism 89, 165
transition from churchyard to cemetery 98
war cemeteries 72–9, 87
cemetery segregation
  interfaith marriage mixed marriage 38
  ethnoreligious and national 5, 100, 114–15, 178, 227, 231
  Jewish 37, 100, 113
  new cemeteries 121
  United States 4
  war cemeteries 74–5
  Western Europe 37
cenotaphs 75
charnel house (*see* ossuary/ossuaries) 22, 24, 148
Chetniks 50, 58, 77
Church of Bosnia 64
coffins 23, 29, 32–3, 130, 141, 143, 144, 148, 152, 204
collective identity postwar Yugoslavia 4–5, 17, 73, 78–9, 84, 88–9, 134, 227–8, 230

Čolović, I. (*see also* epitaph, Serbian laments) 159
columbarium 31–2, 45, 140–1
Commission for Commemoration and Burial 90
Commission for Religious Questions (CRQ) 15, 69–70, 72, 102–5, 107, 113, 115, 117, 119, 121–7, 129–34, 136–8, 143, 187, 209–12, 231
Commission for the Arrangement and Commemoration of Historical Places 79
Commission for the Cultivation of Revolutionary Traditions 69
Communist Party of Yugoslavia (CPY) 4–6, 16, 43, 50, 51, 55, 65, 68, 73, 78, 80, 93, 185
community/ies of the dead 3, 5–6, 10, 17, 96, 98, 110, 124, 126, 147, 157, 171, 173, 177–8, 185–7, 193, 196, 198, 222, 229, 235
Constas, N. 32, 152
Constitutions
  Croatia 1990 56
  Democratic Federated Republic of Yugoslavia 1946 71
  Federal Peoples Republic of Yugoslavia 1948, 162
  Socialist Federal Republic of Yugoslavia 1974 52, 63, 65, 162
conversion 38, 40, 54, 64
corruption 30, 45
Council for Affairs of Religious Cults/CARC 44, 69
Council for Communal Affairs 210
Council of Affairs of the Russian Orthodox Church/CAROC 44, 69
CPY (Communist Party of Yugoslavia) 4–6, 16, 43, 50, 51, 65, 68, 73, 78, 80, 93, 185
cremation
  background 8, 31–2
  burial rituals 141
  Catholics 31, 38, 140
  Communists 17, 45
  culture 138
  increase 31
  Islam 140

Jewish 37–9, 140
Kodeks Pogrebne Usluge 138
opponents 31, 37–9
Orthodox 140
popularity 31, 110
proponents 31, 126
Soviet Union 45, 140
Nazi 38
crematorium
  Novo Groblje Cemetery 140
  Père Lachaise, Paris, France 31
  planned and extant crematories 141
  Vlakovo municipal cemetery, Sarajevo 121
Croatia, historical context 53–7
Croatian Democratic Community (HDZ) 56, 200
Croatian Spring 51, 55–6, 118, 127, 135
cult of the dead/death 32–3, 41, 115, 140, 212
Čupina, M. 1–3
Curl, J. 30

Dapčević, P. 126
Day of the Dead (*see also Zadušnice*) 137, 212
Dayton Peace Accords 60, 63, 66–7
Defense of Monuments of Culture 90
Democratic League of Kosovo (LDK) 63
demonstrations Albanians in Serbia 62–3, 210
desecration
  against African American graves in the United States 205
  against Jewish graves 38, 204–5, 217
  by or against communist regime 209–10
  definition 205
  during and after wars of Yugoslav dissolution 217–228
    in Bosnia & Hercegovina 218–21
    in Croatia 217–18
    in Kosovo/Kosova 216, 221–8
  escalation of 185
  as ethnic conflict in Socialist Yugoslavia 210–215
  forms of 204, 216
  grave and cemetery desecrations 201–9, 219
  as grave robbing, body snatching 201, 203
  as hate crime 204–5
  Ministry of Communities and Return renewal 223
  Nazi and Ustasha symbols 3
  OSCE, graveyard reconstruction and repair 222
  political significance 207
  strategies for 206
  Sufi shrines, Northern Africa 4
  United States 4, 205
  as vandalism 73, 203–4
District People's Council, Zagreb 102, 106
Djilas, M. 96
Djureinović, J. 10, 190
Dobrović, V. 92
Doughty, C. 18–19
Drašković, V. 59, 218
Dubrovnik 57, 107, 211, 217
Duizings, G. 178
Dušan, Tsar Stefan 187

Enlightenment 23, 26, 151
epitaph
  Balkan Muslims 153–5
  as form of private and public communication 159
  grave marker text 153–4, 199
  on grave markers, early 153
  on grave markers, Protestant 153
  on graves, pre-Islamic Arabic 153
  on graves, signs of Islamization 153
  increase of epitaphs on grave markers 159
  Qur'anic citations on epitaphs 153
  Serbian laments 159, 197–200
eradication/removal of graves 77
ethnic cleansing 66, 208
ethnicization of the dead 186, 189, 214, 228
ethnoreligious segregation in cemeteries 111, 114–15
exclusion from burial rites and cemeteries
  by Communists 77–8, 96
  by religious groups 22, 25, 32, 38, 42, 101, 118
exhumation
  Bleiburg 189
  German War Graves Commission 190
  historical 4, 25, 34–5, 83, 128–9
  Kodeks Pogrebne Usluge 138–40

Kujundžić, V. 140
Law on Cemeteries 91
mass graves 186
Orthodox graves 218
prevention of vampirization 129
repatriation 75-6
Sarajevo 221
Second World War 189-90
secondary burial 128-9, 144
Srebrenica 189-90
of war dead 83-4, 91

Federal and Republic Archives 15
Federation of Bosnia & Hercegovina 67-8, 221
First World War 43, 50, 53-4, 58, 60-1, 64, 73-5, 77, 94, 163, 194, 223
French Revolution 23, 25, 28-9, 148
funding
 cemetery maintenance and care 82, 111, 118, 209, 239
 creation of cemeteries and memorials 22, 29, 76, 79-82, 84, 92, 109-10, 131
 decentralized laws regarding 81
 lack of/inadequate 16, 79, 91, 109-10
 local for cemeteries and memorials 79
 local for Partisan Cemetery, Mostar 81
 Local People's Councils for graves and cemeteries 80
 maintenance costs 81, 83, 103-4, 107, 118-19, 222
 Partisan cemeteries 82
 profit from burials 30
 profit from cemetery land/grounds 104
Funeral Associations 128
funeral service, ZAGS 44-5
funeral societies 126-8, 131

Gaj, L. 162
Gal, S. 14
Gazi Husrev-Beg library, Sarajevo 220
Geiger, V. 77
Gemeinschaft/Gesellschaft 97-8
Geneva Conventions, 1949 206
German War Graves Commission (*see also Volksbund Deutsche Kriegsgraberfursorge*) 190
Gladstone, W. 18
Glenny, M. 164

Golubnjača [The Dove Hole] (*see also* politicization) 188
Grace (Krstovdan) Incident 213-16
Granešina, Croatia 108
Grant, S. 75
grave markers
 abstract 93
 in burial culture 178
 burial rituals 14-15
 change over time 154-61
 early 148-9
 emblems of political affiliation 228
 epitaphs increase 159
 homogeneity during Communist era 157
 inclusive religious symbols 232
 and language 161-7
 maps 191
 mixed marriage 18, 168-71, 211
 multigenerational 155-6
 Muslim 41, 141, 149-50, 152-6, 160, 171-9, 192
 as nationalist symbols 5
 options during Communist era 158
 pebbles on Jewish graves 151
 photographs on grave markers 152-3, 174, 176, 182-3, 235-7, 240
 politicization of grave markers 179, 191-201
 politicization of script on grave markers 166
 religious affiliation 149
 renovation of grave markers 157, 191, 200-2
 sculptures and figurines 154, 234
 soldiers' 192-3, 196
 soldiers', five-pointed star, hammer and sickle 84
 under communism, epitaphs, symbols, photographs 157-8
 Veteran's Association 7
grave ownership (*see also* leased graves) 30
Greenberg, R. 162
Guide to Funeral Services (*Kodeks Pogrebne Usluge*) 138-9

Habermas, J. 11, 13
Hadith 40, 41
Hadžihalilović, S. 220

Hague Convention 206
Halevi, L. 9, 41, 174
Hameršmitd, A. 201
Hayden, R. 169
HDZ (see Croatian Democratic Community)
Hermann, V. 217
Herscher, A. 10, 206, 211, 214, 221
Hevra Kadisha 39, 127
Hitler, A. 38
Hobson, R. 169
Holy Council of the Serbian Orthodox Church 211
Hoxha, A. 62, 221
hygiene 5, 26–32, 34, 45, 99, 101, 129–32, 142, 144

identity
  Albanian 61–2, 192
  Bosniak 67, 200, 225, 232
  bošnjaštvo 64
  collective identity 4–5, 17, 73, 78–9, 84, 88–9, 134–5, 227–8, 230
  Croatian 56, 63–5, 194
  national vs religious 46, 71, 227, 229
  Serbian 164, 166, 187, 212
  Yugoslav 78, 161
Illyrian movement 162
Imperial War Graves Commission, 1920 94
Independent State of Croatia (NDH) 65, 188–9
interethnic and interfaith marriages (see also mixed marriages) 26, 38, 65, 97, 108, 168
Interwar Yugoslavia (see also Kingdom of Yugoslavia) 49, 51, 101, 118, 163
Islam in Europe
  aniconistic policies 173
  graves, egalitarian 149
  historical background 39–43
Islamic Religious Community (IVZ) 104–5, 115, 123
Islamization/Islamic nationalism in Bosnia & Hercegovina 65, 67, 153
Izetbegović, A. 65, 66, 119

Jasenovac, Croatia 87, 210
Jashari family 63
Jeftić, Archpriest S. 210–15

Jewish diaspora 35–6
Jim Crow Acts 4
JMO (see Yugoslav Muslim Organization)
JNA (see Yugoslav People's Army)
Joseph II, Emperor 100
Jovanović, A. 126
Jovanović, M. 129
Judaism in Europe 35–9
Jupp, P. 25

Karadžić, R. 66
Karadžić, V. 162
Karge, H. 10, 79, 85, 87
Kelly, C. 45
Kingdom of Serbia 58
Kingdom of Serbs, Croats, and Slovenes 50, 54
Kingdom of Yugoslavia (see also Interwar Yugoslavia) 54, 61, 64
KLA (see Kosovo Liberation Army)
Kodeks Pogrebne Usluge (Guide to Funeral Services) 138
Kosovo Liberation Army (KLA) 63, 221, 224
Kosovo/Kosova, historical context 60–3
Kosovska Mitrovica, Kosovo 211
Krajina (see Vojska Krajina)
Kselman, T. 150
Kujundžić, V. (see also Exhumation) 140
Kulen Vakuf, Bosnia & Hercegovina 88, 95

laments, lamentation 33–4, 159, 197
landmines 217, 220
language
  BCMS (Bosnian-Croatian-Montenegrin-Serbian) 162–3
  BCS (Bosnian-Croatian-Serbian) 16, 162–3, 239
  common language 162
  Croatian Literary Language 1967 162
  Declaration on the Name and Position of the Croatian Literary Language 162
  for education and tourism 164–5
  on grave markers 161–7, 192
  and identity 167–71
  linguistic complexity 161–7
  linguistic diversity as obstacle to unity 162

Serbo-Croatian/Croato-Serbian 161–3
Vienna Linguistic Agreement, 1850 162
Laqueur, T. 8, 10, 18, 97–8, 110, 227
Lawler, A. 10, 73, 85, 87, 227–8
laws
  Agents, policies, and laws 68–72
  Commemoration of Historical Events and People 90
  Law on People's Councils (*Narodni Odbori*) 1946 99, 102, 105
  Law on Agrarian Reform 1945 72, 127
  Law on Burials and Cemeteries in Serbia 1961 140
  Law on Cemeteries, Bosnia & Hercegovina 1960 90–1, 115, 117, 127
  Law on Cemeteries, Croatia 1965 82, 102–3, 113, 155
  Law on Cemeteries, Ferizaj, Kosovo 1961 106
  Law on Cemeteries, revised, Serbia, 1965 140
  Law on Cemeteries, Serbia, 1961 106
  Law on Expropriation 1947 72
  Law on Funeral Activity and the Maintenance and Administration of Cemeteries 119
  Law on Legal Status of Religious Communities 1953 72, 106, 132, 137
  Laws on Graves for Soldiers 81
Lazar, King 188
LCY (*see* League of Communists of Yugoslavia)
LDK (*see* Democratic League of Kosovo)
League of Communists of Yugoslavia (LCY) (*see also* Communist Party of Yugoslavia) 51, 67
leased graves 30–1, 34, 37, 82, 148, 157
Lenin's Mausoleum 44–5
Limani, M. 214
Ljubunčić, H. 70

Malcolm, N. 41
marginalization 67, 208
mass graves
  commemorating deaths of those killed by Communist regime 201
  France 28
  individual and mass graves, ossuaries 82
  Jasenovac, Croatia 210
  ossuaries for civilian victims of war 86
  PLA, funding from SUBNOR 79
  Srebrenica, Bosnia & Hercegovina 189–90
Massey, R. 169
Matica Hrvatska 136
Matich, O. 152
matične knijige birth, marriage, and death records 70, 72
Mbembe, A. 207–8
McAllester, M. 224
Memorandum of the Serbian Academy of Arts and Sciences 1986 52, 59, 164, 188
Menachemsen, N. 204
Merridale, C. 46
Mihailović, D. 58
Military Frontier (*see* Vojska Krajina)
Miloradović, G. 96, 142
Milošević, S. 52, 59, 60, 63, 188, 224
Ministry of Communities and Return, Kosova 222
Misirača, D. 87
Mitrofan, Monk 33
mixed marriages (*see also* interethnic/interfaith marriages)
  burial complications 15, 118, 120–1, 124, 169
  communist encouragement of 161, 168–9
  grave desecration 211
  grave markers 18, 148, 168–72, 184, 240–1
monuments and memorials
  abstract design (*see also* Symbols) 92–3
  Bleiburg massacre, Mirogoj Cemetery, Zagreb 201
  commemoration of ethnoreligious dead (*see also* SUBNOR) 87–8
  design and construction 79
  exclusion of anti-regime war deaths 77–8, 96, 200–1, 228, 231
  exhumation 77
  Kulen Vakuf massacre 88
  Monuments of the Revolution, District of Slavonska Požega 83

monuments to victims of fascism 81–2, 85, 87, 90, 92, 94, 231
Partisan 1–2, 68, 73, 76, 79–80, 83, 86, 88–92, 96, 165–6, 182–3, 208, 227–8
Second World War 5, 76, 85, 88, 201
Srebrenica, Bosnia & Hercegovina 189–90
symbols 149, 151, 155, 166
mortuary and mortuaries 23, 42, 101, 119, 126, 130
Mytum, H. 148

nationalism
  and religion 6, 56, 58, 64–5, 177, 212, 233
  ethnoreligious 124, 161, 189, 233
  nineteenth century 40, 50
  rise of in Socialist Yugoslavia 18, 52, 56, 65, 162, 164, 185, 188
nationalization (*see also* laws)
  of cemeteries 119–20
  of church properties 72, 102, 106–7, 114–17, 120, 123, 126
  effect on cemeteries and funeral industry 43–4, 105, 128, 132, 155, 233
NATO 60, 63, 66, 203, 221–3
Nazis 3, 38, 50, 65, 76, 179, 204
NDH (*see* Independent State of Croatia)
necropolitics 207–8
Nemanjić Dynasty 212
Netherlands 25–6, 37–8, 153
Niebyl, D. 10
Nora, P. 10
Novi Pazar (Sandžak of), Serbia 100, 114, 123, 130, 173–4, 210, 230
Novi Sad Agreement, Serbo-Croatian 162–3

O'Dell, E. 208
Office of the Islamic Union, Kosova 221
Old Serbia 213–14
Omerdić, M. 220
Operations Flash and Storm 57
Organization for Security and Cooperation in Europe (OSCE) 222–4
Orthodox Church 32–5
  In Bosnia & Hercegovina 116
  Russian Orthodox Church 44–5
  Serbian Orthodox Church 10, 52, 58–9, 61–2, 126, 140–1, 188–9, 210–14, 221
ossuaries
  creation by SUBNOR 84
  individual and mass graves 82
  Orthodox cemeteries 34
  Ossuary to the People's Heroes in Veliki Park 91
  Vraca Partisan Cemetery and Memorial Park, Sarajevo, Bosnia & Hercegovina 92
ossuary, ossuaries (*see also* charnel house) 1, 5, 6, 22, 24, 26, 34, 36, 37, 73, 78–9, 82, 84–7, 89, 90–1, 92, 96, 148, 164, 227
Ottoman Empire 13, 40, 53, 64, 100, 152–3

Paris Peace Conference 61
Partisan cemeteries
  to create collective identity 230–1
  creation of "communities of the dead" 96
  "generally Yugoslav" (opštejugoslovenski) 94, 95
  overcome/alleviate grief 83–8, 230
  for tourism and education (*see also* language, script) 89
  unequally valued 86
Partisans (PLA/People's Liberation Army) 6–7, 50, 68–9, 79–80, 82–3, 86–7
Party of Democratic Action (SDA) 66–7
Patriarch German 211
Patriarchate of Peć 212, 224–5
Pavičević, A. 129, 141
Perica, V. 55
Petrović, E. 128
Petrović, R. 169
Pijade, M. 126
pilgrimage 42, 53, 90, 186
plague 22, 32, 34, 37
Politicization
  cemetery politicization 5, 96, 217, 228, 231
  of the dead 179–81, 185, 188, 228, 231
  exhumation of mass graves 186
  Golubnjača [The Dove Hole] 188
  of mass graves 186–91

nationalist narrative of bones and graves 228, 231
of partisan cemeteries and graves 68, 86, 96, 179–81
repoliticization of mass graves 185
Ustasha rehabilitation through politicization of the dead 189
of war dead 76–8, 91, 148, 179–84, 185, 189
Pollack, C. 190
Protestant Reformation 24–6
Public/Private dichotomy 11–15
Public/Private forms of mourning 11, 14, 17, 73, 79, 88–9, 97, 133, 136, 144, 168, 190, 197, 240
Public Health Act of 1850, Great Britain 30
Putnam, R. 168

Qur'an
 epitaphs on graves 152–3, 173, 194
 regarding burial culture 39, 41

Rabbinical Board of the Committee for the Preservation of Jewish Cemeteries in Europe 35
Radić, R. 71
Radulović, J. 188
Rambouillet international peace negotiations 60
Ranković, A. 55, 58–9, 62, 116, 134–5
Ravnikar, E. 92
reburial (*see also* Exhumation) 6, 110, 128–9, 189–90
Reconstruction Implementation Commission for Serbian Orthodox Religious Sites 222
registration of births and weddings, ZAGS 44
Reis-ul-Ulema 65, 115
relics 32, 140, 187–8
religious minorities 57–8
Resurrection 22, 31–2, 35–7, 42, 98, 140
Riedelmayer, A. 218, 221
Ritig, S. 54, 55, 70, 103–6, 209
Roma 87, 114, 118, 205, 222, 235–40
Rubić, D. 121
Rugg, J. 8, 25, 30
Rugova, I. 63

Salis-Seewis, Bishop 54
Šamec, I. 108
Savez Udruženje Boraca Narodnooslobodilačkog Rata (*see* SUBNOR)
Schauble, M. 189–90
Schlesinger, Rabbi E. 35, 37
Schulz, F. 8–9
Scientific Revolution 23, 26, 203
Scott, J. 177
Script
 Arabic script on Muslim graves 152
 Cyrillic 56, 161, 163
 Cyrillic, Graberje, Croatia (*see also* Desecrations) 211–12
 Cyrillic vs. Latin 163
 in education and usage 163
 equality of, Novi Sad Agreement 163
 and ethnoreligious or political identity 161
 Latin script 161
 mixed marriage 18, 184
 mixed script 166–7
 and national identity 164
 SUBNOR, script on monuments 165
 and symbols on grave markers 164–7
SDA (*see* Party of Democratic Action)
SDS (*see* Serbian Democratic Party)
Second Balkan War 1913 40
Second Vatican Council 55
Second World War
 exhumation 189–90
 institutionalized memory 4–6, 78–9
 Jews 38, 204
 Kulen Vakuf 88
 monuments and memorials 85, 190–1
 occupations 58, 61
 Partisans 6, 50–1, 71, 76, 189, 231
 politicization of dead 76–8, 179, 185, 189
 Ustasha 56, 188
secularization
 Bosnia & Hercegovina 115–20
 burial practices 26
 secular cemeteries 17, 25, 97–8, 121, 124, 227
 secular control 115
 Serbia and Croatia 100–9
 Western European 8–9, 23–4
Šehman, K. 108–9
Šehović, S. 114

Sekulić, D. 169
Self-Managed Social Agreements 83
separation of church and state 13, 25, 70–2, 104, 229
Serbia
  historical context 57–60
  League of Communists of Serbia 52
  Ministry for Kosovo and Metohija 222
  Serbian Writer's Association 188
  Serbian Democratic Party (SDS) 66
  Serbian Republic (RS) declaration of independence 66, 187, 194, 239
Šešelj, V. 59, 119, 197
Shoup, P. 67
Silajdžić, H. 67
Slavonia, Eastern and Western, Croatia 53, 57, 59, 101, 111, 123
Smolkin, V. 44, 139
Soviet Union 9, 16, 51, 71, 76, 78, 86, 96, 105, 140, 179–80
  CARC/Council for Affairs of Religious Cults 44, 69
  CAROC/Council of Affairs of the Russian Orthodox Church 44, 69
  New Economic Policy 44
  Red Funerals 43
  Red Square graves 44
  religious funerals 46
  War Communism 43
Sremec, M. 134
St. Ilija Parish Church, Zenica, Bosnia & Hercegovina 120
stećci (stećak) 40
Stepinac, A. 55–6
Strossmayer, Bishop 54
SUBNOR (Savez Udruženje Boraca Narodnooslobodilačkog Rata)
  commemoration of ethnoreligious dead 87–8
  creation of ossuaries, common mausoleums 84
  creation of secular all-Yugoslav funeral ritual 142
  exhumation of unknown soldiers 84
  graves of soldiers, maintenance, preservation, establishment 68
  inclusive of religious traditions 143
  Law on Graves for Soldiers, Bosnia & Hercegovina 81
  Partisan cemeteries 180
  rulebook for military funerals 142
  segregated sections for soldiers buried in non-Partisan cemeteries 180
  structure 69
  Veteran's Organization 68
Subotić, J. 10
Sušić, M. 41
symbols
  abstract design 92–3, 96, 227, 230
  alternative political symbols 181
  in burial culture 46
  images/effigies on graves 152–3
  mixed marriage 71, 240
  National
    Albania
      black double-headed eagle 7, 191–2
      maps 191–2
    Bosnia & Hercegovina
      fleur-de-lis 194, 196, 200
      shield, blue and gold 194–6, 202
    Croatia
      braided cross 194–5
      šahovnica (checkerboard flag) 56, 192, 194, 201–2
    Serbia
      double-headed white eagle 59–60, 194, 198
      ocilo (Serbian cross) 197–8, 223
  Political
    Communist party symbols on grave markers 179–81
    five-pointed Partisan Stars 84, 92, 180, 200, 230, 224
    hammer and sickle on grave markers 84, 224, 230
  Religious
    Catholic symbols on grave markers 150–1
    forms of crosses on grave markers 149–51
    in the Soviet Union 45
    Islamic Crescent Moon and Star 152, 171, 173, 232, 234, 240
    Muslim soldiers 192
    Orthodox Cross 151, 197
    Protestant symbols on grave markers 150–1
    Star of David 151

script and symbols on grave markers (*see also* script) 165-7
sculptures and figurines on grave markers 154, 234
shapes, symbols, images, and epitaphs 148-54, 175
under communism, epitaphs, symbols, photographs 157-8

Tauber, E. 121
tehvid 42, 129
Tihić, S. 89-90
Tito, J. B. 50-2, 54-6, 58-9, 69, 86, 92, 124, 133-4, 143, 211
Tjentište, Battle of Sutjeska 80
Tomb of the People's Heroes, 1948, Kalemgdan Park, Belgrade 96
Treaties of Versailles, Trianon, Lausanne, Sèvres, and Neuilly 75
Treaty for the Protection of Minorities 61
Tudjman, F. 56, 59, 164, 200
Tvrtko I 64, 194

UNESCO United Nations Educational, Scientific and Cultural Organization 206, 224
United Nations brokered/imposed Peace Agreement of 1991 57-9
United States 4, 9, 60-1, 74-6, 96, 168, 203, 205
Ustasha 54, 56, 58, 65, 77, 87, 188-9, 201, 211

vakuf (waqf) 65, 100, 105, 116
vampirization 33, 35, 129
Van Onselen, C. 4

Vanderstraeten, R. 153
Veteran's Association (VA) 7, 68, 79
victims of ethnic violence vs. victims of fascism 87-8
Victims of Fascist Terror (Žrtva Fašističkog Terora) (ŽFT) 86, 92
Vincent, F. 205-7, 214, 225, 227
Vivod, M. 59
Vojska Krajina (Military Frontier), Croatia 53, 57, 59, 111, 123, 217
Vojvodina, Serbia 4, 51-3, 58, 60-1, 63, 76, 100, 104, 111, 138, 169, 188, 232
Volksbund Deutsche Kriegsgraberfursorge (*see also* German War Graves Commission) 76

Walton, J. 155, 201
warchitecture 206
Wars of Yugoslav dissolution 4, 6, 18, 53, 185
Wenzel, M. 220
Winter, J. 10, 73, 84

Yugoslav Muslim Organization (JMO) 64
Yugoslav People's Army (JNA) 57, 59, 209, 217

Zadušnice (*see also* Day of the Dead) 34, 212
ZAGS, registration of births and weddings 44
Zenica, Bosnia & Hercegovina 116, 120, 127, 128, 171
Zmaj, J. 140

www.ingramcontent.com/pod-product-compliance
Lightning Source LLC
Chambersburg PA
CBHW071800300426
44116CB00009B/1149